The Development

of

Modern English

Second Edition

The Development
of
Modern English

Second Edition

By
STUART ROBERTSON

Revised by
FREDERIC G. CASSIDY
University of Wisconsin

PRENTICE-HALL, INC.
Englewood Cliffs, N. J.

L.C. Cat. Card No.: 53-13011

First printing .... *January, 1954*
Second printing .... *September, 1954*
Third printing .... *June, 1955*
Fourth printing .... *October, 1957*
Fifth printing .... *December, 1958*

PRINTED IN THE UNITED STATES OF AMERICA

20833

Reviser's Note.

IN THIS edition *The Development of Modern English,* by Stuart Robertson, has been to a great extent rewritten. I have kept, of course, those substantial parts of the original whose value time has not altered; but, on the other hand, I have not hesitated to modernize, to rephrase, to reject, or to add, whenever I felt that the book could be thereby improved.

The field of language study has seen much new work and many ramifications, within the past few years. So far as these touch upon or alter our knowledge of English, I have taken cognizance of them. Some developments, however, are still so tentative that we have no warrant as yet to discard, for them, what is established.

It is impossible to acknowledge in detail here my debt to the many scholars upon whose work I have depended; references to these works within the book must suffice. For what I have learned from them, I hereby express my grateful and sincere thanks.

F. G. C.

Preface to the First Edition

THIS BOOK attempts to present the historical background necessary for an understanding of the English language as it is spoken and written today. The author has endeavored to introduce the general reader and the student who is beginning the systematic study of English to a selected portion of the mass of facts and doctrine that linguistic scholarship, of the last half-century particularly, has made available. In the belief that, for the general reader and the elementary student alike, the field of contemporary language is of paramount interest and value, the emphasis of the book has throughout been placed on present-day English. It has been the author's purpose, however, to deal with the English of our own day in the light of the perspective that is afforded by a survey of the past. He can merely express the hope that his judgment as to the fitting proportion to be observed between past and present has been reasonably sound.

The question of proportion has been present too in the problem of the relative amounts of space to be devoted to the various specialized fields of linguistic study. Naturally the attempt has been to preserve a just balance among the topics that appear as chapter headings, and not to allow the greater attention that is paid to some of them today (phonetics, for instance) to dictate that an undue amount of space be given to these. Among the topics, American English is not so much given a separate treatment as made the point of emphasis in almost every discussion of contemporary English. Hand in hand with the presentation of facts has inevitably gone indulgence in speculation on their significance. The author trusts, however, that fact is presented as fact and theory as theory, so that the reader, accepting the one, will at the same time be given the basis for determining whether the accompanying interpretation or commentary is worthy of consideration. Into the attitude toward language that the book sets forth it is impossible to go here, except perhaps to suggest the writer's belief that a woeful general ignorance of the facts is chiefly responsible for the curiously wrong-headed notions about the standards and sanctions of language that accompany most discussions of that ever fascinating topic, one's native speech.

The author's indebtedness to others is indeed vast, but exceedingly difficult either to measure or to acknowledge. He has of course endeavored to give credit for all ideas that are not common property, by citations in the text or in footnotes, but he is conscious that such acknowledgment is sadly inadequate. The footnotes have been put to other uses too: to supply additional illustrations of points made in the text, to suggest supplementary or additional lines of inquiry, and occasionally to give references that might be helpful in pursuing these or other topics. References for additional reading in connection with the general topics of each chapter have also been added at the end of the chapter. These lists consist, for the most part, of books and articles of recent date and, almost entirely, of matter in English; they do not pretend to form a complete bibliography of the subject, but are designed to indicate supplementary material of a kind that the reader will be likely to find useful.

To the works of three men, of three different nationalities, the author feels most deeply indebted: Jespersen, Bradley, and Krapp. The first named, particularly, is in large measure, though of course quite innocently, responsible for much of the speculation as well as for many of the facts about language that the book contains. The author can only regret the impossibility of singling out and acknowledging his debt to many another writer and work. He must, however, make the usual obeisance, and in no perfunctory fashion, to that wonderful storehouse of information, *The Oxford English Dictionary*.

There are nearer and more personal obligations that should also be recorded here. To his colleagues, the author is grateful for many expressions of interest and helpfulness; to two of them, Miss Jane D. Shenton and Mr. Ellis O. Hinsey, both of whom have read and criticized the entire manuscript, he would particularly express his thanks.

S. R.

PHILADELPHIA,
November, 1934.

Contents

Contents

more precisely, language is an arbitrary system
of vocal symbols used in human communication

Chapter 1

Introduction: The Nature and Origin
of Language

LIKE most words that are often used, the word *language* has many senses. We will do well to begin our discussion by sorting out the main ones and seeing how they are related to one another. The English *language*, the *language* of mathematics, deaf-mutes' *language*, "the subtle *language* of a woman's eyes"—all these legitimate senses differ so much that some of them, at least, must represent special uses, extensions, or generalizations that have grown up in the course of time, presumably from some basic core of meaning. What is that core? Without indulging in the etymological fallacy of thinking that the earliest meaning of a word must necessarily be the "right" one, we may yet note that *language* is derived from *lingua*, the Latin word for tongue, which in this case correctly emphasizes speech as the basic thing in language. For our present purposes we may define as follows: *Language is the vocal and audible medium of human communication.* And, having stated this definition, we must next consider each part of it, clarifying where necessary.

To say that language is *vocal and audible* immediately puts aside everything written—and that is as it should be. For writing is a *record* of language, and is therefore on a different plane altogether. People spoke long before any means of record was invented, and the records we make today (in print, or on disks, wires, tapes, photographic film, and so forth) would have no meaning if they could not be translated back into speech. True, they do not always need to be translated so; communication may take place altogether on this second level, as when we correspond with people we have never seen or heard, or when a deaf person learns to read silently the new "visible

1

1. spoken - not written or otherwise recorded
2. a human activity
3. a rational rather than merely social and emotional aspect of com

speech." [1] For to a practiced reader the words on a page need not suggest sounds at all. He has learned to respond directly to what he sees: he has a short cut through the eye that eliminates the ear. This does not change the system, however, which began as a record of speech, and is always potentially retranslatable.

The dots and dashes of the Morse Code are on still a third level, since they are substitutes for the letters with which we spell out our records of speech; and with them are the gestures of the deaf-mute, also substitutes for the letters of a system of writing. In short, our definition recognizes that the basis of language is speech, whatever other structures may be built upon it.

Since gesture has been mentioned, we may ask here whether it is not language. The American Indians had a system of signs once widely used as a kind of diplomatic code by tribes whose dialects were mutually unintelligible. The gestures were conventionalized, and they served for communication, but (unlike deaf-mute gestures) the system bore no relation whatever to vocal sounds. Thus, though it was certainly language in the broader sense, it does not come under our definition. Had vocal communication never been discovered, this kind of sign language might have had to serve for all human communication, though it is hard to imagine how it could have undergone the high degree of elaboration that speech permits of.

Gesture surely preceded speech as a means of human communication and will never be wholly displaced. Some nations and individuals use it more than others, and the gestures themselves differ in meaning from place to place—for example, a nod of the head, which to us means "yes," means "no" in some parts of the East; we clap our hands in applause, but in the Orient this means a summons. However, we all communicate by gesture to some extent. A frown or a shaken fist will everywhere be recognized as threatening. We indicate the sizes of things with our hands ("about so long"), and some shapes and movements are far easier to show than to describe (a spiral staircase, or the playing of a concertina). Gesture, then, though it may serve alone up to a point, is usually no more than an

[1] R. K. Potter, G. A. Kopp, and H. C. Green, *Visible Speech,* New York (Van Nostrand), 1947. A cathode ray tube is used, and sounds are known by the distinctive shapes they make before the eye.

aid to speech, which can be far more detailed and precise, and which can proceed with perfect efficiency (as gesture can not) even when the speakers do not see each other.

Returning to our definition, we find that the use of the word *human* raises a second question: Is it correct to deny the name of language to the sounds made by the "lower animals"? Such sounds are certainly vocal and audible, and many animals appear to be able to communicate a variety of notions to each other by means of sound. Crows and other birds post sentinels to give the cry of alarm when danger threatens, and the barnyard hen makes quite different noises when searching for food for her chicks and when warning them that a hawk is near.[2] But even if there is some likeness in kind, the difference comes in degree, and there it is vast. The language of even the most primitive humans known is enormously more complex than the range of distinctive sounds made by the highest apes.[3] Human speech employs the symbolic process, by which a sound or sound-group is made to "stand for" something with which it may have only a conventional connection—that is, a connection which depends solely upon the tacit agreement, among speakers of the same language, that those particular sounds ("words") will always be interpreted in the same way when used in similar conditions.

Our use of this process is very highly developed; the animals do not appear to use it at all. Their signals seem to refer to broad situations and to concrete things present to their senses; besides, their range of distinctive sounds is too small to permit much elaboration. When (as in the case of bees) they communicate relatively detailed information, this is done by actions, not by speech.[4] Human speech, on the other hand, always has enough distinctive sounds (phonemes) so that their combinations may produce many thousands of "words," which may, in turn, be attached by general agreement to as many things and concepts. It is the possession of this kind

[2] But note that she does not specify a hawk—merely a source of danger. The significance of the cry is extremely general. It is usually held that "animal language" is instinctive, while human language is learned.

[3] For a list of published "vocabularies" of animal sounds, see G. Révész, *Ursprung und Vorgeschichte der Sprache*, Bern (Francke), 1946, p. 47.

[4] Karl von Frisch has shown that the bees perform elaborate dances to indicate to others that they have found nectar. Cf. "The Language of the Bees" in *Smithsonian Institution Annual Report for 1938*, Washington, 1939. Reprinted from *Science Progress*, Vol. 32, No. 125, July 1937.

of language which separates us widely—one might say essentially—from the rest of the animals.[5]

The third limitation in our definition, that language is a *medium of communication*, will probably raise the largest question, since it is clear that language is not used exclusively for communication. What Madame de Staël has written of the French language surely applies to all others too:

> It is not only a means of communicating thoughts, feeling and acts, but an instrument that one loves to play upon, and that stimulates the mental faculties much as music does for some people and strong drink for others.[6]

Children discover very early, and adults never forget, that language may give kinesthetic enjoyment through the mere exercise of the vocal organs, and (what is far deeper) esthetic pleasure by expressing whole complexes of inward sensations.

When we talk at length to animals—as Alice in Wonderland does to her cat Dinah, which is not even present—we do not expect to be understood; like a baby babbling, or like Wordsworth's solitary reaper singing to herself, we often make sounds merely for the enjoyment of utterance. In short, language has an important expressive function, as well as the communicative one. Much of what we say in social intercourse, while ostensibly communicative, is no more than vaguely so and is quite as much expressive. The words we use in greeting or in being pleasant to people are not to be taken literally; they, and the tone in which they are said, are mostly a means of establishing a friendly atmosphere.

It is probably safe to conjecture that expressive sounds preceded communicative language, since they require a single speaker only, and the noises made are not necessarily conventionalized. As a speaker repeatedly made sounds, however, he might well find them falling into habitual patterns—like the songs of some birds—and another creature, hearing them in connection with particular situations, might interpret them accordingly. Thus the person expressing himself would quite incidentally be communicating. When, for ex-

---

[5] Physiologically, the capacity for speech depends on the existence of certain centers in the brain. See Sir Arthur Keith, *A New Theory of Human Evolution*, London (Watts), 1948, esp. pages 208-209.

[6] Translated from the French quoted by Jespersen in *Mankind, Nation and Individual*, Oslo (Aschehoug), 1925, p. 7.

ample, he howled with hunger, smaller creatures would keep out of his way. So expression would pass insensibly into communication as the expression became more willful or as one creature's expression brought a reply from another. Cries evoked by pain, fear, anger, love-longing, and such elemental sensations were surely as much the property of primitive man as of modern man and the lower animals. Out of some such crude beginnings must have come the highly developed structure of language—a primarily social thing as we know it, and primarily communicative rather than expressive.

This leads us to ask what theories have been offered of the origin of language, and to glance at some of the better-known ones. The first, now completely discredited, is that which finds the origin of language in a divine fiat. Thus, Plato, in what is perhaps the earliest extant explanation of the beginnings of speech, insists that "names belong to things by nature," and hence "the artisan of words" must be "only he who keeps in view the name which belongs by nature to each particular thing." [7] The implication is that the original perfect language, which humans must rediscover or re-create, is the work of the ruler of the universe, the great "law-giver." Imperfections in human language are thus explained as failures to discover the original "natural" or divine words. Curiously parallel to this is the view of the origin of language that was long the orthodox Hebrew (and Christian) theory, likewise maintaining that language origi-nated in a divine act. It was supposed that God gave to Adam a language fully developed—this was, of course, believed to be Hebrew —and that the confusion of tongues at the building of the Tower of Babel accounted for the variations in human speech. This ex-planation, it is surely unnecessary to add, has long since been given up, by theologians as by linguists. Language is looked upon today as one of the things achieved by the human creature in the course of his long development—but one so fundamentally human, as we have said, that it is a distinguishing characteristic setting him apart from the lower animals.

Of the more recent theories based on this assumption one en-counters two types, resulting from two approaches. The earlier approach sought, by examining the vocabulary of languages as we know them, to isolate the most primitive (least conventionalized) types of words, and to build a theory of origins on these. The more

[7] *Cratylus,* New York (Putnam), Loeb ed., p. 31.

recent approach has been through speculative reconstruction of the broader situation which might have led to the discovery or application of vocal communication. As an example of the first we may look at the echoic (or as it is nicknamed, the "bow-wow") theory. This maintained that primitive language was exclusively onomatopoetic; that is, that its words were directly imitative of the sounds of nature or of animals, all the word-stock being thought to have originated in a way parallel to the child's calling a dog "bow-wow" or a duck "quack-quack." There is undoubtedly some truth in this; but it should be noticed that sheer echoisms are not words; they become words when they are conventionalized in terms of the sound-patterns of the imitator's language. Thus to a German the cock crows "Kikeriki"; to a Frenchman "Cocorico"; to an Englishman "Cock-a-doodle-doo"—not because cocks crow differently in Germany, France, and England, but because these forms are the imitations conventional to each language. Furthermore, once an echoism, duly conventionalized, has entered a language, it is subject to the same kinds of language-change as any other word, and may thus be altered in the course of time until its echoic origin is no longer perceived. The word *cow* is not obviously echoic, because its vowel sounds have changed (with all similar sounds) within the past six hundred years. In Old English, however, its ancestor was *cū*, which more clearly suggests its probable echoic origin.

The obvious objection to the "bow-wow" theory is that it does not explain more than a part, and not the largest part, of language. Not even early or "primitive" languages have been shown to be composed chiefly or altogether of onomatopoetic words. The languages of primitive or savage peoples, indeed, turn out upon examination to be quite as conventional as those of civilized peoples. Thus the "bow-wow" theory, though it contains some truth, claims too much.

Similarly, other discarded theories may contain an element of truth. The principal ones are the so-called "pooh-pooh" (or interjectional) theory, which derives language from instinctive ejaculatory responses to such emotions as pain or joy; and the "ding-dong" theory, which holds that language began with a mystically harmonious response, on the part of man's hitherto silent vocal organs, to a natural stimulus which was fated thus to call forth its perfect expression—"everything that is struck, rings." The obvious criticism of the interjectional theory is the difficulty of bridging the gap between interjections (which on the whole are relatively isolated phenomena in speech) and the main body of language. Indeed, it has been held that this is precisely the chasm that separates animal speech, "exclusively exclamatory," from that of men.[8] It is difficult to see how the theory of interjections accounts for much more than the interjections themselves. The other theory is reminiscent of the ancient Greek belief that words exist by nature, rather than by convention, and that there is a necessary and inherent connection between words and the ideas for which they stand. In its eighteenth- and nineteenth-century phases, this theory (once maintained but later rejected by Max Müller) seems no more acceptable as a complete explanation of the origin of language than it does in its Platonic form.

To this account of past theories may be added, in brief summary, the speculations of two twentieth-century students of language. Otto Jespersen's hypothesis[9] based in part on the study of the language of children and of primitive races but chiefly on the history of language, is that emotional songs were the germs of speech. In particular he felt that the emotion of love[10] called forth the earliest songs, that these songs—and others evoked by different emotions (a chant of victory, for example, or a lament for the dead)—were inevitably accompanied by what were at first meaningless syllables, and that the circumstance that the same sounds were used on similar occasions brought about the first association of sound and meaning.

Sir Richard Paget, assenting to the general belief that the earliest form of human communication is gesture, has proposed the *oral gesture* theory. This holds that

. . . human speech arose out of a generalized unconscious pantomimic gesture language—made by the limbs and features as a whole (including the tongue and lips)—which became specialized in gestures of the organs of articulation, owing to the human hands (and eyes) becoming continuously occupied with the use of tools. The gestures of the organs of articulation

---

[8] Cf. Grandgent, C. H., "The Why and How of Speech," *Getting a Laugh*, Cambridge, Mass. (Harvard), 1924, p. 78.

[9] *Language*, pp. 412-442.

[10] Professor Arthur E. Hutson reports that his students have dubbed this, by analogy, the "woo-woo" theory.

1. Jespersen, Otto }
2. Paget   } P-14

were recognized by the hearer because the hearer unconsciously reproduced in his mind the actual gesture which had produced the sound.[11]

This theory differs from others in considering gesture not as a concomitant of speech, but as the source or at least the articulating factor of speech; it proposes a causal relationship where none had been seen before. There is, of course, no way of either proving or disproving this. Even if we agree that gesture preceded speech as a means of communication, the one need not be accepted as the cause of the other.

The conclusion of the whole matter is that the origin of language is an unsolved and doubtless insoluble enigma.[12] Whatever the origin may have been, it is too remote to admit of more than conjectures about it, of differing degrees of plausibility. Yet the fact that he may never arrive at the truth should not prevent the scientist from making and testing hypotheses. If he gains nothing absolute, at least he dismisses untenable theories and keeps the question alive. As Jespersen has pointed out,[13] "questions which . . . *can* be treated in a scientific spirit, should not be left to the dilettanti." Thus while it is right to reject premature solutions, it is "decidedly wrong to put the question out of court altogether"—as some recent linguists have tended to do.

There is no historical reason or logical necessity, then, to find a single explanation for all types of words. Some were no doubt exclamatory, others imitative; most have changed so entirely from their early form that it cannot be recovered. All we can feel fairly safe about is that at some point the human creature discovered something that the lower animals had not discovered: the symbolic process. His noises could be made to stand for things not present

---

[11] *Human Speech.* New York: Harcourt, Brace and Company, 1930, p. 174. Quoted by permission. By an interesting coincidence, the same theory was arrived at independently and almost simultaneously in Iceland, by Alexander Jóhannesson; see his *Origin of Language.*

[12] There are, of course, a great many more theories than have been mentioned here. Sturtevant, for example, argues that "voluntary communication can scarcely have been called upon except to deceive; language must have been invented for the purpose of lying." *An Introduction to Linguistic Science,* New Haven (Yale University), 1947, p. 48. For a brief summary of theories, see Gray, *Foundations of Language,* p. 40. A full, detailed discussion may be found in Révész, *op. cit.,* pp. 30-112, covering biological, anthropological, philosophical, and other theories. (In German.)

[13] *Language,* pp. 96-99.

to his senses. Gradually he elaborated this into a system, conventionalizing more and more and combining the symbolic sounds in new ways.

But if the *how* of language can never be known, there can be little doubt as to the *why*. Language must have arisen out of a social necessity—the need for communication between man and man. As soon as human creatures began to live in interdependent groups this need must have been a very powerful stimulus. Perhaps, for a time, communication was achieved by gesture alone. But this would have had serious limitations, through darkness, any obstruction that kept one person from seeing another, or the occupation of the limbs that did not leave them free for gestures. Sound, on the other hand, was subject to none of these difficulties, and vocal sound was accessible to almost everybody. And once meaningful speech had been discovered it must have proved its worth as a unifying possession of the whole community. Everyone who could use these symbols would be a member of the group; those who could not, or whose speech-symbols were different, were outsiders. Thus language in the abstract becomes concrete, and we can speak of *a* language, or *the* English language, as the possession of a certain "speech-community." Many of the deepest things in our natures become attached to the particular language which, by accident of birth, happens to be our own. And contrariwise, a difference in language prevents us too often from realizing that other men are, in most ways, very much like ourselves.

Writing. Though it must never be forgotten that speech is the real language, and that writing is only a secondary way of recording it, the importance of writing should not be overlooked. History itself depends on the existence of records, and it may safely be said that the discovery and application of means of recording and passing on human knowledge without the necessity of direct contact between man and man has always been the mark of a high level of human society. If speech itself lifted mankind above the beasts, writing has raised him at least one stage further above his primitive forebears. It therefore seems appropriate to say something here about the evolution of writing, of the alphabet which we use, and of the relationship between speech and spelling.

Systems of writing, viewed chronologically, may be divided into the pre-alphabetic (including *ideograms* or *pictographs*, and *hieroglyphics*) and the alphabetic (including *syllable-scripts* and *single-*

sound scripts). The first of these, strictly speaking, do not deserve the name of writing at all, for ideograms or pictographs are really drawings. These little pictures do not stand for words or names; if they did, they would have to be interpreted always in the same way, as writing is. They stand rather for ideas; they are symbols that may be put into words in a variety of ways. We do not have real writing until a further stage has been reached, in which the drawing —more and more simplified and conventionalized by repetition— stands for a word, or for a part of a word, usually the initial sound or syllable.

Picture-writing, which was apparently developed independently by different peoples in widely separated parts of the world, came eventually into connection with the spoken tongue—though theoretically it might have grown up apart from it, just as the sign language of the American Indians had an existence separate from the spoken dialects. Since it must be assumed, however, that spoken language preceded writing, it seems well-nigh inevitable that sooner or later the two would come into contact with each other. For it would be unthinkable that peoples possessing a well developed set of auditory symbols would continue indefinitely to work out a new set of visual symbols in complete independence of the auditory ones. Drawing became writing when the picture ceased to stand for an idea and came to stand for a combination of sounds. The transition was undoubtedly gradual and came about, probably, "by means of the rebus method . . . by the same sort of process which we apply when we allow a picture of the sun to stand for the first syllable in *sundry*, or let the picture of an eye stand for the pronoun *I*." [14] But of course even after the written symbol came to represent the sounds of some one spoken word by which an idea could be expressed, it also directly signified the idea itself. It was not until the written sign stood only for a sequence of sounds (irrespective of its meaning) that the transition from word-script to sound-script, or from ideogram to *phonogram*, was complete. This was the beginning of the true alphabet. The Egyptian hieroglyphics represent a transitional stage—a mixture—since some of them are ideograms, others phonograms.

The full possibilities of the alphabet were not realized, however,

[14] Pedersen, *Linguistic Science in the Nineteenth Century*, p. 143. For a very good treatment, with illustrations, see also Sturtevant, *op. cit.*, Chapter III.

until the clumsy device of using a symbol for a syllable (consisting perhaps of several consonants and a vowel) gave way to the use of a separate symbol for each individual sound. The Semitic alphabet was a syllable script which represented the consonants definitely but left the vowels vague, so that it appears to consist of consonant-characters only. Characters were no longer so numerous as in the older scripts—the Egyptians bequeathed to a Western Semitic people (the Phoenicians) a means of reducing their number—but the alphabet, as we understand the term, was not yet quite evolved. The final contribution was that of the Greeks: the resolution of syllables into their separate vowels and consonants, and the use of individual characters for the sounds thus analyzed. All known alphabets are descended from the Semitic, but only the Greeks revolutionized the alphabet in the way just indicated, by discarding its syllabic nature. Of the Mediterranean peoples who learned the Greek alphabetic system, one nation—the Romans—continued its use from pre-Christian times through the entire Christian era. Because it was inherited by the Romance languages and borrowed by other Indo-European groups, such as the Germanic, the Latin alphabet has long since dominated the modern world.

Of the four stages in the evolution of writing just outlined—the pre-alphabetic word-script, the syllable-script, and the Semitic and the Greek alphabets—Henry Bradley has acutely observed[15] that the third has peculiar interest for the light it throws upon the general relations of spoken and written language. Arabic, he points out, is to this day usually written as a consonant-script, though vowel marks may be added. Yet it is evident that the consonantal outlines can be apprehended, by one familiar with the language, as readily as if the full phonetic indication of the word were given—perhaps more readily, because the practiced eye takes in the simpler symbol more quickly and just as completely. So too the modern stenographer can read the consonantal outline of familiar words without vowel-markings quite as swiftly as the fuller ones. Medieval Latin manuscripts, Bradley further suggests, were often highly abbreviated, and yet were undoubtedly read with greater rapidity than they would have been if the words had been written in full.

Bradley's point is, of course, that it matters not a jot to the accomplished reader whether his native language is phonetically

[15] *On the Relations between Spoken and Written Language*, p. 6.

spelled or not; "what is important is that the group of letters before him shall be that which habit has led him to associate with a certain word." Nor need one limit this to one's *native* language. Certain Latin abbreviations commonly used in English have just as immediate meaning as native ones: thus *e.g.* does not require to be translated into *exempli gratia* and then into *for example,* or *i.e.* into *id est* and then into *that is.* In both instances the eye conveys the meaning without even the suggestion of a phonetic middle stage.

A simple diagram may make this clearer:

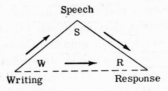

When we speak there is a direct line from the sound-stimulus to its response (S - R). Writing, in its origin at least, substitutes visual characters for sounds, and we have to translate them back into sounds in order to produce the response (W - S - R). But the process is abbreviated when we learn to go directly from the visual stimulus to the response (W - R). Slow readers take the longer route; fast ones take the short-cut.

Just how often the second supersedes the first it is probably impossible to say. Certainly in reading poetry and in reading such prose as that of Milton or Browne, DeQuincey or Coleridge, it may be assumed that the middle stage exists; it would surely be deplorable if it did not. Probably even in the rapid reading of the less poetic types of prose there are some words that call up sound pictures—that is, which the ear responds to as well as the eye. But it seems equally probable that for many words there is no such association; many written or printed words would seem to symbolize their ideas directly.

Bradley's observation should cast doubt upon what is often taken as axiomatic: that the sole function of writing is to represent the *sounds* of language. For, as he argues further,[16] systems of writing that were originally phonetic tend to become at least partly ideographic, as English and other European languages have done—for

[16] *Ibid.,* p. 10.

*Edgar H. Sturdevant — Hitite —
One of grand old men of American
letters and linguistics. (Deception
Theory)*

example, in such matters as the capitalization of proper names, the use of quotation marks, the use of the apostrophe to denote possession, and (most strikingly) the ideographic employment of different spellings to discriminate between words once phonetically distinct but now homophones—such as *rain, rein,* and *reign; or, oar,* and *ore; so, sow,* and *sew.* Even poetry, which normally depends upon sound and therefore necessitates translation from writing to speech, is at times ideographic, as in the use of "eye-rhymes," or in the poems of such writers as E. E. Cummings, in which the typography is deliberately a part of the effect and cannot be entirely rendered into sound.

But even if the writing of Modern English is in some few respects ideographic and has got out of touch with sound to a considerable degree—even if the experienced reader can read directly from eye to brain without involving the ear—the system of spelling is still, in its origin and in actuality, far more dependent on the alphabet than not. And that is altogether as it should be. Alphabetic writing has the enormous advantage over ideographic that it can get on with a very small number of characters: our alphabet has a mere twenty-six letters, while Chinese scholars have been struggling to reduce their picture-writing system to a thousand. The alphabetic system, obviously, is enormously easier to learn and therefore more useful. Universal education becomes a rational ideal only if a system that can be rapidly learned by the mass of people is at hand.

At least one more fact of writing requires attention. In a developed culture, the body of scholarly and artistic writings becomes a repository that can hardly be matched in a culture that has no writing, however carefully the memories of the learned may be developed and trained. The world of the written word, therefore, while ultimately based on speech and always referable to it—capable of being translated into sounds—does have a certain undeniable autonomy. It is in this world, the world of literature, that a language is submitted most fully to intellectual and esthetic influences—in short, to cultivation; and in so far as standards of "correctness" or "acceptability" emerge, they come from those members of a community who are not merely literate but who know the language at its more highly developed levels.

If, then, the language of literature, of ideas, of the more complex emotions reflects its influences upon the spoken language, there should be no cause for surprise. Obviously this cannot happen in a simple culture that has no writing or literary tradition. But it does happen in a higher culture, as we shall see in subsequent chapters. Literary purposes, or the adherence to literary ideals—however wrongheaded they may sometimes have been—have continually affected the English vocabulary, idiom, usage, syntax, morphology, and even the sounds of the language. As we come to these successively it will be well to keep in mind the separate but related spheres of speech and writing, the first fundamental to the second, but the second nevertheless having a real existence, without which the first would only be poorer.

REFERENCES FOR FURTHER READING

Bloomfield, Leonard, *Language*, New York (Holt), 1933.

Bradley, Henry, *On the Relations between Spoken and Written Language, with Special Reference to English*, London (Oxford), 1919.

Graff, Willem L., *Language and Languages*, New York (Appleton), 1932.

Gray, Louis H., *Foundations of Language*, New York (Macmillan), 1939.

Jespersen, Otto, *Language: Its Nature, Development, and Origin*, New York (Holt), 1924.

———, *Mankind, Nation, and Individual from a Linguistic Point of View*, Oslo (Aschehoug), 1925.

Jóhannesson, Alexander, *Origin of Language*, Reykjavík (Leiftur), 1949.

Kennedy, Arthur G., *Current English*, Boston (Ginn), 1935.

Paget, Sir Richard, *Human Speech*, New York (Harcourt, Brace), 1930.

Pedersen, Holger (trans. by J. W. Spargo), *Linguistic Science in the Nineteenth Century*, Cambridge, Mass. (Harvard), 1931.

Révész, G., *Ursprung und Vorgeschichte der Sprache*, Bern (Francke), 1946.

Sapir, Edward, *Language: An Introduction to the Study of Speech*, New York (Harcourt, Brace), 1921.

Sturtevant, Edgar H., *An Introduction to Linguistic Science*, New Haven (Yale University), 1947.

Vendryes, E. (trans. by P. Radin), *Language: A Linguistic Introduction to History*, New York (Knopf), 1925.

1. Emotional songs were basic in the derivation of what became speech.

2. The Oral gesture Theory (bottom of page 7)

Chapter 2

The Ancestry of English

WE DO not at present know whether human languages spring from a single common starting point or from more than one. Nevertheless, we can demonstrate today that of the hundreds of languages and dialects spoken in the world, many fall into historically related groups, usually called "families." Most of the languages now spoken in Europe, for example, and in parts of the world colonized by Europeans, are agreed by students of language to be members of a single family and to have descended from one hypothetical speech ancestor—Indo-European, otherwise known as Indo-Germanic and sometimes as Aryan.[1] This ancestor language is no longer spoken—indeed, no actual records of it remain and what we know has had to be laboriously reconstructed from the features preserved in its off-spring.

Because English is one of its members, the Indo-European family is at the center of our present interest, but there are many non-Indo-European families of languages in the world. Those that have been most directly in contact with Indo-European include the following: Finno-Ugrian, comprising Finnish, Lappish, Hungarian (Magyar), and others; Altaic, including Turkish, Mongolian, and Manchu; Hamitic, made up of certain African languages, among them Egyptian; and Semitic,[2] the best-known members of which are Hebrew and Arabic. There are many more-distant families—for example, the

---

[1] "Aryan" is best avoided; it is ambiguous, having been used as a synonym of Indo-Iranian as well as of Indo-European. Furthermore, it has been used as a racial designation, which gives the false implication of a connection between race and language.

[2] The terms *Semitic* and *Hamitic* reflect the old belief that from the different languages spoken by the sons of Noah sprang the great groups of languages later spoken in the world. In line with this belief, the Indo-European was once called the *Japhetic*.

15

Kinesthetics - study of features

Sino-Tibetan (or Indo-Chinese), whose members are found in Tibet, Burma, Thailand, and China. The total number of families of languages is in the hundreds, but the majority of these are limited dialects, spoken chiefly in Africa and the Americas, whose relationship to any of the larger groups has not yet been shown. The number of native American Indian language-families alone is thus estimated at over one hundred and twenty. If more evidence were available as to earlier forms, it would doubtless be possible to reduce this number greatly; it is even conceivable that, with fuller knowledge, all the families now recognized might be grouped together as branches of a common unit. But a great many languages have never been studied adequately, many are totally unknown, and though there is vigorous activity in the field of language study today, a very great deal of work lies ahead before linguists can begin to demonstrate such broader relationships, if ever they can. In any consideration of the ancestry of English, therefore, we must be satisfied at present with the conception of an Indo-European starting point.

Before beginning with the Indo-European theory, however, it may be well to inquire into the factors that account for the splitting up of a language into subdivisions and new groupings. We have used the metaphor of a "family," of "ancestor" and "descendants," because it is convenient, though not literally accurate. Languages are not organisms living by generations and having individual offspring. This much truth there is in the metaphor, however: that though in the course of time the elements of a language are constantly subject to natural change, they do not change altogether or all of a sudden. Thus, as one may recognize the features and traits of parents in their children, a historical study of language shows some features preserved where others have changed; and if several languages exhibit common characteristics, they must have come by them either through coincidence, or by borrowing, or through derivation from a common source. The chief labor of the historical linguist goes into solving such questions and explaining observed similarities and differences.

Languages split up for at least three reasons, which may work separately or together: *natural change, geographic division*, and *contact with other languages*. The first depends on the fact that language is normally learned by imitation—by hearing and repeating. But since this imitation is never exact—and indeed need not be so, for a fairly close imitation will usually get the same result as a precise one—in the course of a few generations a language may easily come to sound quite different in many respects. Spelling alone could show us, for example, if there were no other evidence, that Shakespeare, at the end of the sixteenth century, said many things quite differently from Chaucer, at the end of the fourteenth. Add to this the changes in vocabulary that come from altered conditions of life, new inventions, and our individual differences of expression, and it is easy to see why we do not speak like our grandparents. In the most conservative societies such changes are reduced to a minimum, and a cultural and educational tradition may (as with us) hold them in check to some extent; but change is a fundamental, unavoidable fact of language.

Secondly, geographic division may foster language division by inhibiting communication. Two groups, let us say, migrate from a common point, but settle on opposite sides of a mountain or river. At the time of parting they spoke alike; but they lose touch, and the rate and type of the natural changes in their speech do not correspond. One group, perhaps, takes to farming, the other to seafaring; or one develops a static society, the other a dynamic. Inevitably such differences will be reflected in speech. The separated groups will speak different dialects, and in time perhaps different languages. But this situation itself will not necessarily last indefinitely. After the original separation and subsequent changes, lines of communication may be established despite the geographic obstruction, and a whole new phase of development may begin. The science of linguistic geography (of which more shall be said later) furnishes countless examples of such developments. One need only glance at the map of Europe to see that natural barriers—the Alps or the Pyrenees—are often also the frontiers of language. On a smaller scale, the separation of Old English (Anglo-Saxon) into dialects, though it began on the continent before the tribes migrated, is emphasized by the fact that the boundaries are rivers: the region of the Northumbrian dialect was from the Humber to the Forth; of the Mercian from the Thames to the Humber: and of the West Saxon, most of the country south of the Thames.

Thirdly, languages change because of contact with other languages. This may come about in various ways, but commerce and conquest furnish the most striking examples. An alien tongue has often been imposed upon a conquered people. Or it may work the other way: the Normans afford the remarkable instance of conquerors twice giving up their own language for that of a conquered people; for they first exchanged their Scandinavian language for the Romance tongue of Normandy, and eventually they gave up the French dialect thus acquired and accepted the Germanic speech of conquered Britain. Commerce involves travel and exploration, and the introduction of things from other lands. Though less sudden than conquest, it is thus an important means of increasing changes in language. From the earliest times we know of, English has been so influenced by other tongues; many of the brave new words that the Elizabethans spouted with such delight had come from brave new worlds that were opening yearly before them.

Let us return, then, to the Indo-European hypothesis. This holds that in the Later Stone Age there lived a people or peoples speaking a tongue that was the common ancestor of the greater number of cultivated languages now existing in the world. This does not imply either that the original Indo-Europeans were racially a unit or that their speech descendants are racially akin. It does, however, assume that the hypothetical language which we call Indo-European was the speech of a people inhabiting a comparatively limited geographical area, and that from this focal point have radiated all the subdivisions of the Indo-European family of languages.[3] What was the focal area from which these languages spread? During the last half-century there have been a number of investigations into the problems of the Indo-European "home" and of the classification of language that the Indo-European theory implies. Partly anthropological and archeological but chiefly linguistic, these investigations have altered the old belief that the home of the Indo-Europeans was in Asia, and most probably in the fabled region of the Garden of Eden, between the Tigris and the Euphrates. It is now generally held that the Indo-European home was in central or southeastern

[3] The migrations from this center are thought to have begun during the third millennium B.C. On the basis of common words for copper that remain in the various branches, Prof. Gray argues (*Foundations of Language*, p. 307), "it seems safe to infer that Indo-European unity came to an end after copper had become known, but before the Bronze Age. . . . The use of bronze was established in Europe by 1700 B.C."—which sets the start of migration as probably before 2000 B.C.

Europe, though some scholars contend that it was farther to the north. Some of the methods used in attacking the problem may be of interest.

The evidence of language is fairly clear as to the climate, the animals, and the plants of the region that the original Indo-Europeans inhabited. Everything points to the temperate zone, and in all probability not to the southern part of that zone. For in many Indo-European languages we find the same words (not, of course, words identical in form, but words strongly alike in both form and meaning, and therefore recognizable as variants of the same original) for such phenomena as snow, winter, and spring; for such animals as the dog, the horse, the cow, the sheep, the bear, but *not* the camel, the lion, the elephant, or the tiger; for such trees as the beech, the oak, the pine, the willow, but not the palm or the banyan.[4] It is urged, further, that the country could not have had access to the sea: there is apparently no common word for "ocean."[5] If it was on the continent of Europe, it is unlikely, for other reasons, that it was near the seacoast: the pre-Hellenic inhabitants of Greece, for example, were not Indo-European, nor were the Etruscans in Italy, the pre-Celtic peoples who inhabited Britain, or the Basques in Spain and southern France; and over the greater part of northern and eastern Europe were the Finno-Ugrians.

A single argument may be given in greater detail to illustrate the way in which the problem of the Indo-European home has recently been approached. Professor Bender[6] observes that almost every Indo-European language shares with its fellows a common word for honey or for an intoxicating drink made from honey. The first stem is Indo-European * *melit*,[7] the second * *medhu*. The former appears, for example, in Greek *méli* (honey) and *mélissa* (bee), Latin *mel* (honey), and Old English *milisc* (honey-sweet) and *mildēaw* (mildew—literally, "honey-dew"). The latter appears, among many

[4] It must be recognized that, singly, these words would offer inadequate proof; the names of trees, for example, are likely to apply to entirely different species in different times and places: the ancient Greek word corresponding to English *beech* meant *oak*, and sometimes *chestnut*.

[5] This, however, is sometimes asserted with more confidence than is warranted; cf. Hirt, *Indogermanische Grammatik*, Vol. I, pp. 77-78.

[6] *The Home of the Indo-Europeans*, pp. 19-20.

[7] An asterisk (*) prefixed to any word indicates that it is a linguistic reconstruction, not a form attested historically.

other places, in Sanskrit *madhu* (honey, mead), Greek *méthu* (intoxicating drink), Dutch *mede* (mead), and Old English *medu* (mead). The inference is that the original home of the Indo-Europeans was a land where the honey-bee abounded; and none of the Asiatic sites that have been seriously considered by linguists falls within the bee-belt. In ways like this, though with full recognition that one or another single argument may be fallacious, the weight of the evidence favors the theory of a central or southeastern European site. Professor Bender argues for Lithuania as the specific region, pointing out that "Lithuanian . . . has preserved into modern living speech more of the Indo-European past than any other language on earth," and that "the Lithuanian stock has dwelt in its present location for at least five thousand years, the duration of the Indo-European period, so far as it is known." [8]

Accepting, then, the concept of an Indo-European starting point, we may proceed to examine the classification of language that follows from this theory. There are nine divisions, groups, or branches recognized today as composing the Indo-European family.[9] These are further divided, according to the sound of the initial consonant that appears (in the various languages) in such words as the Latin *centum* and the Avestan *satem*, the word for "hundred," into the *centum* group (Tokharian, Hellenic, Italic, Celtic, and Germanic) and the *satem* group (Indo-Iranian, Armenian, Balto-Slavic, and Albanian). Upon what cause this observed difference depends is unknown, and it may be doubted whether it betokens important early differences between the languages; but if, as is possible, the *s* represents a palatalization[10] of the *k*, it may suggest something about the relative conservatism of the branches, and possibly about the sequence of the migrations.

The relationships among the nine branches are complex; they group together in one way on the basis of some features and in quite

---

[8] The question, however, is not settled—at least, so far as the specific region is concerned. See, for example, the new arguments made by Professor Jóhannesson, *Um frumtungu Indógermana og frumheimkynni*, 1941.

[9] This number would be increased to ten if Hittite were considered to be on a par with the other members; but according to the Indo-Hittite hypothesis of Prof. E. H. Sturtevant it is not. See the diagram on p. 33.

[10] Palatalization means that a sound (such as that of *k*) which is articulated in the back of the mouth cavity, changes, becoming articulated in the area of the hard palate farther toward the front of the mouth, and therefore also changes its quality.

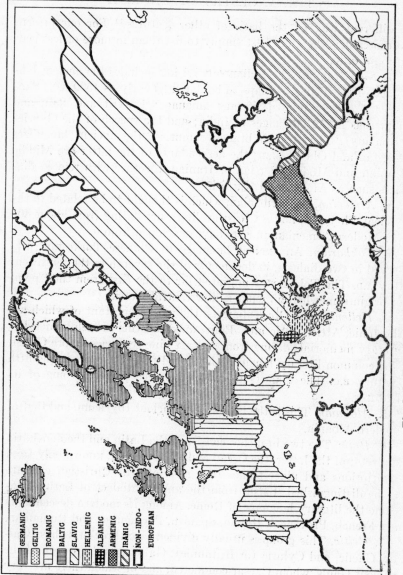

The Indo-European Languages in Present-Day Europe

GERMANIC
CELTIC
ROMANIC
BALTIC
SLAVIC
HELLENIC
ALBANIC
ARMENIC
IRANIC
NON-INDO-
EUROPEAN

a different way on the basis of other features.[11] For our present purposes it is therefore best simply to list them in more or less geographic order.[12]

1. *Indo-Iranian*. The Indian subdivision includes the ancient language of the Vedas, perhaps to be dated as early as 1500 B.C.; Sanskrit, a closely related literary language; Prakrit and Pali, and numerous living languages of India; and the speech of the Gypsies (Romany). The Iranian branch comprises the ancient languages Avestan and Old Persian; the descendants of the latter are Middle Iranian and Modern Persian or Iranian, together with related dialects such as Afghan and Kurdish.

2. *Armenian*. Old Armenian, which is thought to be related to the ancient Phrygian, had a Christian literature dating from about 400 A.D. Modern Armenian dialects have developed from it.

3. *Tokharian*. An ancient language of Chinese Turkestan, preserved in two dialects, in documents of the seventh to the tenth century A.D. The Tokharians migrated far to the east from their point of origin somewhere in what is now central Russia.

4. *Hellenic*. The Greek dialects, the most important of which are the Ionic, Attic, Doric and Æolic, make up this branch, which has literary memorials dating from at least nine centuries before Christ. The common literary language developed from the Attic in the fifth century B.C. The dialects of modern Greece preserve some of its features.

5. *Albanian*. This is the language of ancient Illyricum, and that of modern Albania.

6. *Italic*. The two branches consist of the Latin and the non-Latin dialects; of the latter, the Oscan and the Umbrian, known only from inscriptions and place-names that antedate the Christian era, are to be distinguished. Latin, from the ancient dialect of Latium, became the literary language of Rome. Among its modern descendants are French, Provençal, Italian, Spanish, Portuguese, and Rumanian.

7. *Celtic*. This group is usually divided into three branches: Gallic, Gaelic, and Cymric (or Britannic). Gallic was the speech of the ancient Gauls, whom Caesar conquered, and of which there are very

---

[11] Several theories attempt to account for these relationships. See the summary of these, for example, with illustrative diagrams, in Prokosch, *A Comparative Germanic Grammar*, pp. 21-22, and Gray, *op. cit.*, p. 310.

[12] See the map on page 21.

scanty remains. Gaelic includes chiefly the Irish, with a medieval and modern literature, and spoken dialects now being deliberately resuscitated as a national language in the Irish Free State; and Scotch-Gaelic, known from about the eleventh century, and still in some use in the highlands of Scotland. Cymric embraces Welsh, known as a literary language from the Middle Ages; Cornish, which became extinct in the nineteenth century; and Breton, or Armorican, a dialect of northwest France.

8. *Germanic* (otherwise known as Teutonic or Gothonic). The three branches of this group are the East Germanic, the North Germanic, and the West Germanic. East Germanic (or Gothic) is preserved in the fragmentary translation of the New Testament by Bishop Ulfilas, made about 350 A.D. and hence the oldest text in any Germanic language. The East Germanic has been extinct since about the seventeenth century. North Germanic comprises the Scandinavian languages, represented in both medieval and modern literature; an easterly division includes Danish and Swedish, and a westerly, Norwegian and Icelandic. The West Germanic branch, from which English stems, will be discussed shortly.

9. *Balto-Slavic.* The Baltic group consists of Old Prussian, Lettic, and Lithuanian. The Slavic (or Slavonic) group is further broken into two subdivisions: one includes Polish and Czechish (or Bohemian); the other Russian and Bulgarian.

The common features by means of which scholars have classified the Indo-European languages as a family, setting them apart from non-Indo-European languages are chiefly two: they are all *inflectional* in structure[13] and they have a *common word-stock*. The term *inflectional* means that such syntactic distinctions as gender, number, case, mood, tense,[14] and so forth, are usually indicated by varying the form of a single word or word-base. Thus, in English inflection, we add -*s* to a noun base to differentiate the plural from the singular, or -*ed* to a verb base to indicate past tense. English inflection uses endings almost entirely, though (as we shall see) inflection may come also at the beginning of words or within them.

The *inflectional* structure is only one type; languages outside the Indo-European system that are not inflectional may be: *isolating,*

---

[13] Not all inflectional languages are Indo-European, however.

[14] If the student is not familiar with these and other common grammatical terms, he had better look them up at once in a good dictionary or grammar.

like Chinese, in which invariable word-forms, mostly monosyllabic, are used, and in which the relation between words is indicated by their relative position ("word-order") or occasionally by variation in tonal patterns; *agglutinative,* like Turkish or Hungarian, in which formal affixes are attached to independent and invariable bases in such a way that base and affix are always distinct; or *incorporating* or *polysynthetic* like the language of Greenland (Eskimo), in which a single word may express not only subject and verb, but also such other concepts as direct and indirect object; hence, what would be, in an isolating language, a sentence of five or six words, may be "incorporated" as a single word.[15] Still other types of structure are to be found.

As to the second criterion of the Indo-European languages, the possession of a common word-stock, it will strike even the novice that, for example, Greek *nuktós,*[16] Latin *noctis,* German *Nacht,* French *nuit,* Spanish *noche,* Italian *notte,* and English *night* have a similarity of form and meaning that seems too striking to be accidental. Unless some of these had been borrowed or loaned from one language to another, such similarity must imply a common origin. Further examples of *cognates* (as such words are called) appearing in different Indo-European languages are:[17]

English	Dutch	German	Gothic	Lithuanian
three	drie	drei	thri	tri
seven	zeven	sieben	sibun	septyni
me	mij	mich	mik	manen
mother	moeder	mutter	——	moter
brother	broeder	bruder	brothar	brolis

Celtic	Latin	Greek	Persian	Sanskrit
tri	tres	treis	thri	tri
secht	septem	hepta	hapta	sapta
me	me	me	me	me
mathair	mater	meter	matar	matar
brathair	frater	phrater	——	bhratar

These are not isolated examples; there are hundreds of other such words preserved in the various branch languages, which gives the classification a sound basis.

[15] Cf. Pedersen, *Linguistic Science in the Nineteenth Century,* pp. 99-100.

[16] This form, the next, and others later on are given as usual in oblique cases, in order to show the full bases. (Bases were often reduced in the nominative case.)

[17] From Whitney, *Language and the Study of Language,* p. 196.

Coming closer to English we may next ask what special character-istics the Germanic languages have in common that serve to differ-entiate Germanic, as a branch, from the other divisions of Indo-European. The four principal ones are:[18]

1. A simpler conjugation of verbs (only two tenses), including a twofold classification (strong and weak);
2. A twofold classification of adjectives (strong and weak);
3. A fixed stress-accent;
4. A regular shifting of the stopped (or explosive) consonants.

Each of these points requires fuller explanation.

As to the first: even a slight acquaintance with Latin or Greek makes it apparent that their conjugation of verbs is far more com-plex than is that of German or English. The terminology sometimes used should not be allowed to obscure this contrast. The fact that in a grammar-book the phrase *I had loved* or *ich hatte geliebt* may be labeled as a "pluperfect tense" does not mean that in structure it really parallels *amaveram*, which is similarly labeled. The English and German examples show "analytical" structure—that is, the three words, though they function as a single group, are still separate units in combination; but the Latin equivalent shows "synthetic" structure—that is, the word is made up of inseparable parts that cannot stand by themselves.[19]

Latin verbs have a very elaborate series of such synthetic forms to differentiate various concepts of voice, mood, tense, person, and number; Greek, being still nearer the complexity of the Indo-European verb, has at least one more complication in almost every category: there are not only the two numbers of Latin, singular and plural, but also a third, the dual; there are not only the two voices, active and passive, but also a third, the middle; there are additional moods, like the optative, and additional tenses, like the aorist. In sharp contrast to this is the system of Germanic, characterized by having only two tenses, one to express past time, the other to express present and future. The inflected passive voice of Germanic, like-

[18] It should perhaps be added that the four chief changes from Indo-European to Germanic give a very incomplete picture of the whole process. Cf. Hirt, *Handbuch des Urgermanischen.*

[19] If we break up the Latin word we find that *am-* means *love*, *-av-* indicates past time (like *-ed* in *loved*), *-er-* indicates completed action (like *had*), and *-am* has the same function as *I*.

wise, was early lost; it is represented in Old English by only a single form, *hātte* (was called), a related form of which survives as the poetic relic *hight;* elsewhere the passive voice was expressed as in Modern English by an analytic combination of an auxiliary verb with the past participle of the main verb (as in the example *I had loved* just mentioned).

The most distinctive feature of the Germanic verb, however, is its development of a new way of indicating the preterit and past participle by means of a dental suffix[20] the *-ed* of English and the *-te* and *-t* of German. The pattern inherited from Indo-European in the verb, then, is called "strong" and the new pattern is called "weak." Both types last into Modern English: the weak (less accurately called "regular") verbs are those with the dental preterit, as *walk, walked;* the strong (or "irregular") are those with internal vowel change, such as *sing, sang, sung.* The latter group corresponds historically to the verbs of other languages, but the former is distinctively Germanic. Because more verbs belong to the weak conjugation, we have come to feel, as the term "regular" suggests, that it is not only the simpler but the normal pattern. When we borrow or create new verbs, they are made to conform to it.

The second distinguishing characteristic of the Germanic languages is the twofold classification of the adjective that developed: it was declined according to one system ("strong") when it stood alone before the noun or was used in the predicate relation, and according to another system ("weak") when used substantively or when it was preceded by a defining element, such as an article or a demonstrative. Since Modern English has lost all declension of the adjective, this distinction between the strong and weak forms cannot be illustrated with contemporary examples. It lasted, however, into Old English, and is still to be found in German. Thus, in Modern English we used the identical form *good* in the expressions *good men* and *these good men.* In Old English, however, the corresponding phrases would be *gōde menn* and *þās gōdan menn*—as in German the corresponding phrases are *gute Männer* and *diese guten Männer.* As with the verbs, it is the weak inflection that is distinctively Germanic, the strong forms corresponding more or less to adjective declension in other Indo-European languages. The loss of the dis-

[20] That is, one including the sound *d* or *t,* which are produced in the dental area of the mouth, behind the upper teeth.

tinction in Modern English need hardly be mourned—it is difficult to see any gain in expressiveness that would justify this peculiar inflectional complexity! Nevertheless, its former presence in English and its retention in German are significant in marking these languages unmistakably as members of the Germanic branch.

III. The third characteristic of the Germanic languages is their accent, fixed rather than free or variable, and a matter of stress rather than of pitch. To English-speaking people it may seem at first sight that accent in any language must necessarily be fixed—that is, that it must come on a particular syllable of a word. But it is clear to linguists that the original Indo-European and the primitive Germanic accent was variable; for example, it might shift, in the inflection of a word, from the base syllable to a syllable of the inflectional ending. Greek and Latin partially preserve this, as when the Greek *poûs* (foot) is declined *podós, podí, póda;* the accent, that is to say, shifts in the genitive and dative from the base to the inflectional ending, and comes back, in the accusative, to the base. Latin also exhibits this freer accent (in contrast to the Germanic) as, for example, in the conjugation of the present indicative of *amō*, where we find *ámō, ámās, ámat, amámus, amátis, ámant.* Or note how in the inflection of *gubernātor* the accent is shifted from the nominative *gubernátor* to the genetive *gubernatóris.* We should be doing something equivalent in English if we spoke of the *góvernor*, and then proceeded to speak of *the govérnor's house.* But this, of course, or anything remotely like it[21] we never do: our tendency is to stress strongly the first syllable of a word (excluding prefixes that are felt as such). The Germanic branch, then, during the primitive period when it was becoming separated from the Indo-European parent language, shifted its accent back to the base syllable, where it became fixed; it is therefore called the *recessive* stress-accent, and this is inherited in Modern English.

The other aspect of the Germanic accent is even more important: many other Indo-European languages retain something of the original "musical" or pitch accent; in the Germanic languages, by contrast, accent has become to all intents a matter of stress. The im-

---

[21] It may be objected that we have shifting accent, in Modern English, in pairs of words like *pérfume* (n.), *perfúme* (v.), or in classical derivatives like *phótograph* and *photógrapher*. But this is clearly different from an accent which shifts in the inflection of a single part of speech.

plications of this distinction are considerable. The accentuation of
English and German is utterly unlike that of French, which in words
of two syllables has more nearly a hovering or distributed accent
than a firm stress on one syllable. Such pronunciations as *wéekènd,
bóokcàse, saúcepàn,* with stress on both syllables, are the exception
in English; in most cases we have come to overemphasize, as compared even with German, the accented syllable, and to underempha-
size the unaccented.[22] Perhaps this is the chief reason why French
as pronounced by an English-speaking person, who can scarcely
help carrying over his usual habits of accentuation, so often sounds
curiously unreal. The versification of Germanic languages likewise
depends upon this distinction between the stressed and unstressed
syllable, and its effect is utterly different from that achieved by the
quantitative system of the classical languages and its partial retention in the Romance languages.

Finally, perhaps the most important effect that the heavy Germanic stress-accent has had upon the development of English has
been that of slurring and frequently altogether dropping unstressed
vowels. Because the accent usually falls on the first syllable of the
word and because English inflections are chiefly in the final syllables,
it has been easy for inflectional endings to become weakened, obscured, and lost—and consequently to simplify the whole system of
inflection. Here is the chief reason, too, for the largely monosyllabic
quality of the native English word-stock.

IV   The fourth distinctive mark of the Germanic languages is their
almost regular shifting of the Indo-European stopped consonants.[23]
That is to say, the original Indo-European sounds remained in general unchanged in all branches except the Germanic; but there their
articulation shifted, a new set of sounds being substituted for them.
The evidence for this shift was discovered by comparing hundreds
of words whose meaning was very close, but whose forms differed as

[22] For this reason it is frequently said that in the pronunciation of Modern
English only those vowels that are protected by the stress have their full quality,
all others tending to be neutralized. Only the most recent of dictionaries make this
clear; it has been customary for dictionaries to use different characters for the
unstressed vowels of such words as *tuba, camel, robin, carrot, circus,* even though
the vowels are not sounded *a, e, i, o, u,* but almost identically, with the sound
whose phonetic symbol is [ə]. (See below, Chapter 4, p. 59 and 73.)
[23] A stopped consonant is one produced by stopping the breath stream momentarily, which stoppage, when released, makes an audible explosion. (See
further in Chapter 4, pp. 61-64.)

between the Germanic and the non-Germanic branches, whereupon it was seen that these differences were not haphazard but clearly followed a pattern. The regularity of these changes was first stated by the Danish linguist Rasmus Rask, in 1814; but their later formulation by Jacob Grimm in 1822 has given the principles the designation "Grimm's Law." It is now more often called the *first Germanic consonant shift*.[24] A full statement of it and of its subsequent modifications would be out of place here. It may, however, be broadly stated as follows:

Voiced aspirated stops			*Voiced stops*			*Voiceless stops*[25]		
bh	dh	gh	b	d	g	p	t	k
V	V	V	V	V	V	V	V	V
b	d	g	p	t	k	f	th	h

Indo-European voiced aspirated stops lost aspiration and became Germanic voiced stops.	Indo-European voiced stops lost voice and became Germanic voiceless stops.	Indo-European voiceless stops lost their stopped quality and became Germanic voiceless spirants.[26]
(Stage 3)	(Stage 2)	(Stage 1)

p → F in Gmc [handwritten]

It is to be understood, of course, that each original set of consonants changed only once; for example, the *b, d, g* that resulted from the shift of *bh, dh, gh* did not shift further. Indeed, had they done so, the words formerly distinguished by these sounds would have fallen together as homophones, losing distinction and producing much confusion. The whole process is understood to have taken place in three stages; after *p, t,* and *k* had shifted, it was possible for *b, d,* and *g* to shift without producing homophones.

Illustrations of the situation "before" may be drawn generally from the non-Germanic languages (Greek, Latin, Sanskrit, Old Irish, and so on), and the situation "after" from any Germanic language (Old Norse, Old High German, Old English, Old Saxon, and so on), the only difficulty being that in some cases further simplifications took place in individual languages, which somewhat obscured

---

[24] The second Germanic consonant shift took place only in High German dialects, and therefore does not affect English.

[25] Sounds are *voiced* when the vocal cords are vibrating during their production, *voiceless* when the vocal cords are not vibrating. *Aspiration* is the quality of a sound produced by puffing the breath out, with slight constriction of the oral or throat passage.

[26] A *spirant* (or *fricative*) is a sound made by forcing the breath, without actually stopping it, through a narrowed outlet in the oral or throat passage.

the earlier shift. For instance, in Greek the Indo-European *bh* became *ph*, and in Latin it became *f*; thus Greek *phrater* and Latin *frater* represent Indo-European **bhratar*, the shift being seen in English *brother*. Similarly, Indo-European *dh* and *gh* were reduced initially in Latin to *f* and *h*, therefore we find such correspondences as Latin *facere*, English *do*, and Latin *hostis*, English *guest*. The changes of the third stage, then, cannot be simply illustrated; the others, however, may be seen in the following tabulation:[27]

Change: *b > p*

Lithuanian *troba* (house)—Old Norse *thorp* (village)
Old Bulgarian *slabŭ* (slack, weak)—English *sleep*
Lithuanian *dubus*—English *deep*

Change: *d > t*

Latin *dentem*—English *tooth* COGNATE
Greek *édein*—English *eat*
Russian *dva*—Old English *twā* (two)

Change: *g > k*

Sanskrit *yuga*—English *yoke*
Greek *(gi)gnṓ(skein)*—English *know*
Latin *genu*—German *Knie* (knee)

Change: *p > f*

Greek *plōtós* (floating)—English *flood*
Latin *nepos*—Old English *nefa* (nephew)
Persian *pidar*—English *father*

Change: *t > th*

Polish *tarn*—English *thorn*
Latin *tū*—English *thou*
Old Latin *tongēre* (know)—English *think*

Change: *k > h*

Greek *deka*—Gothic *taíhun* (ten)
Latin *canem*—German *Hund* (dog)
Irish *cridhe*—English *heart*

Later philologists than Grimm found it necessary to modify his statement of the consonant-shift. Chief of these modifications, called Verner's Law, bears the name of the Danish linguist who first

---

[27] Initial consonants regularly illustrate this shift, as do most medial and final consonants; the exceptions to the latter will be dealt with under "Verner's Law," pp. 31-32.

showed (in 1875) how the seeming exceptions to Grimm's Law, if once understood according to a principle of accent, turned out to be regular, not erratic. His postulate was that when the first consonant-shift began it found the early Germanic stress on the same syllables as in Indo-European, and that it was this stress on many medial and final syllables that accounted for the presence of voiced consonants instead of the voiceless consonants which might otherwise have been expected. Thus the primitive Indo-European *voiceless stops (p, t, k)*, no matter in what position in a word they happened to be, changed to *voiceless spirants (f, þ, h)* in early-primitive-Germanic. In later-primitive-Germanic, however, a split developed: those which came in initial position in a word, or immediately after a stressed vowel, changed no further—but those which came in any other position changed to *voiced spirants;* thus *f, þ, h,* (and *s*) became respectively ƀ, ð, ʒ, and *z*.[28] Verner argued that it was the difference in the pattern of stress that was responsible for this change of internal consonant sounds, and that when the Germanic stress shifted back, soon after, to the base syllable of all words (see p. 27), the cause of the consonant-split became obscured.

The English verb *to be* furnishes a good illustration of Verner's Law, since in the forms *was* and *were* we find an *s* in correspondence with an *r*. The difference is explained thus: In early-primitive-Germanic the singular and plural forms had both had *s* (*wǽs, *wēsún*); in later-primitive-Germanic the *s* became *z* unless it was initial or just after a stressed vowel (*wǽs, *wēzún*); then the stress shifted to the base syllable (*wǽs, *wǽzun*). Further changes took place in the West Germanic stage of development, and when we come to Old English we find that the four voiced spirants, ƀ, ð, ʒ, and *z*, have become respectively *f, d, ʒ,* and *r*. Thus the forms of *to be* appear as *wæs* and *wǣron*. One may follow the process further in English by mining in the *Oxford Dictionary* (or any other which has good etymologies) under such words as *seethe, sodden; freeze, frore; rear* (the verb), and *raise*.

A few broader illustrations may also be given. Germanic, in the situation described, has *d* when *th* would be expected as the simple

---

[28] These four symbols represent respectively a bilabial, an interdental or labiodental, a velar, and an alveolar—all voiced spirants. For further light on these terms, see Chapter 4.

shift from Indo-European *t;* thus English *old* (Old English *eald*) is cognate with Latin *altus*,[29] English *yard* (Old English *geard*) with Latin *hortus,* English *sad* [30] with Latin *satis.* Likewise Indo-European *p* and *k,* instead of appearing as *f* and *h,* become *b* and *g* respectively under the conditions of Verner's Law.[31] Verner's brilliant discovery showed all the more clearly that the greatest progress was made in the solution of problems when investigators proceeded on the assumption of basic regularity ("laws"), the exceptions to which were themselves to be explained by the assumption of regular processes of development and change. Linguistic geography has since shown that qualifications must be made to this, but as a broad working hypothesis it marked a great advance over the less rigorous methods which preceded it.

Of the four distinguishing Germanic characteristics that have been reviewed, it is probably accurate to suggest that the accent contributed most to make Germanic words distinctive and to give the modern Germanic languages a unique place among European languages. The stress-shift that took place, as Verner's Law implies, after the first consonant-shift had begun, was even more important than the other process in changing the character of Germanic words.[32] The result of the stress-shift was that, in general, the Germanic accent was fixed on the base syllable of the word, except that in nouns and adjectives, and in verbs derived from these, it rested on the first syllable, whether prefix or base. As a result of both consonant-shift and stress-shift, the Germanic branch emerged as a highly individualized and easily identifiable member of the Indo-European family of languages.

In order to understand the specific position of English, we must now return and consider the subdivisions of the Germanic branch. To the eastern group belongs Gothic; to the northern belong Old Norse and the modern Scandinavian languages; the western became divided into the high and low groups (according to their geographic distribution in southern uplands or northern lowlands), the former

[29] Representing an Indo-European **alt-ós.*

[30] Originally meaning "sated"; cf. German *satt.*

[31] An excellent, detailed treatment of these two laws may be found in Wright, *Old English Grammar,* sections 229-239.

[32] For a discussion of the relative significance of these two processes, see Jespersen, *Growth and Structure of the English Language,* Leipsig (Teubner), 1935, pp. 22-28.

being chiefly represented by modern standard German, the latter by Low German ("Plattdeutsch"), Dutch, Frisian, and English. In all these divisions of Germanic there are remains from early centuries. The accompanying diagram shows schematically the relations of the

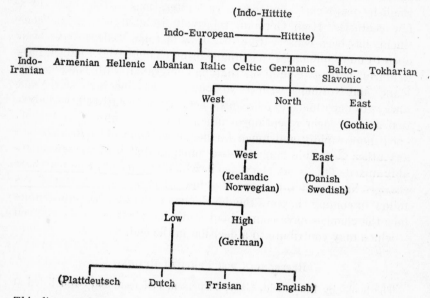

This diagram shows:

a. The nine main branches of the Indo-European family of languages;
b. The position of Hittite (above, in parentheses) according to the Indo-Hittite theory (unless Hittite is considered the tenth branch, on a par with the other nine);
c. The subdivisions of the Germanic branch, with the position of English in relation to the other sub-members.

The diagram shows only lines of descent; if it also showed the many inter-relations through borrowing, it would include numerous lateral lines—e.g., between members of the Italic and the Germanic branches.

various branches of Indo-European,[33] and the subdivisions of the Germanic branch. English, as we see, is a member of the Low German subdivision, and is therefore to be contrasted with modern German, which belongs to the High German subdivision; yet both

[33] For a short exposition of the Indo-Hittite hypothesis, see Sturtevant, *op. cit.*, secs. 229-235, and Fig. 8.

are West Germanic languages, and in that respect contrast with Swedish or Norwegian, which are North Germanic.

To point out that English is genetically a Germanic language does not, however, by any means tell the whole story. For English, compared with modern German—or with its own earliest stage, Old English—has clearly undergone vast alterations in the course of a few centuries. High German, relatively isolated within the continent, has been conservative; the Low German dialects have been open to more influences that might bring change. And English, particularly, with a population that had migrated, with conquest by Danes and Normans, with its surrounding seas opening it early and always to maritime and mercantile activity, with early Christianization and an eager reception of much of Roman culture, has developed more rapidly and much farther away from old patterns than any other Germanic language—so much so that it is now considerably mixed. This is not the place in which to question whether these changes have tended more or less toward improvement. But as we follow in coming chapters the development of English, we may note how the changes have come about and what their effects have been —which may contribute to a decision in the end.

REFERENCES FOR FURTHER READING

The books by Bloomfield, Gray, Jespersen, Pedersen, and Sapir listed at the end of Chapter 1. Also:

Baugh, Albert C., *A History of the English Language,* New York (Appleton-Century), 1935.

Bender, H. H., *The Home of the Indo-Europeans,* Princeton (Princeton University Press), 1922.

Brugmann, Karl, and Delbrück, B., *Grundriss der Vergleichenden Grammatik der Indogermanischen Sprachen,* Strassburg (Trübner), 1886-1900, 3 vols. Also translated.

Bryant, Margaret M., *Modern English and Its Heritage,* New York (Macmillan), 1948.

Emerson, O. F., *History of the English Language,* New York (Macmillan), 1894.

Hirt, Hermann, *Handbuch des Urgermanischen,* Heidelberg (Winter), 1931.

———, *Indogermanische Grammatik,* Heidelberg (Winter), 1927.

Jespersen, Otto, *Growth and Structure of the English Language,* Leipsig (Teubner), 8th ed., 1935.

Jóhannesson, Alexander, "Um frumtungu Indógermana og frumheim-kynni," Fylgir Arbók Háskóla Islands (1940-1), Reykjavík (Gutenberg), 1949.

Meillet, A., *Introduction à l'étude comparative des langues indo-européennes*, Paris (Hachette), 7th ed., 1934.

Schmidt, P. W., *Sprachfamilien und Sprachenkreise der Erde*, Heidelberg (Winter), 1926.

Wright, Joseph and Elizabeth M., *Old English Grammar*, Oxford (Oxford University Press), 3rd ed., 1925.

Whitney, W. D., *Language and the Study of Language*, New York (Scribner), 1867.

Chapter 3

The Early Growth of English

LANGUAGES are studied historically according to the "periods" of their development, during which they exhibit distinguishing characteristics; thus, English is divided into the Old,[1] Middle, and Modern periods. Obviously, such a division, while convenient, is arbitrary, since people do not leave off speaking one form of a language one night and start speaking another form the next day. Though it does not go always at the same pace, language development is continuous. The division into periods is made when the historical linguist, looking backward, sees that by about a certain date the gradual changes have mounted up until the language as a whole is decidedly different, or has entered a new phase of development. We shall date the periods of English as follows:

I.
    Old English   450–1100   *full inflexion*
    Middle English   1100–1500   *leveled "*
    Modern English   1500–the present *lost "*

The history of the English language begins, then, with the incursions of the Jutes, Saxons, and Angles[2] about the middle of the fifth century. These invaders came from neighboring regions in what is now Schleswig-Holstein; they spoke, not one language, but related Low German dialects. The Jutes came first and occupied the smallest territory, principally Kent and the Isle of Wight. The Saxons occupied practically all of England south of the Thames, with the excep-

---

[1] Some use the term "Anglo-Saxon" rather than "Old English." The terms are synonymous, and the use of one rather than the other is largely a matter of fashion. At present, "Old English" is more generally favored; and, indeed, it does fit better with the names for the other two periods.

[2] A fourth tribe, the Frisians, should perhaps be mentioned too. They inhabited much the same regions in Britain as the Jutes, though some settled also in Anglian territory.

tion of these Jutish territories, and of Cornwall, which remained in the possession of the Celts; north of the Thames they also occupied the regions which later became Essex and Middlesex (the final syllables of which still bear the Saxon name). The Angles took for themselves what was left: the greatest part of what is now England, and Lowland Scotland as far as the Firth of Forth, with the exception of the west coast.

Here then is the explanation of the division of Old English into dialects that have left their trace in the provincial speech of England until this day. The dialectal groupings have been somewhat shifted, but a threefold division is still preserved.[3] The speech of the Jutes became the Kentish dialect of Old English; the principal dialect of the Saxons was known as the West Saxon; and the Anglian tongue split into two dialects, the Mercian in the Midlands and the Northumbrian in the North. The later history of the dialects may be briefly suggested: Kentish and West Saxon fell together as the Southern dialect of Middle English; the Mercian became the Midland, its principal subdivision (East Midland) being the ancestor of literary Modern English; the Northumbrian became the Northern, the popular tongue on both sides of the Scottish border.

Literary supremacy has swung from the North to the South and eventually come to the Midland. In Old English times the first centers of learning and culture were in Northumbria; the first important literature in English, dating from the seventh and early eighth centuries, was therefore in the Northumbrian dialect. By the end of the ninth century another center was established, in the south, in Alfred's kingdom of Wessex—therefore the body of later Old English literature is in this West Saxon dialect. In Middle English times, no one dialect could claim to be supreme until the East Midland (and specifically the dialect of London) finally asserted itself by the end of the fourteenth century as the most favored. Standard Modern English represents, for the most part, the further development of this dialect—which has not been, however, without important rivalry from the Northern, particularly in the late Middle and early Modern periods.

[3] See the maps on page 38. The Middle English map is based on Map II in Moore, Meech, and Whitehall, "Middle English Dialect Characteristics and Dialect Boundaries," *Essays and Studies in English and Comparative Literature,* Ann Arbor (University of Michigan), 1935.

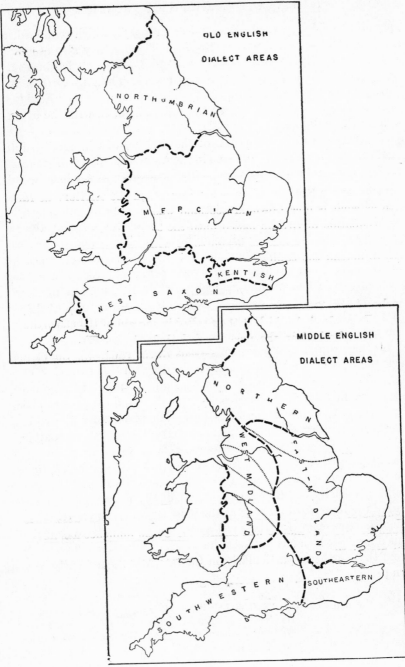

OLD ENGLISH DIALECT AREAS

NORTHUMBRIAN

MERCIAN

KENTISH

WEST SAXON

MIDDLE ENGLISH DIALECT AREAS

NORTHERN

WEST MIDLAND

EAST MIDLAND

SOUTHWESTERN

SOUTHEASTERN

To outline the general development of the language in its Old and Middle periods requires us to return to pre-Saxon Britain, and to retell a familiar story. When the Germanic invaders came, Britain was inhabited by the Celts, who had dwelt there for centuries. Their language, too, was Indo-European, but the Celtic and Germanic branches were by this time so far differentiated as to have little in common. Celtic Britain had been invaded by the Romans in 55 and 54 B.C., as we are told in the *Commentaries* of Julius Caesar, but no serious attempt to conquer the island was made till almost a century later. By the end of the first century A.D., however, the conquest was complete, and a Roman colony which embraced the territory as far north as what is now Lowland Scotland was established. This military occupation of Britain lasted until the early fifth century, when the far-flung Roman legions began to be withdrawn from the provinces to defend the capital against attack by the barbarian Goths. Britain, the most distant western outpost of the empire, was the first to be abandoned. The Celtic inhabitants, left defenseless against the attacks of the Picts and Scots on the west and north, appealed in vain to Rome for help. At last they called in the aid of the Germanic sea-rovers who had in the past harried their shores. The call was answered; but the upshot was disastrous to the Celts, for the Germanic tribes who came to help against the Picts and Scots soon coveted the island for themselves, turned against their Celtic allies, and succeeded in dispossessing them of the greater part of their lands. Many Celts were reduced to slavery, others were driven to the western extremities of the island, some fled across the Irish Sea and others across the English Channel to what is now Brittany. By the middle of the sixth century the Germanic settlement of most of Britain was complete.

We shall return in Chapter 7 to consider the influence of the earlier languages of the island—Celtic and Latin—upon the invaders. It is enough here to say that it was slight: the Celtic influence has never been great; the important Latin influences began later. The Celts were either the subjects or the enemies of the Anglo-Saxons, the Celtic border-chieftains often helping the Danes[4] later in their attacks on the English. Nor should it be forgotten that the word "Welsh" is not Welsh at all, but the Anglo-Saxons' designation of

---

[4] "Danes" was the term applied by the Anglo-Saxons, but to them it included Scandinavians whether from Denmark, Norway, or elsewhere.

their Celtic rivals, a special application of the word meaning "foreigners." About the Danes, later their enemies for two centuries, the English also felt strongly; yet the language of the Danes, being Germanic too, was obviously akin to English, and a great many more Danish words were borrowed than Celtic.

The attitude among the Old English, however, seems to have been on the whole linguistically conservative. Words for new things, new ways, and new knowledge that came in from abroad were quite as likely to be translated into Old English terms as to be directly borrowed. Though such words as *cirice* (church), *munuc* (monk), and *scrin* (shrine) were, it is true, borrowings or "loan-words," others such as *gōdspell* (gospel, literally "good-message") from Greek *euaggelion* (evangel), and *þrynnes* ("three-ness") from Latin *trinitas* (trinity), show clearly a part-by-part translation. Many others, too, show a sense-for-sense rendering into Old English terms: *elpendbān* (elephant-bone) for ivory, *palm-æppel* (palm-apple) for date, *leorning-cniht* (learning-youth) for disciple. The first force to qualify this inhospitable attitude[5] toward word-borrowing was the coming of Christianity, which brought in a new and vigorous flow of Latin influence, drawing England into the cultural orbit of Ireland, Italy, and France. It was Irish priests who taught the English to write in the Roman alphabet, and they, too, having converted Scotland in the latter part of the sixth century, reconverted Northumbria in the seventh. From Italy came St. Augustine in 597 to convert the kingdom of Kent, whose lead the other kingdoms followed. Even in the darkest days of the ninth century when the heathen Danes had won more than half of England, the link was not broken: Latin remained the language of learning, keeping open a way for later French influences, and for its own great contribution later on.

As has already been said, though language is ever changing, change is restrained by a cultural or educational tradition, and accelerated by its absence or decay. In the prehistoric period (that is, before our earliest records begin in the seventh century) Old English underwent a considerable number of changes. Thanks to the personal interest and efforts of King Alfred the Great at the end of the ninth

[5] Modern German still exhibits it to some extent. Whereas English, French, Italian, Spanish, and other languages base their scientific terminology on Latin and Greek, German has translated or re-formed most of these terms, to the great complication of international interchange of scientific knowledge.

century, however, it attained for a while a measure of stability. Alfred himself translated, and stimulated others to translate, some of the basic documents of Roman and Christian learning. Translations include Boethius's *Consolation of Philosophy*, one of the most influential books of the Middle Ages; Pope Gregory's *Pastoral Care*, a book of directions to the clergy for performing their duties; Orosius's *History of the World*, containing much classical historical lore; Bede's *Ecclesiastical History of the English People*, the great source-book of English history, which the Northumbrian monk had written in Latin. In addition, though they come down to us in later manuscripts, the Gospels were probably translated under Alfred, and he surely had a hand in starting the compilation of the famous *Anglo-Saxon Chronicle*, annals which were kept up from his time till well after the Norman Conquest. Some of Alfred's letters also survive (a passage from the most famous is analyzed below), and the excellent eyewitness account of northern explorations, the *Voyages of Ohthere and Wulfstan*, which the king evidently wrote down from the mouths of the explorers themselves. These various works are mentioned in some detail because they give us a fine body of materials for the understanding of early England and the study of the English language. Besides, with schools newly set up, a scribal tradition could be established, which gave a certain literary status to early West Saxon, the Old English dialect of Alfred and his kingdom.

The attacks of the Danes began, according to the *Chronicle*, in 787. By the time Alfred came to the throne a century later, they had won all of north and most of eastern England. Only the brilliant leadership of the young king saved the land—and the language; nor did the Danes win the throne till more than a hundred years after his death. Though the Danes began as pirates, ravaging the coasts and sailing away with their booty, they later settled and amalgamated with the English. Thus it is that their influence on the language was far more inward and homely than that of Norman French or of Latin, both of which were the languages of higher cultures dominating English, whereas the Scandinavian was more nearly on a par with the English.[6] It does not appear, however, during the time of King Alfred.

---

[6] See the map facing page 1 in Taylor, Isaac, *Words and Places* (1874), which shows in terms of place-names the areas settled by Celts, Danes, Norwegians, and Anglo-Saxons.

Alfredian Old English shows us, very well preserved, the characteristics of a Germanic language. It was highly inflectional, distinguishing three numbers, three genders, and five cases, as well as three moods. In common with other Germanic languages it had lost the inflected passive voice, it distinguished only two tenses, and it had weak adjectives and weak verbs in addition to the strong. On looking at a passage of Old English, too, one notices at once that the word-order is frequently unlike the regular subject-verb-object order of Modern English; for in Old English the verb often precedes the subject (inverted order) or follows the object (transposed order).

The readiest way to summarize these first impressions of Old English is to analyze a typical passage of its prose. Here is a selection—part of Alfred's preface to his translation of the *Pastoral Care*. *Good*

When I then this all remembered, then wondered I exceedingly
Đā ic þā ðis eall gemunde, ðā wundrade ic swīðe swīðe

of the good wise men who formerly were throughout England, and
þāra gōdena wiotona þe giu wǣron giond Angelcynn, ond

the books all completely learned had, that they of them then
þā bēc ealla be fullan geliornod hæfdon, þæt hīe hiora þā

no part did not wish into their own language to turn.
nænne dǣl noldon on hiora āgen geðiode wendan.

But I then soon again myself answered and said. "They not
Ac ic þā sona eft mē selfum andwyrde ond cwæð. "Hīe ne

thought that ever men (should [NOT A FUNCTION WORD] so reckless become, and
wēndon þætte æfre menn sceolden [OUGHT TO HAVE RIGHT] swǣ rēccelēase weorðan, ond

the learning so fall away; for the desire (i.e., intentionally)
sīo lār swǣ oðfeallan; for þǣre wilnunga

they it neglected, and wished that here the more wisdom in (the)
hīe hit forlēton, ond woldon ðæt hēr þȳ māra wīsdom on

land should be the we more languages knew."
londe wǣre þȳ wē mā geðīoda cūðon."

The king expresses his perplexity that so little of the learning that had flourished in the land before the ravages of the Danes had been handed down in the form of English translations of worthy books. He concludes that the refusal of the older generation of scholars to do this work of translation was deliberate, and was dictated by their feeling that learning would increase with the study of languages.

A few remarks, then, on this passage in the light of what has been said of the general characteristics of Old English. Study of its vocabulary will reveal that much more of it is familiar to us, as part of the Germanic inheritance, than appears at first glance. Indeed, perhaps only a single noun, *geðiode* (language), and a very few adverbs and conjunctions, such as *swiðe* (much), *þā* (then, when), and *ac* (but), are wholly strange. Several others, of course, are preserved in Modern English only as archaisms—*eft*, *cwæþ* (quoth), and *wēndon* (weened)—or as roots the meaning of which has somewhat changed—*giu* (cf. yore), *giond* (cf. yon), *cūðon* (cf. un-*couth*, formerly meaning un*known*), and *weorðan* (be, become, as in "Woe worth the day," i.e., "Woe be to the day"). Notice too that in a number of cases the form seems nearer to German than to Modern English: *woldon* (cf. *wollten*), *weorðan* (cf. *werden*), *wǣron* (cf. *waren*), *geliornod* (cf. *gelernt*), *wendan* (cf. *wenden*).

The far greater complexity of inflection also finds abundant illustration here. In this short passage, the definite article, which in Modern English appears invariably as *the*, has five variants: *sīo* (nom. fem. sing.), *þære* (gen. fem. sing.), *þȳ* (instrumental neut. sing.),[7] *þā* (nom. plur.), and *þāra* (gen. plur.). Adjective declension, utterly lost in Modern English, appears in such forms as *rēccelēase* (plur.) and *gōdena* (gen. plur. and a weak form). Several lost inflectional endings of the noun may be noticed; for example, *londe* (dat. neut. sing.) *wiotona* (masc. gen. plur.), and *wilnunga* (dat. fem. sing.). Other types of plural inflection than the regular -*s* ending of Modern English are to be seen: *bēc*, an umlaut plural [8] later regularized into *books*, and *geðioda* (languages). In the verb, too, a far higher state of inflection is evident, as in the infinitive endings of *wendan* and *weorðan* and the plural endings of *forlēton* and *cūðon*.

Finally, our selection gives a vivid picture of the more varied word-order that accompanies the greater degree of inflection in Old English. German might parallel this order: "When I this all remembered, then wondered I much at the good wise men who formerly were throughout England and the books all completely learned had" —but Modern English, never! Note, throughout the passage, how infinitives and participles are detached from their auxiliaries, how a

---

[7] Such a phrase as "*the* more *the* merrier" preserves this adverbial use of the old instrumental case; it parallels the Latin ablative of degree of difference.
[8] See below, Chapter 6, page 119.

predicate is detached from its subject, and how a pronoun object may precede rather than follow its predicate. Most striking of all, probably, is the transposed order that is the usual rule in subordinate clauses. The use of transposition is perhaps the most powerful single element in making the passage appear, to the modern reader, thoroughly un-English.[9]

With this glimpse of the language in its Old English stage, we may pass on to the developments in the Middle English period. As has been indicated, the transition from the one to the other was gradual; further, it is clear that it did not proceed at a uniform rate in all the dialects. In the north, changes were earlier and more rapid than in the south, so that by the year 1100, which we have taken as the dividing line, the northern dialect, even in its literary form, had already distinctly assumed the aspect of Middle English. The southern dialect changed more slowly, and in its literary form remained till at least 1150 essentially what we know as Old English.[10]

What, then, are the changes which distinguish the new Middle English phase of the language from the Old English? All parts were affected, but the most fundamental difference was in the widespread "leveling" of inflectional endings, that is, a great reduction in their number and complexity. This simplification, and others such as the loss of "grammatical" gender in favor of "natural" gender[11] and the increase in the use of normal word-order, had clearly begun before the Norman Conquest. It is therefore easy to overrate, as many have done, the immediate effects of this political and social upheaval upon the language. It is true that the Normans under William extended their power rapidly and vigorously through the land, and that Norman, as the language of the new nobility, displaced English from its

[9] However, the substantive þæt clauses are not *completely* transposed. It seems to be here that the transposed order gave ground most readily, and opened the way for the final establishment of the normal order in most types of dependent clauses—doubtless aided later by the influence of French.

[10] The distinction between speech and the literary language must never be forgotten. The latter is traditional and conservative, keeping up past ways long after they have changed in daily speech. Middle English was probably being *spoken* before the year 1000. See Kemp Malone, "When Did Middle English Begin?" Curme Volume of Linguistic Studies, *Language Monograph No. 7*, Baltimore, 1930.

[11] See Bradley, pp. 47-50; Classen, pp. 38-39; and especially Samuel Moore, "Grammatical and Natural Gender in Middle English," *Publications of the Modern Language Association*, Vol. 36, No. 1 (March 1921), pp. 79-103. See also Chapter 6, pp. 118-119.

aristocratic position. But it must not be supposed that any large number of the English people began at once to speak Norman. Though English "lost face," and decayed as a language of learning, it remained the only speech of the great mass of people. The chief effect of the Conquest at first, then, was, by removing the conservative restraints, to accelerate changes that had already begun.

The Middle English period covers four centuries, however, during which time the enemies, Saxon and Norman, became gradually welded into a single nation with a single speech. If the immediate influence of the Normans on English was chiefly negative, it began within a century to be positive, and this appears very strikingly in the number of Norman French words, and later Parisian French, that English absorbed. The Old English word-stock was virtually unilingual: the Middle English became bilingual. *As a result of Normans*

Yet even the borrowing of Norman words had begun before 1066.[12] The English King Æthelred married in 1002 the daughter of the Duke of Normandy, and their son, later known as Edward the Confessor, found many influential posts in the English church and state for French clergymen and French nobles. It is to be noted, too, that French influence continued, though in a new form, after the loss of Normandy by the English in 1204. As early as the twelfth century, the French of Paris, as learned by English students and priests, had begun to supplement the earlier influence of the Norman dialect, and eventually it became a more important force. Thus, the influx of French words that had begun before 1066 was gradually increased through most of the Middle English period, and particularly accelerated between 1250 and 1400.[13]

These words cover almost every aspect of life, but, as might be expected, the new objects, ways, and ideas of a more complex society constitute the majority: legal, military, religious, political, intellectual, artistic, and the like. In the simpler, more everyday matters English has held its own: of all the numerals, only *second* is borrowed; of all the external parts of the body, only *face* and *palm*. However, these are the exceptions—everywhere else we are struck with the widespread adoption of French words.

[12] *Castle, mantle, purse,* and *trail* are French borrowings in Old English writing (F. Kluge, *Englische Studien,* Vol. 21, pp. 334-335).

[13] Baugh, *History of the English Language,* p. 219, cites Jespersen's statistics on the borrowing of French words, and interprets them.

It should be added that because a French word was acquired, an English one was not necessarily lost. Quite often both survive with slight differences in meaning, the English being the humbler or less pretentious; thus we have *table* as well as *board*,[14] *labor* as well as *work*, and *chair* as well as *stool* (formerly as general a term as its German cognate *Stuhl*). A striking illustration of this aspect of the bilingual vocabulary is the often-quoted observation of Wamba, the jester in *Ivanhoe*, to the effect that while the Saxon serf calls the animals he tends by one set of words (*ox, cow, calf, sheep, swine,* and *deer*), the Norman master knows them, when their flesh appears as food, by another (*beef, veal, mutton, pork, bacon,* and *venison*).

One more general comment on the Middle English vocabulary. The borrowings from French, though the most numerous and influential, were not the only ones: a thin trickle of Celtic continued; and later in the period (as recent work for the *Middle English Dictionary* has shown) increasing numbers of Latin words were added.[15] During this period, too, came the bulk of the Scandinavian influence, not only on vocabulary, but on grammar. Still, the French influence was overwhelmingly the greatest.

Harder to assess is the subtler influence of French (and Latin) upon syntax and idiom—a subject that scholars have tended to neglect. But even in Old English prose there is a decided difference between the simplicity of original pieces—sometimes elliptical to the point of obscurity—and the style of pieces translated from Latin. The effects of classical rhetoric, even when crudely handled, are clearly visible in the Old English sermons; and the more complex sentences, the elaborations, the sense of structure, come to be imitated. One might mention here one strong evidence of the French and Latin[16] influence on morphology: many of the new, complex expressions of tense and voice that grew up in Middle English (and before) were renderings or imitations from words in those languages which the English were reading or trying to translate, and for the subtleties of which Old English conjugation did not provide.

[14] Retained, in a similar sense, in *bed and board, boarding house.*
[15] See Hereward T. Price, "Foreign Influences on Middle English," *University of Michigan Contributions in Modern Philology,* No. 10, April 1947.
[16] Latin was both a direct and an indirect influence (through French) on English—indeed, it is often impossible to know in particular instances whether some word or grammatical feature came to English from French or from Latin, when both languages were the property of the educated man.

The Middle English period, then, was one of transition, when a language already tending to lose its inflections was hastened in that process by political upset and loss of prestige; when, its grammatical machinery having been much simplified, it began to increase its resources of vocabulary and idiom, chiefly under the powerful influence of the French language; and finally when, with Englishmen rising in the world who had never abandoned their vernacular, and whose popular support had to come from speakers of that same vernacular, the English language emerged once again, deposing its French rival.

Professor Baugh shows vividly, with dated citations, how English becomes reinstated as French falls away, particularly in the fourteenth century.[17] In 1258 comes the first royal proclamation to be made in English as well as French. By the 80's of the same century many voices of complaint are raised in the universities because the Fellows are speaking neither Latin nor French, but English. By 1300, writers begin to use French less because, they say, though some can still understand it, everyone understands English. On several occasions during the first half of the fourteenth century public announcements made in the traditional Latin or French are explained to the people in English. In 1362 the Chancellor for the first time opens Parliament with a speech in English, and in the same year the Statute of Pleading is enacted, officially establishing English thenceforward as the language in which lawsuits are to be conducted. In 1399, nevertheless, at the deposition of King Richard II, the articles of accusation are read to Parliament in Latin and English. Thus Latin generally sustains itself as the traditional language of law and learning, but French yields progressively to English as the actual language of all daily affairs.

Literary history, too, illustrates this gradual rise from eclipse to reinstatement. For a century after the Normans came, Norman French took the place of English as the language of pure literature, while Latin continued to be, as it had been before the Conquest, the language of monkish chroniclers and scholars. From about the middle of the twelfth century, however, the Anglo-Norman literature is paralleled by writings in English, and by about 1200 we have the composition of two substantial works in English, the *Ormulum* and Layamon's *Brut*. The recovery was slow, but in the fourteenth cen-

[17] *Op. cit.*, Chapter VI, and particularly pp. 176–192.

tury came a decided quickening, and by the end of that century, with Geoffrey Chaucer, English poetry reached a level which it was not to achieve again before Elizabeth's day. Chaucer—as any great literary artist does—saw for himself and made abundantly clear to others the resources of the language in which he chose to work.[18] We may do well to look at a passage from the most English of his works,[19] and to see what the language had come to look like in the five centuries since King Alfred:

> With hym ther was his sone, a yong Squier,
> A louyere and a lusty bacheler,
> With lokkes crulle, as they were leyd in presse.
> Of twenty yeer of age he was, I gesse;
> Of his stature he was of euene lengthe
> And wonderly delyuere and of greet strengthe;
> And he hadde been sometyme in chyuachie
> In Flaundres, in Artoys, and Pycardie,
> And born hym weel, as of so litel space,
> In hope to stonden in his lady grace.
> Embrouded was he, as it were a meede
> Al ful of fresshe floures whyte and reede;
> Syngynge he was or floytynge al the day;
> He was as fressh as is the monthe of May.
> Short was his gowne with sleues long and wyde;
> Wel koude he sitte on hors and faire ryde;
> He koude songes make and wel endite,
> Iuste and eek daunce and weel purtreye and write.
> So hoote he loued that by nyghtertale
> He sleep namoore than dooth a nyghtyngale.
> Curteis he was, lowely and seruysable,
> And carf biforn his fader at the table.

Perhaps the first thing that strikes us is the word-order—how much like that of Modern English it has become. Adjectives, it is true, are more often given prominence at the beginning of the line, with consequent inversion of the verb and subject: "Embrouded was he," "Short was his gowne"; but contrast "Syngynge he was." Except for a few words (and discounting the differences in spelling) the vocabulary is so familiar that it can be made out almost at sight. *Lusty, bacheler, euene,* and one or two other words have unfamiliar

[18] Like his contemporary, John Gower, Chaucer might as well have chosen to write in Latin or French, the traditional languages of culture. He also knew Italian. But he chose English—to our eternal pleasure and benefit.

[19] Description of the Squire, *Canterbury Tales,* Prologue, lines 79-100.

senses, and *delyuere, chyuachie, nyghtertale* are now obsolete; but
these are decidedly in the minority. Excluding the proper names we
find 23 different words of French origin: 12 nouns, 5 adjectives (including one participle), 5 verbs, and 1 adverb, all but two of which
(*iuste* and *chyuachie*) are still in Modern English. Since there are,
in the same passage, 52 different words of English origin in the same
parts of speech (16 nouns, 13 adjectives, 15 verbs, and 8 adverbs), it
is clear that in these categories the French element is close to one
third of the total.[20] However, the pronouns (22), articles (8), prepositions (20), conjunctions (24), and numerals (1), have remained
almost exclusively English, and since they are the words most frequently repeated, they preserve the predominantly English cast of
the language. Fewer and less complex inflections are found here than
in Old English: in nouns in this passage we find the regular plural
(*lokkes, floures,* and so on) and an old genitive (*lady*) ; in verbs we
find the infinitive sometimes still inflected (*stonden*) but more often
not (*sytte, ryde, make, write*). The auxiliary verbs and most of all
the personal pronouns preserve the fuller inflection of Old English—
as they still do in Modern English.

Not only did the fourteenth century see English firmly and finally
established as a literary language, but it saw the elevation of one
dialect into a commanding position. Hitherto there had been rival
claimants among the three groups of dialects, Northern, Midland,
and Southern. Beginning with the fourteenth century, however, a
single subdivision of one of these, the East Midland dialect of the
capital, the court, and the universities, assumed a peculiarly favored
position as the literary standard, and it was never seriously threatened thereafter.[21] The causes of this elevation of East Midland are
not far to seek. All things worked together to bring it about; if
England was to be a really united realm, the speech of London could
scarcely fail to be, in time, the standard for the whole country.

[20] These figures are not absolute; they refer to this passage alone. However, they do not differ greatly from the figures for the French element in
Chaucer's works as a whole. Note that they refer only to certain categories of
words.

[21] The nearest approach to a rival literary language and a second literary
center is, of course, to be found in the literary use of Lowland Scots, and in
Edinburgh as a rival of London—particularly in the work of the Scottish
Chaucerians of the fifteenth century, and again, in the early nineteenth cen-
tury, in the circle of Sir Walter Scott and the contributors to the *Edinburgh
Review* and to *Blackwood's Magazine.*

But one very important additional reason why London English became the standard dialect just when it did is quite certainly the influence of Chaucer. The happy accident that he was a Londoner born and bred, and wrote for a court that, though probably still bilingual, used the local dialect when speaking English, helped immeasurably to give the East Midland dialect [22] a place apart from the others. It is easy to exaggerate here. In the past, phrases like "the father of the English language," "the first finder of our fair language," and "the well of English undefiled" have tended to magnify unduly the contribution of Chaucer to the English language. For even if he had never lived, London English would surely still have become the basis of standard English. On the other hand it is evident that a great part of English poetry, throughout the fifteenth century, is in direct imitation of Chaucer. The chorus of praise that arose from his contemporaries, and the eagerness of his successors to acknowledge him their master, are almost evidence enough of his powerful influence. But the point need hardly be labored, since the wonderful genius of Chaucer has never been more clearly perceived than in the twentieth century.

The fifteenth century saw the standardization of the literary language carried further, though there were still occasional references to the fact that dialectal differences are a stumbling-block. Thus, Caxton, who was probably made more conscious of such difference through his long residence abroad,[23] complained that "it is hard to please every man because of diversity and change of language." [24] Yet at that very time the products of his printing press were helping to remove this cause of complaint. One of the earliest and most famous of the books printed by Caxton, Malory's *Morte d'Arthur* (1485), is thoroughly representative of the standardization as well as of the simplicity and flexibility that the language had attained in late Middle English times.

One final note of summary, then, before closing this chapter on the three periods of the development of English. It has become

---

[22] It should be pointed out that the London and the East Midland dialects are not quite synonymous. Chaucer, and London English generally, used occasional Southern forms that are later displaced in the standard speech by East Midland ones.

[23] Emerson, *History of the English Language*, p. 81.

[24] From the prologue to his version of the *Æneid*; quoted by Emerson, *op. cit.*, pp. 81-82.

almost customary to speak of them as, respectively, the "period of full inflections," the "period of leveled inflections," and the "period of lost inflections." Yet, as we have seen, such designations are more neat than accurate. For the inflections of Old English had already undergone considerable leveling (compare Gothic), before the time of the earliest records; thus they were by no means "full." So too, it would be more accurate to call Middle English the period of "leveling" (rather than "leveled") inflections—yet both the other periods could claim the term to some degree. And though inflection has been greatly reduced in Modern English, it is certainly not "lost"; it is still very much alive within its restricted sphere, though the sphere itself may still be gradually narrowing. We shall return to the consideration of such matters in the later chapters on Modern English. But first we must look successively, and in greater detail, at the sounds, the forms, the vocabulary, and the syntax of English.

REFERENCES FOR FURTHER READING

The histories of the English language by Baugh, Emerson, Jespersen, and others listed at end of Chapter 2, and in addition:

Aiken, Janet R., *English, Present and Past*, New York (Ronald), 1930.

Bradley, Henry, *The Making of English*, New York (Macmillan), 1904, reissued 1951.

Classen, E., *Outlines of the History of the English Language*, London (Macmillan), 1919.

Jordan, Richard, *Handbuch der Mittelenglischen Grammatik*, Part I, Heidelberg (Winter), 2nd ed., 1934.

Kurath, Hans, and Kuhn, Sherman M., *Middle English Dictionary*, Ann Arbor (University of Michigan), 1952-. (Being published in sections.)

McKnight, G. H., *Modern English in the Making*, New York (Appleton), 1928.

Zachrisson, R. E., *Romans, Kelts and Saxons in Ancient Britain*, Uppsala, 1927.

Chapter 4

English Sounds and Sound-Change

IN THE definition given at the beginning of this book, language was said to be basically "vocal and audible." Any records of language—writings, carvings, and so forth—must be transposed back into sounds before we have the real thing. All recorded language, thus, is at the mercy of the means used to record it, for it can be recovered or restored only in proportion to the accuracy or effectiveness of the recording device. The handicap in studying languages of the past, then, is that they can be known only at second hand. Besides, only an infinitesimal part of language has been recorded at all. Scholars labor over ancient manuscripts and inscriptions not as the best but as the only means they have; we cannot bring back the voices of the past.

The importance of the sounds of language as a key to its development was not fully realized until a little over a century ago. Great progress, it is true, had already been made in comparative grammar and philology, but language study did not find its feet and become a scientific discipline until the discovery of sound-development as a basis of regularity.[1] The understanding of phonetics made it possible at last to explain rationally, and without resort to continual "exceptions," the changes that had left their mark on languages down through the course of time, and to recover unsuspected relationships between languages. If we intend to understand the development of English with any accuracy, we must pay first attention to its sounds.

Representation of Sounds. How are we going to deal with them, how refer to them, how describe them? The natural recourse would

---

[1] See Pedersen, *Linguistic Science in the Nineteenth Century*, especially the first and last chapters.

be to the alphabet, since we use that for spelling, and since each letter has a name.[2] But the more we look at the alphabet, the more we realize that it will not do. In the first place, some consonants are ambiguous: *g* has different values in *gin* and *begin*; *s* has different values in *ease, lease,* and *sugar.* Secondly, the alphabet has super-fluous consonants: there is nothing spelled with *c* that cannot be quite as well represented with *k* or *s*; and *q* and *x* could be replaced by *k* and *ks* respectively. Thirdly, to express various sounds we have no single letter at all, but are forced to make clumsy combinations such as *th* and *sh,* which do not equal the sum of their parts. Actually, *sh* represents a single sound, not *s* plus *h*; and *t* plus *h* will not produce either of the sounds which *th* has to spell (cf. *thin* and *then*). There are many other overlappings, too, with the result that nearly half of the letters do not have a constant value.

Yet the consonants, even so, are far more stable than the vowels. Ask any schoolchild how many vowels there are in English, and the immediate response is, "Five." This testifies the extent to which learning is tied to reading and writing—and how, in this case, it distorts the entire situation. There *are* five vowel *symbols* in English, but how many sounds? We know that *a* sounds different in *able, apple, all;* that *e* sounds different in *even, egg, event;* and so on for the other vowel symbols—where they have sounds at all, for often they, like many consonants, are written emptily. The fact is that English spelling has, in the course of time, become so unphonetic that, in order to learn to spell well, one has to make a positive effort *not* to try to connect the letters with single sounds. Since spelling gets a good deal of attention in the early schooling of most people, we are, in effect, trained to ignore or to misapprehend the actual sounds of speech.

Thus we have to start all over when we study phonetics; we have to put conventional spelling deliberately out of mind, close our eyes to the printed page, and begin to listen to sounds and their qualities. And when it becomes necessary to write down these sounds, we have to use something better than conventional spelling: a system in

[2] The *names* of the letters do not tell us their sounds; note *h, w, v,* etc. The sound of American "zee" is *z* (without a vowel); in England, France, etc., the same sound is named "zed." So, the other letters have names made of more than one sound.

which each symbol has only one value, and the number of symbols is limited by the number of distinctive sounds that are to be dealt with—in short, a *phonetic alphabet.*

Significant Sounds. The next problem, then, is to discover how sounds are made, what qualities they have, and which ones are significant in classifying them. It is true that there are sounds we cannot hear—the "silent" whistle blown to call a dog, for example; there are also sounds we are unable to make vocally. These, being outside the limits of our physiological equipment, obviously cannot function as speech sounds, and may therefore be left aside. But even within the range of actual speech sounds, it must not be forgotten that no two can possibly be *exactly* alike. Nobody is so precise or consistent that he can repeat a sound perfectly. The differences, it is true, may be so slight that only an instrument more sensitive than the ear could distinguish them; in which case, again, they may be left aside.

On the other hand, sounds may be audibly different, but insignificantly so. That is, in the language which we happen to be speaking, if no difference in meaning depends upon that difference in sound we may for all practical purposes ignore it—and so we do, consciously or (more often) unconsciously. This is another way of saying that we can make a great many more speech sounds or variations in sounds than need to be distinguished if communication is our sole purpose; and furthermore, that each language has its own limited range of sounds within the total of possible sounds. The phonetician cannot limit himself arbitrarily; in his field of inquiry he must include the entire range of speech sounds,[3] and must pay attention to all the distinctions that are observable. Only so can he hope for accurate description and classification.

The phonetician describing the sounds of one single language will report all the variations he finds; but if he wants to know further what the functional patterns of sound are in that language—in other words, its structure—he must become a phonemicist: he must separate those sounds which are significant structurally from those (also observed) which are not significant. The clue to that separation has already been hinted at: those distinctions that make a

---

[3] Pike would have him investigate non-speech sounds too. See his *Phonetics,* Chap. II.

difference in meaning. In short, we come to the concept of the *phoneme*, the unit of meaningful speech-sound.

Suppose we compare the two sentences *He heard a bus* and *He heard a buzz*. They mean very different things, yet that difference in meaning depends wholly on the contrast between the last two sounds, *s* and *z*. In many American Indian and some other languages these sentences would sound identical because, in them, the difference between *s* and *z* is non-significant. Speakers of those languages simply would not hear this distinction as we do, since they habitually discount it in their own speech. They could, of course, learn to understand the different meanings of *bus* and *buzz* if once they could be made to hear the difference in sound. Contrariwise, speakers of English are mostly unaware that there is a difference between the *k*-sounds of *keel* and *cool;* yet it is a regular difference which we make every time we say the words, which we can hear (and even feel with our tongues) if we take the trouble, and which, in some languages (e.g., Hungarian) is phonemic—that is, differences in meaning depend upon it.

Meaning, then, becomes the chief clue for separating the significant from the non-significant variations in the sounds of any language, and understanding what and how many phonemes it has.[4] We shall consider this in detail later on, but first we must return to the role of the phonetician and to the questions raised before: how sounds are produced, and how they may be classified.

Production of Speech Sounds. Most speech sounds originate with the breath being exhaled from the lungs.[5] If we leave a clear exit for this breath there is no audible sound, but we can disturb it in a variety of ways to produce speech sounds. Upon this fact rests the first basic division of sounds into *continuants* and *stops:* in *continuants* the breath is not completely cut off at any time, but may continue to be exhaled as long as it lasts; in *stops* the breath is completely cut off for a moment at some point in the throat or mouth.

As the breath leaves the lungs, then, and comes up through the *trachea* (or windpipe), it must pass through the voice-box, or *larynx,* the first place in which it is possible to modify it for purposes of

[4] Phonemes cannot be discovered by themselves, of course; they can be identified as such only in relation to other phonemes in the total phonemic pattern.

[5] A few sounds are inhalatory, the classic examples being the "clicks" of Zulu.

speech. The larynx consists of a cartilaginous tube, somewhat pinched toward the front (this is what we feel as the "Adam's apple"). Along the inner sides of this tube are muscular folds (the *vocal cords* or *vocal bands*), attached at front and back. When re-

Transfer information To NoTes.

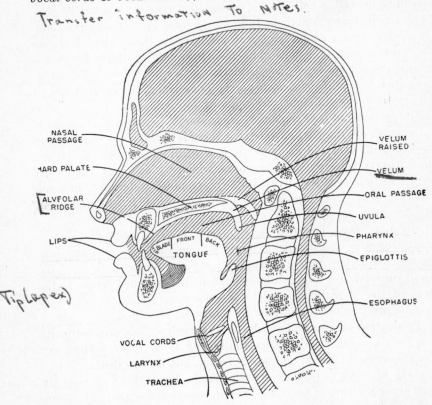

laxed, they lie along the inner sides, letting the breath go through undisturbed; but they can be brought together more or less tightly across the air passage,[6] and the breath then makes them vibrate rapidly, producing a buzzing sound which is known as *voice*.[7]

In a great many languages, of which English is one, this feature

[6] The opening between the vocal cords is called the *glottis*.

[7] In the larynx is also produced another quality of sounds: *pitch*, which depends on the rate of vibration of the vocal cords (the faster they vibrate, the higher the pitch). Pitch is of essential importance to many languages—Annamese, Thai, etc.

is the basis of important distinctions. The example of *bus* versus *buzz*, just given, is a case in point, since the only serious difference between the sounds of *s* and *z* is that in *z* the vocal cords are vibrating, while in *s* they are not; thus *z* is said to be *voiced*, and *s* *voiceless*. If the student will make these two sounds in succession, he may *feel* the vibration by holding the Adam's apple between thumb and forefinger, or *hear* it by stopping the ears. This feature of speech sounds may be used (along with others) in classifying them.

The breath-stream, having passed through the larynx, comes next to the *pharynx* (the cavity at the back of the throat). Here there are two exits, the mouth passage (or *oral cavity*) and the nose passage (the *nasal cavity*), by either or both of which it may escape. If it goes through the first, *oral* sounds will be produced; if through the second, *nasal* sounds; if through both together, *nasalized* sounds. By making various kinds of stoppages and constrictions, we can control what happens here. Through the accidents of our physical structure,[8] there are far more ways of stopping or modifying the breath-stream orally than nasally—consequently there are far more oral sounds in any language than nasal.

The organ that opens or closes the nasal passage when the breath reaches it is the *velum* (or soft palate), which, as its name suggests (Latin *velum* = veil), is a muscular process hanging inside the back of the oral passage. If the finger is run backward along the roof of the mouth, it can easily feel where the hard palate leaves off and the velum begins. (The velum can also be seen easily with a mirror if the mouth is well open.) This velum can be drawn back and upward (*retracted,* or *raised*), in which case it shuts off the nasal passage. In normal breathing, however, and in making nasal sounds, the velum is lowered, hanging relaxed and letting the breath pass behind it and out through the nose. The opening-and-closing action of the velum may be felt if one repeats slowly the word *ink:* it is up for the vowel; then down, opening the nasal passage for the nasal; then up, closing it for the *k*. (Note also the action of the tongue.)

If oral sounds are to be made, the velum is retracted, and the breath passes into the mouth. Here it may be affected by the move-

[8] By this is meant that, after all, our so-called "speech-organs" are only secondarily for speech. Their primary use is for breathing, eating and drinking; they have been adapted secondarily to speaking. The *kinds* of sounds that are employed for speech, then, are contingent upon equipment that was made for other ends.

ments of the tongue (which can hunch and bend itself into many positions),[9] the hard palate, the gums, the teeth, the lips, and various combinations of these, which will be considered more fully in a moment. Furthermore, the resultant sounds are clearly of different types: some involve a complete momentary stoppage of the breath— *stops;* others only partly constrict it, producing a hiss or buzz— *spirants* or *fricatives;* others are characterized by a clear tone —*resonants* (or *sonorants*) ; and there are still other types.

Classification of Sounds. But before coming to these matters in greater detail, we must pause to consider methods of describing and classifying sounds. In our everyday talk we refer to a "hard" *g* or a "broad" *a*, to "sharp" sounds, "warm" tones, and so on. In a sort of way we know what people mean by such terms, but they are usually quite subjective, rather vague, and not the same for everybody. Yet the very thing we need is a description that can mean the same for everybody. Certainly, there must be far clearer ways of referring to sounds, once one has found out objectively what their properties are.

We could, of course, throw ourselves entirely upon the science of acoustics, and describe sounds in terms of their physical properties: the frequency of sound waves, their intensity, their duration, and so on. For purposes of exact measurement under laboratory conditions this has great advantages—but it is too complex a system for use outside the laboratory. The fact is that speakers of any language hear differences in sounds with considerable accuracy and yet may know nothing about their acoustic properties. Neither do they necessarily know much about the physiological production of speech, but, at least, each of us has our speech mechanism present for observation at any time, and consequently it has always proved more convenient for phoneticians to use this approach to begin with, as we have just done.

It will be recalled, then, that two different kinds of things about the speech sounds have already come to our attention: the effect they make to the ear (a buzz, an explosion, a tone, and so forth), and what organs are functioning in producing particular sounds (such as the larynx, velum, tongue, palate, gums, teeth, or lips). By combining these two kinds of information, we can describe the char-

---

[9] The tongue has four functional sections: the *tip,* the *blade* (including the tip and the part just behind it), the *front,* and the *back.* See the diagram, p. 56.

PHONETIC ALPHABET
for the sounds of English

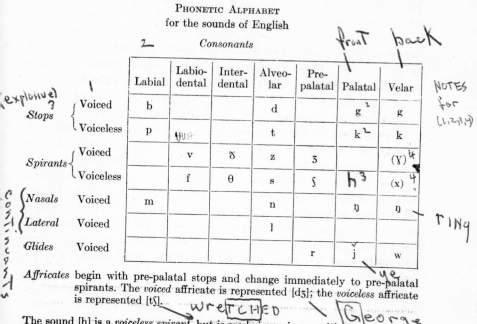

2   *Consonants*

		Labial	Labio-dental	Inter-dental	Alveo-lar	Pre-palatal	Palatal	Velar
Stops	Voiced	b			d		g	g
	Voiceless	p			t		k	k
Spirants	Voiced		v	ð	z	ʒ		(ɣ)
	Voiceless		f	θ	s	ʃ	h	(x)
Nasals	Voiced	m			n		ŋ	ŋ
Lateral	Voiced				l			
Glides	Voiced				r	j	w	

Affricates begin with pre-palatal stops and change immediately to pre-palatal spirants. The *voiced* affricate is represented [dʒ]; the *voiceless* affricate is represented [tʃ].

The sound [h] is a *voiceless spirant*, but is made in various positions.

Vowels

	Front	Central	Back
High	i (yː) / ɪ (ʏ)		u / ʊ
Mid	e / ɛ	ɜ ɝ / ə ɚ / ʌ	o / ɔ
Low	(æː) / æ / a		ɒ / ɑ

The vowels are made in an area corresponding to the palatal and velar; *front* and *back* therefore refer to the tongue, and *central* to that part of the tongue where front and back are adjacent.

Characters in parentheses represent sounds used in Old English but not in Modern English.

SEE CHART ON P-419

acteristic sounds of English and classify them.[10] In doing this, we always need to ask three questions: 1, whether the vocal cords are vibrating (voiced vs. voiceless sounds); 2, whether the breath is completely or only partly impeded (stops vs. spirants, resonants, and so on); 3, where the characteristic modification is provided (the point of articulation), and by what action of the vocal organs.

As we identify and discuss each sound, the symbol used for it will be given.[11] We shall use a "broad" alphabet; that is to say, one having separate symbols for only the strikingly distinctive sounds.[12] The symbols for the consonants are phonemic; for the vowels, most symbols are also phonemic, but a few which are necessary to show existing differences in British and American regional pronunciation have been added; these are sub-phonemic (or *allophonic*) and will be noted when used. This alphabet is easy to learn, it will allow us to deal with sounds simply and accurately, and it will eliminate the numerous inconsistencies of our spelling and the shortcomings of the systems still used in most of our dictionaries, which are often clumsy and even misleading. Knowing this alphabet, the student will also be prepared to read further in important studies on language.

Vowels and Consonants. The broadest division of sounds usually made is that between vowels and consonants. The terms themselves suggest something of their nature: vowels are, normally, voiced sounds (our word *vowel* is from Old French *vouel*, from Latin *vocalis*, meaning *voiced*); and consonants go with vowels (Latin *consonare* means *to sound with*) to form syllables. This is not the whole story, however, for the fact is that many consonants are voiced too, and some can function as the core of the syllable—in short, no sharp line can be drawn between vowels and consonants.

[10] English is not pronounced the same everywhere in the world, yet one type must be taken as the standard for present purposes. The pronunciation of the North and West of the United States is chosen here as that which differs least over the largest area.

[11] The symbols are those of the International Phonetic Association, supplemented where necessary from other established sources. (The only character given a different value is [ʌ], which is here placed higher and farther forward, to represent its American pronunciation better.)

[12] No alphabet can be exact enough to cover all possible differences in sounds—and even if it were possible, such an alphabet would be impracticably unwieldy. The most useful alphabet is one which indicates all broad distinctions, and has additional diacritics that can be used when necessary to indicate narrower distinctions.

Nevertheless, it is convenient to make a division, and this is usually done by classing as vowels those sounds which are relatively *open*—that is to say, which have no constriction (or almost none) in the oral passage (or in the nasal, when that is involved), and in which, therefore, the chief characteristic is *voice,* a clear resonance originating in the larynx. Consonants, by contrast, though they may be voiced, are, as a group, more *close* than vowels—that is to say, they are characterized by some degree of constriction or obstruction, with consequent noise, occurring ordinarily in the oral passage. Obviously, the openest vowels would be in contrast with the closest consonants; but the vowels with the smallest oral opening come very near to the more open, resonating consonants, making the dividing line somewhat arbitrary.

Consonants. Let us begin our observations with the consonants. It will be useful to take the various classes of sounds in some order (stops, spirants, affricates, nasals, laterals, glides), and to begin each time in the front of the mouth and move toward the back, noticing where each sound is articulated, and how. As we go along, one other thing must be discussed: whether all the distinctions noticed are phonemically significant. Our alphabet should have, basically, one character for each phoneme; and no more characters than the number of significantly different sounds. Non-significant variants (allophones) which we notice can be grouped with their phonemes, but will not ordinarily be given separate symbols.[13]

Stops. We start then with [b][14] as in *bob.* When we make this sound, it is evident that it begins with the lips pressed together to hold in the air being forced up from the lungs.[15] Since the velum is retracted, the breath cannot get out through the nose. It therefore is compressed momentarily behind the lips, and when they are

---

[13] Another way of looking at the phoneme is as the sum of all the phonetic variations (allophones) which do not affect the meaning of the word in which they are used.

[14] The usual way of indicating a phonetic symbol is by placing it in square brackets: [b]; phonemic symbols are placed between virgules (or "slant-lines," or "diagonals"): /b/. Since our transcription is broad, most of the phonetic symbols are also phonemic; but since some sub-phonemic symbols will be needed, we shall, to avoid the confusion of mixing phonetic and phonemic symbols, treat all symbols as phonetic, and use only brackets.

[15] The lungs themselves do not expel the breath; the muscles of the rib-cage compress it while the diaphragm pushes from below, this double pressure forcing the air out of the lungs.

parted, releasing this pressure, there is a sudden explosion of air. Clearly, then, [b] is one of the *stop* sounds, and since the closure for it is made with both lips, it is a *bilabial* stop. If we say [b] a few times, holding the Adam's apple or (better) closing the ears, we can notice that the vocal buzz is present as the air is released. It is therefore a *voiced* bilabial stop, and we have described it in terms of its auditory effect and of the speech organs chiefly involved in producing it.[16]

Is [b] always the same, regardless of where it appears in a word? The first [b] in *bob* does not vary, but for the second we need not—at the end of a phrase we often do not—part the lips or have the explosion; yet it sounds perfectly normal so. When there is no explosion, where does the air go? Testing this, we discover that the unexploded air comes out through the nose; in other words, instead of opening the lips, we lowered the velum. The acoustic effect is noticeably different—anybody can hear it with a little practice—yet no speaker of English would make a difference in *meaning* depend upon the variation between the exploded and the unexploded [b]. Therefore we may say that the variation is not phonemically significant, and we may use the same symbol [b] for both.[17]

What are the other stop-sounds of English, and where are they made? The closest to [b], because it is also bilabial, is [p], as in *pop*, and it differs chiefly by being voiceless. We must consider [b] and [p] as different phonemes on the basis of such contrasts as *bin:pin, bent:pent, bark:park*, and many others; the whole distinction in meaning depends on whether, in one case, the vocal cords are vibrating, or, in the other, they are not. As to other variations in [p], we may notice the same possibility as with [b] of leaving it unexploded in end position, but again, no distinction in meaning results; thus the exploded and unexploded varieties belong to the same phoneme. Next, if we contrast such words as *pin:spin, pan:span*,

---

[16] There are, of course, all kinds of other features that would have to be mentioned in a very full, exact description. Our descriptions here are deliberately reduced to the essentials, since this is only an introduction to the phonetics of a single language. For a recent example of a detailed description, see the analysis of the phoneme /t/ in Hubbell's *Pronunciation of English in New York City*, where on pages 23-25 the eight allophones of /t/ found in cultivated pronunciation are described, and on pages 26-27, the eight allophones found in uncultivated pronunciation.

[17] In a "narrow" transcription we might distinguish the two *b*'s: exploded [b], unexploded with nasal release [b^n].

we may notice another variation: that when it is alone, [p] is followed by a puff of breath (aspiration), but when it is combined with s there is no such puff. This is a real phonetic distinction between aspirated and unaspirated [p]—but since we can find no pairs of words in which a difference in meaning depends on the presence or absence of this aspiration,[18] it does not call for a different phonemic symbol.[19]

The student, up to now, should have been following exactly every step of our explanation by testing in his own pronunciation the sounds and the words we have mentioned. The same tests should be made throughout the rest of this description, even though, in the interest of brevity, they are not specifically asked for hereafter. It is essential that sounds be made normally, that they be listened to carefully for their quality, and that their method of production be analyzed and tried out with the student's own vocal apparatus.

If we continue backward in the mouth cavity, attempting to make stoppages with the tongue along the way, the next point at which we discover any that are used in English is at the back of the upper gums where the teeth are set in. This is called the *alveolar ridge* (or *teeth-ridge*),[20] and may easily be felt with the finger. It makes a convenient place for the tongue to press itself, impeding or stopping the breath—in fact, more sounds in English are determined at this point than anywhere else. If we make and break a closure here, as in such words as *did, dead, dad*, we hear the *voiced alveolar stop* [d]: and, as in *tit, tat, toot*, the *voiceless alveolar stop* [t]. In all of these the final consonants may be unexploded, but the distinction is no more phonemic than with [b] or [p]. Like [p], [t] has aspirated and unaspirated allophones—contrast *tick:stick, tongue:stung.*

Going still farther back in the mouth cavity, we find two other stops, [g] and [k], which may be made either with a palatal or velar articulation. Attention has already been called to this fact with regard to the *k*-sounds in *keel* and *cool* (p. 55 above), and, as was pointed out, the difference is not phonemic. Similarly with [g]—compare *geese:goose*. These sounds are palatal (relatively front) or

---

[18] In the pairs of words given, of course, the difference in meaning depends on the presence or absence of *s*. The difference in *p*'s is incidental.

[19] We could show it phonetically, in a narrow transcription, by spelling [pʻɪn] vs. [spɪn].

[20] Latin *alveoli* = pits, here referring to the sockets of the upper teeth, which form a ridge in the bone beneath the gums.

velar (relatively back), varying according to the environment they happen to be in—that is, they adapt themselves to the position of the vowel. Since the *ee* of *geese* is made with the front of the tongue and the *oo* of *goose* with the back, the first [g] is palatal and the second is velar. Thus [g] stands for a *voiced stop, palatal* or *velar*, and [k] for a *voiceless stop, palatal* or *velar*. As with the other two voiceless stops [p] and [t], initial [k] is normally aspirated, but in combination with *s* it is not—contrast *kit:skit, care:scare*, etc. The difference here is no more phonemic than before.

One other stop-sound, a sort of "catch in the throat," is heard in several varieties of English speech (for example, in Scotland, in Cockney of London, in parts of New York City) and therefore perhaps deserves passing mention. It is usually a substitute for [t] (sometimes for [k] or other sounds) in such words as *battle, mitten, stocking*. This sound is made by a closure of the vocal folds within the larynx itself, and is therefore called a *glottal stop*. In many American Indian languages this is an important sound, a phoneme in itself; but in English it is no more than an allophone of the *t*-phoneme, or some other.

Spirants. We next turn to the class of *spirant* (or *fricative*) sounds, again following their points of articulation from the front to the back of the mouth. English has none made with the lips alone, but the upper teeth and lower lip form a narrow aperture through which the breath hisses to produce [v] (as in *vale, live*) and [f] (as in *fail, life*), respectively voiced and voiceless. Thus [v] is a *voiced labiodental spirant*, and [f] a *voiceless labiodental spirant*. These have no notable allophonic variations.

The next spirants encountered are made just below or behind the upper teeth, the breath passing over the tip of the tongue, which is just between the teeth (or a little behind)—wherefore these are called *interdentals*. Conventionally, both the voiced and voiceless varieties are spelled *th*, which obscures the fact that there are two distinct sounds, and that they are single sounds, not combinations of *t* and *h*. The phonemic contrast between them is less easy to prove than for some others, but *teethe*(vb.) :*teeth*(n.), *mouth*(vb.) :*mouth*(n.), and *sheathe:sheath*, show it clearly. The phonetic symbols for these two sounds are borrowed respectively from Old English and from Greek: [ð] is a *voiced interdental spirant*, and [θ] a *voiceless interdental spirant*.

Moving the tongue back and up till it makes a small aperture with the alveolar ridge, we next come to the contrasting sounds of *buzz:bus, zinc:sink*. The symbols for these are, respectively, [z], the *voiced alveolar spirant,* and [s], the *voiceless alveolar spirant.*

Still farther above and behind the gums is the next point of articulation, between the alveolar and palatal areas; therefore the spirants made there are called pre-palatals (also alveolo-palatals or post-alveolars). Sample words are *azure:ashes, rouge:rush,* and the symbols are [ʒ], a *voiced pre-palatal spirant,* and [ʃ], a *voiceless pre-palatal spirant.*

In the palatal and velar areas we find no spirant sounds that are used in standard Modern English. Those of us who know Modern German, however, will recognize the sounds spelled *ch* as in *ich, doch,* respectively palatal and velar, and both voiceless. These sounds existed in Old English, and they are preserved in Scottish dialect in such words as *night, loch.* The difference between palatal and velar (as with [g], [k], and so on) is not phonemic, thus the symbol [x] (borrowed from Greek) may be used for both varieties: *voiceless palatal* or *velar spirant.* The voiced variety of this sound survives in neither dialectal English nor Modern German, but again, it was used in Old English, therefore it will be helpful to list it here and assign the symbol [ɣ]—a *voiced palatal* or *velar spirant.*

Finally, there is one spirant which requires only a slight degree of stricture to produce: [h] as in *hiss, hot, who.* This sound is not always articulated in the same position, but varies (without any noteworthy acoustic difference) according to the environment—usually the position of the vowel that accompanies it. It may be made in the glottis, or in various parts of the oral passage, when there is just enough constriction and enough breath pressure to produce audible friction. There is no vibration of the vocal cords, therefore it may be described as a *voiceless stressed-breath spirant.* Because it requires this stress of breath, it is an unstable sound, and easily disappears in unstressed positions; emphasis will, on the other hand, preserve it, or even introduce it where it does not belong historically.

Affricates. We next come to two sounds that are made by combining a stop with a spirant made in the same or nearly the same position, so that they combine smoothly in articulation: the *affricates.* Since both the stops and the spirants have voiced and voiceless variants, it is not surprising that the affricates have them too. The voiced one combines a stop very much like [d], but made farther back, with [ʒ]; the voiceless combines a similar [t] with [ʃ]: thus we have [dʒ] as in *ridge*, a *voiced pre-palatal affricate*, and [tʃ] as in *rich*, a *voiceless pre-palatal affricate*. Some phoneticians prefer to make a single character for each of these, rather than to combine the symbols for the stops and spirants. They analyze these sounds as unitary phonemes, on the basis of such contrast with the spirants as *pledger:pleasure*, *catch:cash*, and with the stops as *badge:bad*, *batch:bat*. But since these affricates do not pattern structurally like the other pairs of voiced and voiceless phonemes, they are not quite on a par, and therefore do not perhaps deserve treatment as unitary phonemes.[21] To symbolize them as we do here is certainly more convenient, since it reminds us of the way they are produced, and does not require extra symbols.

Nasals. Since the nasals are normally voiced, there will be no symbols necessary for voiceless ones. It will be remembered that nasals are characterized by the breath going out through the nose passage—which requires that the velum be lowered. If breath is not to escape simultaneously from the mouth, the oral passage must be closed. As it happens, there are no places within the nasal passage where muscular control may be applied to modify the breath stream. (We are not camels, or we might be able to close our nostrils tight and produce nasal stops or spirants there, corresponding to labial sounds in the mouth!) The difference in the quality of nasals, in consequence, must be controlled elsewhere, and it is in fact determined by the place where a stoppage is made in the oral passage. When this is shut off it forms a kind of resonance chamber, something like an organ pipe, and as the breath passes by at the back to enter the nasal passage, resonance is set up.[22] Thus, by stopping the mouth passage at various points we can give a different quality of resonance to the breath that is going out through the nose.

Lowering the velum, then, and beginning at the front of the mouth, let us make a succession of closures and see what nasals there are in English. Comparing such words as *sum*, *sun*, *sing*, *sung*, we soon find

[21] See the discussion of this point in Bloch and Trager, *Outline of Linguistic Analysis*, p. 49.
[22] Any hollow body is potentially resonant; when the body of air inside it is disturbed, it resonates, or gives off sound-waves, which may become audible.

that there are four, made respectively with lip closure, alveolar closure, palatal closure, and velar closure. The latter two, however, as with the variants of [g] and [k], do not differ phonemically; we therefore need only three symbols, as follows: [m], *voiced bilabial nasal;* [n], *voiced alveolar nasal;* and [ŋ], *voiced palatal* or *velar nasal.*[23]

Laterals. The next type of sound is that made neither with a stoppage, nor with a spirant hiss, nor a combination of these, nor nasal resonance, but with oral resonance—and yet with the breath-stream impeded, so that it cannot be considered a vowel (though it sometimes functions syllabically): the sound of *l.* Notice that, in saying it, the blade of the tongue (particularly the tip) touches behind the alveolar ridge, but the *sides* do not touch (as they do in producing [t], [d], or [n]). Thus the breath may pass out freely over one or both sides of the tongue, i.e., *laterally.* If we now contrast *leak:luke, lean:loon,* we will hear a difference—and feel it too —coming from the different positions of the tongue. The names often used for these are "clear" *l* and "dark" *l,* but since they are not phonemically different, we use the single symbol [l] for *voiced alveolar lateral.*

Glides. The last class of consonants to be considered is that of *glides* (also called semi-vowels). As the name suggests, these are characterized not by a fixed point of articulation, but by movement. They start or end in a certain position, which gives them their distinctive character, but (except in final position) this position is shifted at once toward that of the vowel which follows them. The first of these is the *r* sound in *rut, trash, forest.* Its characteristic position is with the tip of the tongue turned back (retroflexed) toward the alveolar ridge or above it (the pre-palatal area). The sides of the tongue touch, but a small aperture is left over the middle for the air to pass through. The sound made while the tongue is moving from this position toward the position of the following vowel is that which characterizes this glide: [r]—a *voiced retroflex alveolar glide.*

A good deal of variation exists in *r*-consonants. Quite apart from

---

[23] Bloch and Trager, *op. cit.,* page 25, refer to these as "nasalized stops." This is hardly an accurate designation, for though they do have oral closures, the breath is never entirely stopped. Such a classification runs counter to the basic division of sounds into stops and continuants.

the strongly "trilled" *r* of Spanish, Italian, and certain other languages, there is a less strongly trilled *r* in emphatic British speech, rarely heard in American; it is made by the breath-stream vibrating the tip of the tongue rapidly against the alveolar ridge. The "uvular" *r*, familiar to any student of French, is made by the breath-stream vibrating the *uvula* (which hangs down from the velum) against the back of the tongue; this is also found in many varieties of German and some north-of-England dialects, but nowhere in standard English. The "flapped" *r* (as in the common British pronunciation of *very*, and *sorry*) is a reduction of the trilled *r*, having only one tap instead of several. The glide *r* that we are now considering—the common *r*-sound of the United States—is a still further reduction, with no trill or flap at all. Even in the words given to illustrate it we may notice that there is more friction with the *r* of *trash* than with that of *rut* and *forest*. These and other quite noticeable variations, however, are non-phonemic; thus the single symbol [r] may be used with safety.[24]

Before leaving [r], we may do well to say a word about its loss in many types of English today—particularly in standard British use and in most places along the U.S. Atlantic coast—where in final position or before a consonant it regularly disappears, such words as *car* and *cart* becoming [kɑ:] and [kɑ:t].[25] It should be noticed that this loss is not uncompensated, since the preceding vowel is perceptibly lengthened (contrast the word *cot* [kɑt] with *cart* above). In those regions where this [r] is regularly lost in final and pre-consonantal positions, it is, however, retained between vowels, as in *carol*, *carry, by car and bus*. It therefore has come to be taken as a "linking" sound, which is felt to be necessary to get from one vowel to the next. The next step is for speakers to put it in between vowels where

---

[24] This consonant *r* must be distinguished from the vowel *r*'s dealt with later. It is true that this, being a glide (or semi-vowel) borders closely on the vocalic *r*'s found in such words as *further, early, butter*. We class the latter as vowels, however, because their *r*-quality appears to be no more than a coloring of what is essentially a syllabic vowel—at least in the pronunciation of most people in the North and West of the United States. The most difficult to distinguish apart are those preceding a vowel—e.g., in *merit:* are we to transcribe [mɛrɪt] or [mɛɚɪt]? The decision depends on finding the point at which the syllabic division seems to come, whether before the *r*, as in the first transcription, or after it, as in the second. For an excellent discussion of this point, see the Appendix to Kenyon's *American Pronunciation*.

[25] The diacritic [:] indicates length in the preceding sound.

it does not belong historically, as in *law*[r] *and order, sofa*[r] *and chair, Emma*[r]*and me,* and after this has been done many times, the [r] becomes attached so firmly to the preceding words that it becomes a part of them even when they are not followed by a vowel: thus we get such pronunciations as [lɔr], [sofɚ], [ɛmɚ], as a regular feature of British standard and eastern New England speech.

Finally, one effect of the loss of [r] that has received a lot of popular attention, but which is usually misunderstood, is that associated with the area of New York City, particularly of Brooklyn. It appears in such words as *earl, girl, first, hurt,* which are humorously rendered in print as "oil," "goil," "foist," and "hoit." A glide-vowel has replaced the lost [r], forming a diphthong with the preceding vowel. Now in the first place, the sound actually made is not [ɔɪ], but [ɜɪ] or [ʌɪ]; in the second place, it is not exclusively an uncultivated usage, and to the cultivated users *earl, first, hurt* are not homonyms of *oil, foist, Hoyt,* which have the diphthong [ɒɪ] or [ɔɪ]; in the third place, this sound may be heard in many parts of the South, and even in the Southwest, and is by no means limited to the New York City area.[26]

The second glide is made when the front of the tongue rises close to the palate, causing constriction and a spirant sound, then moves away toward the position of the following vowel. The symbol is [j]; the sound is that of *y* in *year, yes, loyal;* and it is a *voiced palatal glide.* It should be noticed that the tongue and palate here are in the same positions toward each other as for the vowel [i], but there is more constriction of the breath passage. (This explains the alternate term "semi-vowel," and also why [j] often takes the place of [i] or [ɪ] in diphthongs.)

The third glide is made when the lips are decidedly rounded, the back of the tongue rises close to the velum, causing constriction, and then both tongue and lips move to the position of the following vowel. The symbol is [w]; the sound is that in *win, won, aware;* it is a *voiced velar glide.*[27] (Like [j], [w] is similar to a vowel—in this case, to [u].)

One more symbol must be mentioned: [ʍ], often used in phonetic

---

[26] See Hubbell, *op. cit.,* sections 9.4, 9.5.

[27] This sound is sometimes classed as a labial because of the lip rounding; but it seems more consistent to classify it—as here—on the basis of tongue articulation.

alphabets to transcribe the *wh* in such words as *whale, white, awhile*. Strictly speaking, this [ʍ] represents a voiceless *w* sound, preceded by the slight friction of [h] made at the same place in the mouth. Others transcribe *wh* in these words [hw], which, strictly speaking, represents a voiced [w] preceded by [h]. The fact is that both [ʍ] and [hw] are actual pronunciations; and furthermore, the latter is often reduced merely to [w], as in London standard English and the speech of many Americans: there is no distinction made between such words as *whales* and *Wales, while* and *wile, when* and *wen;* they have become homonyms, and there is no longer any separate phoneme for *wh*. Thus we are presented with two questions: What is the preferable way of transcribing *wh* in such words as these, and, Is a separate phoneme to be recognized for *wh*?

It may be said that [ʍ] is certainly not the general pronunciation even where it is still in contrast with [w]; [hw] is far more common in the United States today. Thus a special symbol [ʍ] hardly appears necessary.[28] It seems preferable to transcribe *whales, while, when* with [hw] and [w], according to which of them is actually said by the speaker concerned. Where the contrast is consistently made, individually or regionally, between [ʍ] and [w], an additional phoneme must, of course, be recognized. This distinction is certainly not kept up as widely as it used to be. However, the facts about it are not sufficiently known, and the situation is obscured by the present tendency of schools to try to enforce the distinction, despite the fact that the drift of the language appears to be toward dispensing with it. (See Chapter 12, footnote 35.)

Vowels. We are now ready to look at the vowels. Since they are characterized by voice, this feature will not need to be mentioned when they are described. There are no vowels in English characterized by nasality (as there are in French); when a vowel *is* nasal, it is only incidentally so—that is, the person who makes it may have the habit of nasal speech, or the phonetic environment may tend to add nasality to a vowel. (The vowel of *can't* and many other words is often somewhat nasalized by anticipation of the *n*.) The different qualities of vowels, then, are controlled by what happens to the breath-stream within the oral passage: what the position of the tongue is with respect to other organs, and so forth.

---

[28] If we wish to indicate voiceless *w*, this can be done with the following diacritic: [w̥].

Length. In the kind of terminology with which most of us are familiar, vowels are often spoken of as "long" and "short." Almost all dictionaries mark them so, and some people still mark the scansion of English poetry long and short. This is an inheritance from Latin, where difference of length did separate vowels and was the basis of poetic scansion. But English scansion depends on stress, and though length (at least as subjectively felt) cannot be altogether ignored, it is a minor feature. So with English vowels. It is not length that makes the difference between the so-called "long *i*" of *sheen* or *bean* and the so-called "short *i*" of *shin* or *bin*. To prolong the vowel of *bin* will not turn the word into *bean,* nor will a briefer pronunciation of *bean* produce *bin:* the *quality* of the two vowels is different. Furthermore, the cold fact is that the length of the vowels of *bean* and *bin* is the same because their phonetic environment is the same, and they take the same degree of stress.[29] The difference in the quality of our vowels, then, depends not on length, but on other factors which we must now examine.

Formation. The vowels get their voice in the larynx, and the breath-stream then is blown through the mouth. The kind of resonance they are given there determines their characteristic quality. The differences are made by the way the tongue behaves, for its tip may rise or fall, and the front and back may hump up more or less close to the palate and velum or to intermediate areas. It never makes a closure, of course (though sometimes the aperture is even smaller than for some consonants), but controls the size and shape of the passage. Since the tongue is anchored to the lower jaw, which can move up and down, this member also takes part in controlling the shape and size of the mouth passage. The action of the lips (whether they are rounded or not), how much muscular tenseness there is in the mouth, and how much pressure (or stress) in the breath-stream, must also be attended to.

Vertical Dimension. Let us take the words *bat, bait, beet* and say them naturally in succession. We notice first that the mouth is open more (that is, the jaw is lower) for *bat* than for *bait,* and for *bait* than for *beet.* Now as the jaw is raised, the lips come closer, and their sides spread apart more and more—a natural adjustment. The tongue is relatively flat and in about the same position for all three

---

[29] See Heffner, *General Phonetics,* particularly pages 208-211. In many other languages, however, length is distinctive for both vowels and consonants.

sounds, but the raising of the jaw brings the front of the tongue successively closer to the palate.[30] On the basis of these observations (and of many others made with similar sets of words) it becomes evident that we may quite accurately speak of the vowels in these words as relatively *low, mid,* and *high* (referring to the successive positions of the front of the tongue), and as *unround* (referring to the shape of the lips).[31] Pronouncing next the words *bar, boat, boot,* we notice that there is the same successive raising of the jaw (though it moves less than before) through three positions, and that this time the lips were protruded for the second and third words, and the round opening was made smaller as the jaw rose. It was not the front of the tongue that seemed active this time, but the back, and it was raised closer and closer to the velum. The vowels in these words, then, might equally well be referred to as relatively *low, mid,* and *high,* and (for *boat* and *boot*) *rounded*—alluding to the distinctive opening of the lips.

Horizontal Dimension. Now if we contrast the pairs of words which we have just seen, at each of the levels—i.e., *bat* with *bar, bait* with *boat,* and *beet* with *boot*—paying attention to the action of the tongue, we can easily feel a shift of articulation from the front to the back for each pair of words. A ready means of classification comes out of these observations: we can refer to vowels at least two-dimensionally, according to their height and according to their being relatively *front, central,*[32] or *back.* Thus the vowel of *beet* is both *high* and *front,* while that of *boot* is *high* and *back.*

Tension. Now if (introducing some new examples) we contrast *beet:bit, bait:bet, boot:foot,* another feature becomes apparent. The vowels in the pairs seem to be articulated in nearly the same position,[33] but the first vowel in each pair seems tenser than the second; and observation verifies that the muscles of the tongue are held more firmly for the first member of each pair than for the second.

[30] The jaw position need not necessarily be changed. "Pipe-talkers," for example, can pronounce all the vowels quite normally without dropping their pipes. The adjustments, in that case, are made by the tongue and lips alone.

[31] Naturally, what is significant cannot be realized until one has observed the similarities and differences in the production of all kinds of vowels. We are here short-cutting what is, actually, a laborious process.

[32] The central vowels are formed with the middle of the tongue (including part of the front and part of the back) facing toward the area between (and including parts of) the palate and velum.

[33] Actually, the second member of each pair is slightly lower than the first.

We may therefore call the vowels of *beet*, *bait*, and *boot* "tense," and the vowels of *bit*, *bet*, and *foot*, "lax."

We are now ready to begin assigning symbols to these vowels, and to describe them in terms of the distinctions just noticed. (In connection with this list see the chart on p. 59.)

[æ] as in *bat*   — low front tense unround
[e] " " *bait*[34] — mid   "   "   "
[i] " " *beet*   — high "   "   "
[ɑ] " " *bar*   — low back "   "
[o] " " *boat*[34] — mid "   "   round close
[u] " " *boot*   — high "   "   "
[ɪ] " " *bit*   — " front lax unround
[ɛ] " " *bet*   — mid "   "   "
[ʊ] " " *foot*   — high back " round

These we have met with already; the others may now be given, following the chart:

[ɔ] as in *bought*—mid back tense round open

This is often called the "open *o*" in contrast with [o], which is called "close *o*." We shall notice later that in British standard (and local U.S.) usage there is a shorter, lax variety of this sound.

[ə] as in the unstressed syllables of *tuba, camel, robin, carrot, circus*—mid central lax unround

There is no usual letter for spelling this sound; as the sample words show, it is spelled with *a, e, i, o,* or *u*. It is the centralized, inert sound toward which all others vowels tend when unstressed; it is found only in unstressed syllables.

[ʌ] as the *u* of *butter*—mid central tense unround, retracted and lowered

This, in contrast with the preceding, is found only in stressed syllables.

[ɚ] as the *er* of *butter*—mid central lax unround retroflex. This is found only in unstressed syllables.

[ɝ] as the *er* of *Ernest*—mid central tense unround, retroflex and somewhat fronted

[34] In *bait* and *boat* there is a tendency to diphthongize the vowels respectively to [eɪ] and [oʊ]. Cf. page 75.

barred i   X is I unstressed

In contrast with the preceding, this is found only in stressed syllables.[35]

[ɜ] as the *er* of *Ernest* when the *r* has been "lost" (as in eastern New England)—mid central tense unround

It is found only in stressed syllables.

[ɒ] as in *doll, fog, moth,* as some people pronounce them, is intermediate between [ɑ] and [ɔ]—low back tense round

The three sample words are all pronounced also with [ɑ] and [ɔ], the differences sometimes being regional, sometimes individual. Thus [ɒ] is an allophone sometimes of [ɑ], sometimes of [ɔ].

[a] as in *aunt, fast, bath,* as some people pronounce them, is intermediate between [æ] and [ɑ]—low front tense unround

The three sample words are all pronounced also with [æ] and [ɑ], the differences sometimes being regional, sometimes individual. Thus [a] is an allophone sometimes of [æ], sometimes of [ɑ].[36]

Three more vowel symbols remain, for sounds of Old English that are not phonemic in Modern English:

[æː] as the *ai,* in *airy, fairy,* as some people pronounce them, is intermediate between [ɛ] and [æ]—low front tense unround, higher and probably tenser and longer than [æ].

(It is sometimes symbolized [ɛː] and called "open e," in contrast to [ɛ], which is then called "close e." In this book, however, the symbol [æː] is used by preference, in order to associate it with [æ], since they are spelled in Old English *ǣ* and *œ*, respectively.)

[yː] as the *ü* in German *müde*—high front tense round, probably long

[ʏ] *as the ü* in German *Müller*—high front lax round, probably short

---

[35] Because *r* in spelling is usually thought of as a consonant this description may seem strange. This and the preceding sound, [ɝ] and [ɚ], do descend historically from a combination of vowel + *r*, and that is still to be heard in some types of pronunciation. But generally in the North and West of the U.S. the vowel and *r* have merged into a single sound, so that what we actually have is a vowel with "r-coloring." These two symbols, though not in the International Phonetic Alphabet, are widely used by American phoneticians.

[36] It may even be a separate phoneme. C. K. Thomas, in his *Phonetics of American English,* finds that in such words as *ask, dance, path,* [a] is in phonemic contrast with [æ] in eastern New England, whereas in the New York City area there is no such contrast.

To conclude with, there are the *diphthongs:* combinations of two vowels in one syllable. The characteristic of a syllable is that it has at its core a peak of sonority.[37] When two vowels come together in a diphthong, therefore, one must be subordinated to the other. When the vowel with higher sonority comes first, the diphthong is said to be *falling;* when it comes second, the diphthong is said to be *rising.* The chief diphthongs of Modern English are:

$$
\left.
\begin{array}{l}
\text{[aɪ] as in } buy \\
\text{[aʊ] as in } bough \\
\text{[ɔɪ] as in } boy
\end{array}
\right\} \text{Falling}
$$

[ɪu] as in *few*[38]   —Rising

Two others (diphthongized forms of [e] and [o]) are coming into wider use:

[eɪ] as in *bay*
[oʊ] as in *blow*

On our chart the vowels are placed so as to indicate their *relative* position of articulation; that is, we can see which is higher, lower, farther front, or farther back than some other. For it is quite impossible to think of any vowel in absolute terms. The articulation varies from individual to individual, and even within the usage of each individual. So long as these variations do not violate phonemic boundaries (which would make sounds fall together, and wipe out distinctions on which meaning depends), variations do not greatly matter. The relative position on the chart is therefore the thing that matters. Symbols in parentheses represent less common sounds, or sounds lost since Old English times.

Phonetic Transcription. Students should master this phonetic alphabet and begin to practice transcribing speech. Almost anything will do to start with, if done under careful direction. It is far better to record heard speech than something written, but if the latter is attempted, one must guard oneself vigilantly against the spelling, by converting the written word into *sounds* before beginning to transcribe. This means that, in effect, each transcriber will be rendering

---

[37] All sounds have sonority or they would not be audible; but the vowels have the most, therefore most syllables are based on a vowel. The most sonorous consonants, however, ([m], [n], [l], [r]) also function quite often as syllabics (as in *bottle, butter, cap'm* (captain), *cotton,* etc.). When syllabic, the diacritic [ˌ] is used, e.g., [batl̩].

[38] This very often becomes [ju], the first element being more constricted than for the vowel [ɪ].

his own pronunciation; thus two results may be equally accurate without corresponding in every detail.

Here, for example, is a transcription of the preceding paragraph:

[fo'nɛtɪk ˌtræn'skrɪpʃən. 'studn̩ts ʃʊd ˌmæstɚ ðɪs fo'nɛtɪk 'ælfəbɛt ən bɪˌgɪn tə 'præktəs ˌtræn'skraɪbɪŋ 'spɪtʃ. ˌɔlmost 'ɛnɪθɪŋ wl̩ du tə ˌstɑrt wɪð ɪf ˌdʌn əndɚ 'kɛrfl̩ də'rɛkʃən. ɪt ɪz 'fɑr 'bɛtɚ tə rɪ'kɔrd 'hɝd ˌspɪtʃ ðən ˌsʌmθɪŋ 'rɪtn̩ bət ɪf ðə 'lætɚ ɪz ə'tɛmptəd wən ˌmʌst 'gɑrd wənsɛlf 'vɪdʒələntli əˌgɛnst ðə 'spɛlɪŋ baɪ kən'vɝtɪŋ ðə 'rɪtn̩ 'wɝd ɪntə 'saʊnz bɪfoɚ bɪˌgɪnɪŋ tə trænˌskraɪb. ˌðɪs 'mɪnz ˌðæt ɪn i'fɛkt 'ɪtʃ trænˌskraɪbɚ wɪl bɪ 'ikwəli 'ækjərət wɪðaʊt kɑrɪsˌpɑndɪŋ ɪn ˌɛvri 'diˌtel.]

Note that this transcription, particularly in regard to accentuation, is *one* man's pronunciation, made upon *one* occasion.

Such words as *knife, palm, pseudo, heir, who, doubt, saw, mutton, could, receipt, solemn,* will make one aware of the "silent" or unpronounced letters; such words as *menu, finger, dreamt, colonel,* will make one aware of the sounds that are pronounced though not spelled in; such words as *through, cough, though, rough, bough, nation, passion, fashion, fascist, scholar, schism, fuchsia, beau, beauty, sceptic, cycle, physics, author, symbol, cymbal, classed,* will make one aware of the unexpected and inconsistent values of groups of letters. All should teach the value of listening, and give practice in transcription.

Sounds Together. As we have taken the various sounds for individual examination, it is evident that they have been treated somewhat arbitrarily. The medical student dissects a particular organ at one time, another at another; yet these organs are part of a larger functioning unit, the living creature, therefore a part of the necessary knowledge about them is, how they work together. When we speak a word or a sentence we do not say a series of discrete sounds or words; the sounds flow together into words, and the words into utterances. Actual language is a continuum; there is no inorganic break between sounds. We must not be misled by the letters of writing—not even by the symbols of a phonetic transcription. Far truer than even the best transcription, in this respect, is the band of continuous marks on a sound-spectrograph record;[39] it shows us, for

---

[39] See the illustrated samples of these following p. 136 in Martin Joos, "Acoustic Phonetics," *Language,* Vol. 24, No. 2 Suppl., Apr.–June 1948.

example, how what we consider a characteristic element of one sound (such as friction) may not have ceased being produced before a characteristic element of the next sound (such as nasality) has begun to be produced. Thus sounds are constantly in a position to influence each other—and not only within words, but within the larger unit of the breath-group. The physiology of their production, with the interaction of various organs, inevitably affects sounds. Let us look at some of the influences that sounds have upon one another in speech.

Stress. The first phenomena to notice are those connected with stress, which is nothing but the extra emphasis put upon some sounds by a more vigorous pronunciation. More muscular energy goes into them, and they are therefore louder and more prominent than the surrounding sounds. In English, any word of two or more syllables has its own stress-pattern. No native speaker of English would hesitate which syllable to stress in such words as *excessive, prepare, only, habit, habitual, policy, unable.*[40]

It may be taken as a principle—whose physiological basis is evident—that the stressed syllables of words are more stable than the unstressed syllables. It is in the latter, therefore, that we find both vowels and consonants changing their quality, becoming "weakened," or disappearing altogether—and there are countless examples of this in English and other languages. A word such as *manly* is an illustration, since it is a combination of *man* and *like* (O.E. *monn + līc*) in which the main stress on the first element reduced the stress on the second until the final consonant disappeared and the vowel changed from [iː] to [ɪ]; or one might notice such a word as *afire* (from O.E. *on fȳre*) in which it was the first element that was unstressed, and that therefore lost its consonant and had its vowel reduced from [ɔ] to [ə].

Perhaps the most sweeping effect of this phenomenon in English may be seen in the loss of inflectional distinctions, by which, chiefly, Old English became Middle English. In early Primitive Germanic, it will be remembered, the recessive stress-accent that differentiated the Germanic branch from the other Indo-European branches had

---

[40] The student should transcribe these words and mark their stress. I.P.A. stress-marks are short vertical strokes placed *before* the syllable to which they apply. For *primary* stress the mark is *above* the line; for *secondary* stress it is *below* the line: ['bizˌwæks], [ˌsænəˈteʃən]. Unstressed syllables are unmarked.

become established. In Old English this inherited accentuation is thought to have increased, so that the base syllable of words took a very strong stress, and the inflectional syllables correspondingly little or none. As a result, the nasals at the end of many of these syllables were obscured, then lost; and the formerly distinct vowels became relaxed and centralized, and finally disappeared. Other influences, it is true, were at work at the same time, but there is very little doubt that the phenomenon of stress was the chief contributor to this thoroughgoing alteration in the language. Thus what began as a sound change led ultimately to a recasting of the entire grammatical structure.

Stress-patterns are not limited to single words, of course. As was mentioned above, polysyllables have their own stress-patterns; but many monosyllables depend on the rhythm of the sentence for the amount of stress they get. Articles, prepositions, conjunctions, and pronouns (*the, a, an, and, but, or, for, yet, in, to, with, who, some, that, by, from,* and so on) are very often thrown, in sentences, into unstressed positions. As a result, many of them have what amounts to two forms—the emphatic, used only occasionally, and the unstressed, used most of the time. Examples of the emphatic forms are: "*A* book, not *five* books!" (Stressed, [e]; unstressed, this would have been [ə]). "This is *the* moment!" (Stressed, [ði]; unstressed, this would have been [ðə]). "Six *and* a half!" (Stressed [ænd]; unstressed, [ən] or [n̩]). "Stand *by* the doorway, not *in* it!" (Stressed [baɪ]; unstressed, [bə]).

The history of a single one of these forms will give a hint of what has happened to a number of them. The indefinite article of Modern English *a* (or *an*) did not exist as such in Old English. It comes, as does the numeral *one,* from Old English *ān.* In Middle English this word split entirely in two. When it was used as a numeral, it was stressed, therefore the original nasal and the "long" vowel were preserved; the vowel took the normal course of changing from Old English [ɑ:] to Middle English [ɔ:] (in Chaucer's day it was spelled *oon*) then to early Modern English [o], at which time it also acquired an initial [w], and the [o] has been centered and unrounded, the final result being Modern English [wʌn]. But when, in Middle English, the word developed a new use as the indefinite article, which came almost always in unstressed position, the [n] was lost (except where it was needed to link on to a following vowel), and the vowel was reduced to [ə], the usual pronunciation of *a* today.[41]

Accommodation. Several other phenomena of sound-change may be summarized under the heading of *accommodation*, since they show the way in which some sounds accommodate themselves to the presence of others.

One of the most important of these was <u>umlaut</u> or <u>mutation</u>. Here it was the stressed vowels that were affected (rather than the unstressed), and the new forms that resulted from their change give us several distinctive grammatical differences today, the plurals such as *mice* and *feet* being the most familiar, but the causative verbs *set* and *lay* (formed by umlaut from the intransitives *sit* and *lie*) being also of daily occurrence. What is interesting at this point is the phonetic process involved in umlaut. The change (which took place during the prehistoric period of Old English) was always brought about by the presence of an [iː], [ɪ], or [j] in the latter part of a word. Now since [iː], [ɪ], and [j] are all *high front* sounds, the tendency was for the vowels preceding them to become more like them—to move higher or farther forward—by anticipation. Thus the presence of *i* in the second syllable of such Primitive Germanic forms as **gōsiz* and **manni* eventually brought about the fronting of the vowel of the first syllable; later this *i* was lost, so that the historical Old English forms became *gēs* and *menn*.

It may be wondered how a sound which has not yet been pronounced can work retroactively in this way; yet the common experience of "getting ahead of oneself" will make it clear. For when we are about to do a series of things we sometimes skip, or alter the sequence so that some part is performed before it should have been.[42] So, in umlaut, the preceding vowels or diphthongs, by changing to positions of articulation higher in the mouth or farther toward the front, accommodated themselves to the anticipated high front sound: [ɑ] (before a nasal) was fronted and raised to [ɛ] (*man:men*), [oː] was fronted to [eː] (*goose:geese*), [uː] was fronted to [yː] (*louse:lice*, from O.E. *lūs:lȳs*), and so on. This "*i*-umlaut" made

---

[41] Actually, the occasional emphatic pronunciation [e] or [eɪ] is an unhistorical sound—a calling of the name of the letter *a*, which occurs when this word is "restressed."

[42] *Metathesis* is another common example of confusion in the order of sounds; in this case they are interchanged: O.E. *urnen* gives us *run*, O.E. *acsian* gives *ask*, O.E. *bridd* gives *bird*.

widespread changes in Old English, yet it was not the only one—there was also a "*u*-umlaut," and Modern German exhibits the same kind of change.

Another phenomenon of accommodation is *assimilation*, the tendency of sounds to become similar to those next to them—so much so that they are sometimes absorbed with them into a single sound. Our most common example of this is on everyone's tongue—we employ it a thousand times a day, yet so automatic is it that most people are quite unaware of it. This is our regular "*s*-plural," which has three distinct phonetic variations. If we transcribe *dogs, cats, dishes,* we get [dɒgz], [kæts], [dɪʃəz]. In Chaucer's day these would have been [dɔgəs], [kɑtəs], [dɪʃəs]—all three with the same ending. But between Middle English and Modern English the vowel of this plural suffix "syncopated" (that is, coming in an unstressed syllable, it disappeared) except where that would have thrown together sounds so similar as to be difficult or impossible to pronounce (in the example above, [ʃ] and [s]). When the vowel went from *cattes,* it threw two voiceless sounds together, so there was no need for assimilation and the [s] remained; but when the vowel went from *dogges* it threw the voiceless [s] next to the voiced [g]—and [s] therefore assimilated to [g] by becoming [z], its voiced correspondent.[43]

Assimilation is an extremely widespread phenomenon. Indeed the word is an illustration of itself, since it comes from Latin *assimilāre,* from *ad-similāre,* in which the *d* changed to agree with the *s* that followed it. In the Early West Saxon dialect of Old English, assimilation also occurred in verb forms, again as a result of syncopation. We would expect the infinitive *hēaldan* to have, as the second person singular of the present indicative, **hīeldest;* instead we find *hīeltst.* Evidently the vowel of the ending syncopated, throwing voiceless [st] against voiced [d]; [d] therefore assimilated to [st], losing voice, and becoming [t]. Our past participles today (despite their spelling) follow a pattern similar to that of the plurals: *walked* really ends in [kt]; *raised* ends in [zd]; and in such words as *guarded, parted,* whose stems end in [d] and [t], there has been no syncopation of the vowel (and consequently no assimilation) because that would have thrown together sounds too much alike to be easily pronounced.

One more phenomenon of accommodation may be mentioned be-

[43] The [s] of *dishes* became [z] for another reason. See below, p. 83.

cause of its widespread effects: _palatalization._ Here, the position at which certain consonants were articulated was changed: it was moved farther forward in the palatal or to the pre-palatal region, when the consonants had formerly been made farther back. Palatalization is due in most cases to the influence of front vowels, toward which the back consonants accommodate themselves. In prehistoric Old English, [k], [sk], and [ɣ] were fronted in this way,[44] but the corresponding sounds in other Germanic dialects remained unpalatalized; so we have, for example, German _Kinn_ preserving the _k_, while English _chin_, from the same source, has palatalized it; similarly German _Nagel_ preserves _g_, while English _nail_ has palatalized it. But the palatalization took place mostly in the south of England, therefore in the north we still find unpalatalized forms contrasting with the southern forms: Scottish _kirk_, standard English _church;_ Northern and Eastern English _garth_, standard English _yard;_ Scottish and U.S. _scoot_, standard English _shoot._[45]

Articulative Intrusion. No sharp line can be drawn between the phenomena of accommodation and those of sheer articulation, in which, though there may be no actual approach of sounds toward each other, changes come about because of the mechanics of their production. For example, the positions through which the vocal organs have to move in producing two sounds in succession may make a third sound creep in between; ultimately it may establish itself there, changing the word. An instance of this may be seen in the word _thimble._ In Old English this was _þȳmel_ [θyːmɛl], but as speakers went, in saying it, from [m] (velum lowered, lips closed) to [ɛl] or [l̩] (velum raised, lips open), the breath stream was suddenly cut off from the nasal passage, compressed slightly behind the lips, then exploded. These are exactly the conditions for producing a _bilabial stop._ The vocal cords were vibrating for [m] and continued vibrating for [ɛl], thus the sound produced was also voiced—i.e., [b]—and it had appeared simply as a mechanical effect of its environment. No doubt, it was light or faint at first, but gradually became a regular part of the word. At last, in the fifteenth century,

[44] We cannot be absolutely sure of the values of these sounds; [k] probably became [tj], then [tʃ]; [sk] probably became [sj], then [ʃ]; [ɣ] probably became [ɣj], then [j].

[45] Scandinavian influence is also present in varying degrees: _scoot_ is probably (and _garth_ certainly) from Old Norse, borrowed into Middle English. Palatalization of these sounds did not occur in Old Norse.

people began to indicate their awareness of this by spelling it in. Another word which illustrates the same kind of development is *thunder* (from O.E. *þunor*). This time it was the alveolar stop [d] that came in, however, following the alveolar nasal [n].

A similar principle is at work in *breaking, diphthongization,* and such phenomena. In prehistoric O.E., for example, the front vowels [æ], [æː], [ɛ], [ɪ], [iː] were "broken" by the effect of a following *h* or a consonant group with *r* or *l*. They became respectively [æə], [æːə], [ɛo], [ɪo], [io], showing that in the process of articulation the back of the tongue had been raised, producing a vowel glide that ultimately established itself along with the original vowel, forming a diphthong. So also, at about the same time, the initial palatal consonants (the [tʃ], [ʃ], and [j], discussed above under *palatalization*), when they preceded the front vowels [æ], [æː], and [ɛ], all of which are relatively low, developed glides that turned them into diphthongs. If we listen carefully to the pronunciation of people around us we can hear just the same kinds of changes in progress today. The historical [e] and [o] of *say* and *so,* well preserved in the North and West of the United States, have become regularly diphthongized in London standard speech and commonly in the east Atlantic area. And the tendency to diphthongize is present with the other vowels too—as, for example, in current pronunciations of such words as *school, field, cough, sad,* and so on.

The appearance of additional sounds due to the sheer mechanics of enunciation raises the question of ease of pronunciation, or "economy of effort," which often appears to be the active principle in phonetic changes. Can the addition of a sound be thought to economize effort? Would it not, rather, increase the amount to be pronounced, and therefore the effort required to pronounce it? To answer such a question fruitfully would require actual measurement of energy expended in alternative pronunciations—a very difficult thing, for which techniques are not yet adequately developed.[46] It may be suggested, however, that it might cost a speaker more to keep some sounds out than to let them come in, where the phonetic conditions tend to produce them naturally. The normal rhythm of speech, too, dominates the individual sounds; "ease," therefore, may involve more than merely the mechanics of adjustment between individual sounds.

[46] See Heffner, *op. cit.,* pages 50-51.

The principle of economy of effort is more obviously at work, however, when sounds are lost—and there are countless examples of this everywhere in language. It is impossible to say how far a set of sounds (words or sentences) can vary from the norm without causing a breakdown of communication. But since no two utterances are ever identical, a part of every one is open at any time to phonetic variation without loss of understanding. It is within this area, so to speak, that sound changes occur—and often simply because an economy of effort results. The principle has already been illustrated in assimilation, syncopation, and the weakening and loss of unstressed sounds. To these may be added *dissimilation, vocalization,* and *monophthongization* (to mention only the most striking).

If we recall the derivation of *assimilation* it will be easy to see what *dissimilation* must mean: a sound in this case differentiates itself from a nearby identical sound, apparently because the two, coming close together, are difficult to pronounce. The classical example of this is in the descendants of Latin *peregrinus,* in which the first r has changed to l (in Italian and French, but not Spanish), giving our word *pilgrim.* In *peregrination,* also from Latin, the original r's remain; but *pilgrim* came in earlier, is a popular, not a scholarly word, and so underwent dissimilation along the way. The offending sound is not always changed to some other, but sometimes tends to disappear altogether, as in the widespread present-day pronunciation of *lib(r)ary, sec(r)etary, Feb(r)uary.*

Vocalization means either the voicing of a sound—one that was not voiced before—or the converting or absorbing of a consonant into a vowel. Not only do voiced sounds require less energy to produce than the corresponding voiceless sounds, but when a voiceless sound comes between two voiced ones the tendency is *not* to stop the vibration of the vocal cords for it, but to let them keep on vibrating—which, of course, vocalizes that sound. Vocalization, naturally enough, sometimes accompanies reduction of stress. The Old English definite articles and pronouns beginning with [θ] were voiceless, and continued so throughout Middle English; but in Modern English they have become voiced: *the, that, them,* and so on. Similarly the final -es of noun plurals and verb singulars has become voiced since Middle English times to -[əz]—e.g., *dishes, passes,* which ended in -[əs] in Middle English.

In Old English there were no letters v and z, so f and s did double duty: when they were not between voiced sounds they were [f] and [s]; when they were between voiced sounds they were [v] and [z]. Sometimes the surrounding vowels absorbed them completely, then fell together and shortened the word; thus Old English *hafoc* became *hawk*, *hlāford* became *lord*. Similarly, Old English *lawerce* gives Modern *lark*, but since the consonant did not disappear everywhere, the Scottish word still is *laverock*. Nor did this occur only in native words: loan-words such as *launder*, *salmon*, *calm* exhibit it too (the *l* in the latter two being preserved in spelling only). *Won't* and *shan't* are examples, coming from *woll* + *n't* and *shall* + *n't*. The loss of a [w] is illustrated in the nautical *gunwale* [ˌgʌnl̩] and *forward* ['fɔrəd]. And our everyday conversation will furnish many other instances of this loss of [l]'s and [w]'s: *all right* becomes ['ɔ'raɪt], *always* ['ɔˌwɪz] or ['ɒləz], *it will do* becomes [ɪtl'du].

Monophthongization is the reverse of diphthongization, since it converts a diphthong into a single vowel. In this case the stressless element is not added but lost, probably as the result of increasing the relative stress on the other element. While the "standard" vowels of Modern English are constantly subject to diphthongization, the "standard" diphthongs are tending just the other way. In parts of the southern United States, particularly, this happens in such words as *fine*, *town*, *boil*, where the second vowel element may be reduced almost to the vanishing point: [faːn], [taːn], [bɔːl]. In the northern and western United States, particularly, historical [ɪu] has regularly become [u] in such words as *tube*, *dune*, *new*, *stew*, following the pattern set earlier by *true*, *blue*, *grew*, *glue*; and the movement is spreading.

Consonant Clusters Reduced. One more common type of simplification comes in the tendency to reduce clusters of consonants. Old English initial clusters have been simplified by the loss of the first member from such words as *hlence* (link), *hnutu* (nut), *hring* (ring), *fneosan* (dialectal *neeze*, meaning sneeze), *gnæt* (gnat), *cnēo* (knee), *wlips* (lisp), *wrītan* (write); and *hwæt* (what) has been going the same way, though some people preserve it. Other clusters that are not initial have been reduced in such words as *lomb* (lamb) and *long* (long). In many clusters of three consonants the middle one tends to go: *castle*, *soften*, *whistle*, *listen*, have lost a [t]; *handkerchief* has lost [d] (and assimilated the [n] to the [k]); such words as *sanctuary*, *postpone*, *government* have virtually lost a [k], [t], or

[n]. The same thing is visible when the name *Saint Clair* is reduced to *Sinclair;* also in the British pronunciation of *St. John* as ['sɪndʒən]. Everyday speech holds countless similar examples—[ŋk] in *don't care,* [ŋg] in *won't go,* [nb] in *handbill,* [n:] or [n] in *don't know,* [mb] in *don't believe,* [rt] in *arctic*—which testify to the persistence of this long-standing tendency and the principle of "economy of effort." The fact that the lost consonant is alveolar in almost every instance, that it follows a homorganic (or nearly homorganic) nasal or spirant, and that it is nearly always another stop or nasal should be noticed.

Juncture. Finally we may note one example of change due to *juncture.* This refers to the phenomena of contiguity between sounds, which join more or less closely (*close* juncture or *open* juncture). Juncture does not necessarily correspond with the conventional divisions between words as we write them; in actual speech we may make our divisions quite otherwise. *Cart rack* and *car track* have exactly the same series of sounds, but in one case the open juncture follows the [t]; in the other it precedes it. Thus, too, in *not at all* we very frequently join the [t] of *at* closely to *all,* with open juncture just before it: [ˌnɑtəˈtɔl]. When this kind of re-division of the words (which represents a prosodic fact) establishes itself, it in effect changes the words. This has happened with *a newt* (from M.E. *an ewte*), in which the [n] has been "captured" by the noun. And exactly the opposite has also occurred in *an umpire* (M.E. *a nompere*), *an adder* (M.E. *a naddre*), in which it is the article that has "captured" the [n]. The old phrase "the tone and the tother" represents the [t] of *that* being captured (twice) by the following words *one* and *other,* reducing *that* in each case to *the*—a clear instance of a change due to shifted juncture.

Summary. The sound changes and the tendencies to which attention has been called in this chapter are by no means the only ones, but merely the most arresting—those which have, at some stage in the development of English, altered the language. It should never be forgotten that English is still in the process of development, and that the same kinds of phonetic conditions which prevailed in the past are still at work. There can be no doubt whatever that some of them will bring about changes in the future. The linguist cannot predict; he can observe possibilities—he may even dare on occasion to speak of probabilities. But he is aware always that many more changes are possible than are ever fully achieved, and that most of the variants observed in speech remain individual, local, or temporary, or that they continue as free but unsignificant variations of a broader, more stable entity. Thus the phonetic variations of allophones may be considerable and quite noticeable—yet they may exist for a long time without affecting the phonemic structure of the language.

The most basic changes in the sounds of a language come when the phonemes change—yet even the loss or addition of a few phonemes will not completely upset the overall structural pattern. The first consonant shift (Grimm's Law) made the Germanic branch different from the other Indo-European branches, but within the group of Germanic consonants it only shifted around, but did not overthrow, the structural relationships—otherwise it would (for a time at least) have destroyed meaning, and thwarted the very *raison-d'être* of language: to transfer meaning. The "great vowel shift" of English, as we shall see, was a similar case.

To understand, then, how sound change does take place one must be aware of the potentialities for it, and nothing shows that better than a knowledge of phonetics. Armed with an introduction to some of the accomplished changes, and keeping our attention on the facts of our own daily speech, we may now move on to a consideration of the history of English sounds.

REFERENCES FOR FURTHER READING

Heffner, R.-M. S., *General Phonetics*, Madison (University of Wisconsin), 1949.

Jones, Daniel, *Outline of English Phonetics*, New York (Stechert), 4th ed., 1950.

Kenyon, John S., *American Pronunciation*, Ann Arbor (Wahr), 6th ed. 1935.

Pike, Kenneth L., *Phonetics*, Ann Arbor (University of Michigan), 1943

Chapter 5

The History of English Sounds

IN THE previous chapter the subject of the sounds of English was introduced and a phonetic alphabet was furnished, by which means these sounds will be symbolized throughout this book. In addition, attention was called to the more important kinds of sound-change that take place in language, with examples drawn from as far back as Primitive Germanic, the ancient ancestor of English, and from as near by as the spoken English of the present moment. We should now be prepared to put this knowledge to a more orderly use by following the development of English sounds from Old English times forward, the better to understand how (in broad outline, at least) the pronunciation we use has come by its rules and its exceptions—how, in short, it has become what it is.

Evidence on Past Pronunciation. But before actually plunging into the discussion of the sounds, it will be wise to ask how scholars can know with any degree of accuracy about the sounds of words spoken hundreds of years ago. It has to be admitted that the pronunciation of earlier periods cannot be reproduced with absolute fidelity. Of some things—the main points—there is very little question; others are doubtful, but no fundamental disagreement exists among those qualified to judge; on some points there may be no conclusive evidence whatever, yet a reasonable surmise is possible; on a very few there is conflicting evidence, and qualified people disagree. A great deal of work, for example, has been done on the pronunciation of Chaucer, and much has been learned about it; nevertheless, the result has been justly summarized by Manley in these terms: "If Chaucer could hear a good student read his poetry, the pronunciation would probably seem like that of a foreigner, but he would, we hope, be able to understand what he heard." [1]

[1] Introduction to J. M. Manly's ed. of the *Canterbury Tales*, New York (Holt), 1928, p. 89.

Taking it as a whole, however, the story of English pronunciation is clearly understood. One basic assumption must never be forgotten: that human physiology has not changed materially within historical times. It follows that any speech-sound possible today was possible in the past (and vice versa) ; and that the way sounds behave, therefore, as we observe them in our own speech, throws the clearest light on the sounds of earlier times.

What, then, are the tangible sources of evidence on pronunciation in the former stages of English? There are at least four: (1) the spelling, in all its phases, whether traditional or unorthodox; (2) the remarks or statements made about sounds in the past, whether casually, or in treatises on pronunciation and spelling; (3) the evidence furnished by the rimes of poetry, by puns, and by other plays on words; (4) the evidence of dialectal and conservative usage.

In pointing out the need of a phonetic alphabet (Chapter 4) we found it necessary to demonstrate the many inconsistencies of present-day English spelling. These faults are more painfully visible when one is teaching or learning the language, because a simple set of rules necessarily becomes vitiated by a crowd of exceptions. To the scholar tracing the history of sounds, however, they furnish useful evidence as to older habits of pronunciation. He is somewhat in the position of the biologist who finds, still existing, not only mammals (the most modern form of life), but reptiles, amphibians, crustaceans, worms, amebae, and other "creatures great and small" which testify to former stages in the development of mammals. The biologist has not only living forms, but fossil forms which are datable; so has the linguist, as he looks back into older books, manuscripts, documents, and inscriptions: the two kinds of evidence supplement and illuminate each other. And all depend upon spelling, which has to be interpreted carefully, but which tells us most of what we know.

The spelling of Modern English, at least, with all its faults, is now relatively standardized. As we go back to early Modern English, and to Middle English, there is less and less of such standardization— more and more variability. In Shakespeare's day a man spelled pretty much as he liked—the Bard himself never signed his name twice alike, if we may judge by the signatures that remain to us. People with good ears or some ideal of consistency (Milton, for example) spelled with regularity and some regard to the actual sounds; others did "what came naturally," and often spelled a word in three different ways on the same page. Then, too, the complexities introduced by dialect are very much in evidence in Middle English, even further increasing the variety and abundance of its spellings. By contrast, the Old English period, even with its dialectal differences, had a far stabler spelling. Not that this proves that pronunciation itself was less varied; it gives testimony rather to the existence of a tradition or a standard, since writing at that time was done by a relatively small group of professionals. Indeed, as Samuel Moore has pointed out,[2] it is just in the discrepancy between the traditional spelling of *most* words and the untraditional spelling of a *few* (lapses, usually, in which the writer inserts a contemporary form—perhaps his own pronunciation—rather than the more orthodox and conservative scribal form), that we find the best evidence of the sound-changes that separate Old from Middle English.

Old English was written first in the runic alphabet, an adaptation (probably) of a North-Italian alphabet which was early spread throughout the Germanic north of Europe. Pre-Christian inscriptions, and early Christian ones, were in runes—for instance those on the Bewcastle and Ruthwell crosses. With Christianization the Roman alphabet was introduced with the Latin language, and the English adapters used the new letters for those English sounds which corresponded best to the values which they had in Latin. In most cases the correspondence was very close, so that few changes had to be made—and those mostly additions.[3] A knowledge of the pronunciation of Latin in the seventh century, therefore, casts light on the pronunciation of Old English.

The sounds of Middle English, similarly, are known in part from a comparison with Latin and French; but also (and chiefly) from the changes in spelling by which writers show that they are trying to keep touch, consciously or unconsciously, between the written and the spoken word, when the former is by its nature traditional, and the latter is undergoing all kinds of alterations.

[2] "Loss of Final *n* in Inflectional Syllables of Middle English," *Language,* Vol. 3, pp. 232-259.

[3] The letters þ and ƿ were brought over from the Runic alphabet, and ð was developed by crossing the staff of a d. Latin had no sounds [θ] or [ð], therefore no characters for them which the Anglo-Saxons might adopt. Latin w as a single letter had not yet been developed, so the Runic ƿ for w was also borrowed. It is usually transliterated to w in present-day Old English texts.

In the Modern English period this continues in a somewhat different form, particularly after the time when spelling has become standardized to some degree. For now, those who have not learned the "educated" way to spell, do so by ear, and their "naïve" spellings therefore reveal many things about actual pronunciation (local, dialectal, and so on) that would be hard to know otherwise. Krapp, and others after him, have thrown a great deal of light upon seventeenth- and eighteenth-century American pronunciation by studying old town records. Such spellings as *arst* for *asked* and *clack* for *clerk* are better clues to pronunciations in actual use than are statements of grammarians and lexicographers, who are likely to be concerned with how they think words ought to be pronounced rather than how they *are* pronounced.

The second source of evidence about sounds is in the statements of contemporary observers, whether they speak only in passing about some feature of pronunciation, or whether they are orthoepists professionally interested in the sounds of language. Of the first kind of observer a classic example is Sir Thomas Elyot, who, in the early sixteenth century, complains of the "corrupt and foul pronunciation" that the sons of noblemen acquire from their "nurses and other foolish women." If it proved no more, such a denunciation would tell us that more than one pronunciation existed at the time, and that there was competition among these for survival. When contemporary observers complain that a sound is—for example—a "horrid innovation," they incidentally reveal to us the *direction* which developments are taking.

The professional writers themselves—the orthoepists—are not to be attended to incautiously. For one thing, they were often too intent on proscribing what seemed bad to them—an attitude not conducive to careful observation. It was late in the seventeenth century before some would admit that English might have *a*-sounds not found in the Classical languages, though they had, in fact, been present for hundreds of years.[4] With the advent of Wallis and Cooper,[5] however, observation began to be more acute and more candid, and continued so through the eighteenth century. Yet evidence from this source must be confirmed from other sources—the rimes of poetry, for in-

[4] H. C. Wyld, *A Short History of English*, p. 161.
[5] Good lists of these orthoepists may be found in Wyld, *op. cit.*, and Zachrisson, *Pronunciation of English Vowels*, Göteborg (Zachrisson), 1913.

stance. Wyld sums it up pointedly: "As we cannot suspect poets and pedants of being in collusion to deceive posterity, we may assume that agreement between them implies the truth." [6]

The third source of evidence on pronunciation is in rimes, puns, and other plays on words. It is true that the accuracy of rimes cannot always be trusted: the poet may have a bad ear, he may be careless and take what is called "poetic license," [7] or he may be using a regional pronunciation; besides, puns quite often get some of their effect by *not* being perfect. Nonetheless, these may teach us about past pronunciation, and help in solving literary and historical problems. It has always been recognized, for example, that Shakespeare was a great punster, yet with all the study that has been devoted to his plays, many of his puns are being perceived for the first time today, former students not having paid strict enough attention to Shakespearean pronunciation. The pun in *Timon of Athens,* III. iv. 305-310, on *medlar* and *meddler* was recognized long ago, but a second pun in the same lines on *hate* and *eat* was not pointed out till 1947, at last clearing up a puzzling passage. [8]

If a writer is generally careful, and consistent in his use of individual rimes, and if his practice is weighed against that of his contemporaries, we may learn a good deal from rimes. Chaucer, for example, is meticulous in this respect; therefore when we find him riming *breeth* (breath) with *heeth* (heath) in the *Canterbury Tales* (Prologue, lines 5-6) which both had ǣ vowels in Old English, though their vowels differ today ([ɛ] and [i] respectively), it is safe to conclude that the difference must have developed *after* Chaucer's time. Furthermore, when we find that such a word as *heate* (heat) is never rimed by Chaucer with another such as *swete* (sweet) though we would rime them today, and that the first had ǣ in Old English but the second had ē, we may conclude (other evidence, of course, being in agreement) that the Old English distinction between these sounds still existed in Chaucer's day, and that their identity as [i] has come about *since* his time.

[6] *Op. cit.,* p. 162.

[7] In defense of poets it may be remarked that readers and teachers who do not know as much as they might about historical pronunciation sometimes explain seemingly bad rimes or meters as "poetic license," when in reality they were perfectly correct at the time when they were written.

[8] See Helge Kökeritz, "Five Shakespeare Notes," *Review of English Studies,* Vol. XXIII, Oct. 1947, pp. 312-313; also several other articles on Shakespearean pronunciation by the same author.

Again, changes in pronunciation since the eighteenth century are to be observed in a study of the rimes of such poets as Pope and Cowper. The neat anticlimax of this couplet

> Here thou, great Anna! whom three realms obey,
> Dost sometimes counsel take—and sometimes tea[9]

falls deplorably flat in present-day pronunciation, yet the lines must once have rimed perfectly. If, as can be demonstrated, the word *obey* has remained virtually unchanged in its sounds, *tea* has altered greatly. The old pronunciation, evidently, was not [ti] but [te]; the comparative method substantiates the conclusion, [te] being also the pronunciation of the word in such languages as French, German, and Spanish, and in certain dialectal forms of English—Irish, for example. A similar change is shown by the lines of Cowper's well-known hymn,

> God moves in a mysterious way, . . .
> He plants his footsteps in the sea . . . ,

for the vowel of *sea* has developed from [æ:] through [e] to [i], and in the eighteenth century it was still in the middle stage. In Pope's famous attack on Addison, these lines occur as a riming couplet;

> Dreading e'en fools; by flatterers besieged,
> And so obliging that he ne'er obliged.[10]

Once more, a surviving dialectal pronunciation helps to make it clear that the sounds of *obliged* were once parallel with those of *besieged*.

The reverse of this situation is often given by the conventional rimes called "eye rimes"—the employment, that is to say, of words spelled alike but sounded differently, where the poet's only justification is the fact that at some former time the words really did rime. It would seem, however, a rather illegitimate extension of poetic privilege to rime such words as *star* and *war* for no other reason than that such a seventeenth-century poet as Henry Vaughan did so. Lines like

> My soul, there is a country
> Far beyond the stars,
> Where stands a winged sentry
> All skilful in the wars.

[9] *Rape of the Lock*, Canto III, lines 7–8.
[10] *Epistle to Dr. Arbuthnot*, lines 207–208.

indicate a parallelism in sounds that no longer exists. On the other hand, when in a popular song of our day, *Home on the Range*, we find *stars* rimed with *ours* and *flowers*, it is neither an eye-rime, nor a bad rime, nor poetic license, but testifies truly enough to the reduction of the diphthong [aʊ] to a single vowel which may be heard in the southwest (whence hails the song) and elsewhere. The second word is pronounced [ɒrz] and the third [flɒrz], so that in the regional pronunciation they do rime correctly enough with [stɒrz].

Finally, because language changes at a different rate in different areas we can learn about past pronunciation by comparing the less conservative types with the more conservative. This may be observed within a single lifetime when the oldest people preserve a sound that the youngest have given up (or have never used at all). One clear instance of this is the "New England short *o*" (a centered and lowered variety of [o]), which was still widely used in the early years of this century in such words as *coat, road,* and *home* but now appears to be falling away.[11]

But even when forms are not in rapid decay, the conservative and the unconservative may be compared by studying dialectal (local and regional) differences; for in isolated and outlying areas changes come slowly, and sounds that were "standard" in the seventeenth and eighteenth centuries (long since altered in today's standard pronunciation) remain alive on the lips of the folk. The whole series of words spelled humorously *bile, rile, spile, jine* (for *boil, roil, spoil, join*) show the survival, at a substandard level, of a remnant of the once standard pronunciation [aɪl], which has since become [ɔɪl]. A careful study of dialectal pronunciation, therefore, is a very valuable source of evidence.

History of Consonant Sounds. We may now come directly to the history of the sounds of English, beginning with the consonants and enquiring which of them have disappeared, which have changed, which are new, which have remained the same. Old English[12] had only two consonant sounds that no longer exist in standard English: [ɣ] and [x], the voiced and voiceless velar spirants. As has been said above (page 65), the first is not to be found at all today, though the second lingers in Scots dialect. Old English words such as *gamen*

---

[11] *The Handbook of the Linguistic Geography of New England* has a map on which this information is displayed: Chart 8.

[12] Unless stated otherwise, Early West Saxon is being referred to.

(game) and *græs* (grass) illustrate [ɣ], which lost its spirant quality and became a stop in late Old English or early Middle English, therefore changing to [g] and falling together with the regular Old English [g]. It has retained this value since.

The second sound, [x], though it had already begun to change in Old English, survived throughout the Middle English period. In the Modern English period, however, it has been either lost or converted into some other sound. It was spelled *h* in Old English, but by the thirteenth century we find the new spelling *gh* (probably introduced by Norman scribes) ; and we are still spelling it this way even where it has long since disappeared from pronunciation. We find [x] in such Old English words as *lēoht, bōhte, rūh, tōh,* and it continued to be pronounced in Middle English—e.g., Chaucer's *lighte, boughte, rough, tough.* But by early Modern English it had either disappeared, as in *light* and *bought,* or had been changed to [f], as in *rough* and *tough.*[13] Initially, before *w,* as in Old English *hwīt, hwā,* it has been reduced to [h], or has disappeared, in Modern English *white, who* (see above, page 70). In some other words it has fallen together with its homorganic stop [k] (just as [ɣ] often fell together with [g]) : O.E. *weahsan,* later *weaxan* (*x = ks*), *eolh;* which became Middle English *wexen, elke;* and Modern English *wax, elk.* Otherwise, in final position it has either disappeared: O.E. *scōh,* M.E. *shoo* (shoe) ; or it has given way to a high back vowel, later lowered: O.E. *holh, sorh,* M.E. *holowe, sorwe* (hollow, sorrow). It will be seen then, that this sound has been losing ground even from Old English times (as in *wax*); that by Chaucer's day, though still strong, it had disappeared from a considerable number of words, or had changed to something similar (*shoe, hollow, sorrow*) ; and that its greatest decay comes in Modern English times, so that it is altogether lost from standard English today (*light, bought, rough, tough*). Needless to say, the words cited are not the only ones which illustrate this development—they are only typical examples.

So much for the losses. Two other Old English consonants have changed somewhat in the course of time, but not completely; that is, though their phonetic quality has altered, they retain their pho-

---

[13] Spellings with *f* begin to appear as early as the fourteenth century, at first added to *gh,* then later superseding it. Apparently the spirant [x] gave way to the more frequent spirant [f], perhaps aided toward the labial type by the lip-rounding of the preceding [u] or [o].

nemic position virtually unchanged from Old English times through to the present. The first of these is [r], which today is usually no more than an effect of retroflexion of the tongue-tip or tension of the tongue blade (with lowered tip), or some kind of simple flap of the tongue—all of which are Modern English reductions of a formerly trilled sound that King Alfred and Chaucer used, and that may still be heard in emphatic speech (though less in America than in Britain). It has been spelled r all along and is still so spelled traditionally, even in those positions (final and pre-consonantal) in which it has been "dropped" or "lost," as in modern British and Atlantic U.S. pronunciation.

The other sound that has changed somewhat is [j], which today is a palatal tongue-glide, but in Old English was closer, tenser, and had definitely the quality of a spirant. Its spelling in Old English—g, or g with a front vowel (ge, gie)—betrays part of the reason for this; for when [ɣ] was palatalized it became [j] and fell together with the Germanic [j], also a voiced palatal spirant. In Middle English this was usually spelled with the character ȝ, later with y, so that though it looks different in O.E. gēar, geoc: M.E. ȝeare, ȝoke: Mn.E. year, yoke, the sound has been somewhat similar all along, though becoming more open, less consonantal—in fact, semi-vocalic.

Though two sounds have been lost, and two have been quite a bit altered, it is striking that only one has been added: [ʒ]. It is true that the affricate [dʒ] which is generally thought to have existed in such O.E. words as ecg, brycg (edge, bridge) contains [ʒ], but it did not become an independent phoneme until early Modern English times, when it developed out of [zj] in such French loan-words as measure, usury, azure, osier. Old French words with initial j (journal, jealous, large, forge) had the sound [dʒ] when they were borrowed in Middle English; today they have the value [ʒ], but when borrowed they tend to adapt themselves to English sound-patterns by substituting [dʒ] for it—as in the recently introduced massage, garage, rouge—which suggests that [ʒ] is still a difficult sound for speakers of English. It gives least trouble in medial position, but in final position the feel of the language is against it, and it is never used in initial position, though very common there in French.

With the exception of the five just dealt with, the consonants of Old English have come down to Modern English virtually without change. We still have the voiced stops [b], [d], [g]; the voiceless

stops [p], [t], [k]; the voiced spirants [v], [ð], [z]; the voiceless
spirants [f], [θ], [s], [ʃ], [h]; the nasals [m], [n], [ŋ]; the lateral
[l]; the glide [w]; the affricates [dʒ] and [tʃ]. Most of these were
spelled in Old English as they are in Modern English, but there were
a few differences: [dʒ] was usually *cg*, as in the examples just given
above, *ecg, brycg*; [tʃ] was the sound of palatalized *c*, as in *ceowan*
(chew), *stenc* (stench); [ʃ] was spelled *sc*, as in *scieran* (shear),
fisc (fish); *k* was rarely used, *c* almost always, for [k].

But though all these sounds were present in Old English, their
status was not in every case the same as it is now. Four of them, at
least, that were not phonemes then, are phonemes now. It has been
pointed out that though [ʒ] existed as part of the affricate combination [dʒ], it was not till early Modern English times that it gained
full phonemic status. Something similar happened too with the
sounds [v], [z], [ð], and [ŋ], for in Old English they were no more
than variations respectively upon [f], [s], [θ], and [n], when these
latter came in particular phonetic positions.

Thus when [f], [s], and [θ] (all voiceless) came between voiced
sounds, they assimilated to them by also becoming voiced; but,
clearly, since they were voiced *only* in intervocalic position, they
never came in contrast with their voiceless correspondents, and did
not constitute different phonemes—they were allophones, no more.
They probably began to split off as new phonemes in early Old English, completing the process in early Middle English;[14] and the proof
of their independence comes when new characters are introduced to
spell them—*v* and *z*, at least, though the substitution of *th* for *þ* or
ð in both their voiced and voiceless values made no gain in clarity.

It was a little different again when [ŋ] split off from the *n* phoneme, for here it was not a difference as between voiced and voiceless
variants, but between alveolar and velar nasal: the latter appeared
(again by assimilation) when the environment was one having back
sounds, and [n] appeared when the environment was one having
front sounds. Thus the word *cyning* (king) was [kyniŋg], the first
nasal being alveolar and the second velar. Eventually, in Middle
English, [ŋ] achieved independent phonemic status. No character

---

[14] See Herbert Penzl, "A Phonemic Change in Early Old English," *Language*,
Vol. 20, part 2, pp. 84–87, for a discussion of this process, and an analysis of the
evidence for it.

for spelling it has ever been introduced, so that we now spell it sometimes with *n*, sometimes with *ng: singer, finger, thinker.*

We may now summarize the situation with regard to the individual consonants. Old English had two sounds that have since been lost ([ɣ] and [x]), two that have changed their quality considerably ([r] and [j]), one quite recently added ([ʒ]), and four that have changed from the status of conditional or positional variants of others to being independent phonemes. The others, though their distribution in words has altered in many cases (some becoming substituted for others, some being lost entirely, some occasionally added to words), have generally remained stable, both as to quality and status.

On the level not of individual sounds, but of words, there were other losses and gains too, though only the most important can be mentioned. Without question, the foremost happening of this type was the loss of -*n* from inflectional syllables, which has already been spoken of (pages 44, 78) and will be again (pages 116-117), since it went so far to mark the boundary between Old and Middle English. Simplification of initial consonant clusters, as a result of which many an [h], [k], and [w], and some [f]'s were dropped, has also been referred to (pages 84-85).

Also referred to (pages 83-84) was the phenomenon of vocalization, by which consonants were absorbed or lost, when they came in a vocalic environment. As might be expected, this happened most often with those consonants that are most like vowels—the glides and the resonants. Thus [w] has been lost in *two, who, sword* (which were all pronounced with the *w* in Old and Middle English); [j] has been lost in the prefix *ge-* ([jɛ]), very common in O.E., reduced to *y-* ([ɪ]) in Middle English, and finally done away with in early Modern English. The [r] sound in final and pre-consonantal position, widely lost today, began to drop out quickly in the seventeenth century, though occasional spellings show that it was weakening as early as in M.E. times.[15] Also mentioned before (page 84) is the loss of [l] from *folk, calf, calm,* and so forth.

The conversion of the resonants into the equivalent of vowels is proved also by their frequent use since early Modern English times as syllabics. Thus we find syllabic [ɹ] today in *butter, madder,*

[15] Wyld, *op. cit.,* p. 162.

lather; syllabic [ḷ] in *kettle, muddle;* syllabic [m̩] in *stop 'em,* and the often heard pronunciation of *happen* as ['hæpm̩], *something* as ['sʌmpm̩], and so on; syllabic [n̩] in *batten, bidden;* syllabic [ŋ̩] in *slacken* ['slækŋ̩], *wagon* ['wægŋ̩]. These vowel-like consonants, when they come together, also may absorb each other, as [l] absorbs [n] in *kiln,* usually pronounced [kɪl] and in *mill,* from O.E. *myln,* the *n* of which is still seen in the surname *Milner;* and [m] absorbs [n] in the loan-words, *damn, hymn, autumn, column,* and so on.

Again, *voicing,* mentioned before (page 56), changed many consonants in early Modern English from the corresponding voiceless forms. Thus M.E. *of* [ɔf] is now [əv]; M.E. *the, that,* began with [θ], rather than [ð], as they do today; the -[s] of plurals and possessives often became -[z]; and [tʃ] became [dʒ]: M.E. *knowleche, cabach, partriche* are now *knowledge, cabbage, partridge.*

Consonants were not only altered or lost, however; here and there they were added where historically they do not belong. Thus an unetymological [r] is seen in *bridegroom* (cf. German *Bräutigam* and O.E. *guma,* "man"), *cartridge* (cf. French *cartouche*), and *hoarse* (from O.E. *hās*); an additional or "excrescent" *n* is to be observed in *passenger* (cf. French *passager*), *messenger* (still *messager* in Caxton), *nightingale* (cf. German *Nachtigal*), *collander* (from French *collader*). So also [b], [d], and other sounds creep in where the phonetic environment is favorable (see pages 81-82). These tendencies are ever present: note, for example, the way in which a [t] is added in folk usage to *once, twice, across,* in exactly the same way as it was added in early Modern English (in acceptable usage, which has lasted till today) to form *whilst, amongst, amidst, against,* and so forth. Nor should the effects of dissimilation, metathesis, and other minor sound changes be forgotten.

With all the alterations that we have been noticing, it may seem that the consonants were greatly changed between Old English times and the present. But this was not the case, either absolutely or relatively. The language has lost velar sounds ([ɣ], [x]) and gained alveolar ones ([ʒ] and [dʒ], the latter much more common than in O.E.), and the changes have reduced the consonantism somewhat. But most of the consonants have been unaffected. The loss of the inflectional -*n* in Middle English—the farthest-reaching of the consonant changes—affected the language more through what it did to the grammatical structure than to the system of sounds; for the sound of [n] was not lost, nor was the phonemic structure disrupted. Relatively, too, the consonants were altered far less than the vowels. Most of the troubles in our spelling today come from the confusion and the incomplete adjustments that followed upon changes in the vowel system. The outlines of these must now be sketched.

History of Vowel Sounds. During the Old and Middle English periods, most of the vowels of English remained stable. When scholars introduce students to the pronunciation of Chaucer it is customary to speak of giving the vowels their "continental" values—which means simply that in modern French, German, Spanish, Italian, and so on, the vowels have continued much as they were in Chaucer's day. By contrast, the English vowels since the fourteenth century, have undergone what Jespersen has termed the "great vowel shift." [16] All the *tense* vowels [17] have changed their quality; but the movement has had a very clearly defined direction, and has proceeded with striking regularity, so that though the system is now out of agreement with the system of Chaucer's day, it still functions quite satisfactorily, very little confusion having occurred in the course of the shifting.

What has happened may be visualized by means of the following diagram:

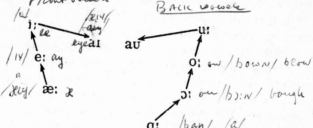

The tense vowels, both the front and the back series, have shifted to the positions of articulation of vowels above them. The highest in each series, unable to go higher, have become diphthongs. Jespersen

---

[16] *Modern English Grammar,* Part I, section 8.11.

[17] In Modern English vowels, tenseness or laxness is phonemically distinctive, though length is not; in symbolizing these vowels, therefore, length has not been indicated. In Old and Middle English vowels, on the other hand, length appears to have been phonemic, and is therefore indicated in symbolizing them. On the following diagram, the vowels represent the starting-points of the movement. The student must note carefully that *the degree of the shifting was not the same for all vowels.*

Raising and fronting vowels (long) – VOWEL SHIFT

No one word goes through all the changes

argues with good reason[18] that this general upward shift could not have taken place until the way was clear for it—in other words, that it must have begun with the diphthongization of [i] and [u], which then permitted the rest to rise serially without losing their phonemic contrasts. Some words illustrating this shift are:

O.E.	M.E.	Mn.E.	O.E.	M.E.	Mn.E.
æ:	— æ: > i		sǣ, clǣne	see, clene	sea, clean
e:	— e: > i		grēne, tēð	grene, teeth	green, teeth
i:, y:	— i: > aɪ		īs, hȳdan	ise, hide	ice, hide
ɑ:	> ɔ: > o		bān, bāt	boon, bote	bone, boat
o:	— o: > u		tōð, sōna	tooth, soone	tooth, soon
u:	— u: > aʊ		mūð, hūs	mouthe, hous	mouth, house

The Middle English spellings given here are Chaucerian, and are not the only ones that were used. As has been pointed out, though we rime *clean* and *green*, Chaucer would not have done so: they had different vowel sounds for him. Also, though he spelled *boon* and *soone* with *oo*, he would not have rimed them: the vowel sounds were different for him. Note that though some shifting begins before Chaucer's day, the shift as a whole is subsequent. Some sounds are still unsettled today, as will be shown later.

The shift of the individual vowels must be examined in further detail, for the diagram and the list of shifted words do not tell the whole story. The sounds [æ:] and [e:] were not only simple vowels, but were the basis also of two Old English diphthongs. The first of these, spelled *ēa*, was phonetically [æ:ə], and it fell in with [æ:] in early Middle English. Thus words such as O.E. *ēast*, *strēam* are found spelled *eest*, *streme* in Middle English, like *see* and *clene*. The second Old English diphthong, spelled *ēo*, was phonetically [e:] followed by a centralized short [o]; and it similarly fell together with the simple vowel [e:] in early Middle English. Thus words such as *dēop*, *ðēof*, spelled *deep*, *thefe* in Middle English, had the same vowel as *grene* and *teeth*. As we have said before, though both these vowels, [æ:] and [e:], whether originally simple vowels or diphthongs, are spelled alike by Chaucer, he keeps them carefully apart in his rimes.

[18] Compare the grounds for arguing that the first Germanic consonant shift began with the simple voiceless stops becoming spirants, so that the other stops could shift afterward without causing homonymy.

Thus they certainly were distinct for him, and they appear to have remained so into the late sixteenth century. In the seventeenth century, however, [æ:] fell in with [e], so that the descendants of words which in Old English had had four different sounds, [æ:], [æ:ə], [e:], [e:o], now all had the same; and loan-words with similar vowels—such as French *beest* and *grese*—had joined the group along the way. Finally, by the eighteenth century, the [e] in this entire group of words seems to have begun to shift to [i], which shift has since been completed.[18a] Diagrammatically this might be represented thus:

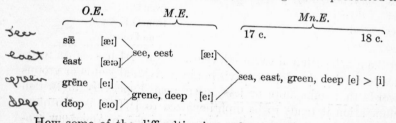

How some of the difficulties in modern spelling have come about will now be better understood. If spelling had changed to keep up with the changes in pronunciation, there would have been only one way to spell [i] in Modern English. But at least two conditions worked against this. The first was that the reduction in the number of sounds did not lead necessarily to consistency in spelling; we have already seen that Chaucer's [æ:] and [e] were spelled interchangeably with *ee* or *e*, and often with *ea* and *eo* preserved. Thus spelling had lost touch both with the actual sounds and with their historical sources. The French loan-words which had come in, meantime, had gone some one way, some another—and a few had even retained their French spelling.

The second condition working against simplicity of spelling was that before the further sound-changes of the seventeenth and eighteenth centuries came about, the standardization of spelling had begun; accordingly there was even less likelihood of the spellings'

[18a] In his *Shakespeare's Pronunciation* (pages 194 ff.) Professor Helge Kökeritz argues plausibly that Mn.E. [i:] did not develop in a straight line from M.E. [æ:], through early Mn.E. [e:] (the conventional view), but that by the early 15th century [i:] had developed independently in a Southeastern dialect, then rose to the standard level, displacing the historical [e:]. In Shakespeare's time, then, two pronunciations coexisted, but [e:] died out by 1700, leaving the field to [i:].

becoming adapted to the sounds: if things were allowed to take their course, only further dislocations could occur. Today, as a result of these conditions, we have at least seven ways of spelling [i], three of which are widely used, but without clear relationship to the original sounds. Thus we find:

ea	(mead, leaf, dear, meat, beaver)	from O.E. æ, ēa, ēo, e, eo
ee	(eel, sheep, feet, creep, fee)	from O.E. æ, ēa, ē, ēo, eo
e	(mere [boundary], dew,[19] fever, yew,[19] mete)	from O.E. æ, ēa, ē, ēo, e
ie	(bier, thief, chief)	from O.E. æ, ēo; French ie
ei	(either[20])	from O.E. ǣg
ey	(key)	from O.E. ǣg
ay	(quay)	from French ay

In the nineteenth and twentieth centuries this [i] has shown tendencies to further development, visible in individual words or groups of words that gain more or less acceptance. Especially in British pronunciation it tends to be diphthongized to [ij]. It is also quite often changed to [ɪ]—there are many examples in American pronunciation, such as been (British [bin], in the United States more often [bɪn]), and the very widespread pronunciation of [krɪk] for creek. Similarly, alongside sleek has developed the form [slɪk], respelled slick, which betrays its origin when a man makes his hair slick, but which has developed other, less obviously connected meanings: smart, or clever, in both favorable and unfavorable senses. The loan-word clique (from French [klik]) has gone the same way, being generally [klɪk] in United States usage.

So much for the front vowel series. What has been noted for them was paralleled in the back vowel series: the shift of O.E. [ɑː] to M.E. [ɔː] and Mn.E. [o]; and of O.E. and M.E. [oː] to Mn.E. [u]; though it is to be remarked that in the back the shifting vowels remained separate, whereas in the front the shifting vowels eventually fell together as [i].

Just as [æː] and [eː] were spelled alike though distinct in sound in Middle English, so [ɔː] and [oː] were distinct in sound, though Chaucer spelled them interchangeably o or oo. After Chaucer's day the [ɔː] from O.E. [ɑː] became [o], and it has remained that in most of the Modern period, though (as was mentioned when the

---

[19] The vowel here became [i], then combined with w to form a diphthong, now appearing as [ɪu] or [ju].

[20] The American pronunciation is meant here, obviously.

sound was first described) it is tending strongly today to be diphthongized to [oʊ].

The other back vowel shift—that of [oː] to [u]—has had an interesting development. In early Modern English it took place in almost all words having Middle English "long o," but the [u] has not in every case remained the end point in the development. In fact, in a good many words there has been the strong tendency to relax the tensity of [u] and to articulate it more toward the center of the mouth—in short, to change it to [ʊ]; and in still other words the centering movement has gone one step further, changing [ʊ] to [ʌ]. This may be diagrammed as follows:

	O.E., M.E.	Early Mn.E.		Late Mn.E.
tooth	[oː] > [u]			
foot	[oː] > [u] (preserved in Scots)	> [ʊ]		
root	[oː] > [u]	> [ʊ] (sometimes)		
soot	[oː] > [u] (preserved in U.S. dial.)	> [ʊ]	> [ʌ] (preserved in U.S. dial.)	
blood	[oː] > [u] (preserved in Scots)	> [ʊ]	> [ʌ]	

Thus within the Modern English period this [oː] has progressed through three stages. Some words have stopped at the first (*tooth*), some have reached the second (*foot*), and others the third (*blood*). The transitional stages may be seen preserved in non-standard usage —as Scots dialect, for example, showing the first stage of *blood* as *bluid*, as in the famous ballad *Edward:*

> Why does your sword sae drap wi' bluid,
> Edward, Edward?

This is, of course, an early example, but the word may still be heard so pronounced in Scotland; so, too, for the first stage of *foot*. Local usage, in the United States exhibits both the first and third stages of *soot*, the second being standard. And with such words as *roof, root, hoop*, [u] and [ʊ] are both widely current in acceptable usage— indeed, it would be rash to predict which will survive in the future if both do not. *Roof* and *root*, at least, are unlikely to reach the third stage, which would make them homonyms of *rough* and *rut*.

Vowels that, in Old English, were already in the highest position

—the front [iː] and the back [uː]—acquired on-glides[21] which eventually converted them into diphthongs that have become the Modern English [aɪ] and [aʊ]. The [iː] sound included words spelled in Old English with *ȳ* as well as *ī*, for the originally distinct vowel [yː]—rounded like German *ü*—had lost its rounding in late Old English and fallen in with [iː]; the O.E. diphthong *īe* ([iːə]) did the same; thus O.E. *hȳdan* and *līehtan* give us today *hide* and *light*. The other high vowel, [uː], seems to have developed in a parallel way. It is interesting to observe that in this case, diphthongization has not taken place in the Scots and North English dialects: *house* is still [hus] in Scottish pronunciation, as it was in Old English times.

The Great Vowel Shift chiefly affected the tense vowels; the lax vowels did not as a rule take part in the upward movement. Their development has less regularity and simplicity about it for the additional reason that lax vowels have been more affected by their consonantal environment. Only the most conspicuous and uniform developments can, therefore, be summarized here.

Old English *a* (as distinguished from *ā*) had, apparently, the same quality, but was briefer: [a]. This sound remained throughout the Middle English period, but was finally fronted, probably in the seventeenth century, to [æ], so that we have such Modern English words as *sand*, *thank*, *have*, and *saddle*, from Old English *sand*, *þanc*, *habban*, and *sadol*. Some of these originally short *a*'s followed another development: they first lengthened in Middle English to [aː], after Old English *ā* had become [ɔː]; and much later, in Modern English times, they went up and forward to [e].[22] This is the history of an exceedingly large number of Modern English monosyllables, in which the spelling still bears witness to the original *a* of the base: *ape*, *shake*, *knave*, *name*, *bathe* are a few examples.

Another low vowel of Old English, the *œ* of such words as *sæt*, *glæd*, *œx*, and *þæt*, has had a more curious history. It is generally thought to have been a front vowel in Old English, to have become a back vowel [a] in Middle English, and then to have gone forward again to [æ] in Modern English.[23] The Modern English spelling is

[21] An on-glide is one preceding the vowel (or consonant) and therefore gliding on toward it; an off-glide follows the vowel. Diphthongs develop from the addition of either on-gliding or off-gliding elements.

[22] Probably first to [æː], then up to [e] or [eɪ].

[23] This is so curious a history that its truth has been doubted. Jespersen, *Modern English Grammar*, Part I, section 8.63, argues that it moved back as far as [a] (though not to [ɑ]) then returned to [æ].

the same as the Middle English, but the pronunciation (except in certain Northern dialects, where [ɑ] is still to be heard) has returned to the [æ] of Old English.

Two other vowels of Old English—the front vowels [ɛ] and [ɪ] —have survived with little or no change in Middle and Modern English when they occur in stressed syllables and are not lengthened. The spelling is usually unchanged: *ebb, help, length, step, west,* from O.E. *ebba, helpan, lengþ, steppan, west,* and so on. Before certain nasal combinations, however, [ɛ] has been replaced with [ɪ]; thus O.E. *sengean, hlence, streng,* have become respectively Modern English *singe, link, string.* In one or two instances the modern spelling retains the *e* in spite of the fact that the sound has long since become [ɪ]; this is true of *England.* Modern [ɪ], however, usually represents the very regular survival of Old English lax *i;* a few illustrations are *drink, fish, if, in, rib,* and *this,* from O.E. *drincan, fisc, gif, in, rib, þis.* In late Old English the sound [ʏ] (spelled *y*) fell in with [ɪ] (just as [yː] fell in with [iː]) and thereafter was spelled *i;* later *y* became the letter with the sound of [ɪ] used in final position, as in *carry* ['kærɪ]. Modern English *fill, pit, sin* (from O.E. *fyllan, pytt, synn*) represent this survival.

There remain the lax back vowels spelled *o* and *u.* The first, in O.E., was phonetically [ɔ]. This sound has persisted with little or no change to the present time, so far as the "standard" pronunciation of British English is concerned. Words exemplifying this are *ox, fox, pot, got,* and so forth. Except for eastern New England, however, the usual American pronunciation is not [ɔ], but a short form of [ɑ]— like the first vowel in *artistic.* Curiously enough, it is also an American tendency to lengthen the Old and Modern English [ɔ] to [ɔː] (instead of introducing the [ɑ] sound) when the [ɔ] is followed by [ŋ], [f], [θ], or [s], and sometimes when it is followed by [d], [g], or [k]. Americans pronounce *song* with a vowel that is perceptibly longer than that used by Englishmen, and sometimes *coffee* and *hog* in a way that dialect writers render *cawfee* and *hawg.* O.E. and M.E. lax *u* ([ʊ]) has usually developed into Modern English [ʌ], a mid-central sound that is without the liprounding characteristic of both [u] and [ʊ]. This is illustrated in *love, sun, wonder* (O.E. *lufian, sunne, wundor*), and so on. The [ʊ], however, is frequently preserved in the neighborhood of labial consonants; Modern English *full* and *pull* illustrate this.

The original diphthongs of Old English have been lost, as such—usually through the emergence of the predominating element as a single vowel; we have seen, for example, how *ēa* and *ēo* conformed with *ǣ* ([æ:]) and *ē* ([e:]), respectively, and developed the same way. It might be added that the corresponding lax *ea* and *eo* were simplified in a parallel way. Moreover, of the several new diphthongs that developed in Middle English, all but two have been made monophthongs in Modern English. Thus [ɑʊ] in such a Middle English word as *faught,* and the closely akin [ɔʊ] of *thought,* have altered to [ɔ]; while in other cases a diphthong made up of [ɔ] + [ʊ] —as in *soule* (soul)—has simplified to [o]. Likewise, Modern English [e] often represents a sound that was a diphthong in Middle English; in fact, two separate diphthongs are represented here, for the spellings *ai* and *ei* stand for sounds that are rimed in Chaucer but that in earlier Middle English were distinct. *Day, may, sail, play,* and *way* are of this group. The exceptions to the process of monophthongization are the borrowed *oi* ([ɔɪ])—in French loan-words like *join, joy,* and *toil;* and [ju], which has a double source—Middle English *eu* (or *ew*) and *iu.* The *eu* was originally [ɛʊ], found in words like *few* and *new;* and the *iu* was originally [ɪu], found in words like *humor* and *rude.* Even here, monophthongization has taken place to some extent in Modern English; for while *few* and *humor* are invariably pronounced with [ju], most Americans substitute the simple vowel [u] in *new.* It may be in order here to emphasize once more the idea that what we commonly call the simple or pure vowels in Modern English are really not so in practice. Modern English lacks, in a strict sense, the pure vowels of Old English or of Modern German; Modern English [e], [i], [o], and [u] all tend, in degrees varying in different parts of the English-speaking world, to be diphthongal.

Reference has been made, so far, to vowels that occur mostly in stressed syllables and in native words. Borrowed words have been mentioned only in passing, because, in the main, the vowels of such words follow the development of native words of like sound. But it should not be imagined that anything like the complete history of even the native vowels has been given. For one thing, the separation into three categories—tense vowels, short or lax vowels, and diphthongs—is somewhat unreal. Something has been said of the interchange of single vowels and diphthongs; and much more might be said of the interchange of lax vowels and tense ones. More striking than such changes, however, and so far-reaching in its consequence that the entire character of English pronunciation has, through it, been altered, is the general obscuring that has occurred in the vowels of unstressed syllables. The matter will be dealt with in Chapter 7 as one of the fundamental causes of inflectional leveling. Here it may be briefly summarized with regard to the phonetic changes involved.

Before the end of the Old English period, every unstressed *a, e, o,* and *u* tended to become a vowel that was usually spelled *e* and was presumably pronounced [ə]. These are typical illustrations: O.E. *oxa,* M.E. *oxe;* O.E. *foda,* M.E. *fode;* O.E. *heorte,* M.E. *herte;*[24] O.E. *swēte,* M.E. *swete;* O.E. *nacod,* M.E. *naked;* O.E. *wundor,* M.E. *wonder;* O.E. *lufu,* M.E. *love;* and O.E. *sunu,* M.E. *sune.* Unstressed *i* ([ɪ]), however, tended to remain unchanged through Middle and in Modern English; note the second syllable of *English, shilling,* and *evil* (except, of course where this *l* has become syllabic and the [ɪ] has consequently been lost). The [ɪ] has also usually been preserved in Middle English borrowings from French: *peril, punish, service.* When *e* ([ə]) was final in Middle English—as it is in most of the above illustrations—it was eventually lost; hence the emergence of the Modern monosyllables *ox, food, heart, sweet, love,*[25] and *son.* Certain endings in which [ə] was followed by a consonant—especially the possessive and plural -*es* and the preterit -*ed*—have regularly syncopated, so that here, too, [ə] is lost. The exceptions perhaps should be noted: a noun ending in a sibilant, such as [s], [z], [ʃ], or [tʃ], does not syncopate its ending in the plural (*busses, vases, rushes, ditches*); nor does the past participle of a verb ending in the alveolar [t] or [d] (*wetted, wedded*). Quite as important as the frequent loss of [ə] that has just been noticed is the tendency, beginning in the sixteenth century and universal in the pronunciation of present-day English, to level all vowels unprotected by stress to either [ə] or [ɪ]. The general rule may be stated thus: Every Modern English vowel occurring in a syllable that receives neither

---

[24] In this pair and the next, the final *e* was in Old English [ɛ], and in Middle English [ə].

[25] This word (and many others) retained final -*e* in spelling, though it is an empty letter, being unpronounced.

primary nor secondary stress approximates one or the other of the relaxed vowels [ə] and [ɪ]. This trend is combated by the conservatism of dictionaries, which has done something to perpetuate spelling-pronunciations, but in natural, colloquial speech, it is a distinctive characteristic of normal English. In the following chapter we shall bring down to the present our examination of the sounds of English.

REFERENCES FOR FURTHER READING

Davies, Constance, *English Pronunciation from the Fifteenth to the Eighteenth Century*, London (Dent), 1934.

Jespersen, Otto, *A Modern English Grammar* (esp. Part I, "Sounds and Spellings"), Heidelberg (Winter), 3rd ed., 1922.

——, *Essentials of English Grammar*, New York (Holt), 1933.

Jordan, Richard, *Handbuch der Mittelenglischen Grammatik*, I Teil, "Lautlehre," Heidelberg (Winter), 2nd ed., 1934.

Kökeritz, Helge, *Shakespeare's Pronunciation*, New Haven (Yale University), 1953.

Kruisinga, E., *A Handbook of Present Day English*, Part I, "Sounds," Utrecht (Kemink), 4th ed., 1925.

Moore, Samuel, rev. by Marckwardt, Albert H., *Historical Outlines of English Sounds and Inflections*, Ann Arbor (Wahr), 1951.

Wyld, H. C., *A History of Modern Colloquial English*, London (Murray), 3rd ed., 1937.

——, *Studies in English Rhymes from Surrey to Pope*, New York (Dutton), 1924.

Zachrisson, R. E., *Pronunciation of English Vowels 1400-1700*, Göteborg (Zachrisson), 1913.

Chapter 6

The History of English Inflections

INFLECTION, broadly speaking, is the process of varying the form of a word to differentiate related meanings or uses. As commonly applied, the term refers to such syntactical distinctions as those of gender, number, case, mood, tense, voice, and so forth. In any strict use, inflection should mean *variation* rather than *composition;* that is, it should imply that there is a certain stable element or nucleus in the word, and that this is given variety of application by internal change or by the addition of certain prefixes or suffixes, which are not separate words or even independent word-elements.

Actually, however, there is some disagreement as to which of the affixes that exist are to be considered examples of inflection, and which are not; and there are some difficult borderline cases. Are we, for example, to consider the *-ly* ending of such words as *quickly* and *smoothly* as an inflectional suffix that transforms an adjective into an adverb? Is this process therefore to be considered as parallel to the addition of the *-s* ending that transforms most of our singular nouns into plurals? Some feel that it is more satisfactory to limit our application of the term inflection to changes that take place *within* the part of speech—that is, without converting one part of speech into another; yet what of such a suffix as *-ess,* which changes the gender (*author, authoress; waiter, waitress*) without changing the part of speech? The fact is that the term is applied on traditional or historical grounds, and is usually denied to new acquisitions or developments such as *-ly* and *-ess,* even though they may parallel the older inflections both formally and structurally.

On the other hand, there is no justification at all for applying the term inflection to such analytical formations as we now have in the future and the perfect tenses of the verb. A synthetic verbal form for the future, like the Latin *habebo* or the French *aurai,* is a strict

109

example of inflection; the German *ich werde haben* and the English *I shall have*, on the other hand, while functionally parallel to the Latin and French forms, are formally and structurally different, and therefore not examples of inflection.

In considering inflection as a structural device of language which, as we know, has been gradually simplified in the course of time, we may wonder how such a complex system can have come into existence in the first place, what kind of structure can have existed before it, why it should have taken the course it has, and so on. The most widely held theory has been that inflection was gradually developed, by way of an intermediate agglutinative stage, from a primitive "root stage" of language. An isolating language like Chinese, accordingly, was looked upon as the type of all primitive language. The separate roots were thought to have become attached to other roots, losing their independent character as they combined with them, and so finally being reduced to inflectional affixes.[1]

But this theory is no longer unquestioned today. At least two serious objections to it may be cited:[2] the fact that Chinese has recently been shown to exhibit traces of earlier inflection, and the impossibility of proving that *most* of our inflectional suffixes go back to independent roots. The "agglutination" theory contains a good deal of truth: it does actually explain the origin of much of our inflection. But it cannot tell the whole story. In any case, far from being the type of an undeveloped, "root-stage" language, Chinese appears to be the exact opposite, a language that has reached the extreme stage of development from synthetic to analytic structure. And furthermore, it is by no means necessary to believe that primitive expression was in terms of simple verbal units; indeed, Jespersen argues plausibly[3] that the earliest expression was in large and not fully analyzed complexes, out of which, ultimately, the smaller units were gradually isolated. Thus, broadly speaking, the development of language may well have followed a sort of cyclical course: from primitive complexity to simplification of form (the "root stage"), and back to complexity again (through agglutination to inflection); then,

---

[1] Something like this is seen in the formation of such a word as *manly* from *man + like*, which two independent forms first agglutinate into *manlike*, then the latter becomes reduced to *-ly*, losing its independence, the synthetic form *manly* being the final result.

[2] Jespersen, "Origin of Grammatical Elements," *Language*, pp. 367-395.

[3] *Ibid.*, esp. sec. 11.

within the historical period, the movement away from inflectional complexity toward the simplicity of form of the isolating type.

Certainly, if one starts with Modern English and goes backward in time, one encounters ever more and more inflection. Middle English and Old English have a much higher degree of inflection, and there is a still higher degree in Gothic, the oldest Germanic language that has been preserved; Sanskrit, of much greater antiquity than any Germanic language, is a still nearer approach to the complexity of Indo-European inflection. A single illustration of differing degrees of inflection may be useful: the case distinctions for the noun, pro-

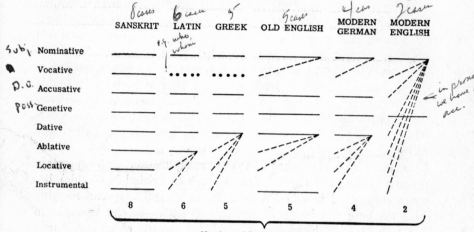

Lines indicate preserved forms; dots indicate weakened forms; dashes indicate syncretized forms.[4]

noun, and adjective. Sanskrit exhibits distinctive endings for eight cases: the nominative, genitive, dative, accusative, instrumental, ablative, locative, and vocative. Gothic, like Greek, has reduced the number to five; certain endings, that is to say, that had expressed particular functions, have ceased to exist, and their functions have fallen together (or "syncretized") with those of some other case-form. (Latin here is more conservative, since six cases are preserved.) Old English lost the distinctive form for the vocative and so exhibits, at most, five variations; Modern English preserves three

[4] This diagram does not show derivation of one language from another, but only relative degrees of complexity of the inflectional patterns.

cases only in one category—the pronoun; the noun has but two case-forms, and the adjective no longer expresses case.

We can no more than speculate about the extent of inflection in the remote past, or about the limit of its simplification in the distant future; but so far as the use of inflection is concerned, English has quite clearly become in the course of time less and less like Latin, and more and more like Chinese.

Inflection may occur in any of three places: at the beginning of the word, in the middle, or at the end; by means, respectively, of prefix, medial change, or suffix. The terms usually employed to designate the three types are *initial, internal,* and *final* (or *end*) inflection.

Modern English contains no genuine example of initial inflection.[5] Such pairs as *manservant* and *maidservant, cock sparrow,* and *hen sparrow*[6] give an idea of how a gender distinction might be shown by initial variation; but in these examples it is full words, not inflections, that are varied. In Latin a certain type of initial inflection is familiar; thus the present tense *cadō* (I fall) forms its preterit by the "reduplication" of the initial consonant to produce an extra syllable: *cecidī* (I fell). The same method is in Greek the typical way of forming the perfect: *lúō* (I loose), *léluka* (I have loosed). Early Germanic also utilized the method of "reduplication" to form certain preterit tenses; but the full forms (such as existed in Gothic) became contracted in Old English, the reduplicative prefix merging with the base and losing its separate identity—as, for example, in *hēold* (held), which developed from **hehald,* the reduplicated preterit of **haldan.* A clearer instance of initial inflection is the frequent use in Old English of the prefix *ge-* with the past participle; but it never became regular as it is in Modern German. Thus, even in the earliest stage of English, only a trace remains of true initial inflection.

The other two types, however, are abundantly represented in all stages of the English language. We have a familiar illustration of internal inflection in such strong verbs as *ring, rang, rung,* and in such "irregular" nouns as *goose, geese* and *man, men.* These two types, incidentally, are in origin quite distinct. *Ring, rang, rung* rep-

---

[5] *To,* as the "sign of the infinitive," is sometimes so considered—e.g., in Aiken, *English, Past and Present,* p. 216—but this interpretation is not altogether convincing.

[6] Krapp, *Modern English,* p. 58.

resents the process known as *gradation* or *ablaut:* that is, the variation of the vowel through a *series* of changes. *Goose, geese* and *man, men,* on the other hand, illustrate the process of *mutation* or *umlaut:*[7] that is, the *single* change produced in a vowel by the influence of another vowel or semi-vowel in the following syllable. The same process has operated in other pairs of related words; for example *blood, bleed; doom, deem; proud, pride; foul, (de)file; fall, fell.*

The third type, final or end inflection, is too common to need particular illustration. It is most familiar in the *-s* ending that we have come to feel as the regular plural sign for nouns, and the *-ed* ending that is the regular sign of the past tense and past participle of verbs. The *-s* ending also indicates the third person singular, present tense, of verbs; and (usually with an apostrophe when written) is the sign of the possessive case. Other inflectional endings of Modern English are *-ing* of the present participle, and *-er* and *-est,* used in the comparison of adjectives. These five endings virtually exhaust the varieties of final inflection that are now in really living use—the ones that we apply without question to the words entering the language or to old words used with a new function or as a new part of speech. Initial or internal inflection would never be employed[8] in either of the categories just mentioned. A noun borrowed from another language, for example, must make its plural by end inflection.[9] Even a well-established mutation plural can scarcely be carried over when the noun is used in a new compound—hence the difficulty of the plural of *tailor's-goose* or *mongoose.* How strong is the preference for the usual types of end inflection is neatly illustrated in the history of *broadcast.* When this word began to be used as a verb, in connection with radio, the popular form of the past tense was *broadcasted,*[10] despite the precedent of the simple (and invariable) verb *cast. Cast* was not a very widely used word, and the sudden nearly universal use of

[7] See Chapter 4, pages 79-80.

[8] Except, perhaps, facetiously or in folk speech. I have seen the noun *fan* pluralized in print as *fen,* on the analogy of *man, men* (*Thrilling Wonder Stories,* Aug. 1950, page 160). Ablaut still has some analogical power in verbs, as in *wink, wank, wunk; wave, wove;* and so on, heard from uneducated speakers.

[9] Unless it brings the foreign plural ending with it—a thing which can hardly happen except with Latin and Greek words; and even with these, the tendency is to anglicize.

[10] A parallel form, *uppercutted,* is used by some sports writers; and *forecasted* may be found in print occasionally.

broadcast naturally conformed to the better-known regular pattern. The radio itself was driven to put on an elaborate educational campaign against *broadcasted*, but has not yet succeeded in killing it in everyday use. Now with television we are beginning to get *telecasted* along with *telecast,* the latter, of course, following the more traditional form.[11]

The fact that only five endings can be enumerated as the varieties of inflection in vital, active use in Modern English is a striking testimony to the simplification that the inflectional system has undergone. And not only in the mere number of endings, but in the number of distinctions that an ending expresses. For in Old English such an ending as *-ne* simultaneously indicated accusative case, singular number, and masculine gender when attached to a noun, pronoun, or adjective base; in Modern English the inflectional endings (except the *-s* of verbs, as in *comes*) express only one distinction at a time.

English is not unique in leveling its inflections—far from it; other European languages have done the same. But English is striking for both the rapidity and the thoroughness with which that leveling has been carried out. Quite apart from the natural tendencies of pronunciation to change, we can see that in England the vicissitudes of politics, dialectal competition, influences from Danish, Norman French, Parisian, Latin—all these must have had a part in simplifying English inflection. When men of different tongues attempt conversation, it is natural for each speaker to employ both his own and the other's language in as simple a form as possible—his own, to make it easier for his hearer, and the other's through his imperfect knowledge of it. Inflectional elements are, on the whole, much less important for conveying one's approximate meaning than the base of a word. Just so, probably, the elaborate inflections of Old English were simplified, and, after frequent repetition, established in the new form.[12] Only the most vital of the inflectional distinctions eventually were preserved. In quite large measure it was a case of survival of the fittest, or at any rate of the most essential.

[11] *Webster's New International Dictionary,* second ed., 1939, lists the participial forms "*-cast* or *-casted*" in the New Words Section. In the printing of 1949 they are moved into the main section.
[12] For a fuller exposition of this point, see Bradley's treatment of "Simplification of Accidence," in *The Making of English,* pp. 17-53.

Analogy — The tendency of a given form or inflexion to follow the existing formations or inflexions of a language.

Analogy. Inflectional leveling once having begun on a considerable scale, it was undoubtedly accelerated and made farther-reaching by the operation of the great principle of *analogy*. This is the extremely important drift in language through which the exception tends to conform to the rule. When once a particular declension or conjugation is established as the normal or typical one—usually through the greater frequency of its forms—the rival types of inflection often yield to its influence, giving up their forms in favor of the "regular" ones. For example, the Old English *gāt* (goat) formed its plural by umlaut: *gǣt;* and we find this still reflected in Chaucer's usage: *goot, geet.* But a full century before Chaucer, the analogical "regular" plural *gotes* had begun to come in, and by early Modern English times the new form had won the contest.

The pull of analogy is, of course, resisted to some degree; otherwise we should have complete uniformity and only a single type of inflection in each part of speech. In reviewing the inflectional history of the various parts of speech we shall observe, as we go along, certain counteracting influences that have served to prevent absolute standardization.

Nouns. The noun, to begin with, affords a particularly striking illustration of progressive simplification. For the Old English noun four vocalic declensions and at least four consonantal declensions are usually recognized (the distinction between the two groups depending on whether the original stem ended in a vowel or a consonant). This classification, however, since it looks at Old English in terms of its Germanic and Indo-European origins, rather than as a language actually in use, gives an impression of more diversity than in fact existed. By King Alfred's day, one of the vowel declensions included most of the masculine and neuter nouns, and another most of the feminine; and the great majority of the nouns of the consonant declensions were of a single type, the *n*-stem. Practically, then, we may say that in Early West Saxon there are only three dominant declensions to be distinguished—two varieties of the vocalic declension, and one variety of the consonantal declension. The others were decidedly minor, with few representatives, and some had already begun to yield under the force of analogy and to "go over" to the major declensional patterns.

For the first group these paradigms are typical:

	MASCULINE	NEUTER
	Singular	
Nom., Acc.	stān, *stone*	hof, *dwelling*
Gen.	stānes	hofes
Dat.	stāne	hofe
	Plural	
Nom., Acc.	stānas	hofu[13]
Gen.	stāna	hofa
Dat.	stānum	hofum

The other two groups—feminine nouns with vocalic stems, and nouns of the consonantal declension—may be represented thus:

	Singular	
Nom.	lār, *learning* (fem.)	guma, *man* (masc.)
Gen.	lāre	guman
Dat.	lāre	guman
Acc.	lāre	guman
	Plural	
Nom., Acc.	lāra	guman
Gen.	lāra (or lārena)	gumena
Dat.	lārum	gumum

One minor group must be added, particularly because of its survival in Modern English—the monosyllabic consonantal stems in which inflection may be represented only by umlaut, or mutation of the vowel of the base. Such a noun is *fōt* (foot) (*masc.*):

	Singular	*Plural*
Nom., Acc.	fōt	fēt
Gen.	fōtes	fōta
Dat.	fēt	fōtum

In spite of the variety of inflection that has been indicated, it is evident that even in the early Old English noun there is a fair degree of uniformity. A few generalizations may be useful: -*um* is the invariable ending of the dative plural, and, for the great majority of nouns, -*a* is the ending of the genitive plural; -*es* is the sign of the genitive singular in the very great majority of masculine and neuter nouns, as -*e* is of the dative singular in almost all nouns, including

---

[13] Only short-stemmed neuters kept this final -*u*; long-stemmed ones (such as *wif* and *word*) lost the -*u*. (*Word* counts as long-stemmed because although the vowel is short it is followed by two consonants.)

feminines. In general, the endings that are established, through frequency of use, as normal and typical at a very early stage are these:

	Singular	Plural
Nom., Acc.	—	—as
Gen.	—es	—a
Dat.	—e	—um

Recalling now from Chapter 5 (pages 97, 106-107) the sound changes that went the farthest toward converting Old English to Middle English (the change of inflectional -*m* to -*n*, the loss of inflectional -*n*, and the neutralization of inflectional vowels), we may see at once how they affected such a pattern of endings. The plural forms became -*es*, -*e*, and -*e* respectively, losing the distinctiveness by which number, case, and (if we compare the declensions) gender had been shown. The process was anything but simple, and sound-changes were complicated by many analogical cross-influences. But the end result was the establishment of a typical Middle English declension for the noun, which may be summarized thus:

	Singular	Plural
Nom., Acc.	—	—es
Gen.	—es	—es
Dat.	—(e)	—es

Case. As we can see, of the six distinctive forms of the typical Old English noun, two—the genitive and dative plural—had been lost altogether, and a third—the dative singular—was going. The last mentioned, the dative singular -*e*, may be found preserved occasionally in Chaucer (after it had presumably been lost or nearly lost in spoken English) for several reasons: the language of poetry is usually more conservative; the vowel is useful for its sound-value and for rime or meter (as in *to the rote*, riming with *shoures sote*;[14] it also tends to survive as a "petrified" form in certain familiar formulas, like *to bedde, in londe, on fyre*. The corresponding ending, it is interesting to observe, is also in a disappearing state in the German of our own day. It might be added that the originally distinctive ending of the feminine genitive (-*e* instead of -*es*) also occasionally appears in Chaucer: thus the title of one of the *Canterbury Tales* is *Nonne Preestes Tale* (Nun's Priest's Tale) instead of

[14] Prologue to the *Canterbury Tales*, lines 1-2.

Nonnes Preestes Tale; and we have already[15] come upon the phrase *in his lady* (i.e., lady's) *grace*, in which the feminine genitive is partly preserved though the vowel has actually been dropped.

From the typical declension of the Middle English to that of the Modern English noun is only a short step, involving the loss of the *e* from pronunciation. Whether the *e* is written in, or omitted, or replaced by an apostrophe, is only a matter of spelling; what is important is whether it actually existed—that is, whether it was pronounced or not. It had probably begun to disappear by Chaucer's day; certainly it disappeared generally between the end of the Middle English and the beginning of the Modern English periods; so that in such a phrase as Shakespeare's *moonës sphere*[16] it is clearly an archaism used for the sake of the extra syllable.

For writing, Modern English has devised through the use of -*s*, -*'s*, and -*s'* a method of distinction which Middle English did not have. But since these three forms are pronounced identically, they have meaning only to the eye and no reality in speech; thus their value is minor at best.[17] The plural -*s* (like the genitive -*s*), is a syncopation of the Middle English -*es*, which in turn represents the "weakening" of the Old English -*as*.

Gender. It will have been observed that gender in the Old English noun differs from that in Modern English by being *grammatical* rather than *natural* (or *logical*).[18] Thus, the words for *stone* and *foot* were masculine, while that for *learning* was feminine, and that for *woman* was neuter—which had nothing to do, as their gender would today, with nature. Part of the explanation of the substitution of the new system for the old lies, of course, in the dropping or leveling of inflectional endings; the change of the genitive of *lār*, for example, from *lāre* or *lōre* to *lores*, meant the loss of a form that had been recognizable as distinctly feminine. The replacing of grammatical

[15] Chapter 3, page 49.
[16] *A Midsummer Night's Dream,* II.i.7.
[17] They have never become fully adopted: note such official forms as Teachers College, Womens Club, and so forth, which omit the apostrophe by preference. At its worst, the uncertainty about them leads to such common monstrosities as the lunchroom sign "Jacks Hamburgers," where plural and genitive have become hopelessly confused.
[18] "Logical" is not a good term, since it poses unanswerable questions. "Natural" (meaning "based on nature") is better, since our classification today is chiefly a matter of animate vs. inanimate.

by natural gender first began long before the end of the Old English period,[19] and by the time that the simplification of noun declension which we think of as typical of Middle English had been accomplished, the replacement was already a completed process.

Number. So far we have been concerned with the normal or typical declension of the noun. It is of course evident that not all Middle and Modern English nouns are declined on this model. The exceptions are survivals of some other Old English declension than that of the masculine and neuter *a*-stems, which tended to absorb the other types; or, less frequently, they are analogical formations. It will be simplest to approach this question from the angle of Modern English.

One noteworthy group of survivors of another Old English declension comprises the mutation or umlaut plurals. The Modern English plurals that represent this declension, uncomplicated by any other type of plural formation, are these: *feet, teeth, men, women, geese, mice,* and *lice.* In Old English, of course, the group was considerably larger; it included for example, such words as *bōc* (book), *āc* (oak), *scrūd* (shroud), the plurals of which have later been regularized, so that we now speak of several *books, oaks,* or *shrouds,* rather than of several *beek, eak,* or *shride* (forms that might well have developed). But how does it happen that the several plurals mentioned above have resisted the pull of analogy and remained in Modern English as a small body of recalcitrants? It is no paradox to say that frequency works both to normalize them and to preserve their abnormality. For frequency is what makes the -*s* plural "normal" and sets up its analogic attraction, so that children at first say *mans* and *foots;* yet the very fact that *men* and *feet* are everyday words makes them appear in use early enough and often enough so that the same children learn that they are "correct," even though exceptional. Possibly, also, ease and euphony have had some influence: *gooses, mouses, louses,* and *tooths* would be both longer and uglier than *geese, mice, lice,* and *teeth*—yet we do say *nooses, houses, souses, booths.*

A second group of irregular plurals in Modern English is made up of the nouns that have the same form in the plural as in the singular. These unchanged plurals are either the direct descendants of the

[19] See Chapter 3, footnote 11.

Old English neuter monosyllables with long stems, or analogical forms that follow that model. Of the first type are *swine, sheep, deer, folk*—the long-stemmed neuters that had no final *-u* in the plural.[20] *Hors* survived in Middle English as an unchanged plural, as we see in Chaucer's line:

His *hors weren* gode, but he nas nat gay,[21]

but it has since conformed, by analogy, to the regular type of plural. On the other hand, Old English *fisc* was a masculine *a*-stem with plural *fiscas*, which would regularly give *fishes* as the Modern English form; yet it has another and commoner plural form, *fish*[22] in Modern English, apparently because of the analogy of such other names of animals as those just mentioned. The unchanged form *fish* having thus been established as the usual plural in Modern English, names of various species of fish—*salmon, trout, bass,* and so on— make their plurals accordingly.

Another type of unchanged plural of Modern English should be mentioned, for though it looks much like that just discussed, its origin is different. When any enumeration or measurement was made in Old English, the numeral was followed by the genitive case of the thing enumerated or measured: for example, *seofon geara* (seven of-years), *þrēo mīla* (three of-miles), *twēntig fōta* (twenty of-feet). But when inflectional endings were reduced and ultimately lost, these genitives became identical with nominative singulars: Middle English *year(e), mile, fote* or *foot(e)*. Such apparently singular words —really the descendants of genitive plurals—are still very much alive in popular speech: for example, The horse is seven *year* old, He lives three *mile* down the road, The ladder is twenty *foot* long. In standard usage, however, they are regularized by analogy: *years, miles, feet*. Nevertheless, when phrases composed of the numeral and the noun are used as modifiers, they usually remain unpluralized in standard as well as other usage: a *ten-dollar* bill, a *five-man* team,

---

[20] See above, footnote 13.

[21] Prologue to the *Canterbury Tales,* line 74.

[22] Sometimes present-day (especially British) usage employs two plural forms for other names of animals. The distinction is thus explained by Miss Rose Macaulay: "Animals seen as sport become to the mind meat, and cease to be reasonable creatures, so that you may feed fishes, but catch fish, ride elephants but hunt elephant, . . . throw bread to ducks, but shoot duck, admire moths, but seek to exterminate moth. . . ." *Staying with Relations,* New York (Liveright), 1930.

"The *Twelve-Pound* Look";[23] and a couple have even survived as compound nouns: a *fortnight* (for *fourteen nights*), a *twelvemonth* —and note also such a formation as a *seven-year-old*.

The *n*-stems, or weak declension, furnish a third group of exceptional plurals in Modern English. Only a single word, however— *oxen* (O.E. *oxan*)—now survives directly in this declension. Even words in everyday use—those, for example, for *sun, moon, eye,* and *ear*—have had their plurals regularized by analogy.[24] Here, incidentally, is one of the best evidences of the strength of analogy: that, of the many numerous and important weak nouns in Old English, one alone should survive into Modern English. In Middle English there were considerably more survivors: *toon* (toes) (O.E. *tān*), *been* (bees) (O.E. *bēon*), and *treen* (trees) (O.E. *trēo, trēowu*, later made a weak plural by analogy) are Chaucerian forms. Milton's *shoon* in

> The swain
> Treads on it daily with his clouted shoon (*Comus*, 1. 635)

is, of course, a belated occurrence of a weak plural, possible only in the more archaic language of poetry or folk speech.

Other exceptional plurals in Modern English are the double plurals, a very few of which have survived. In them we see combined two pluralizing devices, giving mute evidence of the uncertainty that must have existed as old patterns weakened and new analogical influences began to operate. *Brethren* is probably an example of the joining of a weak plural ending -*en* to an umlaut plural (Old English *brēðer). *Children* exhibits an old *r*-stem plural (O.E. *cildru*) to which the weak -*en* was analogically added after the force of the *r* had been lost. The Biblical and poetic *kine*, like *brethren*, adds a weak plural to an umlaut plural, whereas the development that might have been expected is singular *cow* (O.E. *cū*), plural *kye* (O.E. *cȳ*). Ordinarily, of course, the regularized plural *cows* is used;

[23] But even with these modifying phrases, the powerful analogy of the regular plural pattern is enough to produce also such forms as a *six-years* course, a *five-days* pass. (See C. C. Fries, *American English Grammar*, p. 43.)

[24] A comparison of certain words cognate in English and German will testify to the comparative conservatism of the latter, which keeps today the weak declension plurals that Old English had, but which in Modern English have gone over to the regular -*s* plural: O.E. *eagan*, Ger. *Augen*, Mn.E. *eyes;* O.E. *cnapan*, Ger. *Knaben*, Mn.E. *knaves;* O.E. *tungan*, Ger. *Zungen*, Mn.E. *tongues;* O.E. *flēogan*, Ger. *Fliegen*, Mn.E. *flies:* and O.E. *naman*, Ger. *Namen*, Mn.E. *names.*

but *kye* is preserved in Scots dialect, and *kine* in archaic uses. Lastly, *breeches* is an example of the combination of an umlaut plural (O.E. *brēc*) and the regular plural.

Apart from all the groups of plurals that have so far been mentioned stand the foreign plurals that are occasionally met with in Modern English. With scarcely any exceptions, nouns entering the language before the Modern English period have conformed to the inflection of native words. In Modern English, however, there are many instances of borrowed words retaining their foreign plurals. The present tendency—and a sound one in most cases—is to regularize these foreign forms by giving them the native plural ending in -*s*. It must be admitted, however, that this might not always have felicitous results, for such forms as *axes, bases, crises,* and *theses* (with the second vowel pronounced distinctly as [i]) would have to give way to the cacophony of *axises, basises, crisises,* and *thesises*. The first two forms, particularly, need to be pronounced as they are in order to make a distinction between the plural of *basis* and that of *base,* and between the plural of *axis* and that of *ax*. But surely, when two plurals, one native and one foreign, are competing in actual use, it is desirable to use the native. Plurals like *banditti, monsignori, prime donne, stadia, gymnasia,* and even *campi* have a certain (mostly academic) vogue, but they have also a decided odor of pedantry or affectation, which lays them open to satiric use. The story is told of a certain celebrated English lady airily remarking, "I don't understand how anyone can ride in those odious *omnibi*" [25]—to be met by the deserved retort, "Ah, there you propound one of the most difficult of all *conundra!*"

Sometimes the problem of rival plural forms is complicated by the retention of both, each having its own area of use: the native plural serving general purposes, the foreign plural specialized (often scientific) purposes. Thus the mathematician or the chemist may prefer *formulae,* but the man in the street is justified in using *formulas;* and so it is with *foci* and *focuses, cherubim* and *cherubs, gladioli* and *gladioluses*. The last instance is further complicated by varying

---

[25] What makes *omnibi* particularly grotesque is, of course, the fact that the -*us* with which the singular of the English word ends is not a singular ending at all in the Latin word from which it is taken. To "pluralize" it in this way, therefore, is quite false.

ways of accenting it. It seems natural to put the stress, in the foreign plural, on the second syllable, and in the native plural on the third, but this inconsistency leads to uncertainty (one hears *gladíoli, gladióli, gladíoluses,* and *gladióluses*) so that many people simply use the unchanged plural *gladíolus* (or *gladiólus*), or the newly developed form *gladiola*[26] or else they dodge the issue altogether and say *glads*—just as others avoid the difficulties involved in the plural forms of *hippopotamus* and *rhinoceros* by using the shortened forms *hippos* and *rhinos.*

One argument for preferring the native plural where there is any sanction for it in acceptable use is that, after all, only a small proportion of the English-speaking world is sufficiently acquainted with Latin, Greek, or Italian inflection to employ the foreign forms correctly. Observe, for example, the confusion between *alumni* and *alumnae,* one which is intensified by the fact that the preferred English pronunciation of these words exactly reverses the sound of the Latin endings.[27] More commonly, however, the difficulty is as to number rather than gender. Thus it is easily forgotten that *phenomena* is a plural; it tends then to be used as a singular, and a new English plural, *phenomenas,* is evolved. So also, though *datas* is little used, *data* (historically a plural) has become so strongly established as a singular in recent use that dictionaries enter it so, and the historical singular, *datum,* is less and less used.

We must remember, too, that even with our native words it is possible for a form etymologically plural to become singular in use; *wages* was once so treated,[28] and *news* is so treated now (present usage exactly reversing that common in Elizabethan English). So *woods,* in American use, is normally singular, though in British use it would be plural. Foreign plurals have sometimes gone the same way, the meaning of the word changing in the process; thus *opera* and *stamina* are both, in origin, Latin plurals. A recent Latin borrowing, *agenda,* is on the way to complete anglicization in an inter-

---

[26] *Gladiola* may represent a respelling of *gladioli* pronounced with the final [ə] on the analogy of *Cincinnati, Missouri,* and the like; or it may represent a back-formation from *gladiolus* taken as a plural. Whatever its source, it is one of the current forms, and has a plural *gladiolas.*

[27] *Alumni* in Latin and *alumnae* in English end in [i]; *alumni* in English and *alumnae* in Latin end in [aɪ].

[28] As in "The wages of sin *is* death."

esting fashion: first the pronunciation of the *g* has changed (from [g] to [dʒ]), and now the tendency seems to be to treat the word as a singular rather than a plural.[29]

The attention that has been paid to exceptional plurals must not be allowed to overweigh our understanding of Modern English pluralization; for on the whole it is very regular, and the drift of the language is all toward normalizing the not very numerous exceptions under the pattern of the regular *-s* plural, greatly reducing the former complexity of English inflection in the noun.

Pronouns. The pronoun, by contrast, is the one part of speech that retains in Modern English a degree of inflection comparable to that which it had in Old English. The personal pronoun is inflected, in Modern English as in Old English, for three cases, three persons, and (for the third person singular) three genders; in addition, two numbers are distinguished in the Modern English forms, and (for the first and second persons) three in the Old English. The evolution of the first, second, and third personal pronouns may be given in some detail.

FIRST PERSON

	Singular	Dual	Plural
Nom.	ic (I)	wit (we two)	wē (we)
Gen.	mīn (mine)	uncer (of us two)	ūre (our)
Dat., Acc.	mē (me)	unc (us two)	ūs (us)

These are the forms commonly used in late Old English and early Middle English. In early Old English separate accusative forms were employed (*mec* for the singular, *uncit* for the dual, *usic* for the plural), but well before the end of the Old English period these had syncretized with the datives.[30] All trace of the dual is lost after the thirteenth century; from the others our modern forms have developed, with the regular sound changes, except that the consonant of *ic* has been lost and the vowel lengthened, and that of the vowel of *ūs* has been shortened.

---

[29] "Agenda Is Determined on Calendar Reform" (headline in *New York Times*, June 17, 1931). "Goethe had taken an intelligent interest in all this phenomena of history" (*Times* book review, Feb. 14, 1932). These are typical instances.

[30] In the dual, however, the two forms *unc* and *uncit* (the latter a form of more recent origin) were often used side by side, for both dative and accusative.

SECOND PERSON

	Singular	Dual	Plural
Nom.	ðū (thou)	git (ye two)	gē (ye)
Gen.	ðīn (thine)	incer (of you two)	ēower (your)
Dat., Acc.	ðē (thee)	inc (you two)	ēow (you)

These, again, are the typical Old and early Middle English forms, the distinctive accusative forms (ðec, incit, and eowic) having been absorbed by the datives.[31] Once more the Modern forms have developed regularly from their Old English prototypes. It is evident, however, that modern usage has treated the second person pronouns differently from those of the first person. A single form, you, does service, for the most part, in Modern English for both nominative and accusative, in both singular and plural numbers. This difference comes from a rather interesting development.

The custom of addressing kings and other great personages by the plural rather than the singular second person pronoun began in the Latin of the Empire, and was spread, through a similar usage in French, throughout Europe; it exactly corresponds, of course, to the present royal and editorial use of we. In English the polite use of ye and you for the singular became common by the end of the fourteenth century; at the same time thou and thee began to be relegated to familiar or affectionate use. The proverb that familiarity breeds contempt is illustrated in their later history; for a misplaced thou— one used where the occasion demanded the formal ye—could only be interpreted as patronizing or derogatory. Thus in early Modern English thou has much the force of the modern German du or the French tu: it may signify affection, intimacy, or scorn. However, the more conservative language of poetry and religion preserved the older thou in certain special categories. It still persists in the language of prayer and it is kept likewise in the speech of the Quakers. The form in vogue among the Quakers, however, is not thou but thee, just as the standard speech has substituted the formerly accusative you for the nominative ye; it is joined, moreover, with the verb not of the second person but of the third (thee goes, for example, rather than thou goest), perhaps through the influence of the similar sound of he or she goes.[32]

[31] Except that incit and inc (like uncit and unc) were frequently used interchangeably for both cases.

[32] Emerson, History of the English Language, p. 323.

The other point in the simplification of the modern second person pronoun is that the former distinction for case, as between nominative and accusative, has also been lost. By the early seventeenth century, the older distinction between *ye* for nominative and *you* for accusative is being obscured; either word may be used for either case, but *you* is decidedly the more frequent. The King James Bible of 1611 preserves the distinction (as in "Ye in me, and I in you"); but Shakespeare, less bound by tradition, frequently uses *you* for nominative and occasionally *ye* for accusative. Milton, too, often employs the two forms without regard to their historical distinction: ". . . *you* must then first become that which *ye* cannot be . . . And who shall then stick closest to *ye* . . . ?" (*Areopagitica*). This interchange of forms, however, is surely not due wholly to a disregard for grammatical distinctions; part of the cause was phonetic—the fact that these pronouns, usually coming in unstressed positions, would have their vowels neutralized or centered, until the [u] of *you* and the [i] of *ye* became virtually identical. The *ye* is sometimes retained in modern poetry, as are *thou* and *thee* ("And O, ye Fountains, Meadows, Hills," Wordsworth: *Intimations of Immortality*); but save for poetical and dialectal survivals, the invariable form for the second personal pronoun is *you*.

Such simplification has not been unattended by ambiguity. Useful distinctions are made possible, obviously, by preserving four forms in the first personal pronoun: *I, me, we, us;* thus, when, in contrast, in the parallel uses of the second personal pronoun, a single form is made to do service for all four categories, it is bound to become overworked! We should not be surprised, then, to find that some attempts have been made to relieve this burden; for while the language-sense of speakers of English no longer appears to value case-distinction, it does definitely value number-distinction. Consequently such creations as *you-uns, youse, you-all* have come into being in the effort to restore the "lost" plural form. For better or for worse, none of them has attained general acceptance: the first two are considered illiterate; the third is a regionalism (though quite respectable as such). There is even some evidence that *you-all* may be extending its domain.

The third person pronoun differs from the other two in being declined for gender (in the singular), and in preserving, throughout the Old English period, separate forms for the dative and accusative singular of all three genders.

THIRD PERSON

		O.E.	M.E.	MnE.			O.E.	M.E.	MnE.
Masc.	Nom.	hē	he	he	*Neut.*	Nom.	hit	hit, it	it
	Gen.	his	his	his		Gen.	his	his	its
	Dat.	him	him	}him		Dat.	him	(him)	}it
	Acc.	hine	—			Acc.	hit	hit, it	
Fem.	Nom.	hēo, hīe	he, ho, hie, she	}she *innovation*	*Plur.*	Nom.	hīe	they	they
	Gen.	hire	hire, here	}her		Gen.	hiera, heora }	hire, here	}their
	Dat.	hire	hire			Dat.	him, hēom	hem	}them
	Acc.	hēo, hīe	he, ho, hie	}her		Acc.	hīe	—	

By following these forms in the tabulation, we can see that the third person singular masculine develops regularly throughout its paradigm into the Modern English, except that, as with the first and second personal pronouns, the distinctive accusative form is lost and *him* does service as both dative and accusative.[33] In the feminine, however, a new nominative form developed to distinguish it from the masculine nominative; for the regular development of *hēo* made it, many times, identical in form with *hē*. The introduction or development of *she*,[34] however, eliminated this ambiguity. In the feminine, as in the masculine, the original dative form survived, absorbing the functions of the accusative with its own, even though it was identical with the genitive, as the modern objective *her* still is.

In the neuter, the form *hit* was nominative as well as accusative, and this may account for its survival (with loss of initial *h*) in Modern English as the objective, especially since *him* had become the masculine objective, which might thus be distinguished as mascu-

---

[33] Whence the appropriateness of the term "objective" for this case, since not even in the pronoun is accusative distinguished from dative by inflection.

[34] This may have been introduced from Old Norse *sjā*, or have developed an initial *s* through analogy with the very common demonstrative feminine *sēo* (also nominative singular), or even have developed phonetically from *hēo*. For the last argument see M. B. Ruud, *Modern Language Notes*, Vol. XXXV, p. 222.

line in contrast with neuter *it*. Among all these regular or nearly regular developments, the exception is the new neuter genitive form *its*—exceptional because while the general tendency is to reduce the number of forms, that is an addition. It does not, however, introduce any new inflectional ending, being made on the analogy of noun genitives in -*s*. The reason for it is clear enough, since the original neuter was identical with the masculine: *his*. The substitution of *its* for *his* came about in the early seventeenth century. The English of the King James Bible, again, is more conservative than the general practice of its day, for *its* is never admitted though it was already widespread in spoken English. The old form *his* is often employed ("If the salt hath lost his savor") ; yet it must have been felt to be awkward, for it often gave place to such paraphrases as "of it" or "thereof" ("The earth is the Lord's and the fulness thereof") where, to us, *its* would be the natural word.

In the plural, the forms of Old English have been considerably altered. The general reason for this is evident: *hīe* or *hī*, as they developed in early Middle English, were too nearly like *he* and *heo;* similarly, *hiera* became identical with the feminine singular form, obscuring a distinction.[35] What has happened, then, is that the Scandinavian forms *they*, *their*, and *them*, entering first in the Northern dialect of Middle English, eventually worked their way southward, taking the place of the original *hīe*, *hiera*, *him*. Though Chaucer still used *hire* and *hem*, he regularly used the new form *they;* and by a generation after his death *their* and *them* had also become firmly established in London English.

In listing the personal pronouns, the origin of the possessive pronouns has also been indicated. Save for *its*, the Modern English possessive pronouns developed from and were once identical with the genitive cases of the Old English personal pronouns. These forms early in their evolution lost almost entirely their genitival function, and came to be inflected and used like adjectives. The genitives of the first and second personal pronouns were declined as strong adjectives in Old English, while the forms *his* and *hiere*, indeclinable in Old English, came to be inflected like adjectives in Middle English. In Middle English too we find the beginnings of the modern

---

[35] That is, both singular and plural forms became *hire*, *here*, or *hir*—the resulting ambiguity, indeed, exists in Chaucer. Compare the similarly ambiguous *ihr* of Modern German.

differentiation between the modifying and the absolute forms of these pronouns. The *n* of *mīn* and *þīn* was dropped except before a word beginning with a vowel, and the forms *my* and *thy* thus created; eventually *my* and *thy* were used even before a word beginning with a vowel, but in the predicate position the old forms *mine* and *thine* are still retained. In the more conservative language of poetry, however, the older forms are admissible in Modern English even in the modifying position, when used before vowels ("Mine eyes have seen the glory of the coming of the Lord"). In addition to the pairs *my, mine* and *thy, thine,* the differentiation for these two uses was accomplished in Middle English for all the other pronouns except *his,* which has but one form in both the modifying and the predicate positions (though the dialectal *hisn* is an understandable analogical formation, which had, indeed, a certain literary use in Middle English, as had also *ourn, yourn, hern,* and *theirn*).[36] The *s* of *his* apparently set the pattern that was followed by the other Middle English forms in -*s* for predicate use, which have become standard: *ours, yours, hers,* and *theirs.*

Aside from the personal pronouns, it is the interrogatives that have preserved more of the original inflection than any other group of pronouns. The Old English forms were these (alike for both numbers):

	Masc. and Fem.		*Neuter*
Nom.	hwā		hwæt
Gen.		hwæs	
Dat.		hwām	
Acc.	~~hwone~~		hwæt
Inst.	——		hwȳ

Except for the *hwone,* all of these forms are represented in Modern English, in the following equivalents: *who, what, whose, whom,* and *why.* The last is the sole remnant of the instrumental case in Modern English, save only for *the* in *nevertheless* and in such phrases as *the sooner the better,* also derived from instrumentals. But it is evident that usage in present-day English treats these forms somewhat differently from what the paradigm might seem to imply: *whose* is applied to both persons and things, but less often to the latter; and

---

[36] The explanation often heard, that *hisn, hern, theirn,* and the like, are composed of the pronoun form to which the word *own* has coalesced, has no historical basis.

whom tends to give way to *who*,[37] except in the most formal and literary use.

Though the personal pronouns have preserved the inflectional distinctions of Old English quite fully, and the interrogatives fairly well, the other pronouns have generally lost them. The most sweeping loss comes in the demonstratives, which were reduced by almost three-fourths. The following paradigms are given chiefly to display the complexity of these forms—and only the most frequently used forms are included even so. The first was used in Old English for both demonstrative and definite article, which two parts of speech come from it into Modern English (*the* and *that*). The second demonstrative of Old English gives us the Modern English demonstrative *this*. Both demonstratives developed distinctive plural forms (*those* and *these*, respectively).

		SINGULAR			PLURAL
		Masc.	*Fem.*	*Neut.*	*All Gen.*
1.	Nom.	sē	sēo	þæt	þā
	Gen.	þæs	þǣre	þæs	þāra
	Dat.	þǣm	þǣre	þǣm	þǣm
	Acc.	þone	þǣre	þæt	þā
	Inst.	þȳ	——	þȳ	——

		SINGULAR			PLURAL
		Masc.	*Fem.*	*Neut.*	*All Gen.*
2.	Nom.	þēs	þēos	þis	þās
	Gen.	þisses	þissere	þisses	þissera
	Dat.	þissum	þissere	þissum	þissum
	Acc.	þisne	þās	þis	þās

These were reduced as follows:

First: In early Middle English, the s- of the first two forms, which differed from all the rest, was leveled to þ-; thus they became *þe* and *þeo* respectively. Obviously, analogy was at work here.

Second: By late Middle English, the masculine singular nominative *þe* became generalized as the definite article for *all* genders,

---

[37] Especially when the form which is theoretically objective precedes the verb. Expressions like "Who did you see?" and "Who did you call on?" are widely current and have won a certain sanction. Cf. Sapir's opinion of the general "drift" of the language in this respect (*Language,* pp. 166-174); his conclusion about *whom* is that "It is safe to prophesy that within a couple of hundred years from today, not even the most learned jurist will be saying 'Whom did you see?'"

numbers, and cases, the other forms (except *þæt*) having lost their final consonants and obscured their vowels. The fact that the definite article is usually unstressed surely brought about this leveling.

Third: By late Middle English, the neuter singular nominative *þæt* became generalized as the demonstrative pronoun for *all* genders and cases, in the singular. The nominative plural *þā*, having developed regularly to *þo*, adapted itself to the prevailing plural pattern by adding -*s*, whence Modern English *those*.

Fourth: By late Middle English, the base forms *þēs* and *þis* of the second demonstrative had become generalized for all genders and cases in the singular, and in the plural there were in addition *þese* and *þise*. From the second and third of these forms (*þis* and *þese*) have come our Modern English *this* and *these*.

Thus, of the first demonstrative, with ten distinctive forms in Old English, only three survive today: *the* as a definite article, and *that* and *those* as demonstratives. Of the second demonstrative, with nine distinctive forms in Old English, only two survive today: *this* and *these*. The definite article, then, has lost all its former inflectional distinctions and is quite inert; and the demonstratives have lost case and gender distinctions, retaining only number distinction. They illustrate better than any other part of speech how English has progressively rid itself of these grammatical complexities.

The remaining groups of pronouns show almost no inflectional variation beyond what has already been mentioned. The reflexives, for example, have no separate forms (as they would have in more highly inflected languages) but are made simply by attaching -*self* or -*selves* to the corresponding personal pronouns. In Old English the personal pronouns served without change as reflexives also, and this custom persisted until early Modern English times; the phrase "Now I lay me down to sleep" illustrates this use. Indeed, in popular colloquial speech something very close to it, the former "reflexive dative," survives today—witness such phrases as "She's gone to buy *her* a new hat," or "I'm going to have *me* a good snooze." But Old English also employed the double forms sometimes, with -*self* added for greater emphasis; and from these evolved the regular reflexive pronouns of Modern English. The indefinite pronouns, being derived from and inflected like other pronouns or adjectives or nouns, likewise possess no separate inflectional forms.

One group of Old English indefinites was, however, identical in form with the interrogatives,[38] and these are of additional interest as the source of the modern relative pronouns. Old English possessed no distinctive relative pronoun. The relative function was variously performed (1) by the demonstrative *sē, sēo, þæt,* (2) by the indeclinable relative particle *þe,* (3) by *þe* joined with the demonstrative, or (4) by *þe* joined with the personal pronoun. The sole remnant of all these forms is *that,* originally the neuter of the demonstrative, but widely used as the relative pronoun for all genders in Middle English, and the only relative which is in general colloquial use today. The other relatives of Modern English—*who* and *which*—developed their relative use much later, though both are from Old English forms, the interrogative indefinites *hwā* and *hwilc* respectively. *Which* was the earlier to develop a relative function; it became, in early Middle English use, a general and indeclinable relative form, like *that.* A familiar instance of its earlier application to persons is the opening phrase of the Lord's Prayer, "Our Father, *which* art in Heaven." The present use of *who* as a relative and the distinction between *who* for persons and *which* for animals and for things were not fully worked out until the eighteenth century.[39] Even yet, as has been suggested, *who* and *which* are used as relatives less freely than as interrogatives; the man in the street unconsciously prefers *that* to *who*—partly, no doubt, because by using *that* he avoids the uncomfortable choice between *who* and *whom.*[40]

Adjectives. Much less space need be devoted to the adjectives than to the pronoun, for adjectives in Modern English (except for degrees of comparison) have completely lost inflection. The Old English adjectives, like the demonstrative, was declined for two numbers, three genders, and five cases, and in addition, as we have seen, it had two sets of inflectional endings, one "strong" and one "weak." These forms, ten in number,[41] were already leveled in early Middle English to just two—a form without ending, and one with

---

[38] The Mn.E. indefinite use of *who* and *what* is illustrated in Shakespeare's "*Who* steals my purse steals trash," and such familiar phrases as "*What* you say is true" (Emerson, p. 340).

[39] The classical illustration is "The Humble Petition of *Who* and *Which*," in the *Spectator* for May 30, 1711. As Jespersen points out (*Essentials of English Grammar,* p. 359), Addison turns historical truth topsy-turvy by describing the relative *that* as an upstart that has recently done injury to *who* and *which.*

[40] The genitive form *whose* has been used for all genders since O.E. times.

[41] There were, of course, many duplications, so that the number of inflectional distinctions is far greater than this.

final *-e.* In Chaucer, the only remnant of the elaborate earlier distinctions is that a form without ending is usually found in the singular of the strong declension; in all other positions the adjective ends in *-e.* With the general loss of final *-e* in late Middle English, the last vestige of adjective declension was eliminated. The only exception in Modern English is the occasional use of a borrowed inflection, as in the phrase *Knights Templars* (from the French).

Inflection for comparison, it is true, has lasted into Modern English, but a rival analytical method has been introduced, greatly narrowing its scope. In Old English most adjectives made their comparatives in *-ra* and their superlatives in *-ost,* from which endings come the regular Modern English *-er* and *-est.* There were, in addition, two minor patterns: (1) adjectives with mutated comparative and superlative forms—for example, *strang* (strong), *strengra, strengest; lang* (long), *lengra, lengest; eald* (old), *ieldra, ieldest*—and (2) a few adjectives in which the comparative and superlative forms had a different base from the positive form. The only survivals in Modern English of the first type are *elder* and *eldest,* which even so have been generally displaced by the regularized *older* and *oldest.* There are several survivors of the second type, however; *good, better, best,* and *little, less, least* are the clearest illustrations.

During the Middle English period, however—and partly, at least, in imitation of French—the use of *more* and *most* began to come into competition with *-er* and *-est.* This new method had become established by the end of the period; it has increased steadily throughout the Modern period, and is still gaining.

Adverbs. The adverb in Old English was inflected only for comparison, e.g., *strange* (violently), *strangor, strangost; holdlīce* (graciously), *holdlicor, holdlicost.* Today these are nearly gone,[42] the analytic method with *more* and *most* having displaced the inflectional method. Nevertheless, inflection was used in the *formation* of the Old English adverb. The regular method was to add the instrumental ending *-e* of the adjective to form the corresponding adverb; for example, *georn* (eager), *georne* (eagerly); *wīd* (wide), *wīde* (widely). Adjectives already ending in *-e* became adverbs without change of form; thus *blīðe* meant either "joyful" or joyfully," and

---

[42] They last only with such adverbs as *fast, hard, wide;* the *-ly* adverbs have virtually given them up, though a century ago such forms as *quicklier, harshliest,* and the like were not uncommon.

clǣne, either "clean" or "cleanly." In addition, a second adverbial termination, *-līce,* was evolved through the circumstance that when certain adjectives ending in *-līc* were made into adverbs—*earmlīce* from *earmlīc* (wretched) and *freondlīce* from *freondlīc* (friendly)— the ending *-līce,* rather than *-e,* came eventually to be felt as the adverbial suffix. It was then added, instead of *-e,* to form other adverbs; thus we have *eornost* (earnest) and *eornostlīce* (earnestly) (rather than *eornoste*). The *-līce* termination, and its modern descendant *-ly,* gradually became established as the normal or typical adverbial ending—so much so, indeed, that it has been added by analogy to many words, native as well as foreign, to which it did not originally belong. There is a special reason for this in the phonetic change that the old adverbs in *-e* have regularly undergone.

In the Middle English period, inflectional final *-e* was regularly dropped. This meant, of course, that adverbial forms which employed this suffix could no longer be differentiated from the corresponding adjectives: Old English *heard* and *hearde* became alike *hard; fæst* and *fæste* became alike *fast.* The modern adverbs *hard* and *fast* are therefore not properly described as "adjectives used adverbially"; on the contrary, they are true adverbs, though identical in form with adjectives. Only a few of them, such as *hard, fast, first,* and *wide,* have resisted the pull of analogy, and (more recently) the push of normalizing schoolteachers. The great majority of the adverbs which once possessed the *-e* suffix and later lost it have conformed to the *-ly* pattern. Even in the cases mentioned, *hardly,* as well as *hard,* and *widely,* as well as *wide,* are possible as adverbs (though with a differentiation in meaning); and *firstly,* by analogy with the other ordinals *secondly, thirdly,* and so forth, is knocking lustily at the doors for admission.[43]

It is difficult to see why some should have persisted longer than others of equal frequency. Why should *quick* have gone over almost always to *quickly,* and *slow* very often to *slowly,* whereas *fast* remains without an *-ly* form? We shall return to this question in our discussion of modern usage; it is enough to point out here that, speaking historically, the new formation of adverbs with *-ly* grew up to compensate for the loss of the old formation with *-e,* in order to

---

[43] On the other hand, *first* has also, by analogy, attracted *second, third,* and so on, into adverbial use.

keep adverbs distinct from adjectives. This process is still going on.

Other case-forms beside the instrumental were used in Old English to make adverbs, the genitive -es (of nouns and adjectives) being next in frequency. Some that have survived in Modern English are *nēades* (needs) as in "He *needs* must go"; i.e., "He must *of necessity* go"); *nihtes* (nights);[44] *ānes* (once) (where changes in spelling and pronunciation have obscured the origin, as also in *twice* and *thrice*); *sūðeweardes* (southwards); and *hāmweardes* (homewards). The adverbial genitive *his weges* (on his way) is preserved in the Shakespearean "Go your ways" and in the present-day colloquialism "He went a long ways." Modern English, in fact, makes frequent use both of the genitive ending used adverbially—for example, *sideways, backwards, always, sometimes*—and of the corresponding prepositional phrase—as in *of course, of old, of late, of a truth,* and so on.

One other case-ending used adverbially may be mentioned, although there are very few survivals of it in Modern English. This is the dative-instrumental -*um*, as in Old English *miclum* (greatly), *wundrum* (wonderfully), *stundum* (from time to time), and so on. The form *whilom*, now archaic, comes from *hwīlum*, originally meaning "sometimes," "at times," but later "in former times." *Seldom* (O.E. *seldum*) is an analogical creation in which an earlier form *seldan* (cognate with German *selten*) has been altered through the influence of the other adverbs with this -*um* ending. The fuller suffix -*mǣlum* (from *mǣl*, meaning time or measure) was used in a number of adverbial forms; for example, *styccemǣlum* (here and there), and *dropmǣlum* (drop by drop). This is preserved in Chaucer's *flokmele* (in a flock) and *stoundemele* (hour by hour), and in a single Modern English example, *piecemeal*.[45]

Verbs. Distinguishing features of the inflection of the English verb have already been mentioned in the discussion of the Germanic verbal system. Thus, in contrast to those of Latin and Greek, Old English verbs had inflectionally distinct forms for only two tenses (present and preterit); two moods (indicative and subjunctive) for

---

[44] In "He goes out nights," the final -*s* is not plural but genitive singular in adverbial use; the expression is thus exactly equivalent to the old-fashioned "of an evening," in which the prepositional phrase replaces the genitive ending.

[45] Gerard Manley Hopkins, who learned much from O.E. poetry, has created *leafmeal* (leaf by leaf)—*Spring and Fall*, line 8: "Though worlds of wanwood leafmeal lie."

these two tenses, and an imperative (for the present only) ; one voice (active) ; three persons; and two numbers. In addition, there were the infinitive and the gerund, the latter historically the dative case of the infinitive, used as a neuter noun, after *tō;* [46] and the two participles, present and past. The early Germanic simplifications are visible here, and, in regard at least to the use of the inflectional method in verbs, English has continued the simplifying trend. On the other hand, while inflectional endings have been more and more leveled, new analytical formations have been constantly replacing the lost synthetic forms, and adding new resources of voice, mood, and tense. The two most striking illustrations of this general development in the verb are the future tense and the subjunctive mood. Early Old English had no future tense; the original synthetic future had been lost in Germanic, and the analytical future of Modern English was only beginning to be built up by the use of the auxiliaries *willan* (wish, will) and, occasionally, *sculan* ("must," later "shall"). Meantime, the present did service for the future also, as it still does in Modern English in such a phrase as "I leave tomorrow" or "The boat sails at midnight." During the Middle English period the use of *shall* and *will* became established—but it has never become regular, and the "rules" usually cited today are a pedagogical fiction that does not correspond to reality. This will be further discussed in Chapter 10; it is enough to point out here that, in his *Modern English Grammar,* Jespersen devotes 65 pages to the complexities of *shall* and *will* without by any means exhausting the subject.[47]

The subjunctive mood reveals a somewhat similar story, though here the earlier synthetic method was not entirely lost before it began to be replaced by the analytical. Little use is made in Modern English of the once prevalent inflected subjunctive, but that is not to say that the subjunctive has little place in Modern English—on the contrary, the subjunctive formed by the auxiliaries *may, might, should, would, could, ought,* and so forth (a method exactly parallel

---

[46] The inflected form very early began to drive out the simple or uninflected form of the infinitive. This accounts for the preservation of the *to* as the "sign of the infinitive," after the distinction in form between infinitive and gerund had been lost in Middle English. The modern "gerund" is of course an entirely different thing; it is simply the present participial form used as a noun.

[47] Part IV, pp. 235-300; also 300-374 *passim.* See also C. C. Fries, *American English Grammar,* pp. 150-167.

to that used in the compound tenses of the indicative) has been constantly given a wider and more subtly differentiated use.[48]

The Modern English verb preserves the distinctive twofold division of the Germanic verb into strong and weak types. The latter group has been the larger in all periods of English, and it grows steadily even now, both because newly created or newly borrowed words are invariably conjugated in this way and because verbs that were once strong not infrequently become weak; thus *swoll* has given way to *swelled*, and *clomb* or *clumb* to *climbed*. There are a few exceptions to the latter type of change: a shorter form, made on the analogy of some existing strong verbs, has replaced a longer weak past tense (as *strove*, *stuck*, and *dug* have replaced *strived*, *sticked*, and *digged*): but on the whole, the simplifying and regularizing tendency is very manifest: the strong verbs have tended both to conform to the simpler pattern of the weak, and to level the variations of the ablaut series within their own conjugation.

This leveling has proceeded in various ways and to different degrees, some verbs being reduced to a single invariable form (as *burst*), others to two (as *wring, wrung; slide, slid; win, won*); still others are in transition, with leveled and unleveled forms coexisting, sometimes competing (as *wake, waked*, with the analogical strong-type *woke*). Simplification of the ablaut variations was making great headway during the early eighteenth century (not only colloquially but also in the writings of the best authors), but the growth of conventional "rules" later in the century arrested it. Several of the verbs which had been reduced were once more given three forms—at least in literary and formal use—while the simplified forms remained in colloquial use. As a result we have today a conflict between the colloquial and the literary, the former tenaciously preserving the simplified ablaut; the latter, chiefly through the schools, seeking to enforce the three-part ablaut. Such verbs as *break, ride, drive*, and so on, which had virtually lost the participle in *-en*, have partially got it back again. But the drift toward simplification is constantly working, and not even the prestige of literary and educated use has been able to stop it.[49]

[48] See Curme, *Syntax*, New York: Heath, 1931, pp. 390-430. A terminological question may, of course, be raised here, whether the term "subjunctive" can apply to these new formations without amending its definition.

[49] For more light on colloquial and regional survivals of verb forms, see E. Bagby Atwood. *A Survey of Verb Forms*.

Returning, now, to Old English, we find that the strong verbs fell into six classes according to their ablaut series; and that there was in addition, a seventh group made up of reduplicating verbs, which may or may not have gradation. All of these are represented in Modern English. Principal parts of a representative example of each of the six ablaut series, in Old and Modern English, follow. It will be noted that the four principal parts of Old English have been reduced to three in Modern English, since the distinction between the second and third forms (preterit singular and preterit plural) has long since been lost; further, as we have seen, the three variants often tend in Modern English to be simplified to two, or even one.

	Old English	Modern English
1.	drīfan, drāf, drifon, drifen	drive, drove, driven
2.	cēosan, cēas, curon, coren[50]	choose, chose, chosen
3.	singan, sang, sungon, sungen	sing, sang, sung
4.	beran, bær, bǣron, boren	bear, bore, borne[51]
5.	etan, ǣt, ǣton, eten	eat, ate, eaten
6.	scacan, scōc, scōcon, scacen	shake, shook, shaken

Reduplication of the initial consonant to form preterit tenses occurred in many Germanic verbs, but the only trace of this in Old English is the resulting contraction of certain verbal forms. The vowel sequence of a fair number of Old and Modern English verbs is nevertheless the result of their former initial inflection. Typical representatives of the reduplicating (or seventh) group are the following:

Old English	Modern English
bēatan, bēot, bēoton, bēaten	beat, beat, beaten
blōwan, blēow, blēowon, blōwen	blow, blew, blown
feallan, fēoll, fēollon, feallen	fall, fell, fallen
grōwan, grēow, grēowon, grōwen	grow, grew, grown

---

[50] In these two forms, r has taken the place of s by a substitution called *rhotacism*. To state the matter more fully, the Indo-European s became voiced [z] in these forms because the preceding vowel was not accented (Verner's Law); later, as in O.E., this voiced s passed to r—not a great change, since these sounds are both voiced continuants, and have very similar tongue position. The Mn.E. forms of course show the analogical replacement of s. Compare the past participles of two other verbs of this group, *lēosan* (lose) and *frēosan* (freeze): *lorn* and *frore* survive as archaic forms in Mn.E., but for general use they are replaced by *lost* and *frozen*. *Was* and *were* (from O.E. *wæs* and *wǣron*) show a similar alternation, preserved to this day.

[51] Mn.E. *born* is a variant form, differentiated in meaning.

Weak verbs in Old English have the preterit in -*de* or -*te* ([dɛ] or [tɛ]), and the past participle in -*d* or -*t* ([d] or [t]) ; in Modern English they end, in both preterit and past participle, in -*d*, -*ed*, or -*t* ([d], [əd] or [ɪd], [t]). This is the surest criterion of the distinction between strong and weak. Other indications differentiating them may be confusing: internal vowel change, for example, may occur in the weak verbs as well as in the strong, though in the former it is due to mutation or umlaut rather than gradation or ablaut; then, too, the formerly distinctive suffix of the strong past participle, the -*en* ending, has been lost in many verbs. Weak verbs are divided, in Old English, into three groups, of which only two are represented by many verbs, the third having been reduced to just four verbs. The following are examples:

	Old English	*Modern English*
Class 1.	bringan, brōhte, gebrōht	bring, brought
	hīeran, hīerde, gehīered	hear, heard
	settan, sette, gesett	set, set
	tǣcan, tǣhte, getǣht	teach, taught
Class 2.	clǣnsian, clǣnsode, geclǣnsod	cleanse, cleansed
	lufian, lufode, gelufod	love, loved
	seglian, seglode, geseglod	sail, sailed
Class 3.[52]	habban, hæfde, gehæfd	have, had
	libban, lifde, gelifd	live, lived
	secgan, sægde, gesægd	say, said

There remain two groups of verbs which, though small, are very important: the *mi*-verbs and the preterit-presents. As to the first: Indo-European verbs used either -*ō* or -*mi* as the ending of the first person present indicative singular. The English strong and weak verbs which we have considered were of the -*ō* type; to the -*mi* type belong a few of our most important irregular verbs: *be, do, go,* and *will*. The *m* seen in English *am*, Latin *sum,* and Greek *eimi,* still shows us a trace of their ancient relationship as members of this -*mi* type; and in Old English (the Mercian and Northumbrian dialects) the form *dōm* (I do) did so also; otherwise it is gone from English. These four -*mi*-verbs—*be, do, go,* and *will*—are also called *anomalous* or *composite,* because their paradigms are made up from parts of different verbs. *Be* has parts from three sources (O.E. infinitives

---

[52] Only one other verb of this class survived in O.E.: *hycgan* (think). It died out in Middle English.

beon, is, and *wesan*) ; *go* used the preterit *eode* in Old English (later *yede*), and now uses instead *went*, which is historically the preterit of *wend*, and equivalent to *wended* in "I wended my way." [53]

The other group of irregular verbs, the preterit-presents, are so called because the present tense of each of them is a former strong preterit which early lost its preterit sense and acquired a present sense instead. To fill the deficiency left in the preterit, this new present then usually acquired a new, weak preterit and past participle.[54]

The preterit-presents that are retained in Modern English are *ought, can, dare, shall, may, must.* The first and last have no separate forms for the preterit; the others have *could, dared* (formerly *durst,* but now regularized), *should,* and *might. Ought* and *must* are peculiar in that, in their histories, preterit forms have *twice* become present in use: the original strong preterits, *āh* and *mōt,* became present in meaning and were succeeded by weak preterits, *ahte* and *moste* (Mn.E. *ought* and *must*) ; these new preterits in turn became present in use as well as past—as is true also of *durst.* The modern meaning of *ought, must,*[55] and *durst* is consequently ambiguous as to tense. *Durst* for past use has largely been replaced by the new form *dared.* One might think that any further development would scarcely be possible for *ought*[56] or *must,* since they have already undergone both strong and weak types of preterit formation; yet young children often say *oughted* and *musted,* peacefully following the normal analogy of weak verbs despite the resultant doubling of the weak

[53] Lest it be thought that such strange goings-on occurred only in the remote past, and cannot be paralleled today, let us consider the similar case of the verb *sound.* Chaucer inherited the present *soune,* preterit *souned;* but the present form, shortly after his time, acquired a *-d,* making it identical with the preterit form. To keep a distinction, the preterit had to add another *-ed,* the result being Mn.E. *sound, sounded.* These became fully accepted. But similar forms of *drown* (and several other words), which in folk use followed the same course (present *drownd,* preterit *drownded*), have failed to achieve respectability. Nor are they ever likely to do so, since the official voices of "correctness" have been raised against them. *Sound,* however, had established itself before the voices began to be heard.

[54] Just as Latin *novi* and Greek *oîda* have become present in meaning ("I know") ; O.E. *wāt* is exactly parallel.

[55] "He *must* go," for example, formerly meant "He *had* to go," but now ordinarily means "He *has* to go."

[56] There is the additional reason, in this instance, that the regular verb *owe, owed, owed* comes from the same source as *ought* and has been differentiated from it in meaning.

THE HISTORY OF ENGLISH INFLECTIONS   141

preterits, and it is perfectly conceivable that such a formation might not stop with children's use, but establish itself in the language at some later period. Similar developments have occurred in the past.

The simplification of inflectional endings may now be summarized. The present and preterit endings of the *typical* Old English verb were as follows:

INDICATIVE

	Present Sing.	Plur.	Preterit[57] Sing.	Plur.
1.	—e	—að	—ede	—edon
2.	—est	—að	—edest	—edon
3.	—eð	—að	—ede	—edon

SUBJUNCTIVE

1,2,3.	—e	—en	—ede	—eden

In addition there were these forms: two imperatives, the singular without ending for strong verbs and in *-e* for weak verbs, and the plural in *-að;* the infinitive in *-an* and the gerund in *-anne;* the present participle in *-ende* and the past in *-ed* or *-od* (for strong verbs, *-en*). The past participle was prefixed by *ge-*, most often, in the weak verbs, and many times also in the strong verbs.

In Middle English these were the typical endings:

INDICATIVE

	Present Sing.	Plur.	Preterit[58] Sing.	Plur.
1.	—e	—e(n)	—ede	—ede(n)
2.	—est	—e(n)	—edest	—ede(n)
3.	—eth	—e(n)	—ede	—ede(n)

SUBJUNCTIVE

1,2,3.	—e	—e(n)	—ede	—ede(n)

[57] The forms given are for the *weak* verb. The strong preterit was more complicated, since two different stems are involved: one for the first and third singular, and the other for the remaining four forms of the indicative; for example, *ic sang, þu sunge, he sang, we (ge, hie) sungon.* In the subjunctive, only the second stem is present: *sunge* for the singular, *sungen* for the plural.

[58] Again the forms of the strong verb were somewhat different from the forms given, which are those of the weak. The preterit singulars were 1 and 3: -, 2: *-e;* the plurals, 1, 2, and 3: *-e(n).* Usually, the two preterit stems have been leveled to one—more commonly, the one originally singular. Occasionally, however, even as late as Chaucer, both are preserved, so that we have such a conjugation as this: singular, 1 and 3, *bigan,* 2, *bigonne;* plural, *bigonne(n).* In

The imperatives and infinitives are as in Old English, except that *a* regularly weakens to *e;* the plural imperative, accordingly, ends in -*eth*, and the infinitive in -*e*(*n*). The gerund is usually the same form as the infinitive, but sometimes a distinctive form like *to seyne* or *to done* occurs in Chaucer. As the ending of the present participle, -*ing*(*e*) replaces -*ende*, possibly through the influence of verbal nouns in -*ing*(*e*), from O.E. -*ung*(*e*). The usual endings of the past participle are, for weak verbs, -(*e*)*d*, or -*t*, and for strong verbs, -*en* (which is, however, sometimes syncopated to -*n* and sometimes altered to -*e*). The old prefix to the past participle, *ge-*, has been weakened to *y-*, and appears with many verbs, both strong and weak. Incidentally, the fact that *y-* in Middle English is not invariably the sign of the past participle—the O.E. infinitive forms *geþēon* (prosper) and *gesēon* (see), for example, occur in Chaucer as *y-thee* and *y-see*— may have tempted later writers to employ it in other verbal forms, though unhistorically, for its archaic flavor. This seems the explanation of such a coinage as Milton's "star *y-pointing* pyramid." [59]

Two final remarks may be made on the transformation of these endings. For the third person singular of the present indicative in Middle English an occasional -(*e*)*s* does appear where one would expect -*eth*. Since the Modern English form is -*s* here, the question is whether these Middle English occurrences are not the source of our regular form. This seems unlikely, however; sometimes these occurrences of -(*e*)*s* are dialectal, and Chaucer uses them but rarely; thus though these are anticipations, the actual source would seem to be a borrowed Northern ending, rather than a development of the Midland -*eth*. Likewise, the Middle English -(*e*)*n* (in the plural of the present indicative) can scarcely be explained as an outgrowth of Old English -*að;* rather it would seem that when a distinctive form was needed for this purpose (because -*að* would normally evolve into -*eð*, the same ending as that of the third person singular), the subjunctives in -(*e*)*n* and possibly the strong preterits of the indicative in -*e*(*n*) (from O.E. -*on*) furnished the model.

The normal Modern English endings may be listed for purposes of comparison:

---

the subjunctive, as in Old English, the singular is usually (but not always) made by attaching -*e* to the preterit plural stem, and the plural by attaching -*e*(*n*).

[59] "On Shakespeare," line **4.**

INDICATIVE

	Present		Preterit[60]	
	Sing.	*Plur.*	*Sing.*	*Plur.*
1.	—	—	—ed	—ed
2.	—	—	—ed	—ed
3.	—s	—	—ed	—ed

SUBJUNCTIVE

1,2,3.	—	—	—ed	—ed

The imperatives, singular and plural, and the infinitive are without ending. The present participle ends in -*ing*, and the past in -*d*, -*ed*, -*t*, -*n*, or -*en*. Archaic or poetic language occasionally substitutes the ending -*est* (always preceded by *thou*) in the second person singular present and preterit indicative, and the ending -*eth* in the third person singular present indicative.

If, then, we summarize the leveling of verbal endings in Modern English, we observe that only one personal ending, the -*s* of the present indicative third person, has survived. To offset this impression of simplicity, however, one must note that Modern English has built up, on foundations laid in Old and Middle English, a most elaborate[61] system of compound forms—a type of structure which has given great importance today to auxiliary verbs. Thus the additions include a future tense using the auxiliaries *will* and *shall;* a complete passive voice using the auxiliary *be;* what amounts to a new mood, the potential subjunctive (with *can, must, may,* and so forth), as well as a reconstruction of the subjunctive-optative; and a differentiation into three distinct types of statement—simple or indefinite (without auxiliary), progressive or definite (with the auxiliary *be*), and emphatic (with the auxiliary *do*). To illustrate the last point: Modern English may vary such phrases as "I give," "I walk," "I gave," and "I walked" in either of two ways: "I am giving," "I am walking," "I was giving," and "I was walking"; or "I do give," "I do walk," "I did give," and "I did walk." Thus, while Modern English, on the one hand, has reduced the number of *different inflected*

---

[60] Once more, the strong verbs are distinct from the weak in the preterit. Now, however, only a single preterit stem is used, which is made distinct from the present by internal vowel change and which takes no ending.

[61] A typical presentation of modern verbal conjugation, that in House and Harman's *Descriptive English Grammar* (New York, Prentice-Hall, 2nd ed. 1950), takes ten pages in its enumeration of the forms now in use in a single verb.

forms to but six for strong verbs and five for weak (as compared with the maximum of twenty-five in Gothic and fourteen in Old English), it has also greatly increased the number and variety of *verbal phrases*. Old English had only five distinctive tenses, whereas Modern English has at least forty—some grammarians count more.[62] The history of the English verb in general is therefore a particularly striking instance of the development from synthesis toward analysis.

This chapter may be concluded, then, with a summary of the great change-over, between Old English and Modern English times, in respect to inflection. When the language first deserved the name of English it was still highly inflected, many grammatical distinctions being indicated by this device of varying the form of words. Today, its descendant, still called English, has greatly reduced its dependence upon inflection, and has either dispensed to a great extent with those functions for which inflection once served, or has developed other devices to perform the same functions.

In Old English a given part of speech was almost always recognizable as such by its form. Old English *ecg, lond, wæter*, for example, could only be nouns; but the Modern English words descended from them, *edge, land, water*, must be in context before we can be sure that they are not verbs, adjectives, or some other part of speech. The difference lay in inflection: *lond, londes, londa*, could not possibly be anything but noun forms; verbs formed on the same base would have had different endings: *-ian, -ode, -ianne*, or the like. Distinctions were even clearer for the article, demonstrative, and strong adjective: any such word ending in inflectional *-ne*, for example, could be nothing but masculine, singular, and accusative; and when word-groups were composed of a noun and its modifiers, agreement within the group made up for any deficiency of distinctiveness in the individual words composing it. Today nearly all of this is gone; individual words can be shifted almost at will from one functional class to another—and agreement of form within the modifier-group has virtually disappeared.

In Old English *sē gōda mann* would have been recognized as masculine nominative singular the moment the first word had been said, and *þæt gōde wīf* as neuter nominative singular; the second and third

---

[62] In addition, now that the English verb has become so freely analytic, new combinations have sprung into being which do not fit the ordinary categories, and are difficult to classify. *He can go* gives no trouble, but what of the equivalent *he is able to go*? Similarly, *I must try*, and the equivalent *I have to try*.

words in each phrase would merely have confirmed what the first indicated. In Modern English, *the good* would equally precede *man* and *wife,* and would reveal neither number, gender, nor case; the nouns would reveal number but not case; the question of gender would not arise at all unless a pronoun had to be chosen to refer to the one or the other.

Even where Modern English keeps inflections they are less revelatory than in Old English; thus *-ing,* and *-(e)d* or *-t* indicate specific verbal functions, but *-(e)s* may show number, gender, or tense and person. Thus such a word as *dogs* may equally well be the third person singular present indicative of a verb (*he dogs my steps*), the plural of the noun (*the young dogs*), or the genitive (*the dog's ears*).[63] Thus, through the function of inflection, the *word* was generally autonomous in Old English: in Modern English, grammatical autonomy has shifted to the *word-group.* We are more dependent upon context than King Alfred was; for us the order of words therefore indicates more—indeed, sometimes everything—about their grammatical function, whereas in Old English that was implicit in the form of the word.

Thus, as the language has changed from inflectional or synthetic structure to analytic structure, individual words have gained simplicity of form or flexibility of function; but within the sentence they have lost freedom of movement, and have become more dependent one upon another. Whether this has led to gain or loss for the language, is not, strictly speaking, a linguistic question at all. Such comment as it may deserve, however, must be postponed until other aspects of the development of English have been examined.

REFERENCES FOR FURTHER READING

The histories of the English Language already listed, and in addition:

Atwood, E. Bagby, *A Survey of Verb Forms in the Eastern United States,* Ann Arbor (University of Michigan), 1953.

Curme, G. O., *Parts of Speech and Accidence,* New York (Heath), 1935.

———, *Syntax,* New York (Heath), 1931.

Fries, Charles C., *American English Grammar,* New York (Appleton-Century), 1940.

———, *The Structure of English,* New York (Harcourt, Brace), 1952.

Krapp, G. P., *Modern English, Its Growth and Present Use,* New York (Scribner's), 1909.

[63] The apostrophe is phonetically insignificant, of course.

Chapter 7

Sources of the Vocabulary

Having dealt in some detail with the sounds and forms of English, we now come to that more familiar matter, the words that compose our vocabulary or lexicon. Words are, after all, the most obvious building-blocks of language, the small, independent units within the sentence. So familiar are we with writing, and with such lists as are found in dictionaries, that we may feel no doubt as to what a word is. It is well to remember, however, that in some languages—many American Indian ones, for example—there is no independent meaningful unit smaller than what we would consider a sentence; or, to put it otherwise, their "words" say what we use a sentence to say. The "word," then, is not so simple to define as one may imagine.

Even in our own language the dictionary-maker sometimes has difficulty deciding whether to enter certain items separately—that is, to treat them as words—or to consider them as simple combinations. Shall he make, for example, a separate listing and definition of *atomic bomb,* or can he assume that to define *atomic* and *bomb* will be sufficient? Anyone who has puzzled over questions of hyphenation, or of "spelling words together" without hyphens, will also have met this problem. Is *board walk, boardwalk* or *board-walk* to be considered as one word or two? The way in which we choose to spell it is certainly not enough to decide the question.

For our present purpose, however, we may accept the decisions of the lexicographer, which are based in varying degrees on history, form, and meaning. Words of the same form but differing in origin and meaning (homonyms) he lists separately—for example *mint,* the aromatic plant, and *mint,* where coins are made. A form having two or more meanings developed from the same source he enters singly— for example *plot,* which means a piece of ground, a diagram, a conspiracy, and so on, all deriving from a single source. If, however, two forms of common origin, and their meanings, have come to differ markedly—for example *dike* and *ditch*—the lexicographer enters them separately. With combinations the decision turns upon whether there is a new identity, either of meaning alone (as with *atomic bomb*) or of meaning and form (as with *boardwalk*, whose difference of meaning from *board walk* is accompanied by a difference in the pattern of stress and juncture). Thus the lexicographer decides what he is to enter in the dictionary.

But, as everyone knows, he does not enter only independent words: he also enters prefixes and suffixes—which in actual language never stand alone. And he is right to do so, for the question of dependence or independence of word-elements is not so important as we commonly think. Apart from it, there is no real difference between a simple word and such a dependent element as a prefix or a suffix: each is a minimal unit in which a particular combination of sounds has a definite meaning or function. This fact is recognized in the terms *free form*, applied to simple words, and *bound form*, applied to affixes; and all such units are included under the term *morpheme*. If we want to analyze a language into the sound-groups that function as meaningful units, the concept of the morpheme will prove more serviceable than that of the word—for "word" excludes some simple units (bound forms) and includes combinations of units. Thus, *good, man, kind,* and *-ly* are all morphemes; but "word" would exclude the fourth and include combinations such as *goodly, mankind,* which are not simple units. The lexicographer, then, lists not only free forms but bound forms—in fact, ideally, all morphemes; and the sum of its morphemes and morpheme-combinations is the vocabulary or lexicon of a language.

Considered from the point of view of its origin, the vocabulary of English is composed of three types of words and word-elements: the *native* (those derived from Old English), the *borrowed* (those from any other language), and the *newly formed* (those made up at any time from materials already in the language). These types are not mutually exclusive; there were, as we shall see, both borrowed words and newly made words in Old English, and there have been some hybrids made of native and borrowed elements combined. The terms are nevertheless convenient. The first two types will be dealt with here, the third in the next chapter.

It should probably be remarked at this point that most borrowed words (like human immigrants) become in the course of time so fully naturalized that they are indistinguishable from the native words—except, of course, to the historical investigator. The man in the street is entirely unaware that *head* is native while *face* is borrowed; to him they are equally familiar and equally English. And, indeed, so they are in their present function and value. But if we are to understand the development of the language, we must ask about origins too.

The accompanying diagrams should help to make clear some of the relationships between native and borrowed words. In the first we see

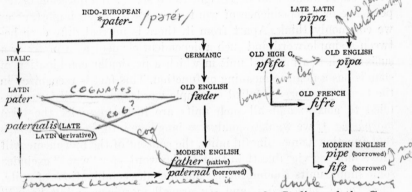

the Indo-European **pater-* descending into the Italic and the Germanic branches, then a derivative Latin form, *paternal*, being borrowed into Modern English, where it exists alongside the cognate native form *father*. In the second diagram we see a Late Latin form *pīpa* borrowed both by Old High German and Old English, descending directly in the latter to give Modern English *pipe*, and coming indirectly through Old French from Old High German to give the Modern English doublet *fife*. Other diagrams could show the very numerous and often very roundabout ways in which borrowed words have eventually found their way into English.

Native Words. Despite the borrowings already made before the Anglo-Saxons settled in Britain, and despite those additional words which they acquired during their first five centuries in the island, the Old English vocabulary was, and remained, overwhelmingly Germanic. The language was as yet decidedly inhospitable to foreign words (see Chapter 3, page 40). A small number did succeed in establishing themselves, but quite as often the things, concrete or abstract, for which Latin and other foreign words stood were rendered into English equivalents. This accounts for a good many new combinations, among them *undersittan* (Lat. *subsidere*), *hēahboda* (Lat. *archangelus*), *oniernan* (Lat. *incurrere*). Not that the process of combination itself was learned from the Romans—far from it; Old English has thousands of words formed by combination that show no foreign influence, and such words are a feature of Old English poetic diction. Indeed, the Old English vocabulary was enlarged far more by this means than by foreign borrowing. In short, the native vocabulary was generally adequate to the life of the times, and it took a social cataclysm, the Norman Conquest, to open it after more than a century to any large number of foreign words. Once this process had begun, however, the vocabulary grew rapidly and English acquired the decided appetite for foreign words which it has exhibited ever since. A great number of the native words (such as the combinations just cited) died, or survived in dialect use only. The resulting shrinkage, as well as the new borrowings, sharply reduced the relative number of native words in the total.

Yet it is a striking fact that these native words are still at the core of the language. They stand for fundamental things: the numerals up to a thousand (while *millions, billions,* and such are borrowed); the most intimate family relations, *father, mother, brother, son* (while *uncle, cousin,* and such are borrowed); most natural phenomena, *fire, water, day, night, summer, winter, moon, star* (though *sky, autumn,* and a few others are borrowed). We shall return to this matter later, but first we must look at some of the multifarious borrowings that have enlarged the English vocabulary during the long history of the language.

Borrowed Words. Three languages have contributed such extensive shares to the English word-stock as to deserve particular attention. These are Greek, Latin, and French. Together they account for so overwhelming a proportion of the borrowed element in our vocabulary that the rest of it seems insignificant by comparison. Practically, too, it is often difficult or impossible to determine the immediate source of the borrowings, for Greek words are likely to be Latinized in form before they are made English, and Latin words are likely to be Gallicized. Thus *texture,* known to be a borrowing direct from Latin, looks as though it came from the French *texture* rather than the Latin *textura; figure*, the immediate source of which is not clear, may just as well have come from the Latin *figura* as from the French *figure*, which it more nearly resembles. So too, *telegraph*, actually a recent coinage in English direct from the Greek words *tēle* (far) and *gráphō* (write), might seem rather to have come from the French *télégraphe*, in turn apparently from a Latin **telegraphus*.[1] *Theater* is an example of a word that is ultimately Greek, but one that was borrowed from the Greeks by the Romans, and in turn taken from Latin into French and from French into English. The spelling *theatre* more definitely suggests the French word as the immediate source of our English one. In the following account of the Greek, Latin, and French elements in English, we shall confine ourselves as much as possible to *direct* borrowings.

The Greek Element. Of *direct* borrowings from Greek into Old and Middle English, however, there were virtually none. Three of the very few old loan words from Greek are *church, devil,* and *angel,* but it is almost certain that each was borrowed through Latin— even *church,* a pre-Christian borrowing, ultimately a Greek word meaning "Lord's (house)," and one that the English retained in preference to any derivative of the Latin *ecclesia. Devil* is likewise a continental borrowing, far older than the migration of the Germanic peoples to Britain, but presumably a borrowing directly from the Latin *diabolus* rather than from the Greek *diábolos* (slanderer). *Angel* likewise comes from the Latin *angelus* rather than Greek *ángelos* (messenger); the Old English form, like the Modern German, was *engel,* the modern spelling and pronunciation being due to the later influence (amounting virtually to a re-borrowing) of the Old French *angele.* Among the Latin words introduced by the Roman (or by the Irish) missionaries into Old English are ecclesiastical terms that had been originally borrowed from Greek: *abbot, alms, clerk, monk, pope, priest,* and *synod.* Later medieval borrowings,

---

[1] Greenough and Kittredge, *Words and Their Ways,* pp. 95-96 and 49-50. Bloomfield (*Language,* p. 494) neatly summarizes the factors that account for the English form of classical borrowings (even synthetic creations like *telegraph*): "Since the Romans borrowed words from Greek, we can do the same, altering the Greek word in accordance with the Roman's habit of Latinization, plus the Frenchman's habit of Gallicizing Latin book-words, plus the English habit of Anglicizing French learned words."

also of course through the medium of Latin and usually French as well, are such words as *diet, geography, logic, physic, rhetoric, surgeon* (for "chirurgien"), and *theology.* Not until after the humanistic movement revived the study of Greek in western Europe did Greek words begin to enter the English vocabulary in great quantities, and even then they were likely to be Latinized in spelling and in their terminations—a convention that has usually been followed since. Thus a Greek *k* is replaced with *c, u* with *y,* and the Greek suffix *-os* with *-ous.* Even in the last three centuries the great flood of Greek words that has been incorporated within the English vocabulary has not always implied *direct* borrowing from Greek. Much of the modern scientific vocabulary is international in character, and often the word has been created, from Greek words or roots, in French and then adopted in English; such words as *barometer* and *thermometer* are examples. Thus, we frequently have a curious kind of indirect indebtedness to Greek as well as an odd combination of word-borrowing and word-creation. Some of our prefixes and suffixes most active in present use are Greek.

How pervasive is the Greek element, direct or indirect, in the Modern English vocabulary may best be illustrated by noting how, in a single department of art or science, words of this type tend to accumulate. Not only do modern drama and dramatic criticism stem directly from the practice of the Greeks and the *Poetics* of Aristotle: their very terminology reminds one of this descent at every turn. Thus *drama* itself is Greek, as is its place of performance, the *theater;* so likewise are its different kinds: *comedy, tragedy, melodrama;* and its parts or elements: *catastrophe, climax, dialog, episode, epilog, peripety, prolog, scene.* In the various natural sciences the preponderance of Greek words is just as striking; it is perhaps sufficient to mention merely the names of such fields as *bacteriology, botany, histology, physiology, physics,* and *zoölogy* (all Greek labels) in order to suggest how the Greek language has permeated their various specialized vocabularies. This effect is quite as striking, perhaps even more so, in fields of science that have been recently developed. Terms used in modern medicine will illustrate: *adenoids, osteopathy, pediatrics, psychiatry,* and *psychoanalysis* are a few of the hundreds of such words. In the field of *electronics* we find such new formations as *dynatron, kenatron, phanotron, pliotron, magnetron, thyratron.*

From the newest activity of physics we get such words—all based on Greek elements—as *atomic, cyclotron, proton, meson, gamma*-rays, *isotope.*

The Latin Element. While borrowings, and particularly direct borrowings, from the Greek have been largely confined to Modern English, our language has been exposed to Latin influence throughout its history. We have already glanced at the Latin influence on the Old English vocabulary, one which began before the migrations of the Germanic tribes to Britain and received its chief acceleration through the later Christianization of the island.[2] The actual number of Latin borrowings is far smaller than might have been expected, for the general attitude of Old English was antagonistic to external influence. After the conquest, however, this attitude was gradually altered, largely through the established practice of borrowing from French; and when in the thirteenth century English reasserted itself as a literary language, Latin began to be freely levied upon to amplify and enrich its word stock.

We should remember that any educated man in thirteenth- or fourteenth-century England would have been virtually trilingual. He would have known English as the language of every day, French as the language of elegance and courtly living, and Latin as the vehicle of all solid learning. The latter two tongues could hardly fail to influence his English, especially when he sought to elevate English for use in public affairs and literature. Many of the pre-Renaissance borrowings from Latin are doubtless due to English translation of the Vulgate Bible, especially the fourteenth-century versions of Wiclif and Purvey. While Old English translators of the Bible had usually turned Latin words into native ones that rendered them almost literally—*mildheortnes* (mildheartedness) for Latin *misericordia* (mercy), and *ðrynnes* (three-ness) for *trinitas* (trinity)—Wiclif introduced such Latinisms as *generation, persecution,* and *transmigration.*[3]

But it was the revival of classical learning in the sixteenth century that first swelled the numbers of English words borrowed from Latin to overwhelming proportions. Whereas the number of Middle English loans from Latin is difficult to estimate because so many

[2] See Chapter 3, pages 40-41.
[3] Cf. McKnight, G. H., *English Words and Their Background,* pp. 111-113.

were made over to look as if they had come by way of French, there can be no doubt that the great mass of borrowings in early Modern English came directly from Latin, even though the convention of Gallicizing the form of the word persisted. Romanic borrowings in Middle English are on the whole much more likely to be from French than from Latin; in Modern English they are much more likely to be from Latin than from French.

Recent borrowings from French are of course frequent enough, and often these words carry an unequivocally French appearance; but their number is far less than the number of borrowings direct from Latin. The habit of treating direct Latin borrowings as if they were French words has continued, but there is nevertheless a fair number of Latin loan-words in Modern English that have escaped this tendency and appear in English unchanged.[4] A few specimens, illustrating also the great diversity in the parts of speech and the inflectional forms borrowed, are these: *affidavit, agenda, alibi, animal, bonus, deficit, exit, extra, fiat, item, maximum, memento, memorandum, omnibus, posse, propaganda, quorum, sponsor, terminus, verbatim, veto,* and *via.* While we cannot get an exact enumeration of the Latin words borrowed into English, it is safe to accept the estimate of Greenough and Kittredge,[5] who, through computing the proportion of words beginning with *a* in Harper's *Latin Dictionary* that have been taken over into English, conclude that English "has appropriated a full quarter of the Latin vocabulary, besides what it has gained by transferring Latin meanings to native words." This indicates, of course, what a reversal has come about in the originally conservative attitude of the language toward word-borrowing.

But such a change could not take place without its extravagances, and, naturally enough, voices were raised against excessive Latinization. In the sixteenth century the new words were dubbed "inkhorn terms" or "inkhornisms," alluding to their origin from the pens of pedants, and implying that they had no real existence apart from this. Shakespeare's familiar satire upon Holofernes in *Love's Labor's Lost* is directed at this kind of excessive Latinizing. It is perhaps more surprising to find a writer so deeply indebted to Latin as Sir

[4] E. L. Johnson, in *Latin Words of Common English,* New York (Heath), 1921 (pp. 63-87), gives many such examples.
[5] *Op. cit.,* p. 106.

Thomas Browne making the same kind of protest when he remarks, "If elegancy still proceedeth, . . . we shall, within a few years, be fain to learn Latin to understand English."

Not that Latinisms alone were flooding in; at the same time came great numbers of words from the vernaculars of those nations whose place upon the world stage the Elizabethans were seeking eagerly to share: thus before the end of the century, and before the appearance of a single all-English dictionary, there were already several bilingual dictionaries of French, Spanish, and Italian, besides Latin and Greek. Furthermore, the first English dictionaries were made not to teach ordinary words, but to explain the new "hard words" to those who wished to understand or acquire these multifarious foreign borrowings. Thus in the era of the Renaissance the victory lay with those who favored free borrowing.

But there were partisans for the opposite cause of "purity." Some argued that the existing vocabulary was adequate to the requirements of the nation, and needed no additions from strange tongues. But this point of view had its extravagances too: witness Sir John Cheke's "purely Anglo-Saxon" version of a part of the New Testament. The compromise which has finally resolved this conflict is based on a sharing of the territory. The native words remain those of greatest force and sincerity, and form a great part of the common ground of all speakers of English; the foreign word carries still a flavor of learning or cultivation. To some the question continues a very live one, as two illustrations will show. Jespersen has traced the curious history of *handbook:*[6] the Old English *handbōc* disappeared in the Middle English period, when its place was taken by the Latin-French *manual* and even (in the sixteenth century) by the Greek *enchiridion.* When *handbook* was reintroduced in the nineteenth century it was treated as an objectionable neologism, "so accustomed had the nation grown to preferring strange and exotic words." In spite of its superior intelligibility—for *manual*, after all, merely *implies* the idea of "book"—*handbook* has only very recently won wide acceptance. A somewhat similar story is that of *foreword.* The scorn felt by the Latinist is voiced in Hilaire Belloc's dictum: "what Anglo-Saxons call a *foreword*, but gentlemen a *preface.*"[7] It should hardly be necessary to add that such a remark, altogether

---

[6] *Growth and Structure of the English Language*, pp. 49-50.
[7] *The Path to Rome*, New York (Putnam), 1915, p. ix.

subjective, says virtually nothing about language, or about the relative values of Latin and English.

In present-day technical and scientific English, Latin shares with Greek as the source of a host of new coinages, or of new applications of words already adopted. A very few examples will suggest the range and variety of these words: *coaxial, fission, interstellar, neutron, mutant, penicillin, radium, spectrum, sulfa;* and there are also a considerable number of hybrid forms, part Greek, part Latin, such as *egomaniac, speleology, terramycin, tonsillectomy.*

The French Element. Although the Latin and Greek influences began even before the Anglo-Saxon period—much earlier than the French—they remained very small until near the end of the Middle Ages. Not till the sixteenth century did they flow plentifully. The influence of French, on the other hand, though it began only toward the end of Anglo-Saxon times, increased rapidly after the Conquest, until by the thirteenth century, when its high-water mark was reached, French had interpenetrated the native element far more intimately than Latin or Greek have ever done. As was suggested above, this is not a matter merely of the number of words borrowed, for in that respect, Latin, at least, is ahead of French. What it means is that far more of the French words have become a part of the essential core of Modern English: they are what Greenough and Kittredge call "popular words," while more of the Latin and Greek terms are "learned words." An examination of the origin of the one thousand most frequently used words in Modern English[8] shows this very strikingly. Analysis reveals the following:

Of Old English origin	61.7%
French	30.9
Latin	2.9
Scandinavian	1.7
Mixed	1.3
Uncertain	1.3
Low German and Dutch	0.3

In short, French borrowings among our most essential words are half as numerous as the native words, and more than four times as numerous as all other words together!

[8] Thorndike, Edward L., *The Teacher's Word-Books*; also *A Study of English Word-Values*, by Lawrence Faucett and Itsu Maki, Tokyo (Matsumura Sanshodo), 1932, based on Thorndike's list and on Ernest Horn's *A Basic Writing Vocabulary*.

Words —
1. natural
2. borrowed
3. newly formed

The French influence came in two waves, first that of the Normans, then second (and much the greater) that of the Parisian or Central French. The Norman borrowings began to come even before the Conquest, and continued for fully a century and a half; but by that time the French of Paris had gained greater prestige, and displaced the Norman dialect as the source of new borrowings. Because of these two sources, however, some French words were borrowed twice, and such pairs, or "doublets," sometimes survive to Modern English. Thus from Norman we get *cattle* and *catch* (with initial [k]), whereas from Parisian we get *chattel* and *chase* (with [k] palatalized and affricated to [tʃ]). The meanings of these doublets, obviously, have parted company, but their unity of origin can still be discerned. Likewise, originally Germanic words with initial [w] that had been borrowed in French passed into English in two forms: the Norman dialect retained the [w] but in Central French this was transformed into [g]. English has sometimes borrowed both variants, so that we have such doublets as *warrant* and *guarantee*, *warden* and *guardian*, and *reward* and *regard*.

Variant English forms of the same borrowed root are not of course always to be explained in the way just mentioned. To digress a moment, it may be of interest to see some of the other possibilities, especially those connected with the Greek, the Latin, and the French sources. Double borrowings of words originally Greek are these pairs, in which the first member is the earlier borrowing and the second the later: *balm, balsam; blame, blaspheme; diamond, adamant; fancy, phantasy; priest, presbyter;* and *palsy, paralysis.* Some of these had variant forms in French—for example *blâmer* and *blasphémer*—and English has borrowed both; in other cases—for example, *phantasy* and *paralysis*—the second borrowing is a learned one, direct from the Greek. Again, *corpse* is a borrowing from Old French, while *corps* is a re-borrowing of the same word with the *s* silent, as the Modern French pronunciation has it. But the doublets *captive* and *caitiff* almost reverse this situation: for *caitiff* is a borrowing from Old French, while *captive,* much nearer the form and sound of the Latin original, is the second borrowing. On a larger scale the possibilities of multiple borrowing are strikingly exemplified in the history of the Latin root that appears in *regem* (king). The adjective form, *regalis,* gives English *regal,* a direct borrowing. But in the usual development of Old French from Latin, intervocalic consonants are lost; hence *real* is a Middle English borrowing from Old French. Another *real* in English represents Latin *rem* (thing); the *real* here referred to, however, occurs as the name of the coin *real,* and in *real-m.* Modern French *roi* has evolved, with the usual phonetic changes, from Latin *regem,* and again the corresponding adjective has been borrowed in English *royal.* Hence *regal, real,* and *royal* are triplets, as are also *legal, leal* (preserved in the Scottish song "Land o' the Leal"), and *loyal.* The use to which Latin *discus* (itself a borrowing from Greek) has been put in English is even more extensive: the Old English direct borrowing is preserved in *dish,* a Middle English variant gives us *desk,* and a borrowing of the Old French form gives *dais;* seventeenth-century direct borrowings of the Latin word are *disk* (*disc*) and *discus,* the last popularized anew when the Greek sport of throwing the *discus* was revived. Duplication, together with the variation in sound and form that results from borrowing at different times and through different channels, may be further illustrated in *capital, chief,* and *chef; candelabra, chandler,* and *chandelier; gentile, gentle, genteel,* and *jaunty.*[9]

A few examples of the kinds of words borrowed by Middle English from French were given in an earlier chapter.[10] It would, however, be erroneous to assume that loan-words from this source are to be found only in particular categories like these. Actually the English vocabulary is permeated by French everywhere. Many—indeed, most —of the earlier borrowings are not felt to be alien in any sense. The common impression that monosyllables in English are of native origin only is refuted by the long list that could easily be compiled of French loan-words of but one syllable. A very few typical illustrations are the following, which, being among the 250 most frequently used words in the language[11] are as thoroughly English as any that could be mentioned: *just, place, part, use, city, large, line, state, sure, change, close, course, fine, pay, please.*

At the same time, it is obvious that borrowings from French do tend particularly to accumulate in certain fields. The first large group of borrowings was made up of ideas associated with religion

---

[9] See also *pipe* and *fife* in the diagram, p. 148 above.
[10] Chapter 3, pp. 45-46.
[11] Thorndike, taken from Faucett and Maki, *op. cit.*

and the church. Importations of the eleventh century are: *cell, chaplain, charity, evangelist, grace, mercy, miracle, nativity, paradise, passion, sacrament,* and *saint.* These words, in general standing for the more formal and outward aspect of Catholicism, have been suggestively contrasted [12] with borrowings of the thirteenth century that testify to a more inward and personal aspect of religious faith: *anguish, comfort, conscience, devotion, patience, pity, purity,* and *salvation* are witnesses to the religious revival on the Continent and the advent of the preaching friars in England.

Other fields than religion in which borrowing from French was early active are of course law, government, military affairs, and the general usages and conventions of polite society. Legal terms of early date are *suit, plead, plaintiff, judge, jury, jail, assets, bail, bailiff, embezzle, lease,* and *perjury.* Typical loan-words for ideas relating to national government are *chancellor, country, exchequer, govern, minister, power,* and *reign.* French borrowings that stand for ideas associated with war and things military are particularly interesting. *Army* had to compete with three Old English words: *here* (the *harrying* body, the term applied by the Anglo-Saxons to the Danish force), *fierd* (the *traveling* body, from *faran,* meaning *to go*), and *werod,* meaning simply "body of *men*"; it was not until the fifteenth century that the older terms were completely displaced. But a great deal of the French military vocabulary was introduced very early. To illustrate the scope and variety of words of this class, a few specimens may suffice: *assault, company, enemy, hauberk, lance, lieutenant, mail, navy, sergeant, soldier,* and *troops.* It may perhaps be significant that the practice of borrowing its military terms from French has been by no means confined to Middle English. *Captain* and *colonel,* for example, are of considerably later date. Other early Modern English borrowings are *attack, barricade, campaign, cannonade, commandant, corps, cuirassier, dragoon, march,* and *massacre.* Some of these represent the renewed general activity in borrowing from the French which came about through the special French influence in the reigns of Charles I and Charles II. This influence upon the English language and English literature continued, of course, into the eighteenth century. In 1710 we find Jonathan Swift complaining that "the war has introduced abundance of polysyllables which will never be able to live many more cam-

[12] By L. P. Smith in *The English Language,* pp. 165, 167.

paigns." [13] The terms he cites are *speculations, operations, prelimi-nary, ambassadors, palisadoes, communication, circumvallation,* and *battalions.* A curious example of the folly of such confident prophe-sying about language! Not one of the words he gives has perished, and only one has been altered, very slightly, in form. Borrowing from the French military vocabulary has continued up to the pres-ent; accessions in this century include such words as *barrage* and *camouflage.*

One other general group of French borrowings has been men-tioned, that composed of words standing for the usages and the con-ventions of polite society. Too much can easily be made of a contrast between "homely" Anglo-Saxon and "polished" French ideas in Mid-dle (and Modern) English; nevertheless, to some extent this contrast does hold good. It has often been pointed out that vigor and sin-cerity rather than grace and finish are characteristic of the "Anglo-Saxon tradition" [14] in literature. In language, the words standing for courtly and graceful ideas are similarly more likely to be of French than of native origin. *Chivalry, honor, court*liness, and *grace* belong here. The French introduced more polished table manners, and words pertaining to eating, like *dinner, supper* (though the homelier *break-fast* remained), *table, fork, plate,* and *napkin;* also, various ways of preparing food for the table, like *boil, broil,* and *roast,* as well as the names of different kinds of food.[15] So today. Everybody knows the modern phenomenon of "menu French," with such words as *hors d'oeuvres, rôti, en casserole, bisque,* and the various *à la's*—e.g., chicken *à la* King.

French, too, are the general names for clothes—*apparel, costume, dress,* and *garment*—as well as most of the more specific ones dealing with the kinds of dress, their styles and materials: *brassière, décol-leté, voile, chemise,* and *lingerie* are a few recent examples. The ear-liest words relating to art are French—*art* itself, and *beauty, color, design, ornament,* and *tapestry*—and so are the more specialized terms of such a field as architecture (for example, *aisle, arch, chan-*

---

[13] The *Tatler,* No. 230 (Sept. 28, 1710). Swift, however, is wrong about the date of some of these words: "the war" he refers to must be the War of the Spanish Succession (1701-1713), but the *Oxford Dictionary* cites earlier uses of all but the first three of the list.

[14] Cf. the eloquent chapter, of that title, in J. L. Lowes's *Convention and Revolt in Poetry,* Boston (Houghton, Mifflin), 1919.

[15] See Chapter 3, pp. 45-46.

cel, column, pillar, porch, reredos, and *transept*). Other art words continue to enter the language in considerable numbers, as witness *cartoon, pastiche, format, montage.* Some of the humbler occupations like those of the *baker, fisherman, miller, shepherd,* and *shoeᵐaker* have kept their native names; but many others, especially the more skilled trades and those introduced with a more complex social life have French designations: the words *barber, butcher, carpenter, grocer, mason, painter,* and *tailor* are typical.

Did all this borrowing, we may wonder, follow any patterns? In what way and to what extent have these French words been naturalized? The general principle is obvious: the older the borrowing, the more thoroughly it tends to follow normal English habits of accentuation and pronunciation (and consequently of spelling). Mere age, however, is not the sole factor; the extent to which the word is used in English is also of prime importance. Thus, the recent importation *camouflage* was very soon, in popular usage, strongly accented on the first syllable, and its final consonant changed from [ʒ] to [dʒ]. Similarly with *rouge, loge,* and others. This, of course, is what might have been expected on the analogy of dozens of words like *message, courage, orange,* and so forth. On the other hand, even a commonly used word may not settle down at once—as witness *garage,* which has different forms both in England and America. In England it has attained first-syllable stress, but both ['gærɪdʒ], with naturalized ending, and ['gærɑʒ], with the French ending, are in widespread use. In the United States the unnaturalized form [gə'rɑʒ] is widely used, the half naturalized [gə'rɑdʒ] is common too and probably gaining; and one also hears the monosyllabic ['grɑdʒ]—probably representing an attempt to move the stress to initial position.

As has been suggested, the tendency throughout the Middle Ages was to make over all borrowings completely to conform to English patterns of sound and accentuation. Obviously this was easiest with monosyllables, but it was the rule also with longer and less common words. Thorough Anglicization of French loans continued to be the rule until about the era of the Restoration. From this time on, however, a deliberate attempt was often made to preserve the original pronunciation; and although this has rarely met with complete success, it is a tendency that has kept in check the older trend toward thorough naturalization. It is interesting that this tendency not to

Anglicize—and the same is true today—comes at a time when the acquisition of French and other foreign tongues is considered a sign of education and social finish. But the attempt to resist naturalization is doomed to failure, sooner or later. The impossibility of preserving foreign forms has been set forth persuasively by Fowler:

> To say a French word in the middle of an English sentence exactly as it would be said by a Frenchman in a French sentence is a feat demanding an acrobatic mouth; . . . it is a feat that should not be attempted.[16]

Whatever the merits of the attempt, habit in the end will prove too strong—and the word will be adapted to English patterns. Its sound will yield first, perhaps its accentual pattern also, though this may resist longer, as in *ballet, cadet, caprice, prestige,* and so on. Last to give in will probably be the spelling: many of our most irregular spellings are French words which we refuse to respell, such as *quay, fruit, gauge.*

Two final remarks may conclude the subject of English borrowings from French. From the association of elegance and good manners it is an easy step to euphemism—which has brought in such words and expressions as *enceinte, d'un certain age,* and *nude.* The last, somehow, in its attempt to avoid the bareness of the fact, has, in English use, a far less decent effect than the plain *naked* which it seeks to avoid. Lastly, we continue to borrow from the French in any field in which they do pioneer work—and not French words alone, but some of the made-up Latin and Greek scientific terms too. Many terms of psychology and psychoanalysis are of this kind. Our terms associated with the automobile include the French *bonnet* (British usage), *chassis, chauffeur, coupé, garage;* those associated with airplanes include *aileron, cadre, empennage, fuselage, hangar, nacelle.* Of foreign words still adopted into English from living languages, those from French, though much fewer than in earlier centuries, are still by far the most numerous.

The Scandinavian Element. Aside from Greek, Latin, and French, only Scandinavian, the language of the people whom the Anglo-Saxons called "Danes," has made a really substantial contribution to the English vocabulary. So substantial is it, indeed, that if we could be more certain of its precise extent, we might have to reckon it as the fourth of the major, rather than the first of the minor ones.

[16] *Modern English Usage,* London (Oxford Univ. Press), 1926, p. 194.

The reader may be referred for an account of this difficult matter to Jespersen's chapter "The Scandinavians," [17] by one peculiarly qualified to deal with it. The resemblances between Old English and Old Norse (or Old Icelandic) were of course much closer than those that now exist between English and Danish or Norwegian. It is consequently often difficult to say whether a given word of Modern English has developed from Old English or from a Scandinavian cognate. Sometimes it happens that the same root appears twice in Modern English, once from Old English and once from Danish. Such doublets as *no* and *nay*, *rear* and *raise*, *from* and *fro*, and *shirt* and *skirt* illustrate this situation, the first of each pair being the native word and the second Scandinavian. But in *whole* (Old English *hāl*) and *hale*, *church* and *kirk*, and *chest* and *kist*, it is equally likely that the second word of each pair represents a native Northern dialect rather than a Scandinavian variant—an additional complication in the difficult task of sorting out the Scandinavian contribution to Modern English. Occasionally, while it is clear that the native *form* has survived, the *meaning* is evidently Scandinavian: thus, *dream* comes in form directly from its Old English ancestor, but this meant "joy," whereas an Old Norse cognate had the meaning "vision"; and *ploh* meant "measure of land" in Old English, while the Old Norse *plógr* meant "plow."

The best indication of the peculiarly intimate relation between Old English and "Danish," however, is that in all probability the pronominal forms with initial *th—they, their*, and *them*—are due to Scandinavian influence. This is the one case in which English has borrowed pronouns from another language. Indeed, "borrowing" seems scarcely the term for the process of gradual assimilation that we must imagine to have taken place. Two conditions evidently made it possible: the chance of ambiguity that would have resulted from the normal development of Old English *hīe, hiera*, and *him* (their likeness to *he, her*, and *him*) ; and the presence in the language already of other pronominal forms in *th—this, that*, and later *the*. But borrowing of pronouns even in these circumstances witnesses most vividly to the close interrelation of the Anglo-Saxon and Danish elements in early English.

Many Scandinavian borrowings have, of course, been lost. A certain nautical vocabulary, particularly terms associated with naval

[17] *Growth and Structure*, Ch. IV, pp. 59-86.

warfare, that the Anglo-Saxons quite understandably took over from their Viking invaders, has not descended to Modern English. To some extent this corresponds to a much later group of borrowings from Dutch, and for a similar reason: the English of the eighth and ninth centuries learned ship-building from the Danes, as their seventeenth-century descendants learned seamanship from the Dutch. Somewhat similarly, early borrowings of Scandinavian law terms have been mostly lost, and their places taken by the much more numerous law terms from Norman French. *Law* itself, however, is one of the survivors, as are the compounds *outlaw* and *by-law*,[18] and a few terms like *hustings, riding* (originally *thriding,* third part), and *wapentake.* These last two are names for the divisions of English counties.

A few miscellaneous illustrations of the Scandinavian element in English may be added. If we can be reasonably sure that a great many of our most familiar words, like *man, father, house, life, summer, come, bring, see, hear, think, sit, stand, wise, well, better, best,* and so forth, are strictly English, it is only, as Jespersen points out,[19] because the survival of a considerable body of early English literature has made it possible to label them as Old English. Many words were doubtless identical in Old English and Old Norse, and many more only slightly differentiated in sound and form. In addition to the numerous words that *may* be Scandinavian, there are many that indubitably *are.* Most of these words stand for the everyday, commonplace things of life: there is no suggestion of a differentiation in culture or interests between Dane and Saxon, as to some extent there is between Saxon and Norman. Typical nouns are *fellow, gate, haven, husband, knife, root, skin,* and *window;* verbs include *bask, call, cast, die, drown, get, hit, scrape, scream, scowl, skulk, take,* and *want;* adjectives are such as *happy, ill, loose, low, meek, odd, rotten, seemly, ugly,* and *wrong.* Like the Celts, the Danes have left a conspicuous record of their occupation of parts of Britain in the form of place-names. According to Isaac Taylor,[20] more than six hundred

[18] This meant "town-law," the first element being that which appears also in places like *Grimsby, Hadd-by,* and *Rugby;* but popular usage has distorted its meaning, through confusion with the more familiar sense of *by,* into "additional or supplementary regulation." Hence, probably, such new creations as *by-play* and *by-proauct.*

[19] *Ibid.,* pp. 64-65.

[20] *Words and Places,* New York (Dutton), 1909, p. 158.

towns in the east of England have names ending in -*by*, from the Danish word for town. Place-names in -*beck*, -*dale*, -*thorp*, -*thwaite*, and -*toft* are likewise of Scandinavian origin. Besides these marks of the original contact between Anglo-Saxon and Dane, there are rather numerous Scandinavian loan-words of later date: *batten* (to thrive), *billow*, *blight*, *clumsy*, and *doze*—all "probables"—made their way from the Northern and Eastern dialects into literary English in the sixteenth and seventeenth centuries; a few words—*equip*, *flounder* (the fish), and possibly the verb *sound*—are thought to have entered English through the circuitous route of Scandinavian elements retained in the speech of the Normans from their original northern tongue and later brought by them to England as part of their French dialect; several comparatively recent borrowings—*maelstrom*, *nag*, *scamp*, *fiord*, *floe*, *geyser*, *saga*, and *ski*—represent either later accretions from English dialects or fresh contacts with Scandinavian languages.

Minor Elements. Turning to the minor borrowed elements in the English vocabulary, it is natural to begin with what is chronologically the oldest: Celtic. The curiously small extent of the Celtic influence (apart from place-names) upon the English word-stock has already been commented on.[21] Besides the words previously mentioned, only a very few others—*ass*, *bin*, *coomb*, *dim*, and *mattock* —may be assigned with any show of probability to this small handful. Of other words (and also of this group) often listed as Celtic, it is quite likely that some come not from the Celts of Britain but from the Irish missionaries to Northumbria, or even that they are Teutonic or Romanic words borrowed in Celtic and later absorbed into English. Later stages of the English language have, however, levied upon the more modern forms of the aboriginal tongues. But the loanwords from Welsh, which we might have expected to be rather numerous, are relatively few: perhaps only *flannel* and *flummery* are really common words; others, like *coracle*, *cromlech*, and *eisteddfod* are distinctly more exotic. Both Scotch-Gaelic and Irish contribute a far greater number of words, which are usually characteristic: *clan*, *claymore*, *pibroch*, *slogan*, and *whisky* are typical of the one group, and *bog*, *colleen*, *pillion*, *shamrock*, and *spalpeen* of the other.

Aside from English, there are two important modern languages of the West Germanic group: Dutch and German. Borrowings from

[21] Chapter 3, pp. 39-40.

both are, however, scanty. Yet it should be remembered that the extremely close relationship of Dutch (and Flemish) with English makes it quite conceivable that some words that we label Anglo-Saxon may just as plausibly be explained as of Dutch or Flemish origin. Numerous English words are still nearly or quite identical with their cognates in the Low German languages; the right of such words to be considered "pure" Anglo-Saxon is, of course, highly dubious. One group that may safely be assigned to Dutch or Flemish influence on Middle English is made up of such trade names as *pack*, from the wool trade; *hops, scum,* and *tub,* probably from the brewers of the Low Countries; and terms of the cloth-making industry (believed to date from the importation of Flemish weavers into England in Chaucer's day): *curl, scour, spool, stripe,* and *tuck.* Far the most important and homogeneous group of Low German—chiefly Dutch —loan-words are those that pertain to ships and the sea: medieval importations are *bowsprit, buoy, freight, keel, leak, lighter, marline,* and *pump;* more recent ones are such words as *avast, belay, boom, bow, commodore, cruise, dock, keelhaul, yacht,* and *yawl.*[22] Besides these nautical borrowings, there is a fair number of miscellaneous words that Modern English has taken from the Low German tongues; a few specimens are *foist, freebooter, groat, heyday, hoist, jeer, plunder, snap, switch, toy,* and *wagon.* Among the many words that may possibly be of Low German origin are some very familiar ones: *boy, girl, bounce, luck, mud,* and *scoff.*

High German borrowings are considerably rarer. Bradley,[23] however, calls attention to one group of words in which the influence of Modern German is conspicuous: the science of *mineralogy* has retained in its English vocabulary, with slight modifications, the terms employed in the land of its origin—*bismuth, cobalt, gneiss, quartz, shale,* and *zinc* are typical. Another group that is likewise noteworthy is that made up of terms used in eating and drinking; for example, *sauerkraut, stein,* and *lager beer.* Such words are, of course, far less numerous than French loans in the same field, and they are less completely assimilated in English. The same may be said of the occasional importations from German in other departments: such various borrowings as *carouse, heroin, hinterland, kindergarten, geopolitics* (from *Geopolitik,* formed of Greek elements), *leitmotif,*

---

[22] Most of these illustrations are from L. P. Smith, *op. cit.,* pp. 191-193.
[23] *The Making of English,* p. 103.

meerschaum, poodle, putsch, umlaut, waltz, and *wanderlust,* though most are in common enough use in English, still bear, in some measure, the marks of their alien origin. Acquisitions from the Second World War, and the events leading up to it,—*anschluss, blitz, flak, lebensraum, panzer, stuka*—are already assuming a historical air, since they have little use apart from the political or military context; *schnorkel,* however, shows signs of greater vitality.

Even apart from French, the modern Romance languages, especially Italian and Spanish, have contributed far more to the English vocabulary than have the Germanic languages that are the closer relatives in our family-tree. Borrowing from Italian naturally began to be active when the culture of the Italian Renaissance impressed itself upon sixteenth-century England. When the traveled Elizabethan Englishman, as Sir Thomas Overbury put it, spoke "his own language with shame and lisping," it was chiefly with Italian that he filled out the supposed deficiencies or improved upon the crudities of his native tongue. Most of these Elizabethan affectations, however, have not stuck, any more than have the Spanish importations that are based upon literary admiration of Góngora and Guevara. Of those that did establish themselves, *attitude, balcony, fiasco, isolate, motto, stanza,* and *umbrella* are typical Renaissance borrowings from Italian, and *desperado, grandee, Negro, punctilio,* and *renegade* from Spanish.[24] As to Italian borrowings in general, it is well known that the chief indebtedness of English to this source is for its musical vocabulary. This extensive stock of words comprises both those in every day use, such as *piano, soprano, alto, opera,* and *tempo,* and those that are more definitely specialized or technical, such as *legato, diminuendo, rallentando, pizzicato, allegretto, scherzo,* and *andante.* Words like these are chiefly of the eighteenth century, the period when Italian music was introduced into England. A somewhat similar, though smaller, group of Italian borrowings comprises terms used in the fine arts, like *chiaroscuro, dado, fresco, portico, replica, studio,* and *torso.* Perhaps half of all our Italian loan-words come to us through French; virtually all the oldest, or Middle English, borrowings are of this indirect kind: *alarm, brigand, ducat, florin, orange,* and *rebeck*[25] (the last two ultimately of Eastern origin) are typical. But words that are shown by

[24] *Ibid.*
[25] Emerson, *History of the English Language,* p. 168.

their very aspect to be direct from Italy have frequently been borrowed throughout the Modern English period; a few random illustrations are *cameo, campanile, dilettante, extravaganza, lava, maca-
roni, rifacimento, spaghetti,* and *virtuoso.*

Spanish borrowings are less common; but such loan-words as
*armada, cargo, castanet, cigar, guerilla, matador, mosquito, quad-
roon,* and *vanilla* testify that this source has been by no means a
negligible one. English-speaking peoples have had commercial (as
well as occasional warlike) contacts not only with the Spanish but
with the Portuguese, as is evidenced by such importations from the
latter as *banana, cobra, cocoa, molasses,* and *pimento.*

It is of course evident that a good deal of history, both political
and cultural, is implicit in the various groups of loan-words. This is
just as true for the minor sources as for the major ones. The indebtedness of Western European civilization to the speakers of
Arabic for the early development of chemistry, mathematics, and
medicine is manifest in such borrowings from this source as *alcohol,
alchemy, alembic, algebra, alkali, attar, cipher, elixir, naphtha,
sugar, syrup,* and *zero.* That the Arabic-speaking peoples were often
the intermediaries through whom Greek culture reached western
Europe at a time when Greek itself was all but unknown is suggested
by the history of several of these words—*alchemy, alembic,* and
elixir; all are ultimately Greek, but all came through the medium of
Arabic. The devious routes by which Arabic words have become
English are illustrated in the history of the doublets *cipher* and *zero:*
both come from the Arabic *sifr* (cipher), but the one via Spanish
and French, and the other through Vulgar Latin and Italian. The
exotic East, always fascinating to the Western traveler, is conjured
up in such other characteristic borrowings from Arabic as *emir,
bedouin, fakir, gazelle, giraffe, harem, hashish, hookah, lute, minaret,
mosque, myrrh, salaam, sheik, sirocco, sultan,* and *vizier.*

Another Semitic language, Hebrew, contributes similar pictures of
the Orient in loan-words like *camel, cassia, cinnamon, hyssop,* and
sapphire, though all of these have come indirectly. A more important
indebtedness to Hebrew, however, is to be observed in religious
terminology. That many of these words also come into English indirectly is, of course, natural enough in view of the part that Greek
and Latin have played in the tradition of Biblical translation; here,
too, is the obvious explanation of why, in spite of the great influence

of the Bible upon the English language, the total number of Hebrew borrowings is comparatively small. Typical words of this sort are *amen, cherub, Gehenna, hallelujah, Jehovah, manna, pharisee, rabbi, sabbath,* and *seraph.*

Another Oriental source—though in this case Indo-European—is Persian. On the characteristic flavor of this group of loan-words, the following rhapsody of Logan Pearsall Smith may be quoted: "To me they glitter like jewels in our northern speech. *Magic* and *Paradise,* for instance; and the names of flowers and gems and rich fruits and tissues—*Tulip* and *Lilac,* and *Jasmin* and *Peach* and *Lapis Lazuli* . . . and *Orange* and *Azure* and *Scarlet.*" [26] Against this one may set less poetical words such as *baksheesh, satrap,* and *seersucker* (through Hindustani).

Among other Asiatic countries, only India has contributed a considerable number of words. From its many languages, often very circuitously, we have taken over such terms as *bandanna, brahmin, bungalow, calico, chutney, curry, indigo, juggernaut, jungle, loot, pajama, pundit, rajah,* and *sandal.* Next most numerous are Malay words like *amuck, batik, gingham, gong, gutta-percha,* and *sarong.*[27] Chinese and Japanese have been levied upon infrequently: *mandarin, pongee, serge,* and *tea* represent the one source, and *hara-kiri, jiu-jitsu, kimono, tycoon,* and *samurai* the other. From minor Asiatic or Polynesian languages have come such words as *atoll, bamboo, cheroot, junk* (the boat), *sago, taboo, tattoo,* and *teak.*

It is clear on the whole that from languages with which there has been less intimate contact—those of remoter peoples whose cultures have touched Englishmen only tangentially—the words borrowed mostly preserve an exotic air, and are therefore not wholly assimilated. This is true of the borrowings even from a European language (and one of the Indo-European system) like Russian: *ikon, knout, pogrom, steppe, tsar,* and *vodka* can be said to be English only in a limited sense, for they would scarcely be used except with direct reference to things Russian. The increasing importance of Russia

[26] *More Trivia,* New York (Harcourt), 1921, p. 85. The etymologies are in one sense, apparently, sound enough, except of course that *lapis* is Latin—though *lazuli* is thought to go back to the same Persian origin as *azure.* Most of the words, however, are far from being *direct* borrowings from Persian; *magic* and *paradise,* for example, are Middle English <Old French <Latin <Greek <Old Persian.

[27] Bradley, *op. cit.,* p. 104, and other sources.

may well, in the future, lead to more borrowing, but at present we have only a few words such as *bolshevik, commissar, intelligentsia,* and *soviet,* the second and third of which are not ultimately Russian. Similarly, words from Turkish: *bey, caftan, effendi, janissary, horde, kiosk, odalisque,* and *turquoise* remain, for the most part, exotic. Or those from various African tongues: *chimpanzee, gnu, gorilla, kraal, oasis* and *zebra.* The languages of the American Indians have given us names for many products of the New World, the commonest of which, however, have come in through Spanish or French: *canoe, chocolate, hammock, potato, tapioca, tobacco,* and so on. Though these are thoroughly naturalized, quite a number of others keep inevitably the suggestion of the story-book Indian; examples are *papoose, squaw, tepee, tomahawk, wampum,* and *wigwam.*

The American Element. Enough has perhaps been said of the major and minor sources of borrowing that have been drawn upon by the English language in general. Clearly, English has given over entirely its early resistance to foreign words. The rule now seems to be that almost every vernacular anywhere on the globe with which the speakers of English have had any important contact at all has been levied upon for at least a few words. Since American English has had its own contacts with other tongues, it is natural that it should have absorbed certain foreign words that it does not share with British English. The most distinctive of these contacts is of course that just mentioned with the various Indian languages. *Chipmunk, hickory, hominy, hooch, mackinaw, moccasin, moose, opossum, pecan, persimmon, raccoon, skunk, squash, succotash, terrapin,* and others would be familiar to any American. Indian words, too, have had some vogue in American political life: *mugwump, powwow, sachem, Tammany,* and so on.

The two European languages that have contributed most to the distinctively American vocabulary are undoubtedly Spanish and French. Spanish borrowings are of course to be found most abundantly in the speech of the Southwest;[28] some that are in fairly general use in the United States are *adobe, bronco, cafeteria, cinch, corral, lariat, loco, marijuana, mustang, ranch, rodeo,* and *vamoose.* Loans from French are due chiefly to contacts with that language in two widely separated regions: Louisiana and the Canadian border.

---

[28] Cf. Mary Austin, "Geographical Terms from the Spanish," *American Speech,* Vol. VIII, No. 3 (Oct. 1933), pp. 7-10.

They include such words as *bayou, butte, cache, chute, lagniappe,*[29] *levee, portage,* and *prairie.*

On the whole, however, it is safe to say that peculiarly American borrowings from foreign languages are far fewer than might be expected. In general, American English has been surprisingly little affected by the speech of immigrants. The prestige attaching to English as the established language keeps the speakers of American English from borrowing, except very occasionally, from the many tongues introduced into the United States in this way. Though the position of natives and newcomers is just reversed, it is evidently the same reason that kept the Anglo-Saxons from levying upon the language of the Celts. The children of immigrants, too, under the pressure exerted by the school and the community, usually give up within a generation the speech of their parents, and achieve precisely the same brand of English as that of their contemporaries of old American stock. The exception is the expected one: where homogeneous foreign-speaking communities have been isolated—the Pennsylvania Germans and the Canadian French are the most conspicuous examples—they have kept up their language for generations, but even then in a form changed by association with English.

Not only has the speech of comparatively recent immigrants left but a slight impression on the general body of American English; the marks of the language spoken by non-English settlers of Colonial America have not been deep. Thus from the Dutch of New Netherlands we have *boss, cole slaw, cruller, Santa Claus, snoop, spook,* and *stoop* (a kind of porch). But only one of these—*boss*—may be said to have gone around the world. On the other hand, as has already been suggested, it is not difficult to cite a number of words of German origin that are part of the general vocabulary—words neither international nor sectional. German terms relating to food are far more common in the United States than in England. To those already given may be added *delicatessen, frankfurter, hamburger, pretzel, wiener,* and *zwieback.*[30] German also are such slang or colloquial Americanisms as *bower* (for the "jack" in cards, for which

---

[29] For an appreciation of the usefulness of this word, see Mark Twain, *Life on the Mississippi,* Chapter XLIV.

[30] Of these, only *pretzel* (labeled "U.S.") appears in the *Shorter Oxford Dictionary* (2nd ed., 1936).

knave is preferred in England), *dumb* (stupid), *bum, loafer,* and *shyster.*[31] It is probable, likewise, that the Irish element in the American population accounts not only for specific words such as *lummox, shanty,* and *shebang,*[32] but also for certain turns of expression,[33] as well as habits of pronunciation,[34] that American English does not share with the English of southern England.[35]

It might be expected that American English would be powerfully affected by the speech of peoples far less akin than the Irish or the Germans to the Anglo-Saxon stock but also represented in great numbers in the American population. Has the speech of the Negroes, the Chinese, or the Jews contributed much to the American vocabulary? Recent investigation by Professor Lorenzo D. Turner[36] has shown that we owe more words to African sources than used to be realized. The best known of these are *hoodoo, voodoo, goober, pinder, yam, juke*-box, *gumbo, tote, jambalaya,* and *banjo.* A very few others owe their present form to the Negro, who brought them in from French, Spanish, or some other source: the best known is *pickaninny.* Chinese immigration has made a negligible impression on American speech; of words from this channel perhaps only *chopsuey,*[37] *fantan, joss, kowtow, tong,* and the slang *yen* (strong desire) are at all generally familiar. As to the influence of Hebrew or of Yiddish, the part of which we can be sure seems unexpectedly small. Yiddish of course is simply a dialect of German, and it is quite possible that some Americanisms attributed to the direct influence of German should really be ascribed to that of Yiddish; *poker* (the

---

[31] Mencken, H. L., *The American Language,* New York (Knopf), 1936, 4th ed., pp. 155-160, cites these and others.

[32] Hutson, Arthur E., "Gaelic Loan-Words in American," *American Speech,* Vol. XXII, No. 1 (Feb. 1947), pp. 18-23.

[33] Mencken. *op. cit.,* pp. 150-152.

[34] On this side of the matter, cf. Krapp, *The English Language in America,* New York (Appleton-Century), 1925, Vol. II, pp. 96-97, *et passim.*

[35] Cf. also McKnight, *English Words and Their Background,* pp. 26-27, and his reference to Joyce, P. W., *English as We Speak it in Ireland.*

[36] See his *Africanisms in the Gullah Dialect,* Chicago (University of Chicago), 1949; also M. M. Mathews's *Some Sources of Southernisms,* University (University of Alabama), 1948.

[37] One or two of the others are likewise dubious: *kowtow* is not peculiar to American English, while *joss* is explained by the *Oxford English Dictionary* as probably from Portuguese *deos* (god), and as Pidgin English rather than Chinese.

game), for example, has been explained in both these ways, as well as in several others.[38] Among the unquestioned loan-words from the speech of Jews in the United States are *kibitzer, kosher,* and *mazuma.* It is altogether likely, however, that Jewish influence on American speech is considerably greater than the number of loans definitely traced to it would indicate; it would be strange indeed if the Jewish population of New York City had made no considerable impression upon the English spoken there. Like the Irish immigrants of an earlier epoch, the German, Polish, and Russian Jews who have come over more recently have probably influenced American idiom and word-formation to a greater extent than is usually realized.

To return to the subject of word-borrowing in the English language as a whole: one rather special aspect of the matter has as yet been merely glanced at—the treatment of foreign proper names. Places in which English-speaking settlers have replaced earlier ones that spoke another language have frequently been allowed to retain the earlier names (or some development of them). Thus, as we have seen, there are very many more Celtic place-names in Great Britain and Indian place-names in the United States than there are common nouns of Celtic or Indian ancestry in the language concerned as a whole. Another angle of the question is the treatment of place-names for parts of the world that are not English-speaking. The earlier practice was either to translate them completely, as was possible with such names as *Black Forest* for *Schwarzwald,*[39] *Low Countries* for *Nederlanden,* or to make them as English as possible by recasting their spelling and pronunciation along more familiar lines. Thus the English called the Italian cities *Firenze, Venezia,* and *Napoli* by the names *Florence, Venice,* and *Naples* (all suggested by the general European use of French revisions of the native names). The Germans, similarly, converted the same Italian names to *Florenz, Venedig,* and *Neapel.* But just the reverse of this is the present tendency in English: to keep the foreign forms—a tendency to which radio, as much as any other agency, has contributed. Announcers and commentators, conscious that geographic names (as well as foreign surnames) will come before the listener's eyes on maps and in the news-

[38] Mencken, *op. cit.,* 3rd ed., pp. 112-113, details six theories of its etymology. See also Mathews's treatment in the *Dictionary of Americanisms.*

[39] As might be expected, German has indulged in this practice much more extensively than English ever has; e.g., the German turning of *Salt Lake City* into *Salzseestadt,* or *Tierra del Fuego* into *Feuerland.*

papers, must choose whether to follow the spelling in pronouncing them, or to disregard spelling and say them in something approaching the foreign way. Since the alphabet has different values in different languages, they choose the latter course and disregard the spelling. News magazines give both the foreign spelling and a more or less phonetic respelling, so that the reader may pronounce for himself and also recognize the radio announcer's pronunciation. Only traditionally intrenched Anglicizations withstand this tendency, and not even all of these—*Leghorn*, for example, is yielding to *Livorno*. Today we do not Anglicize as formerly; in other words, borrowing of names is less complete.

Native vs. Borrowed. We must now return to summarize the subject of the native and the borrowed elements in English. So much has been said about the foreign additions made through the centuries that the impression may remain of a language in which the native element is reduced to a small fraction, overpowered by the new adoptions. Is such an impression justified? Could we not simply count how many words of each kind appear in the dictionary and have our answer?

It is not so easy as that. The dictionary contains words of many kinds—common, rare, current, archaic, obsolete, technical, slang, literary, vulgar, and so on—and a bare word-count would ignore such essential matters as the degree of use of words and the number of meanings which they have developed. If a flat count could be made, for example, rare words and the indispensable words of every day would be put on a par. At that rate, the complicated and technical words, the majority of which are formations of Latin and Greek elements, would easily win the contest. A more realistic test would be to limit the count to a part of the dictionary that is in active use. A count of this kind, based on 20,000 words in common, present use,[40] makes the Anglo-Saxon element less than one fifth, and the Greco-Latin (including the French) element more than three fifths. The larger the number of words counted, the greater would be the proportion of borrowed words, especially those from Latin and Greek. Individual vocabularies obviously vary in a somewhat similar fashion with the interests and the education of the person in question.

A still more revealing method, however, is that of counting not

[40] R. G. Kent, *Language and Philology,* Boston (Marshall Jones), 1923, pp. 5-6.

different words only, but rather counting every word every time it is used, in a piece of writing or of conversation. If this is done, the proportions just cited are almost reversed. The reason is plain: almost all prepositions, conjunctions, articles, pronouns, and auxiliary verbs —exactly the words most often repeated—are of native origin, as are also the greater number of familiar nouns, adjectives, and verbs. Of the 500 words most frequently used in present-day English, according to Thorndike's well-known word count[41] the native words are 72 per cent, the borrowed 28 per cent; and furthermore, the derivatives of the native words are three times as numerous as those of the borrowed words. In general, one fourth of the task of expression in English is accomplished, so it is said,[42] by just nine words: *and, be, have, it, of, the, to, will,* and *you;* and one half of the task by these and thirty-four others, likewise exclusively of native origin. No wonder then if counting every word every time it occurs in a passage of literature reveals that the writer of the most highly Latinized style still employs many more native than borrowed words. The exact proportion will of course vary both with the individual writer and with the subject on which he writes. Kent's figures show[43] that while poets of the last hundred years have employed only from 10 to 20 per cent of classical words, the percentage in recent technical writing sometimes runs as high as 40. Shakespeare is given credit[44] for using 90 per cent of native words and only 10 per cent of foreign ones, while in the King James Bible (on the basis of three gospels) the proportion is 94 and 6. In contrast with these proportions are those for writers of a notoriously Latinized vocabulary: Samuel Johnson's figures are 72 and 28, and Gibbon's 70 and 30. Midway between the extremes stand such writers as Milton with 81 and 19,

[41] Thorndike, taken from Faucett and Maki, *op. cit.*

[42] McKnight, *English Words and Their Background*, p. 158. A study by Godfrey Dewey, "Relative Frequency of English Speech Sounds," *Harvard Studies in Education*, Vol. IV (1923), gives the first nine words used in written matter as *the, of, and, to, a, in, that, it,* and *is.* Another calculation, based on spoken English—French, Carter, and Koenig's *Words and Sounds of Telephone Conversations* (Bell Telephone System Technical Publications, June, 1930)—gives them as *I, you, the, a, on, to, that, it,* and *is.* The first frequency-group in Thorndike's list (see footnote 1) has 24 words, only one of which (*are*) is not native.

[43] *Op. cit.*, pp. 55-57.

[44] Emerson, *op. cit.*, and Krapp.

Pope with 80 and 20, Addison with 82 and 18, and Tennyson (who prided himself on his "Saxon" English) with 88 and 12.

The English vocabulary, then, as it has been used by different writers and for different purposes, exhibits considerable diversity in the elements of which it is composed. The difference between the 6 per cent of borrowed words in the King James Bible and the 30 per cent in Gibbon is really very great—enough, certainly, to give the two styles quite divergent colorings. This is the more evident when one considers that the native words include almost all the necessary machinery of the sentence, the words that are vital to grammatical structure but relatively colorless in meaning. The borrowed words, on the other hand, are almost always essential to meaning. It can easily be demonstrated [45] that while to remove the borrowed words from almost any passage of English prose or verse may leave the sentence structure intact, it will almost inevitably rob the passage of many of the words that carry the essential meaning. By the exercise of a little ingenuity one could fairly easily construct sentences of Anglo-Saxon words only, though hardly of borrowed words only; but with that part of the vocabulary alone one could not go far in the realm of ideas.

Profit and Loss. This brings us to the disputed question of profit and loss in word-borrowing—not really a linguistic question at all, and one in which it is all too easy to prove one's preconceptions, yet one perhaps not out of place in a broad treatment of the language. We have seen that Anglo-Saxon, if not positively hostile to borrowing, tended rather to conserve and to build on its own resources. But the Norman Conquest and the dominant influence of French in succeeding centuries changed all that. In the time of the Renaissance, consequently, a flood of foreign words, Latin, Greek, Italian, French, Spanish, poured in and were generally welcomed. Not that they could all be assimilated—far from it; such "dictionaries of hard words" as Cockeram's (1623) are graveyards of foreign words that died aborning.[46] Nevertheless, many were added and have proved themselves in use since. And the new "open door" policy of the Eng-

[45] See Kent's specimens of "Latinless English," *op. cit.*, pp. 156-158.

[46] Some examples from Cockeram's *The English Dictionarie: or, An Interpreter of hard English Words* (1623), are: *"abarsticke,* insatiable; *basiate,* to kisse; *cucuriate,* to crow like a cocke; *deblaterate,* to babble much; *exilitie,* slendernesse"; and so on.

lish language toward foreign words is still in force today. The French element came early and was ineradicably mingled; the rest followed as new horizons opened and the life of the nation expanded. In the nineteenth century the British Empire, with its outposts throughout the world, continued the expansion. By now there is hardly a language from which English has not borrowed something.

The most obvious disadvantage of the multiple word-stock, it has been said, is that a great many pairs of words that are alike in meaning are totally unlike in appearance and sound. This is particularly the case with nouns and the adjectives corresponding to them in meaning. *Eye—ocular; house—domestic; land—agrarian; moon—lunar; mouth—oral; son—filial; sun—solar;* and *sea—marine* are a few of the many pairs of this kind that might be mentioned. Virtually the same state of affairs exists with other pairs in which the noun is a familiar, homely word, though not a native one, and the adjective is decidedly more learned: *city—urban; country—rural; letter—epistolary;* and *sound—phonetic* are typical. There is something undeniably awkward in this situation. Yet, after all, the language does not force one to use the more learned member of the pair; a phrase containing the more familiar member is usually in common use: *ocular—with the eye; lunar—of the moon;* or else the familiar noun may be converted without change into an adjective: *domestic* or *house servant, agrarian* or *land reform, rural* or *country road.* So perhaps the difficulty here is less real than it seems.

A more serious objection is that the practice of borrowing has weakened the resources of the native vocabulary in certain definite ways. As will be pointed out again, the earlier capacity of the language for forming particular compounds has been seriously curtailed. Not infrequently, too, a borrowed compound has driven out a native one, as when the French borrowing *despair* replaced Old English *wanhope*, with the result that *hope* was left without a formal equivalent for the contrasting idea. Even here, however, it may be argued that there is still the possibility of effective literary contrast in words that are opposite in meaning and unlike in form; Lamb's phrase "in hope sometimes, sometimes in despair, yet persisting ever . . ." (in "Dream Children") illustrates this.

And what of the points in favor of the vocabulary expanded with borrowings? The great wealth of synonyms, or near synonyms, is usually reckoned the most noteworthy asset of Modern English.

Finely discriminated shades of meaning are made possible by the existence of hundreds of pairs of words that are almost, but not quite, synonymous. One need consider only paired adjectives like the following (of which, in each pair, the first is native and the second borrowed) to be impressed by the point: *hearty, cordial; deadly, mortal; bloody, sanguinary; motherly, maternal; lively, vivacious; watery, aqueous.* Often there are more than two words among which to choose the one that is exactly right in connotation and denotation: *manly, male, masculine, virile; womanly, feminine, female; kingly, royal, regal;* and *earthly, earthy, earthen, terrestrial.* The existence in English of so many words to choose from does not make the language easy to handle well; nevertheless, to one who seeks to use it well, this plenitude does offer great possibilities for precise and complete expression.

One further implication of the existence of pairs like *deadly, mortal; bloody, sanguinary;* and *fatherly, paternal* is that there exist in the English vocabulary two planes—one made up of everyday, familiar words, and the other of rarer, more learned ones. The first we acquire before we are aware: we cannot remember when we did not know them. The second we connect with reading or with schooling, and perhaps we can even recollect when first we met one particular word or another.[47] These two planes cannot be strictly equated with native and borrowed, but certainly the majority of the familiar are native and the majority of the learned are borrowed words. Thus it is possible in English to speak of two general types or styles of expression, each depending in large degree upon the part of the vocabulary employed—the more familiar or the more learned. The first style is characterized by directness, brevity, and plainness; the second by eloquence, grandeur, and sonority. The literary man has every reason to be grateful that the English language is not an instrument of one string; that, on the contrary, two styles exist which together offer infinite possibilities of effective contrast. Perhaps it will not take us too far afield—though the matter is literary rather than linguistic—to illustrate the more extreme use of each of these styles under skillful hands.

Ornate, Latinized, polysyllabic diction is represented at its best in the prose of Sir Thomas Browne. Here is a typical paragraph from

[47] The distinction is that of Greenough and Kittredge, *op. cit.*, the chapter "Learned and Popular Words."

the famous concluding chapter of *Urn-burial*, which Saintsbury has called "the longest piece, perhaps, of absolutely sublime rhetoric to be found in the prose literature of the world": [48]

> Pyramids, arches, obelisks, were but the irregularities of vainglory, and wild enormities of ancient magnanimity. But the most magnanimous resolution rests in the Christian religion, which trampleth upon pride, and sits on the neck of ambition, humbly pursuing that infallible perpetuity, unto which all others must diminish their diameters, and be poorly seen in angles of contingency.

Let us set alongside this another passage of seventeenth-century prose, one distinctly in the other tradition of style. John Bunyan had no stated theory of prose style; his diction is simple and full of native words because he knew the King James Bible so fully and because he strove to present his ideas most directly. Here are the opening sentences of *Pilgrim's Progress:*

> As I walked through the wilderness of this world, I lighted on a certain place where was a den, and I laid me down in that place to sleep; and as I slept, I dreamed a dream. I dreamed, and behold I saw a man clothed with rags, standing in a certain place, with his face from his own house, a book in his hand, and a great burden upon his back.

Analysis of only a single aspect of the two styles represented here—the length of the words employed—reveals one explanation of the totally different impressions they create. The fifty-seven words of the passage from Browne include twenty-six polysyllables: ten words of two syllables, seven of three, six of four, two of five, and one word of six syllables. On the other hand, the seventy-two words of the passage from Bunyan include only eight that are not monosyllables; and of these, seven are words of two syllables and only one word contains as many as three syllables.

In short, both of these styles can be superb in their quite divergent ways. As Lytton Strachey observed when comparing the Latinized diction of Sir Thomas Browne with the simpler, "Saxon" English: "It would be foolish to claim a superiority for either one of the two styles; it would be still more foolish to suppose that the effects of the one might be produced by the means of the other." [49]

Both the ornate and the simple styles have the defects of their

[48] *Cambridge History of English Literature*, Vol. VII, p. 275.
[49] See his essay "Sir Thomas Browne," *Books and Characters*, New York (Harcourt), 1922, p. 41.

qualities. The one may tend toward obscurity or an inflated emptiness of content; the other may be plain to the extent of a poverty-
stricken and childlike bareness. What perhaps is most in need of
being pointed out is that the more monosyllabic type of English diction has its own beauty and eloquence, and may be and has been
used for the finest effects of poetry as well as prose.[50] Laments such
as those of Jonathan Swift on the barren poverty and flatness that
have come to the English language as a consequence of the shortening of words are easily refuted by an appeal to the great poets. To
confine ourselves to a single illustration, let us observe the almost
completely monosyllabic diction of a famous scene in Shakespeare,
called by the finest of modern Shakespearean critics "perhaps the
most tear-compelling passage in literature" [51]—the scene from *King
Lear* in which Lear wakes from sleep to find Cordelia bending over
him (Act IV, scene vii). Here are Lear's first words and Cordelia's
replies:

Lear.   You do me wrong to take me out o' the grave.
           Thou art a soul in bliss; but I am bound
           Upon a wheel of fire, that mine own tears
           Do scald like molten lead.
Cordelia.   Sir, do you know me?
Lear.   You are a spirit, I know; when did you die?
Cordelia.   Still, still, far wide!   (ll. 45-50)

Three dissyllables in fifty-four words!—and much the same proportion holds in this later excerpt from the same dialog:

Lear.   . . . nor I know not
           Where I did lodge last night. Do not laugh at me;
           For as I am a man, I think this lady
           To be my child Cordelia.
Cor.   And so I am, I am.
Lear.   Be your tears wet? Yes, faith. I pray, weep not.
           If you have poison for me, I will drink it.
           I know you do not love me; for your sisters
           Have, as I do remember, done me wrong:
           You have some cause, they have not.
Cor.   No cause, no cause.
                                       (ll. 68-75)

---

[50] E.g., the marvelously poignant last line to Milton's sonnet "To His Deceased Wife": *I waked, she fled, and day brought back my night.*
[51] Bradley, A. C., *Shakespearean Tragedy*, New York (Macmillan), 1930, p. 61.

Much the same observation might be made of two great speeches in
the last scene: Lear's words (Act V, scene iii, ll. 8-19) beginning

> No, no, no, no! Come let's away to prison;
> We two alone will sing like birds i' the cage . . .

and his dying utterance (ll. 306-312):

> And my poor fool is hang'd! No, no, no life!
> Why should a dog, a horse, a rat have life,
> And thou no breath at all? . . .
> Do you see this? Look on her, look, her lips,
> Look there, look there!

This last speech—according to Bradley, "the most pathetic speech
ever written" [52]—is utterly different, in the monosyllabic simplicity
of its diction, from the last words of Hamlet or of Othello (as the
same critic points out); but it is surely at least equally moving.

The attempt has been made to demonstrate that both the longer,
borrowed words and the shorter, native ones have their own kinds of
usefulness and effectiveness. In a similar way one might show further
that the language is the gainer through the possession of both instru-
ments, largely by reason of the possibilities of contrasting one with
the other. The classical illustration of this contrast is the passage in
Macbeth (Act II, scene ii, ll. 60-63):

> Will all great Neptune's ocean wash this blood
> Clear from my hand? No; this my hand will rather
> The multitudinous seas incarnadine
> Making the green one red.

in the last two lines of which the Latin and the Anglo-Saxon diction
seem deliberately set off in opposition to each other. It is of course
the same contrast, in less striking fashion, that is always to be found
in the English language in actual practice.

Need any preference be given to the native word over the borrowed
or the borrowed word over the native? As we have seen, the history
of the English vocabulary discloses the fact that different eras, as
well as different individuals, have answered this question variously.
Roughly speaking, Old English clung to the native word, Middle

[52] *Op. cit.*, p. 292.

English often preferred the borrowed one, while in the Renaissance the question was hotly debated, and "Latinist" and "Saxonist" ranged themselves into opposing camps. But on the whole, the more liberal attitude toward word-borrowing prevailed in the Renaissance and, after the conservative interlude of the eighteenth century, has prevailed in general through the Modern English period. Not that it is quite satisfactory to generalize to this extent. If the eighteenth century on the whole leans to a simpler and more native diction, it is to be remembered that its prose literature contains, in addition to the more Anglo-Saxon style of a Swift, and Addison, or a Goldsmith, the more elaborate manner of a Johnson, a Gibbon, and a Burke.

The Renaissance debate between Latinist and Saxonist has its occasional echoes in our own day. The advice is frequently given to the student of English composition that "other things being equal, the native word is the better word." This is probably sound enough, if one could be sure when other things are equal. Better advice, quite certainly, is that of William Hazlitt, who maintained [53] that in the choice of words, the principle should be "the best word in common use." Words should be chosen, that is to say, not on the score of etymology but on that of familiarity and the accuracy with which they convey meaning. It will often happen that the accurate and the familiar word is also the native word. So much the better; but the basis of the choice is still not the etymology. *Begin* is a better word than *commence* not because it is the native word and the other the borrowed one, but because, in addition to having precisely the same meaning, it is the more homely and the more familiar. So much faith one may reasonably put in the theory of preferring native to borrowed words. Fortunately it is true, as we have indicated, that the native word, the shorter word, and the familiar word are often one and the same. But this is obviously a very different matter from the policy of seeking out the "Saxon" word as such and substituting it for the borrowed word that is now in more common use. That way lie folly and a pedantry quite as bad as that of the writer of the most inflated academic style. The language is and has long been so thoroughly committed to a composite word-stock that it can never be restored to the standard of "purity." To substitute *folkwain* for

[53] In "On Familiar Style."

omnibus or *steadholder* for *lieutenant* is eccentricity that borders on lunacy.[54]

One word more as to the implications of the composite vocabulary to which Modern English is permanently committed. While it is true that the native and the borrowed word-stocks have to some extent their separate excellences, and even more certain that their combined resources may be skilfully exploited, it must be admitted also that there is something unattractive in the picture of a vocabulary often sharply divided into two parts. The extent of the gulf may easily be exaggerated. For one thing, not all borrowed words are on the same basis. Indeed, in speaking of "native words" it is often customary, and certainly justifiable enough, to include with them Teutonic words of long standing even though not Anglo-Saxon—especially Danish and Dutch words. Furthermore, many French borrowings like *aunt, beef,* and *car* are quite obviously not to be compared with Greek or Latin loan-words like *euhemerism, ratiocination,* or *hyperesthesia.* Nevertheless, it still remains true that there are in general two groups of English words that have little in common, and that they are made up of the native words on the one hand and the borrowed ones on the other. As a result, there is something "undemocratic," as Jespersen has well maintained,[55] in a large portion of the vocabulary, especially the literary vocabulary, of English. Both Jespersen and Bradley have pointed out that some of these are merely eye-words, existing solely on the printed page and without fixed pronunciation. There are many that have a well-established pronunciation but that after all are intelligible only to those with some knowledge of Greek and Latin. Such words can never compete on an equal basis with words that are firmly rooted in an English soil and that strike an immediate response in the hearts as well as the minds of English-speaking peoples. Probably in no other language is it so necessary as it is in English to take definite precautions against using "big" words—words that require some sort of translation in order to be completely understood. It can scarcely be thought of as a source of strength that the danger of "overwriting" and pretentiousness is an ever-present one to him who deals in Eng-

---

[54] For a statement of the issues involved in "Saxonism," see the article of that title in Fowler's *Modern English Usage,* pp. 514-515.

[55] *Growth and Structure,* p. 146. And cf. Bradley's *On the Relations between Spoken and Written Language, with Special Reference to English,* London (Oxford), 1919, p. 26.

lish words. This is not to deny the variety and the richness that the enormous composite vocabulary of English presumes; it is merely to affirm that even in words, there is such a thing as the embarrassment of riches. There are superfluities and ugly excrescences in our dictionaries that could well be pruned away. Be it repeated, however, that the disadvantages of the situation are of less moment than the advantages. If in English the danger of failing to strike the right note is particularly great, it may still be argued that to the real master of the instrument, the more complicated mechanism offers an opportunity for both rich and clear expression that is quite unequaled elsewhere.

REFERENCES FOR FURTHER READING

Björkman, Erik, *Scandinavian Loan Words in Middle English,* Halle (Niemeyer), 1900-1902.

Carr, Charles T., *The German Influence on the English Vocabulary,* S.P.E. Tract No. XLII, Oxford (Clarendon), 1934.

Clark, G. N., *The Dutch Influence on the English Vocabulary,* S.P.E. Tract No. XLIV, Oxford (Clarendon), 1935.

Daryush, A. A., *Persian Words in English,* S.P.E. Tract No. XLI, Oxford (Clarendon), 1934.

Förster, Max, "Keltisches Wortgut im Englischen," *Festgabe für Felix Liebermann,* pp. 119-142, Halle, 1921; and "English-Keltisches," *Englische Studien,* LVI (1922), 204-239.

Johnson, E. L., *Latin Words of Common English,* New York (Heath), 1931.

Kent, R. G., *Language and Philology,* Boston (Marshall Jones), 1923.

Krapp, G. P., *The English Language in America,* New York (Appleton-Century), 1925.

Llewellyn, E. C., *The Influence of Low Dutch on the English Vocabulary,* Publ. of the Philological Society, No. 12, Oxford (Milford), 1936.

Mathews, Mitford M., *A Dictionary of Americanisms,* Chicago (University of Chicago), 1951.

McKnight, G. H., *English Words and Their Background,* New York (Appleton), 1923.

Mencken, H. L., *The American Language,* New York (Knopf), 3rd ed., 1923, and 4th ed., 1936.
See also *Supplement One,* 1945, and *Supplement Two,* 1948, which bring this work up to date.

Praz, Mario, "The Italian Element in English." *Essays and Studies by Members of the English Association,* XV (1929), pp. 20-66, Oxford (Clarendon).

Pyles, Thomas, *Words and Ways of American English,* New York (Random House), 1952.

Serjeantson, Mary S., *A History of Foreign Words in English,* New York (Dutton), 1936.

Smith, Logan P., *The English Language,* New York (Holt), 1912.

Smock, J. C., *The Greek Element in English Words,* New York (Macmillan), 1931.

Taylor, Walt, *Arabic Words in English,* S.P.E. Tract No. XXXVIII, Oxford (Clarendon), 1933.

Chapter 8

The Making of Words

IF THE native element in English is still the part most frequently used, and if the vocabulary drawn from foreign sources has supplemented this enormously, there is yet another source of words: new formations. This does not mean absolutely new creations, words whose components have had no meaning before; for if such there be, they are exceedingly rare. The stock example of a word newly created is *gas*, which was devised in the seventeenth century by the Dutch chemist Van Helmont and adopted for international use. Yet though it had no formal etymology, we know that the word was suggested to its inventor by the Greek *cháos*—so it can hardly be considered an entirely new creation: it clearly carries over part of the form and meaning of the Greek word.

According to Mark Twain, Eve gave the name *dodo* to the bird for the excellent reason that, to her, "it *looked* like a dodo." Here Twain is, of course, getting humor out of a logical circularity, for the name could not have had appropriateness unless the syllables already bore some meaning for Eve. Words and things have no necessary connection; the aptness of a name is therefore something in the mind of the namer, based on observations he makes when applying the name, and on the established structure of his language. In this case, whatever we may think of Eve, the name *dodo* must have had a definite suggestive force for Mark Twain!

Our point is a serious one. Since it has been calculated that there are hundreds and thousands of monosyllables (to say nothing of polysyllables) that *can* be pronounced within the range of English sounds, but which at present are not used as words,[1] one might con-

---

[1] The number of *possible* monosyllables in English was actually calculated by Herbert Spencer; his figure was 108,264. Jespersen, who refers to this, *Mono-*

clude that there is still a great deal of room for absolutely new creations; and no doubt there is some. But the fact is that so many
similar syllables already exist as meaningful words that the new
syllables, by association, would seem at least partly meaningful.
Thus "dat," if it were offered as a verb, would tend to suggest *bat,
pat, dab,* and other such verbs, unless one sought deliberately to
avoid all existing associations. Yet, actually, when new words are
made, such associations are ordinarily sought, not avoided. An example of a recent word whose creator is said to have desired absolute
newness is *Kodak*—originally a trade-name, though it has come to
mean, more generally, a camera of a certain type, not necessarily
made by Eastman. But this word is exceptional; the vast number of
trade-names and other new words directly avail themselves of existing meanings—*Uneeda, Technicolor, Hadacol,* and so on; a few
subtler ones are deliberately indirect, but still seek to suggest: *Dreft*
(drift? draft?), *Drene* (dream? drain?). Nor is this at all surprising;
the word with associations may be remembered more easily. Sheer
creation of words with no previous associations, then, is a rarity
today, and must be consciously sought. Indeed, it is hard to con-
ceive of a time when pure word-creation can have been common; but
if ever there was such a time, it must have been at the very dawn
of human language—much farther back than any records can
possibly take us.[2]

There is another general species of word-creation that extends so
far back into the earlier stages of language that it was formerly
taken[3] to be the only kind of primitive speech, and hence to explain
the very origin of language. This group of words is made up of the
"onomatopoetic" terms—words, that is to say, that "make their own
names." If it were literally true that certain natural, human, or ani-

---

syllabism in English, New York (Oxford), 1929, pp. 8-9, finds the total too
small, and estimates as his own calculation, "rather more than 158,000 monosyllables"; "only a small part . . . occur as actual words in the language"
(p. 13).

[2] This is not the type of word which dictionaries are obliged to label "etymology unknown"; this phrase does not mean that the word to which it is
attached has no past history, as would be the case with a new creation. Words
of unknown etymology have probably been borrowed, or have developed by
one of the recognized processes of word-formation from elements already in
the language; but their source or development cannot be described because
adequate historical evidence is lacking.

[3] Cf. Chapter 1, pp. 5-6.

mal noises *make* the names by which they are known in language, one would be justified in calling this type of formation, in a very strict sense, pure creation. In point of fact, however, no word of any language ever exactly reproduced the sound which it imitated. Hence it seems more accurate, as well as less cumbersome, to label this method of word-making "echoism" (Sir James Murray's term) rather than onomatopoeia, and to recognize that there is an element of conventional symbolism in the echoic words as a group. Yet there is evidently a very real degree of root-creation in these words. Certainly, for *whiz, hiss, fizz, sizzle, twitter,* and *titter,* we need look up no "etymology" in the usual sense of the term; all we do need is the physical context of the sound being imitated in order to recognize that the word is echoic. Not that all echoic words are so nearly accurate. Heavier noises seem less adequately conveyed by such terms as *bang, crash,* and *whack;* but the difference is one of degree rather than kind, [æ] having evidently been taken to stand for a somewhat more solid and resounding noise than [ɪ].[4] In a similar way, *cuckoo* may pass for a satisfactory rendering of the cry made by the bird, and hence for the name of the bird itself; but *bob-white* employs a more far-fetched echoism.[5] Likewise, *miaow* serves more realistically for the cat than *bow-wow* for the dog.

A great deal more might be said on the use of imitation—echoic or symbolic—in the creation of words. If it has not been proved, and it seems altogether unlikely to be proved, that imitation made the first beginnings of human speech, it is evident that it still runs through all human language. Words like *mama, papa,* and *baby* are found in almost all tongues, and the usual explanation of a cognate relationship or of borrowing will scarcely apply.[6] What is almost certain is that the labials [m], [p], and [b] are almost the first sounds any child acquires and that their repetition alternately with open-mouth sounds (vowels) gives the words in question. Imitation, then, on the part of the parents perpetuates their use and conventionalizes their meanings—meanings that are thereupon gradually acquired by the child, also through imitation. There is an obvious

[4] Cf. Bloomfield, *Language,* sec. 14.9, especially p. 245.
[5] Echoism here is affected by *folk-etymology;* see below pp. 253-256.
[6] Jespersen, for example, denies that *papa* and *mama* in English, German, Danish, Italian, and so on are *borrowed* from the same words in French, though it is conceivable that a French fashion may have dictated their continued use beyond the age of the nursery. (*Language,* p. 159)

use of imitation in such echoic words as have been cited in the preceding paragraph, whether the particular interpretation of the sound that forms the word is peculiar to English (as in *fizz, hiss,* and *titter*) or whether it is a borrowing from another language. In point of fact, the imitations that different languages provide for the noises made by animals do vary widely: compare English *tweet-tweet* for the bird's chirp with the French *cui-cui* and the Russian *tsif-tsif.*[7]

In these words and many others, as we may note, the imitation takes an iterative form. Sometimes this is obviously a part of the echoism; again, it may indicate an attempt to suggest repetition, intensification, or some extension of the action or sound imitated. These iteratives have different forms. In the first type, the base is exactly duplicated—so in *tweet-tweet, cuckoo* (despite the spelling), *mama;* in the second type there is an ablaut-like alteration of the second element—so in *bow-wow, tick-tock, zig-zag.* Here, the first part in each case appears to be the meaningful base, while the second (the iteration) is chiefly phonic. In a third type, however (which perhaps should even be classified separately), the second part is also meaningful, whether by accident or by intent: at any rate, the effect is sometimes of linked rime-words—so *tip-top, ship-shape,* passing into *walky-talky* (a portable radio that can send and receive), and its recent offspring *peepie-creepie* (a portable television camera). Though many of these iterative words come in at the level of slang, or at least the colloquial level, many others are of long standing in the language and have achieved acceptance and even literary use. A few typical ones are: *sing-song, tittle-tattle, hoity-toity, pitter-patter;* some are borrowed, as *mish-mash* (from German); other loan-words that are not iterative come into English, however, in that form, as Japanese *hara-kiri* becoming *hari-kari,* African (Senegalese) *mama dyambo* becoming *mumbo-jumbo;* Indian (Urdu) *ya Hasan, ya Hosain* becoming *hobson-jobson;* Latin *hoc est corpus* (probably) becoming *hocus-pocus.* Some recent slang iteratives are *hotsy-totsy, okey-dokey, heebie-jeebie, palsy-walsy, killer-diller, Jeepers-Creepers,* in which the effect of intensification is evidently sought.

When we proceed from echoic imitation to more remote symbolism, we are on dubious ground. Yet it seems quite certain that sound symbolism is more frequently present in the creation of words

[7] Cf. Chapter 1, p. 6.

than people commonly realize.[8] It is not, of course, confined to our language, but Middle and Modern English have been particularly rich in it and may furnish some illustrations. The close vowel [ɪ] is used again and again to stand for small size or slightness: *little, kid, slim, thin, imp, slip, pigmy*.[9] Sometimes the higher and tenser sound [i] is used to suggest a further degree of smallness. Thus, *teeny* is a child's word for *tiny* (*teeny-weeny* or *eentsy-weentsy* means something still more minute), and *leetle* is, in provincial speech, a more intense kind of *little; wee*, and the very common diminutive endings spelled *-y* and *-ie*, and pronounced [i] are further illustrations. Consonants have their symbolic associations as well as vowels. The use of the breath with some force is suggested by *bl* (*blow, blast, blub, blab, bubble, bluster*),[10] an awkward kind of movement by *fl* (*fling, flounce, flounder, flop, flump, flurry*); and the abrupt cessation of sound or movement by the final voiceless stops *p, t*, and *k* (*pop, clip, snip, rap, pat, crack*). Smith points out the neat differentiation between the type of noise or action just mentioned and that symbolized by a final *sh*, in which the sound or movement "does not end abruptly, but is broken down into a mingled mass of smashing or rustling sounds, as in *dash, splash, smash*, etc." [11] Similarly, *hush* indicates cessation of noise, and *sh!* commands silence.

Yet we dare not look for symbolism of this kind everywhere. To do that would be to repeat the erroneous conception of the Greeks as to the *etymology* or the "true meaning" of the word, the doctrine that there is a natural correspondence between sound and sense. It is easy to be deceived here: the words that we are familiar with are apt to strike us as having in their very sounds an inherent appropriateness to the ideas for which they stand—thus with Eve naming the dodo. So, too, the words that evidently *are* in some degree echoic or symbolic are likely to seem the inevitable and perfect combina-

---

[8] One of the few adequate treatments of it is Chapter XX of Jespersen's *Language* (pp. 396-411); for briefer accounts, see Bradley, *Making of English*, pp. 156-159, and L. P. Smith, *English Language*, pp. 101-104. Illustrations from all three sources are used here.

[9] But not always; cf. *big*.

[10] Perhaps the violent expulsion of breath stands symbolically for the idea of a disgusted rejection in another group of *bl* words: *blasted, blamed, bloody, blessed* (ironically used), *blowed, blighted, blooming, blistering, blithering*, and so forth.

[11] *Op cit.*, p. 103.

tion of sounds for the designated purpose. Yet what seems to the native speaker an obvious bit of appropriate symbolism may leave the foreigner cold. He is likely to prefer the rendering of his own language as more accurately descriptive—as, in fact, in every way a "better" word—that is (though he may not realize it), one which better suits the conventions to which he is accustomed. So the German will prefer *flüstern* to the English *whisper*, while to the Frenchman both will seem inferior to *chuchoter*. Such considerations should lead one to go cautiously both in finding symbolism and in deeming even unquestioned examples of it to be the perfect fitting of sound to sense.

The illustrations already cited show how echoism shades into a more conventional symbolism. Echoism and symbolism (together with the rare case of arbitrary recombination of sounds) between them evidently account for a surprisingly large number of words. However, a still more common way of adding to the vocabulary is by making some new use of words or word-elements already existing in the language. The general line of demarcation for the two great types of word-making is that between root-creation on the one hand and what has been called "adaptation," or differentiation, on the other.

Gradation. A type of adaptation which was in earlier times responsible for the similarity in form and sound of a number of groups of words related in meaning is that known as gradation. In Old English the so-called ablaut series of the strong verbs are instances of this kind of variation in form with corresponding variation in meaning. Verbs of the modern language like *ring, rang, rung,* and *drive, drove, driven* perpetuate these gradations, though the number of variants in each series has been reduced from four to three through the loss of one of the two distinctive preterit forms, and often to two through the falling together of preterit and past participle. But gradation is not confined to the variation of verbs. The principle is rather this: A consonantal framework, like *r-d, s-ng,* or *b-r,* stood for a certain generalized idea, and was given specific application by the variation in form of the medial vowel. Thus, one gradation-group included the noun *song,* as well as the verbal forms *sing, sang, sung;* another included not only *ride, rode, ridden,* but also *road* and *raid* (for the *road* was the place of riding, and the *raid* an all too frequent objective—in Old English, "to ride a raid" was an idiom parallel to "to sing a song"). The third, represented by the framework *b-r*, is one of the oldest Indo-European roots; in English it appears not only in *bear, bore, born* and *borne,* but also in the nouns *bairn, birth, bier, barrow,* and *burden.* However, fruitful as this means of building new words was in older stages of the language, it is evident that gradation, as an active principle in word-formation, is virtually defunct. Occasionally we find new forms patterned on the living verb ablauts[12] (*brung* for *brought, fit* for *fought*), but they are either subliterate or are used for humorous effect.

Compounding. A commoner device for word-making—one that has flourished at every period of the English language—is compounding,[13] which consists in joining two or even more words to form a new entity. It is striking that almost any combination of the parts of speech may be employed in this way, though some combinations are far more common than others, some are unusual, and some have not been favored equally in every period. Among the most common are, (1) that of noun with noun: Old English *hwælweg* (whaleway, sea), *brēostcearu* (breast-care, anxiety), *sæclif* (seacliff), and many such might easily turn up today[14]—indeed, some are still used, and certainly the pattern is vigorously alive in *rail-road, chest-cold, house-top, week-end, wood-shed,* and thousands more; (2) that of noun with adjective: Old English *īsceald* (ice-cold), *heortsēoc* (heart-sick), and the more recent *coal-black, air-tight, foot-sore, leak-free,* and so on; (3) that of adjective with noun: *black-berry, hot-house, sweet-meat, big-shot;* (4) that of adverb with noun: *up-shot, over-head, down-fall, off-color, after-thought, under-dog;* (5) that of verb with adverb: *dug-out, walk-over, tie-up, kick-off, shoo-in.* Other combinations—but far less common—are: (6) that of noun with verb: *keel-haul, hand-pick, side-swipe;* (7) that of verb with noun: *cry-baby, play-boy, starboard* (from the Old English words meaning "steering-side"), *pay-dirt;* (8) that of

---

[12] Cf. above, page 137, and also E. Bagby Atwood, *A Survey of Verb Forms in the Eastern United States,* Ann Arbor (University of Michigan), 1953.

[13] We shall limit the term to full-word compounds—those composed of parts that can stand separately. Words composed of a full word and an affix (which cannot stand separately) will be dealt with next, under "Derivation."

[14] Indeed, the poets Gerard M. Hopkins and John Masefield have frequently imitated these "kennings," as they are called.

adjective with verb: *short-cut* (e.g., hair), *close-haul, high-flown*, passing over into the next type; (9) that of adverb with verb: *over-throw, under-staff, off-set, by-pass;* (10) that of noun with adverb: *hands-off, head-on, hindside-to;* (11) that of adverb with adjective: *over-due, ever-green, under-ripe.*

The part of speech so formed may be different from that of either of its components: the adjective *shipshape* is made up of noun and noun, the noun *upset* of adverb and verb (actually by conversion of the previously compounded verb), the noun *lean-to* of verb and adverb; the adjective *off-hand* of adverb and noun; the verb *atone* of preposition and numeral. Finally, it is not at all uncommon to find three words forming a compound, as in *nevertheless, notwithstanding, hand-to-mouth, out-and-out, brother-in-law.* And even complete clauses—particularly in oft-repeated greetings—combine into words: *howdyedo, fare-thee-well, goodbye* (reduced from *God-be-with-you*).

It should be observed that a number of our early native compounds have died out or have been replaced with French or Latin borrowings that are not compounds, as when *treasure* replaced *gold-hoard* and when *medicine* superseded *leech-craft.* Latin (to some extent) and French lack the compound-making ability of English; extensive borrowing from them, therefore, did nothing to support the device in English. Some go further and argue that the ability of English to form compounds has actually been impaired by the additions from French and Latin. But this claim is dubious, to say the least; for the borrowed words, once naturalized, have themselves entered freely into new compounds (e.g., *treasure-chest, medicine-bottle*), and the "displaced" Old English compounds have been more than compensated for numerically by new compounds. Among the examples just cited the reader must have noted many that are obviously very new. The only pattern that has suffered some diminution of use is that—very vigorous in Old English—of adverb and verb (or verbal form) as in *output, income, uprising, downtrodden.* Yet at least in Scottish[15] and United States usage (the former more conservative, the latter perhaps strengthened by the Germanic influence in American speech) this pattern is by no means dead—witness the recent *uptake, outgo, upkeep,* and *outcome* (introduced into literary use by Carlyle, long objected to, but now fully ac-

[15] Bradley, *op. cit.*, p. 124.

James Moncrief Brailsford, III

cepted).[16] Perhaps the only broad generalization that can safely be made about these compounds is that the less common patterns do not find as much favor at the literary level as in everyday use. Compounding generally, however, still flourishes as a major means of adding to the vocabulary.

Before leaving this subject it might be appropriate to point out that the natural tendency to economize effort is constantly at work reducing compounds—not merely by abbreviation of words (of which we shall see more later) but also by phonetic change.[17] Accentuation plays a part, for example, when words that were fully stressed to begin with—such as *hót hóuse* and *ráil róad*—lose some stress on one element and alter their pitch pattern as they combine: *hóthòuse, ráilròad.* (We do not often indicate this by respelling, but *spoon full* becoming *spoonful* is an example, or *awe full* becoming *awful.*) Eventually the reduction of stress on one word of the combination may change it to the point where it is no longer able to stand alone. The classical example is what has become of the word *like,* now a mere suffix in *friendly, softly,* and other such words; parallel is the reduction of *on* to the prefix *a-* in such words as *aback, aright, away.* When this happens, of course, only the historian of language is aware that the new word was once a compound; it has lost the obvious, analyzable form of compounds. Many a word today is much farther changed even than these from its former state—for example *lord* from Old English *hlāf-weard* (bread-keeper), *barn* from Old English *bere-ærn* (barley-place), *world* from Old English *wer-eld* (age of man); less hidden are the components of *hussy* (a reduced form of *housewife*), *daisy* (for *day's eye*), *don* and *doff* (for *do on* and *do off*). Accompanying these changes of form, of course, are noticeable changes of meaning: *holiday* is no longer equivalent to *holy day* or *bonfire* to *bone fire.* We may note in pass-

---

[16] The "fixing" of Modern English word-order, so that modifiers do not obscure the framework of subject-predicate-object (or complement), may have something to do with this. Certainly, today the adverb more often follows the verb, as in class (5) above, p. 191. In Old English the opposite order, "up-tie," "over-walk," "off-kick," and so forth, would have been much more natural. The most startling such combination that I have heard was produced by a policeman in St. Louis in 1950. When questioned as to the speed limit in Missouri, he replied, "There's no limit, as long as you don't *reckless-drive.*" (This, of course, is really a verb analyzed out of the adjective-noun phrase *reckless driving.*)

[17] Cf. Chapter 4, p. 82 ff.

ing that the accentual pattern of compounds is more decisively changed when they are used in modifying position—indeed, some words do not appear to form a compound until they are so used—for example, *one-way* street, *fair-weather* friend, *all-out* attack.

Derivation. Another very common process of word-making is that by which a new entity is *derived* not from independent words (as in compounding) but from a single full word plus a prefix or suffix. As we have just seen, some elements of compounds lose their independent status and become prefixes or suffixes; in such cases, the historical descendants of elements that formerly produced compounds now produce derivatives: Old English *cyndelīc* was a compound, from which the modern *kindly* is descended, but *stupidly* is a derivative or derived form, made after the suffix -*ly* had come into being. Only if one looks historically at *kindly* and *stupidly* does this distinction become clear; seen synchronically the words appear to be of like formation. A similarly subtle line is drawn between derivation of this kind and inflection: to form a past tense in Modern English by adding -*ed* to a newly created verb (e.g., *televised*), or to add -*er* to make a new noun of agency (e.g., *televiser*), is to do something that could be done, and has been done, in all stages of the language; the line separating these two processes, so that one is called grammatical inflection and the other derivation, is more traditional than real.

But not all prefixes and suffixes remain both so vital and so unchanged in their use as -*er*. There was, for example, in Old English a feminine suffix for nouns of agency, -*estre*. In the form -*ster* this lingers on in *spinster* (originally "spinning woman"), *tapster*, and the proper names *Webster* and *Baxter*.[18] The last two meant, of course, "weaving woman" and "baking woman"; variant forms of the masculine gave *Baker* for the one and *Webb*, *Weber*, and *Weaver* for the other. (*Hunt* and *Hunter* are somewhat similar doublets, representing Old English *hunta* and *huntere*—both "hunter.") The feminine suffix -*stere* was fairly common in Middle English: Chaucer

---

[18] The *Oxford Dictionary* explains that Old English *bœcestre* is one of the few instances in which the suffix was used also as masculine; this was so because it was a rendering of a Latin designation (*pistor*) of men exercising a function which among the English was peculiar to women. (It should be added that Jespersen has attacked this, and indeed the usual explanation of the -*ster* suffix as a whole. His opinion, which has been widely accepted, is that it was from the first used for both sexes. See his *Linguistica*, Copenhagen, 1933, pp. 420-429.)

uses *beggestere, tombestere, frutestere,* and *hoppestere.* In Modern English, apparently, *-ster* has so far lost its sense of feminine suffix of agency that it is necessary to supplement it with a borrowed suffix of the same significance, *-ess,* as is done in *seamstress* and *song-stress.* Perhaps confusion with the same final sounds in a borrowed word like *minister* or *register* has helped to obscure the original significance; at any rate, *gangster, huckster, teamster,* and *youngster* illustrate a new use of *-ster* that owes nothing to the basic meaning of Old English *-estre.*

Many prefixes and suffixes can be used freely in forming new words, and the sense given to the new formation is precisely what the prefix or suffix has always had. Thus, *-ly* can be freely attached to nouns to manufacture new adjectives, like *manly, womanly,* and *gentlemanly.* The native negative prefix *un-*—though in rivalry with the Latin *in-,* so that it is not always easy to say which is appropriate in a given case—can be used very often indeed to make an adjective take an opposite meaning. Another *un-,* though of separate origin, has a similar effect upon the meaning of a verb to which it is attached, so that *undress* and *unfold* are the opposites of the simple verbs. Curiously, however, *un-* seems to have no effect on the meaning of a few verbs already indicating something negative or destructive: *ravel* and *unravel, loosen* and *unloosen* (like *annul* and *disannul*), mean much the same thing.

Though a number of Old English affixes, such as *ed-, ge-, -els,* and *-ol,* have disappeared in the course of time, others still used in making new words are *be-, mis-, -ness, -less, -ful, -y,* and *-ish.* A few of these, however, have taken on a connotation that is not at all implied in their earlier use. The use of *be-* in older formations like *beset, bespeak,* and *bestir* seems to be without the derogatory suggestion that it has acquired in such words as *befog, bemuddle, bemuse, bedizen,* and so forth. Even more clearly, *-ish* has changed both from its original use of merely forming an adjective from a noun (as in Old English *folcish,* meaning "folkish," corresponding to the later borrowing *popular*) and from its later use after an adjective to limit its quality (especially in adjectives of color, like *reddish* and *brownish*). The present implication of *-ish* is decidedly uncomplimentary: we can no longer use Chaucer's word *heavenish,* but we *can* use *hellish*—and *devilish, knavish, fiendish, foolish,* and *thievish.* *Boyish* and *girlish* will perhaps still pass muster as terms that need not be malicious; but *mannish* is far from the equivalent of *virile* or *manly*, and *womanish* is akin to *effeminate* rather than *womanly*. Borrowed suffixes, incidentally, are quite as likely as native ones to take on connotations that limit their use for new formations. The suffix *-ard*, immediately French but ultimately German, has gone in this way: its use is limited to such contemptuous terms as *dullard, coward, sluggard, bastard,* and *drunkard*.

The mention of a borrowed affix introduces another consideration. Derivation in Middle and Modern English has made a very extensive use of foreign prefixes and suffixes as well as native ones. Most speakers of English probably are conscious of no difference in quality between the affixes enumerated above that we have inherited from Old English and the very numerous ones that we have borrowed. A few examples of the latter class are these: Latin *pro-, post-, pre-, ante-, super-, -ation,* and *-ative;* French *dis-, en-, -al, -ment, -able, -ous,* and *-ary* (all, of course, ultimately Latin); Spanish or Italian (through French) *-ade;* Greek *a-, hyper-, -ist, -ize, -ism, -ic, -itis,* and so forth. Almost all of these would be used with considerable freedom in building new words. The purist's sense of shock at the sight of a new word consisting of native base with borrowed affix (or conversely) is not experienced by the man in the street. Granted that hybrid combinations of this sort are often needlessly indulged in, it is still evident that to rule them out as a class would be to rob the language of some of its finest and best-established words. To take a single type, consider only how the native suffix *-ful* has been combined with foreign words: a very few are *useful, graceful, merciful, beautiful, grateful,* and *plentiful*. If the word is sufficiently established as English, it can be joined with any native affix that is really living, no matter what its own ultimate origin may have been. Thus, *class* and *cry* are French borrowings, but their status is far from that of aliens; their union with the native prefix *out-* in *outclass* and *outcry* can occasion uneasiness only to the pedant. Our illustrations have been of foreign root and native affix; but the opposite combination is just as familiar, as is evident when one considers how easy it is to multiply words of the type of *amazement, rebuild, goddess, co-worker, dishearten,* and *anteroom*.

One reason for what is, from one point of view, the incongruity of such compounds as those cited above is of course very obvious. Not all affixes remain in living use. Sometimes a foreign affix has to be used to remove a deficiency in the supply of native prefixes and suffixes, or a native one has to be used much more widely. Thus *-th*, once used in forming such indispensable nouns as *wealth, health, filth, youth, growth, warmth, strength,* and *breadth,* has fallen into disfavor. *Growth* appears to be the latest of this group, dating from the Elizabethan period; but Francis Bacon's *lowth*[19] has not stuck, nor have more recent attempts to use the suffix *-th*—like *greenth* (Horace Walpole), *illth* (Ruskin), and *coolth* (H. G. Wells).[20] The *-th* has been forced to defer to *-ness,* which is not only one of the oldest, but still the most active, of native suffixes; we have not only *greenness, illness,* and *coolness,* but even *warmness* and *broadness* by the side of *warmth* and *breadth,* and *youthfulness* and *mirthfulness* in addition to *youth* and *mirth.* Words that once had the suffixes *-ship, -head,* and *-dom* have likewise conformed to the modern preference for *-ness;* and only very exceptionally do new formations (*chairmanship, boredom*) use these suffixes. Only *-ness,* incidentally, seems to have withstood the remarkable progress of *-ism,* a suffix that English borrowed through French and Latin from Greek. The very mention of it, with its suggestion of the prevalence of *"isms"* in our time, is perhaps enough to indicate how our native affixes have often yielded ground to borrowed ones.

Insofar as this represents a loss to the resources of the language, the literary artist may well regret that several of our native affixes are no longer active: they cannot be used to derive new words. The things that they expressed can still be said, of course, but there is one way less of saying them. A particularly regrettable loss of this kind is that of the old prefix *for-,* which was once widely used with an intensive or privative sense. It is still found, certainly, in a number of words like *forbid, forgive, forgo,* and *forlorn,*[21] but others,

[19] Apparently on the analogy of *highth,* the older and still a popular form of *height.*

[20] These are cited by Smith, pp. 91-92, and by McKnight, *English Words and Their Backround,* pp. 173-174. (But the *Oxford Dictionary* dates *coolth* from 1594; Wells's use of it, then, is either a re-creation or a revival.)

[21] Cf. the similar force of German *ver-* in words like *verboten* and *verloren.* This *ver-* is, of course, cognate with English *for-,* but it has remained active, as *for-* has not. For another interpretation of some of the *for-* compounds, disagreeing with that in the *Oxford Dictionary,* see a note (pp. 780-781) in F. N. Robinson's edition of Chaucer (Houghton, Mifflin).

like *forspent* and *fordone*, have become archaic, and still others are completely gone. A line in Chaucer's *Book of the Duchess* (1. 126),

And she, *forweped* and *forwaked*,

("wept out" and "watched out"—i.e., "worn out with weeping and watching") illustrates the fine expressiveness of these old formations. That the sense of the prefix has been quite lost is illustrated by the fact that the meaning of *forlorn* has changed from the etymological one of "completely lost" to the vaguer one of "wretched"; and though the participle *forlorn* survives, the other parts of the verb *forlose* are gone.[22] *Forgo*, too, is used with so little appreciation of the force of its prefix that it has been possible to confuse it with *forego* (go before, precede), now familiar only in *foregoing* and in the (Shakespearean) phrase "foregone conclusion." Indeed, the spelling *forego* is quite frequently used (and accepted by dictionaries) for the meaning "do without," evidently because *fore-* is in living use and *for-* is not.

The objection of the purist to the hybrid compound has sometimes been successful in recasting the word—more frequently where the objection was to native affix plus foreign base; for foreign affixes, curiously enough, display more vitality than native ones. Even the most vigorous of native suffixes, *-ness*, has often given way in the interest of harmonious derivation, as when *morbidness* yields to *morbidity* and *simpleness* to *simplicity*. No satisfactory distinction between the rival negative prefixes, native *un-* and borrowed *in-* (or *im-*, *il-*, or *ir-*) has been worked out; but the tendency has been for *in-* to supersede *un-* as the prefix for many compounds in which the base is a borrowing. Thus, *unglorious, unpossible, unpatient, unfirm,* and *unexperienced* were quite reputable words in Middle or early Modern English; but only *inglorious, impossible, impatient, infirm,* and *inexperienced* will pass muster now. On the other hand, *unpleasant, undesirable, unprogressive,* and many others witness the retention of *un-* before a borrowed word. Occasionally both native and borrowed affixes may be used, and the variants may then be differentiated in one way or another. A regional preference is seen in the British

[22] "Forlorn hope" is an early Modern English borrowing from Dutch, meaning a "lost band (of soldiers)," and therefore preserving the old sense of *forlorn*; but even this expression has changed meaning, until it does not necessarily mean "lost" today but sometimes only "desperate."

insanitary, meaning the same as American *unsanitary;* more often the difference is one of meaning: thus *unbelief* and *disbelief, mistrust* and *distrust,* are by no means synonymous; nor have *uninterested* and *disinterested* been so regarded in the past, though a present tendency, even in fairly careful use, seems to disregard this useful discrimination in meaning.

Something further may appropriately be said on the topic of hybrid formations, whether by compounding or by derivation. The extreme puristic position would be that not only words made up of native and borrowed parts, but also words that bring together constituents from more than one foreign language, should alike be ruled out. Even this position, it may be remarked in passing, is something of a compromise for the "Saxonist," who would discard all foreign elements from the language; but there is of course no need to take this last point of view very seriously. The objection to the hybrid compound, however, is less fanatical in character, and deserves at least a hearing. The opinion has been frequently voiced that *automobile* is an objectionable formation because the first part is Greek and the second Latin. It is true that the word has come to be less and less commonly used; in American English, *machine* (or the shortened *auto*) was the popular substitute a generation ago, and *car* is the present favorite. But this is obviously because *automobile* is felt to be longer than need be,[23] rather than because it is a hybrid. It is most unlikely that people in general realize that such a word as *aquaplane* is a "good" compound while *hydroplane* and *seaplane* are "bad" ones. The three words, of course, are equally acceptable.

Actually, hybrids are to be found in all periods of the language, even in the less mixed and more conservative vocabulary of Old English; *priesthood* (O.E. *prēosthād*) is typical of a fruitful species of hybrid established very early. In Middle English this kind of formation[24] and also its opposite variety (native base plus foreign element) are very common—a fact which testifies the extent to which the language has become saturated with foreign borrowings. Thus the present addition of hybrid formations to the vocabulary has

[23] Speakers of English are not the only ones who have this feeling; the word is abbreviated also in French and German to *auto,* and to *bil* in the Scandinavian languages. See Jespersen, *Mankind, Nation, and the Individual,* p. 124.

[24] Jespersen (*Growth and Structure,* p. 106) observes that most other languages frequently indulge in this too, but much more rarely in the other type than does English.

long-standing precedent. The present-day objector must realize this at least unconsciously, since his complaint is usually limited to particular words which have stirred his opposition—one sometimes wonders why. Forty-odd years ago, Krapp[25] noted the purist's objection to *racial* on the ground that, in the words of the authors of *The King's English*, "the terminal *-al* has no business at the end of a word that is not obviously Latin"; today this objection seems something of a curiosity, for *racial* has found its way into excellent and general use. One wonders whether such critics would object not only to *tidal* (English and Latin) and to *postal* (French and Latin) but also to *phenomenal* (Greek and Latin). In the interests of consistency, of course, they should; but (perhaps happily) consistency has never been attained in such matters.

Another termination that the purist would seek to restrict in use is the Greek suffix *-ist*. Clearly, *-ist* is even more active than the Latin *-al*, and it seems utterly futile to attempt to limit its use to words in which it is joined with a Greek stem. The objection breaks down in practice, certainly, for Latin-Greek formations like *socialist, florist, jurist,* and *nihilist* are quite as well established as consistently Greek ones like *economist* and *atheist*. *Scientist*, as perhaps not every American knows, was long objected to as a reprehensible American innovation.[26] If any principle is to rule in these matters, it would seem to be that each word should be considered on its individual merits; the necessity for the word and the utility of the word should surely outweigh any considerations of "linguistic harmony." *Deist* proved to be a useful companion to *theist*, though one was "correctly" formed and the other not. Since *physician* meant "practitioner of medicine," there was room for *physicist* ("correctly" formed, by the way).

A word that has recently gained currency within the teaching profession is *educationist*. This is perhaps a fair example of the kind of formation that, from one point of view, would have "made Quintilian stare and gasp." But has it not a *raison d'être? Educator*

---

[25] *Modern English*, p. 273.

[26] Nevertheless it is not of American origin. Actually, it was a creation of William Whewell, who in his *Philosophy of Inductive Sciences* (1840) writes, "We need very much a name to describe a cultivator of science in general. I should incline to call him a Scientist." Smith, L. P., "Needed Words," *S.P.E. Tract No. XXXI* (1928).

was too general and *educationalist* too lengthy, as well as outmoded. What was wanted was an agent-noun that would correspond to the specialized meaning that *education* has acquired in the present curriculum of the American college. *Pedagogy* has fallen into disfavor and *Education* (often the capital *e* distinguishes it from the general *education*) has replaced it. Hence, while an *educator* is concerned with *education*, it is an *educationist* who is concerned with *Education*. If it be objected that there is a slight flavor of contempt about the word as it is used in some professional publications, it may be replied that possibly that is not unintentional. A word in *-ist* frequently seems to be used by those to whom the idea for which it stands is repellent; such is a common connotation for words like *nudist, Fascist, nihilist, faddist, plagiarist, tourist, publicist, elocutionist, purist, alarmist, militarist, pacifist, defeatist,* and *extremist* (and even *chemist* is described by the *Oxford Dictionary* as perhaps contemptuous in origin). The educationists may console themselves with the thought that many a name intended to be derogatory has in the course of time become favorable as general opinion toward its bearers changed.[27]

What has been said on the hybrid compound is not a plea for unrestricted freedom in introducing new words the parts of which are taken from various languages. There is no reason why consistency of the kind indicated should not have been followed in the coining of new scientific terms. *Univalent* and *unimolecular,* for example, are as good in every way as the competing hybrid terms *monovalent* and *monomolecular.* Likewise it would seem to be only sensible to use the Greek prefix *hyper-* rather than the Latin *super-* to intensify the meaning of an obviously Greek formation. *Superheterodyne* is a quite unnecessary monstrosity, and *superheterodyne-plus* makes matters just a little worse. But the English language is altogether too much of a hybrid in general for the principle of purity in word-formation (as well as in vocabulary on the whole) to have wide application. Consider, to take a stock illustration, the implication of such a form as *re-macadamized.* Here is a word that will not strike most of its users as in any way objectionable or eccentric. Yet *re-* is Latin, *mac* is Celtic, *adam* is Hebrew, *-ize* is French (originally Greek), and *-d* is English. This of course is an extreme case; but on

[27] See below, Chapter 9, pp. 243-244.

a smaller scale such mixtures are by no means exceptional in English. In the light of this, "purity" in word-formation must seem an impossible objective.

Not that such formations are often conscious or controlled; indeed, one senses rather in many recent formations a spirit similar to that of the Elizabethans, a stomach for words however outrageous or grotesque. We, too, strut and attitudinize in words. From *cafeteria* we detach *-teria* and with cheerful indiscrimination make *serveteria, gasateria,* and so on; from *automat* (itself a stump-word or back-formation) we detach *-omat* and make *laundromat;* from *auditorium* we detach *-torium* and make *lubritorium;* and—surely the apical example—from *hamburger* we detach *-burger* and make *steakburger, cheeseburger, deerburger, Ike-burger,* and many others. Actually, *hamburger* comes from *Hamburg-er,* and has no ham in it; the new suffix *-burger* must be defined as meaning "sandwich made with a round bun," and the base to which it is added may refer to its contents, to someone famous, or to whatever strikes the creator's whim. In such formations, in which the analogy itself is mistaken, logic has been banished and chaos is come again. The modern spirit, however, seems to spout up such words with a prodigious satisfaction that laughs at logic.

Back-Formation. Compounding and derivation add longer words to the vocabulary, but there are also several processes which form new words by shortening. One of these is "back-formation" (the term was Sir James Murray's) in which the existing word is mistakenly analyzed, and its supposed base (for it is taken to be a derived form) becomes the new "back-formed" word. The most typical variety is this: From a noun ending in *-er, -ar,* or *-or* a new verb is created, on the assumption that what preceded the supposed suffix of agency is a verbal stem.[28] Thus the new verb *edit* has been produced by back-formation from the noun *editor,* though the *-or* is an integral part of the word as it was borrowed. The probable etymology of *beggar* is that it comes from the French *Beghard,* the name of a mendicant order. If this is correct, the verb *beg* is a back-formation, and a very early one; the assumption was, of course, that the *-ar* of the word borrowed in Middle English in the form *beggar* was a suffix like the *-er* of *baker.* Similarly, the noun *pedlar* is a great

---

[28] For the theory, and numerous illustrations of this type, see Jespersen, "A Few Back-Formations," *Englische Studien,* LXX (1935), pp. 117-122.

deal older than the verb *peddle*. This kind of formation is indulged in popularly much more freely than in more elevated speech. Thus *burgle*, from the noun *burglar*, said to have been created by W. S. Gilbert for the line (in a song in *The Pirates of Penzance*)

> When the enterprising burglar's not a-burgling,

would probably seem out of place in formal use; and the status of *buttle* (from *butler*), *sculp*[29] (from *sculptor*), and *ush* (from *usher*) is even more dubious. Often, of course, such creations are humorous nonce-words, as in *bish* for "officiate as bishop" in a question quite naturally asked concerning a bishop whose activities had appeared to be more largely financial and political than ecclesiastical: "When does the bishop bish?"[30]

Back-formation, however, has also produced many fully accepted words. The verbs *diagnose* (from *diagnosis*), *rove* (from *rover*), and *grovel* (from *groveling*, quite naturally misunderstood as a present participle, when it is, historically, an adverb employing the old termination *-ling*—like *darkling* and *sidling*, from which also the new verbs *darkle* and *sidle* have been formed) are quite reputable, as are also the nouns *greed* (from the adjective *greedy*) and *gloom*[31] (from *gloomy*). But there are many more words of this kind that remain jocular, slangy, or colloquial. A few examples are the words *jell* (from the noun *jelly*), *enthuse* (to be enthusiastic), *reminisce* (to indulge in reminiscences), *emote* (to express emotion), *orate* (from *oration*), *peeve* (from *peevish*), *frivol*, and *resurrect*. The English commentator would doubtless add to the list of back-formations of questionable standing the verb *donate*, a back-formation from *donation* that the *Oxford Dictionary* terms not only "chiefly U.S." but (in the sense of "grant, give") "vulgar" as well.

Another type of back-formation is seen in the dropping of a final *-s* that has been misunderstood as a plural ending though it actually belongs to the stem of the word in question. Thus *pease* (preserved in *peaseporridge*) is historically a singular. Middle English *pese*

[29] The appearance of this newspaper headline (referring to an interview with Mrs. Clare Sheridan on her return from Russia) is a little startling: "Trotsky Described by Woman Who Sculped Him."

[30] Quoted by Robert Withington in *American Speech*, Vol. VI, No. 4 (April, 1931), p. 279.

[31] This seems to be true of the word at least in its modern sense of "darkness," a sense which apparently we owe to Milton. For a fuller statement, see Bradley, *Making of English*, pp. 233-234.

(Old English *pise* from Latin *pisum*) had *pesen* as its plural; *peas* singular and *peasen* plural were still in use in the seventeenth century, but *pea* has long since become the accepted singular, and *peas* is forced to do service as a plural. *Shay* (*chay*) is a seventeenth-century shortening of *chaise*, through the same process; but in this instance the omission of the final -*s* has never become standard. *Skate, riddle, burial, cherry* (cf. French *cerise*), *sherry*, are further illustrations of the loss of an original final -*s* that has become reputable. The popular tendency to create a new singular for apparent plurals in -*s* is seen in such forms as *Chinee* and *Portugee*. British and American usage differ in regard to *innings:* in cricket it is an *innings*, but in baseball an *inning*.

Shortening. By far the most common form of word-formation by shortening is that of simple abbreviation. A word may be lopped at either end: what remains over is the new word; and both the old and the new may then subsist at different levels of the language, or they may compete against each other for sole acceptance. One type may be described in the words of Jonathan Swift, from an unfavorable comment on processes active in the English of his day that appeared in the *Tatler* for September 28, 1710 (No. 230): "The next refinement, which consists in pronouncing the first syllable in a word that has many, and dismissing the rest; such as *phizz, hipps* [for *hypochondriacs*], *mobb, pozz* [for *positive*], *rep* [for *reputation*] and many more, when we are already overloaded with monosyllables, which are the disgrace of our language." It happens that, of these shortenings, only *mob* (from *mobile vulgus*) is standard English today; it was on the way to becoming so, in fact, in Swift's own day, for he observes elsewhere in this essay: "I have done my utmost for some years past to stop the progress of *mobb* and *banter*, but have been plainly borne down by numbers, and betrayed by those who promised to assist me." *Phiz, rep*, to be *hipped* on something, and the variant form *hypo*, however, are still recognizable as colloquialisms; and the general process of shortening by clipping off the final syllable or syllables is one that has created many abbreviations that have, often in standard use as well, superseded the fuller words. *Piano* (for *pianoforte*), *gin*[32] (for *geneva*), *miss* (for *mistress*), *wag* (from *wag-halter;* i.e., "one fit to be hanged," a "rascal"—the sense

---

[32] Likewise, *brandy* (for *brandywine*), *grog* (for *grogram*), *hock* (for *Hockheimer*), *rum* (for *rumbullion*), and *whisky* (for *usquebaugh*).

of "wit" is comparatively recent), *curio* (for *curiosity*), *hobby* (for *hobby horse*), *gas* (for *gasoline*), *brig* (for *brigantine*), *fad* (for *fadaise*), and *fan* (for *fanatic*) are typical.

Jespersen makes the interesting suggestion[33] that "stump-words," as he labels them, are really of two classes: those abbreviated by the adult and those abbreviated by the child and later adopted by adults. According to this theory, the adult omits the latter part (or parts) of the word, and the child the first. The shortenings so far alluded to would then be adult shortenings only, the abbreviation being dictated by the feeling of the speaker or writer that the word might be clipped off as soon as enough of it has been given to make it intelligible. *Photo* conveys the meaning as fully as *photograph*, and *auto* as fully as *automobile*. It is certainly true that school abbreviations like *prof* for *professor*, *gym* for *gymnasium*, and *trig* for *trigonometry* are conscious and un-childlike shortenings in that the part retained is not the part most heavily stressed; no more is it in many another modern word such as *bus, phone, plane* (for *airplane*). In support of Jespersen's idea, the observation may be offered that *professor* as pronounced by a little girl of five became not *prof* but *'fessor*, just as *expression* became *'spression*, and *remember* became *'member*. The process is clearly different, since the child was evidently attempting to repeat as much of the word as she had remembered. However, though Jespersen's suggestion is a keen one, it cannot be accepted without qualification, for it would imply that all stump-words which omit the beginning of the word (and they are quite numerous) must have originated in childish mispronunciation. A few examples that have become standard, and that do not bear this implication out, are: *wig* (*periwig*), *drawing-room* (*withdrawing-room*), *still* (*distillery*), *sport* (*disport*), *spite* (*despite*), *mend* (*amend*), *tend* (*attend*), *lone* (*alone*), *fend* (*defend*), and *fence* (*defence*). The process, as we can see, has sometimes enriched the vocabulary by adding a shorter word which neither supersedes the longer one nor is synonymous with it: there is a useful differentiation in meaning or use between *tend* and *attend, mend* and *amend*, and *lone* and *alone*.

Conversion. Still another process by which the vocabulary is increased is by the *conversion* of one part of speech into another—also known as "functional shift." As the terms imply, the form of the

---

[33] *Language*, pp. 169-171.

word remains unchanged, but it is used in a different grammatical function, which, in effect, makes it a new word. Certainly, a new part of speech has been added. This process, though it has existed at all stages of the language,[34] has flourished most in Modern English; indeed, the easy convertibility of words today has gone far toward changing the meaning of the term "part of speech."

Though this kind of interchangeableness is not peculiar to English —we find it very early in the development of the Indo-European family—it is natural that widespread inflectional loss in English, together with the marked phonetic changes that have accompanied the loss, should have made the parts of speech, particularly in more recent English, much less fixed quantities than they are in most languages. When, through the loss of inflectional endings, it is no longer possible to tell a noun from a verb by its form, or an adjective from a noun, it is hardly to be wondered at that verbs should be used freely as nouns, nouns as verbs, and adjectives as nouns. A recent development of the language of the movies will illustrate. The word *feature* may be used alone as a noun; it may be used in the modifying position, in *feature picture* (in both cases with the sense of "principal item on the program"); or it may be used as a verb, in the phrase "to *feature* (a certain player)." This kind of thing could hardly have been done in Old English. To form a verb from a noun one added a suffix, or made other changes in its form. Thus from the noun *dōm* (judgment) was formed the verb *dēman* (to judge). But when we want to do the same thing today we merely take the noun *doom* and convert it without further ado to the verb *doom*.

Such a free interchange of functions is a marked characteristic of Modern English, Elizabethan as well as contemporary. The variety of it that perhaps meets us most commonly is the conversion of noun into verb. *Bell, bridge, color, ditch, ink, paper,* and *stone* are a few random examples of the numerous nouns, native and borrowed, that may be used as verbs. Jespersen lists twenty-three nouns for various parts of the body[35] all of which have been used in Modern English also as verbs. A few of these, like *to chin* and *to jaw,* are not in elevated use; a few others, like *to lip* (kiss), *to tongue, to fist,* and *to knee* (kneel) are Shakespearean rather than contemporary;

[34] Cf. a recent study by Donald W. Lee, *Functional Change in Early English,* Menasha (Banta) 1948.
[35] *Growth and Structure,* p. 167.

but most of the list, like *to eye, to elbow, to shoulder, to hand, to skin, to stomach,* and so forth, are in reputable present-day use.

A striking contemporary aspect of the shift under consideration is the tendency to make technical or occupational verbs out of nouns that are often awkwardly lengthy. There are the commercial verbs *to requisition* and *to recondition,* the librarians' verb *to accession,* the publishers' verb *to remainder* (to dispose cheaply of the unsold *remainder* of an edition), and the electricians' (or aviators'?) verb *to contact,* which, despite much condemnation heaped upon it, has found more and more use in connection with all kinds of negotiations. Another recent converted form, with specialization of meaning, is the verb *to service.* As a verb, *service* seems to have acquired, in American use at any rate, the curious significance of "oil, grease, or overhaul generally" almost any kind of mechanism. A similar transfer is the verb *process;* almost anything can now be *processed,* from cheese to army personnel—indeed, the implications of an impersonal, mechanical *process* carry over far too truly when it concerns human beings.

Incidentally, a noun need not be long in the language before it can be turned into a verb—witness what has happened to the recent borrowings from French, *sabotage* and *camouflage.* They are not only nouns, as when they came in, but verbs too, and quite as often.

Verbs can be turned into nouns with somewhat less facility than nouns into verbs, but the process is even more a distinguishing peculiarity of Modern English. The way was fully open for it, as for the reverse process, when the final *-e,* the last remnant of the former varied inflectional endings of verbs, disappeared in the late Middle English period. Nouns of course can be formed from verbs by the addition of suffixes like *-tion* and *-ment,* or by the use of the participial *-ing;* the availability of these for derivation somewhat lessens the number of nouns that might otherwise be made by conversion. There is also the alternative of employing a borrowed noun to correspond in meaning, though not in its base, to a native verb: thus we have pairs like *to win, victory; to climb, ascent; to break, fracture* —though, to be sure, *win, climb,* and *break* can themselves be used as nouns. Similarly, the use of nominal suffixes like *-tion* and *-ment* and *-ing* does not throw out the possibility of turning the simple verb directly into a noun: one may speak of a *combine* as well as a *combination,* a *visit* as well as a *visitation,* a *move* as well as a *move-*

ment, a *kill* as well as a *killing,* and a *meet* as well as a *meeting.* It will be noticed that nouns made directly from verbs have rather frequently a somewhat colloquial or slangy character: a *show,* a *sell,* a *hit,* an *assist* (the baseball term), a *catch,* a *spin,* a *kick,* a *read,* a *shave,* a *smoke,* a *say,* a *think,* a *bathe,* and a *find* are scarcely possible in elevated diction. Not that the verb made into the noun *must* bear any such stigma. There is perhaps no suggestion of this kind about most of the numerous verbs of motion that are commonly used as nouns[36]—a group that will also serve as well as any other to illustrate once more the easy interchangeability of verb and noun: *walk, run, leap, jump, hop, limp, stumble, stroll, saunter,* and so forth.

What are we to think of the effect of conversion, based as it is on a lessening of the formal distinction between parts of speech? Is there not some loss of intelligibility or expressiveness? Strictly speaking, this is not a linguistic question at all; yet it certainly concerns those who value the language as a communicative and artistic medium. The older school of philologists, inheriting a long tradition (with an obvious strain of Platonism) saw all linguistic change as evidence of decay—particularly when, as here, categories formerly distinct were merged and their separateness was lost. The widely held belief that categories of grammar corresponded to modes of the mind no doubt mingled in this view, so that the change in grammatical patterns appeared to indicate an actual weakening of the resources for thought. But modern opinion no longer holds these views. We know too much about the great variety of ways in which language works, the world over, to hold much with theories of "universal grammar." Nor can we any longer deplore change as such. We know that change in language is inevitable, and the eighteenth-century attempts to "fix" the language and to prevent change seem as pitiful as the attempt of King Canute to stay the flowing of the tide. It is obvious that functional shift may produce ambiguities which would not have been possible if the parts of speech had remained always formally distinct. But such ambiguity occurs only occasionally and seems a small price to pay for the added flexibility and resource of vocabulary that conversion makes possible. If words

[36] To illustrate the relative age of verbs and nouns, it may be said that the *Oxford Dictionary* assigns the verbs *run* and *hop* to the Old English period, while the earliest quotations for the nouns are dated "1450" and "1508" respectively.

had to be understood by themselves the confusions would be numerous; but in actual use words are in contexts which obviate all but a
very few uncertainties.

Furthermore, some who make much of this objection are thinking
of the language as something written, and are therefore prone to
forget that many parts of speech that seem alike to the eye are
clearly distinct to the ear. The two obvious illustrations are the
voicing of the final consonant when *abuse, house, use,* and the like[37]
become verbs; and the familiar differentiation in stress (and consequently in vowel values) between the nouns *conduct, contract,
perfume, present,* and *subject,* and the verbs spelled the same way.[38]
A similar differentiation between noun and adjective is accomplished
by the two accentuations of *minute,* and a differentiation for meaning within a single part of speech in the adjective *gallant,* according
as it is stressed on the first or on the second syllable. So also the
adjective *cleanly* and the adverb of the same spelling have distinct
vowels in the base syllable.

Conversion as between nouns and verbs is the chief but not the
only type; as has been said, almost any interchange is possible. We
must satisfy ourselves, however, with only one example of each:
noun becoming adjective, *head* man; noun becoming adverb, *factory*
made; verb becoming adjective, *crack* shot; adjective becoming
noun, rent a *flat;* adjective becoming verb, *dull* a knife; adjective
becoming adverb, *pretty* good; adverb becoming noun, *ins* and *outs;*
adverb becoming verb, *to near* one's goal; adverb becoming adjective, *under* dog.[39] When the variety and extent of functional shift
are fully appreciated, one begins to see that the inherited part-of-
speech categories which suited Classical grammar leave something
to be desired when they are applied to Modern English, so much
more fluid is its structure.[40]

For a last glimpse of the blurring of parts of speech and the facile
shifting of the same word from one function to another, let us look

[37] But *knife, roof, race, promise,* and *practice* have the voiceless consonant
(and hence the same pronunciation) whether they are verbs or nouns; and an
attempt, fashionable some years ago, to pronounce *rise* as a verb [raɪz] but as
a noun [raɪs], does not seem to have made much progress.

[38] For the history of this, cf. Jespersen, *Modern English Grammar,* Vol. I,
section 5.71.

[39] For further examples see Krapp, *Modern English,* pp. 197-199.

[40] Cf. C. C. Fries, *The Structure of English,* New York (Harcourt, Brace)
1952, especially Chapter V, "Parts of Speech."

at the vagaries of the adjective, and at the use of the noun in the position of the adjective. In "the *good* die young," *good* has become a noun; and so has *bad* in "gone to the *bad*"; only nouns can be modified by *the*. The formal change is complete when what was once a qualifying adjective is used without the following noun and thereupon assumes the function of the noun completely: *private* (soldier), *general* (officer), *epic* (poem), *champagne* (wine), *muslin* (cloth), *common* (ground), the *blue* (devil)*s*, not a *red* (cent), in the *red* (ink), from the *blue* (sky), and out of the *deep* (sea), illustrate the process. Usually, an adjective made into a noun in this way may be given the plural -*s* like any other noun; we may speak of our *betters*, of the *whites* of our eyes, or of eating *greens* or *sweets*. Adjectives similarly are often turned into verbs, sometimes with a verbal ending to distinguish the new part of speech (to *toughen, tighten, roughen*), but often without visible change: it is possible to *rough* (e.g., one's opponent in football) as well as to *roughen*, and (without distinction of meaning) to *loose* and *loosen*, and to *black* and *blacken*. *Black*, incidentally, may be a noun, as well as an adjective or verb, as may also another adjective just mentioned, *better* (*better* half, one's *betters*, to *better* one's condition).

The use of the noun in the position and with the function of the qualifying adjective, on the other hand, has raised objections; to have one noun modify another seems to some grammarians reprehensible. But the formation is one that is separated by an impossibly thin line from the well-established full-word compound consisting of noun plus noun, written with or without a hyphen, as may be seen if *street car* is compared with *railway* or *roadway*; or *street car conductor* with *railway-carriage* or *roadway hotel*. Modern English would be the poorer if it were not to use the noun in this way in innumerable phrases like *bond salesmen, art alliance, silver dollar, department store*, and *sports writer*.[41] True, it may be justly maintained that this is sometimes carried to extremes by American newspaper headline writers, who indulge in such locutions as *mystery*

---

[41] Phrases of three or even more nouns, like *spring football practice, city school system, cod liver oil*, and *Philadelphia Gas Works Company* are common enough; Graff (in *Language and Languages*, p. 134) cites *Rexall milk of magnesia tooth paste* as an extreme but perfectly idiomatic extension of this process. In German, a single polysyllabic compound would be the equivalent for such phrases, while in French—cf. *huile de joie de morue* with *cod liver oil* —the prepositional phrase must be employed.

woman, murder car, miracle man, and the like. The exigencies of space are probably the prime reason for this; probably also the abruptness of *mystery woman* (rather than *mysterious woman* or *woman of mystery*) is felt to gain the reader's attention more effectively. Sometimes, too, there is no adjective corresponding to a noun (*valley,* for example) and the alternative prepositional phrase (*in the valley*) seems awkward or too long. In any case, "headline English" as it is called is now a mode apart, accepted within its sphere despite occasional ambiguities and excesses.

Words from Names. Another type of shifting adds to the vocabulary when names (which refer to particular people or places) become converted into words (which refer more generally or typically). One group which immediately suggests itself is that made up of scientists' names that have been employed as units of measurement, especially in electricity; the international character of such names is implied in the fact that *ohm* was originally a German personal name, *watt* a Scottish name, *faraday* an English name, *volt* an Italian name, *ampere* and *joule* French names, *angstrom* a Swedish name, and so on.[42] Miscellaneous examples in other fields of the taking over of a surname without any change and using it as a common noun are *boycott, davenport, derrick, hansom, mackintosh, pompadour, raglan, sandwich, shrapnel, silhouette, theremin,* and *zeppelin.* Occasionally, Christian names have had a similar use; for example, *timothy* (hay) (from Timothy Hansen, its originator), *guy* (from Guy Fawkes), and *bobby* (policeman) (from Sir *Robert* Peel, reorganizer of the London force). Sometimes, the name is used unchanged as a verb; "to *lynch*" and "to *burke*" (reminiscent of the infamous Burke and Hare murders in Edinburgh a century ago) are cases in point. *Boycott* of course is also a verb, and it deserves mention besides as having a European currency: it has been naturalized in German, Dutch, French, and Russian[43] (in the last two languages, with separate forms for the noun). More commonly, the proper name is fitted with the suffix *-ize* for use as a verb: *pasteurize, macadamize, bowdlerize, mercerize,* and *mesmerize* are typical. Such words, of course, have often but a temporary vogue: *hooverize,* for example, refers to a policy advocated by the former president in his capacity as Food Administrator during the first World War, and now forgot-

---

[42] Aiken, *English, Present and Past,* p. 83.
[43] John O'London, *Is It Good English?* New York (Putnam), 1925, p. 68.

ten, and *fletcherize* to the scheme of chewing each morsel of food a specified number of times—advice given by a certain Dr. Fletcher many years ago.[44] Though some of these terms are used without derogatory significance, it would seem that in coining such a word a very frequent purpose is to hold the individual up to ridicule. Thus, *comstockery*, a word created by Bernard Shaw just before the attempted suppression of *Mrs. Warren's Profession* in New York in 1905,[45] definitely connotes a ridiculous degree of prudishness. Somewhat similarly, a *spoonerism*, immortalizing the memory of the Rev. W. A. Spooner (d. 1930), means an unintentional but humorous distortion of the words in a phrase by interchange of initial sounds, as when "Is the dean busy?" becomes "Is the bean dizzy?"

Spoonerism, the last term mentioned, is very likely suggested by *malapropism*, the usual label of a kindred blunder in the use of words —caused, however, by ignorance rather than inadvertence. The word itself, as is well known, comes from the name of the Mrs. Malaprop in Sheridan's *Rivals*, who was addicted to a "nice derangement of epitaphs." It may be taken as typical of the use that has not infrequently been made of the names of persons who have existed only in literature. *Pander*, from Pandarus, the uncle of the heroine in Chaucer's *Troilus and Criseyde* who acts as go-between for the lovers, has passed into common use, in a sense which Pandarus himself regretfully foresaw. It is something of a tribute to Chaucer's influence that only in English has this development taken place; there are no corresponding terms utilizing the name of Pandarus in other European languages, though the story itself has had an international vogue. In *lilliputian* and *quixotic* we have adjectives of similarly literary ancestry. A very special kind of immortality is thus bestowed upon the creations of authors. Its final mark, perhaps, is the transformation of the initial capital into a small letter. An exactly parallel transformation occurs also with the names of places which have become known for a particular quality or for some historical happening. A few examples will suffice: *rubicon, waterloo,* and from the second World War, *dunkirk*.

Blending. Another process of word-manufacture—one much in

[44] Dr. Fletcher's death was reported in the daily press in 1919—the cause was acute indigestion.

[45] Cf. Heywood Broun and Margaret Leech, *Anthony Comstock, Roundsman of the Lord*, New York (Boni), 1927, pp. 18 and 231.

vogue today—is seen in the type of word called a "blend" or "portmanteau word." [46] The portmanteau word, it is said, comes into being when a speaker, confronted by the choice of two words for a single occasion, happens to possess "that rarest of gifts," a perfectly balanced mind.[47] The first sounds of one word are usually blended with the last sounds of another, when the two have some element of sound in common, though it be no more than a single vowel or consonant. Everyone has unintentionally telescoped words in this way, and it is exceedingly likely that the vocabulary has been enriched, to an extent far greater than is usually recognized, by words created through this process. Thus *flaunt* is almost certainly the amalgamation of *flout* and *vaunt*, *slide* of *slip* and *glide*, and *twirl* of *twist* and *whirl*. Telescoping, sometimes of a slightly different character is probably to be found also in *crouch* (*cringe—couch*), *flush* (*flash—blush*), *squash* (*squeeze—crash*), *splatter* (*splash—spatter*), *squawk* (*squall—squeak*), and so forth.[48] One writer particularly is associated with the deliberate creation of portmanteau words (the term itself being his invention): Lewis Carroll. Among his many coinages, two blends—*chortle* (*chuckle—snort*) and *galumphing* (*gallop—triumphing*)—have met comparatively wide acceptance.[49] Contemporary newspaper and magazine writers often create new words in this manner. Sometimes the result is a felicitous or useful addition; often, however, the effect is that of a rather weak pun. We are all familiar enough with such recent examples as *airmada* (*airplane—armada*), *motorcade* (*motor-car—cavalcade*), *cinemactress* (*cinema—actress*), *motel* (*motorist—hotel*), and *smog* (*smoke—fog*).[50]

[46] Professor Margaret Bryant, in *Modern English and Its Heritage*, sections 39.6-7, offers (but does not fully carry out) a distinction between these terms which I have not found elsewhere.

[47] Lewis Carroll, in the preface to *The Hunting of the Snark*. (*Snark* is itself presumably a blend, from *snake* and *shark*.)

[48] Some of these, and many others, are listed in Louise Pound's "Blends, Their Relation to English Word-Formation," *Anglistische Forschungen* (Heidelberg), 1914. See also Jespersen, *Language*, pp. 312-313; McKnight, pp. 165-166; and Harold Wentworth's *Blend-Words in English*, Ithaca (abstract of Cornell thesis), 1933.

[49] Possibly *slithy* (*lithe—slimy*) might be added.

[50] *Anecdotage*, *shamateur*, *alcoholiday*, and *socialite* (for *social—registerite*) are further specimens. Words of this kind, among others, are given in Robert Withington's article "Some Neologisms from Recent Magazines," *American Speech*, Vol. VI, No. 4 (April, 1931), pp. 277-289. Similar lists will be found in subsequent numbers; but see especially Joseph J. Firebaugh's "The Vocabulary of Time Magazine," *ibid.*, Vol. XV, No. 3 (Oct. 1940), pp. 232-242.

Some may eventually establish themselves; others will no doubt prove ephemeral. Blending, true to its general aura of self-conscious smartness, is greatly favored in trade-names today. Blends permit the advertiser to proclaim in a single word two or more of the components or qualities which he alleges his product to have; thus *Polishine, Bovril, Fastred, Floorite*, and many more.

Acronyms. Another type of word, one which has come into very great favor within the past few years, has been given the name *acronym* (literally, "tip-name"), that is, one composed of the initial letters or syllables of a phrase, sometimes with additional vowels to make it pronounceable.[51] Probably the most familiar example is *OK*, and we may note that even when it is phonetically respelled *okay* (or *okeh*), it still originates as the initials of a phrase.[52] As a device of abbreviation, to avoid saying or printing long titles or names of organizations, the acronym is hundreds of years old, but its modern flowering in American use came in the 1930's with President Roosevelt's "alphabetic agencies" such as *WPA, CCC, FDIC,* and others (pronounced as a series of letters) and *NIRA, FERA* (pronounced both as a series of letters and as the "word" they spelled: [naɪrə], [firə]). The second World War gave a new access of life to the acronym and brought a new refinement into its use— one by no means always felicitous: the initials were not merely pronounced as such, but were made to form a word. The British *WRNS* (Women's Royal Naval Service), called the "wrens," and the corresponding American *WAVES* (Women Accepted for Volunteer Emergency Service), furnish examples; also the American *CB's* (Construction Battalions), nicknamed the "seabees," and the *SPAR's* (the Coast Guard's women's auxiliary corps, the word being made from the motto of the service, *Semper PARatus*), both composed with consciously punning intent. So also such a word as *flak*, though it appears to be echoic, is really an acronym, adopted from the German *FLiegerAbwehrKanone* (anti-aircraft artillery); and the British

---

[51] Some definitions of *acronym* (e.g., that of *Webster's New Collegiate Dictionary*) include under this term words composed of the first part of one word with the last part of another; but these already come under the prior terms *blend* and *portmanteau word*.

[52] Not "orl korrect," as is generally thought, but "Old Kinderhook." See the various entries in M. M. Mathews's *Dictionary of Americanisms*, Chicago (Univ. of Chicago Press), 1951, and his references to the work of Professor Allen Walker Read in clearing up this question.

ack-ack, though the *k* sound is probably echoic, is based on the letters *AA* (for *Anti-Aircraft*). So besieged was the American soldier by official acronyms that he replied with one of his own, the adjective that explained everything, *snafu* (from *Situation Normal, All Fouled Up*).

But the acronym reaches the peak of its possible development when organizations consciously name themselves so that their initials will form a word suggesting their purpose or function. *WAVES* appears to have been one of this type; so were *CARE* (*Committee for American Relief in Europe*), *CROP* (*Christian Rural Overseas Program*), and *SHAPE* (*Supreme Headquarters of the Allied Powers in Europe*). All these types of acronyms are now in lively use, and though there has been a certain element of faddism in their employment, they have apparently come to stay. Indeed, they follow the general tendency of language in our time, along with abbreviations, blends, "headline English," and so on, to attain rapidity and concentration. Nor is this tendency limited to workaday language; recent experimental writing by literary artists has frequently had analogous aims.

Authors' Contributions. An account of word-formation in English almost necessarily implies some recognition of the part that individual speakers or writers have played in the development of the vocabulary. The great body of the word-stock is clearly anonymous, in the sense that no one knows who created or even first gave literary currency to many words. An appreciable proportion of it, however, is on a different footing in that the word is definitely associated with an individual who is chiefly or solely responsible for its use. Since the completion (in 1928) of the *New English Dictionary* (generally called simply the *Oxford Dictionary*), which seeks to give for every word the quotation which represents its earliest known use in the language, the part of the individual in the making of the vocabulary can be studied on a scale that was impossible before. It is evident, of course, that the first literary use of the word (even when that has been incontrovertibly ascertained) is not necessarily the same thing as the original creation or the first borrowing of the word; quite certainly, many words are used in speech long before they find their way into writing. Besides, in the very nature of the case, it is only definitely literary or learned words, almost never popular ones, that have been traced to the individual who stood sponsor for them.

When these deductions have been made, however, it is still surprising
how many words may be attributed, with at least a fair show of
reason, to the creative genius of a man whose identity is known.
Enough has been learned, at any rate, of the part of individuals in
word-making to justify some review of the matter here.[53]

The etymological meaning of *poet* is "maker," and in a very literal
sense some of the great English poets may be said to be the *makers*
of the language. To the first great poet, however, though in the past
he was often called both the maker of the language and the father
of our poetry, very few words indeed can be definitely assigned. The
assumption is that Chaucer was the first to borrow and give literary
currency to a great many French words; but when it comes to
definite evidence, very little can be produced. All that can be said
is that many words—for example, these in *-tion: attention, duration, fraction,* and *position*—are first found in Chaucer and not
again until the sixteenth century, and that a number of these, in all
probability, are to be reckoned his. Bradley observes further that
there is little evidence that even Chaucer's phrases have passed into
common use: "Hardly any of his phrases—except 'After the scole
of Stratford-atte-Bowe'—can be said to have become part of the
language . . ." [54] Professor Weekley, echoing this without the qualifications that Bradley gives it, states roundly, "Except for the 'Stratford-atte-Bowe' cliché, he is never quoted," and goes so far as to
explain the assumed lack of quotability by saying, "Chaucer wrote
his *Canterbury Tales* very much in the same words that he would
have used, barring the rime, in relating them to his friends round the
fireside, and probably seldom paused to polish a line. . . ." This, as
all good Chaucerians know, is utter nonsense. And surely, to produce
evidence of Chaucer's phrases in common use, it is not only the
professed Chaucerian who is familiar with other phrases from the
Prologue than "the Stratford-atte-Bowe cliché"—for example, "a
verray parfit gentil knight" and "as fresh as is the month of May,"
from the first two portraits. The novelist who entitled a recent book

---

[53] Accounts of the "makers of English," to all of which the present summary
is indebted, will be found as Chapter VI in Bradley, Chapter V in Smith
(*English Language*), and Chapter VI in Ernest Weekley, *English Language*.
Smith's "Needed Words" and George Gordon's "Shakespeare's English" (*S.P.E.
Tracts, Nos. XXXI* and *XXIX*) are also useful

[54] P. 227.

Up Rose Emily was presumably counting on a general familiarity with the delightful line in the *Knights Tale*,

Up roos the sonne, and up roos Emylye;

and the poet who has used the title *Now with His Love* is obviously assuming that his readers can supply the other half-line—"now in his colde grave" (from the same tale).[55]

Chaucer's contemporary John Wiclif evidently performed a similar service for the English vocabulary, but his borrowings were quite naturally from the Latin of the Vulgate Bible rather than from French. His adaptations of Latin words seem, on the evidence of the *Oxford English Dictionary*, perhaps more numerous than Chaucer's French borrowings, and the fact that he appends notes explaining many such words would indicate that he considered them novelties. Another famous fourteenth-century version of the Bible, that of John Purvey, likewise introduced noteworthy innovations. The two translators of the early sixteenth century, Tindale and Coverdale, working either from the original Greek and Hebrew, from the German version of Martin Luther, or from recent Latin renderings of the original tongues, often created new English equivalents that replaced older words reproducing the Vulgate rather than the Greek or Hebrew text. To Coverdale we are indebted for such familiar terms as *lovingkindness, tender mercy, blood-guiltiness, noonday, morning-star,* and *kind-hearted;* and to Tindale for *peacemaker, long-suffering, broken-hearted, stumbling-block,* and the first literary use of *beautiful.*

The great King James version of 1611 retained much of the vocabulary that had been established through the long tradition of English Biblical translation preceding it, including a good deal that was archaic in the early seventeenth century. It is therefore less notable for innovations than for perpetuating words that would otherwise have fallen into disuse. Since the English people have known the King James Bible as they have known no other book, it is not surprising that its diction has impressed itself upon common

---

[55] Likewise, evidence of a belief that some of the lines of the *Prologue* are generally familiar may be found in these two titles: Elizabeth Roberts's *Jingling in the Wind* and Bliss Perry's *And Gladly Teach*—to say nothing of the punning *And Madly Teach,* by Mortimer Smith (1949).

speech to an overwhelming degree. Shakespearean phrases are the only rivals—and they tend, on the whole, to be more "literary"—for the hundreds of words and groups of words from this source that are familiar counters in the currency of Modern English. To illustrate, let us observe these quotations from the shortest of the gospels— that according to St. Mark—limiting ourselves strictly to the briefer of familiar phrases (it might be added that some of them are even more familiar, perhaps in a slightly different wording, from their appearance elsewhere in the Bible): "new wine in old bottles," "house divided against itself," "light under a bushel," "clothed and in his right mind," "virtue had gone out of him," "shake the dust off your feet," "a millstone about his neck," "the tables of the money-changers," "a den of thieves," "the stone which the builders rejected," "the image and superscription," "marrying or giving in marriage," "the widow's mite," "wars and rumors of wars," "Lo, here and lo, there," "Ye have the poor with you always," and "the hour is come."

To return from the translators of the Bible to those other "makers" of English, the great poets. Spenser, Chaucer's successor in the imperial line, is noteworthy, like the translators of the Bible of 1611, for preserving expressions that had become archaic or even obsolete in his own day. This statement of the case, however, is insufficient, for it is clear that he resorted also to the use of dialect and to deliberate invention. He may be called the first English writer who, apart from the necessities of translation, self-consciously created words. Most of his creations, of course, have perished; and a few that are still familiar are likely to have an archaic air, like *drowsihead, elfin,* and *dreariment. Blatant* and *braggadocio* perhaps should not be so described; and certainly not *briny, horsy,* and *shiny,* if these are his,[56] as seems likely. The general character of Spenser's contribution to the language may be suggested by the fact that he kept alive the significance of *y-*, the weakened prefix of the past participle; the forms *ycladd* (clothed) and *y-drad* (dreaded), occurring in the first two stanzas of the *Faerie Queene,* are typical of the archaic verbal forms scattered lavishly throughout the poem. Without them, perhaps archaisms (like *y-clept* and *hight*) that are still occasionally used would be quite unintelligible.

Shakespeare's supremacy in word-making is as unquestionable as

[56] George Gordon, *op. cit.,* p. 272.

his supremacy in other aspects of the use of language. Bradley, however, expresses a useful caution when he points out that the number of new words attributed to Shakespeare (because not yet found in an earlier writer) undoubtedly exaggerates the extent of his verbal innovations. Nor do the illustrations that Bradley cites of presumably Shakespearean creations—e.g., *control* (as a noun), *dwindle*, *homekeeping*, and *lonely*—seem especially characteristic. On the other hand, it would be strange if many a scene or a speech that is particularly Shakespearean in the inspired boldness of its conception, like the lines from *Macbeth* quoted in the preceding chapter, lacked invention in the use of words.[57] And, in fact, in these very lines, the words *multitudinous* and *incarnadine* (as a verb) are apparently new. We are perhaps on safer ground still when we call attention to the daring originality of Shakespeare's compounds; Bradley well observes that "Shakespeare abounds in splendid audacities, such as '*proud-pied* April,' 'a *heaven-kissing* hill,' 'the *world-without-end* hour.' "

On the whole, there is small reason to quarrel even with the more extravagant descriptions given by others who have studied Shakespeare's legacy to the language. Smith remarks that there are more new words in the plays "than in almost all the rest of the English poets put together," and Weekley that "his contribution to our phraseology is ten times greater than that of any writer to any language in the history of the world." This is the less debatable if one is thinking not merely of individual words—since we have seen that the extent of Shakespeare's creativeness here is by no means certain— but of groups of words or phrases that are much more surely Shakespeare's and his only. The point is too generally familiar to require extensive illustration, but a brief list may not be out of place. The following quotations are from a *single* act of a *single* play (*Hamlet*, Act III), and a number of others might be added from the same

---

[57] *Ibid.*, p. 267. In this admirable book, Gordon calls attention not only to the "verbal audacity and word-creativeness" of Shakespeare, but to something that he feels has been more neglected: "his genius in the manipulation and development of meaning." To cite but a few of his quotations, Shakespeare was apparently the first to speak of *cudgeling* one's brains, *breathing* one's last, *backing* a horse, *catching* a meaning or a cold, and *getting* information or an ailment; and the first to call the world *dull*, an answer *abrupt*, speeches *flowery*, and plain faces *homely*. First, that is, so far as our written records go —though some of these probably were used colloquially before he wrote them down.

source: "to be, or not to be," "that flesh is heir to," "consummation devoutly to be wished," "there's the rub," "this mortal coil," "the law's delay," "the undiscovered country," "the native hue of resolution," "the glass of fashion," "the observed of all observers," "trippingly on the tongue," "tear a passion to tatters," "it out-Herods Herod," "to hold . . . the mirror up to nature," "make the judicious grieve," "metal more attractive," "miching mallecho," "the lady doth protest too much," "as easy as lying," "pluck out the heart of my mystery," "very like a whale," "fool me to the top of my bent," "the very witching time of night," "it smells to heaven," "the primal eldest curse," "no relish of salvation," "a king of shreds and patches," and "hoist with his own petard." [58]

Milton's contribution both of new words and new phrases is evidently much less extensive than Shakespeare's, but often markedly characteristic. Words like *emblazoning, dimensionless, ensanguined, irradiance,* and *infinitude* have the eloquent sonority that might be expected of the poet of *Paradise Lost. Pandemonium,* a word that has later undergone a curious transference in meaning, is the name coined by Milton for the hall of the fallen angels; it obviously follows the analogy of *Pantheon,* as it has been noted that the very architecture of the building Milton describes likewise does. "The *anarch* old" is the splendidly descriptive phrase that Milton applies to the ruler of Chaos, that welter of warring elements. In quite another sphere, Milton coined the useful term *sensuous* to take the place of *sensual* after that word had taken on baser associations; it is the famous definition of poetry as "simple, *sensuous,* and passionate"—a noteworthy instance of sophisticated word-creation. It is well known that Milton is less "quotable" in short passages, not only than Shakespeare, but also than some poets of much smaller stature, such as Alexander Pope; it is not surprising, therefore, that his legacy of phrases that have become common property should be small. Everyone knows, however, a few Miltonic phrases, like "light fantastic toe" (*L'Allegro*), "dim religious light" (*Il Penseroso*), "writ

---

[58] As another and curious illustration of the extent to which Shakespearean phrases are familiar, H. G. Castor points out that from the nine and a half lines of *Macbeth* beginning "Tomorrow and Tomorrow and Tomorrow," nine recent book titles have been taken. These include *All Our Yesterdays, A Walking Shadow, A Poor Player, Told by an Idiot, The Sound and the Fury,* and so on. *Saturday Review of Literature,* Vol. X, No. 13 (Oct. 14, 1933), p. 180.

large," "they also serve" (*Sonnets*), "His [God's] Englishmen," "not without dust and heat" (*Areopagitica*), "darkness visible," "human face divine," "fallen on evil days," and "confusion worse confounded" (*Paradise Lost*).

In later English poetry there is no one to compare with Shakespeare and Milton, in phrase-making as in other respects. The quotability of Pope, already alluded to, largely consists after all of well turned single lines or couplets that have become bits of proverbial wisdom without being particularly notable examples of *verbal* inventiveness. Perhaps the one later poet who even remotely approaches Shakespeare as a "lord of language" is John Keats. When the "Shakespearean" qualities of Keats are referred to, it is presumably first of all his ability in word- and phrase-making that dictates the use of the term. Particularly in the creation of compounds, Keats, more than any other later poet, recalls Shakespeare; it has been well remarked that some of these compounds—the tiger moth's *deep-damasked* wings, and the nightingale's *full-throated* ease—are themselves poems in miniature. There is of course a Spenserian streak in Keats; and like Spenser, he in some measure "made" his own language. As with Spenser too, his archaisms have scarcely taken permanent root, and his own innovations—like the words *aurorean* and *beamily* referred to by Smith—are not always felicitous. Keats's attitude toward words on the whole more nearly resembles the Renaissance feeling that language is for the individual to deal with and create as he sees fit than does that of any other poet of later times. Again it is not only in the single word but in the phrase that his memorable creativeness is to be seen. In the "astounding four lines" (as Hilaire Belloc has called them) that conclude the seventh stanza of the *Ode to a Nightingale,* he has created phrases—"alien corn," "magic casements," "perilous seas," and "fairy lands forlorn"—that are a permanent part of the language.

The Victorian poets contributed relatively little to word-creation, though Tennyson's compounds are sometimes exceedingly happy: *evil-starred* is one that has been widely adopted. *Fairy tale* and *moonlit* are also said to be innovations of Tennyson's, and "rift in the lute" is a familiar phrase that we owe to him. Browning's creations have a characteristic grotesqueness that limits their usefulness: *crumblement, febricity,* and *garnishry* are typical. *Artistry,* however. is a formation of his that has (though not without protest) won a permanent place. More than can be said about Tennyson or Browning as word-makers might be said about an American poet of the nineteenth century, Walt Whitman. Whitman, of course, was convinced that "the new vistas need a new tongue"—in a word, an American language—and he did not hesitate to include in his poetry even the less polished of current Americanisms. In individual word-creations, however, which his theory of poetic diction would also justify, he dealt with somewhat surprising conservatism.[59] Many of the innovations he introduced—words like *camerado*, *libertad*, and *Americano*—smack of one influence particularly, the Spanish of the American Southwest.

Our account of the "makers" of English has so far dealt chiefly with the poets. Prose-writers too have sometimes been responsible for the introduction of words that bear the stamp of individual creation. Before the Modern English period, Wiclif, Malory, and Caxton are noteworthy names, not only in literary history in general, but in this special aspect of the use of language; and a similar observation might be made of such sixteenth-century writers as Sir Thomas More, John Lyly, and Robert Greene. The two last-named writers represent particularly the Elizabethan love of sheer oddity and the Elizabethan experimental attitude toward language. Perhaps the best illustration that can be given, however, of the prose-writer who creates his own vocabulary is a writer of the seventeenth century, whose name figures more often in the pages of the *Oxford English Dictionary* than that of almost any other author: Sir Thomas Browne.

Browne's Latinisms are not always individualized. Other English writers of the Renaissance might perhaps equally well have taken from Latin such words as *clamation* (shouting), *dissentaneous* (contrary), *donative* (gift), *fictile* (molded), *exenteration* (disemboweling), *incrassated* (thickened), *ligation* (suspension), and *prescious* (foreknowing).[60] In Browne's time, that is to say, a good deal of the Latin vocabulary was potentially English—in the sense that the right to seize upon a Latin word and, with perhaps some slight

[59] Cf. Louise Pound. "Walt Whitman's Neologisms," *American Mercury*, Vol. IV (Feb. 1925), pp. 199-201.

[60] These have all been cited as Browne's, but the evidence of the *Oxford Dictionary* makes this attribution, for several of them, more than dubious. However, it is of course likely enough that Browne took over a Latin word independently, even when an earlier use of it in English has been found.

change of ending, use it like an English one was generally taken for granted. Browne does not always use the Latin (or Greek) coinage because the English vocabulary is insufficient; sometimes, he seems to add the English equivalent by way of translation (*"improperations* or terms of scurrility," *"areopagy* and dark tribunal of our hearts"). Quite often, however, the Latin term follows; and though it adds nothing to the sense, it is abundantly justified by the rhythm of the phrase ("one common name and *appellation,"* "the hill and *asperous* way"). Many of his original creations have not found another user. A few characteristic ones are *favaginous* (honeycombed), *paralogical* (fallacious), *digladiation* (fighting with swords), *quodlibetically* (in the manner of scholastic disputation), *pensile* (hanging), and *exantlation* (exhaustion).[61] But equally characteristic creations by him have found a permanent place in the language: *antediluvian, hallucination, insecurity, incontrovertible, precarious,* and *retrogression.* Moreover, at least a few of Browne's innovations have lost all sense of the merely ornamental; *electricity, literary,* and *medical* are, from any point of view, a necessary part of Modern English. If the later history of Browne's word-coinages is a case of the survival of the fittest, the extent both of the original list and of the survivors still offers eloquent testimony to his genius as a maker of words.

Browne may be taken as an extreme example of the free use that seventeenth-century writers made of Latin as a source of new English words. To some extent, the use of French (more for direct borrowing, however, than for English adaptation) in the Restoration and in the early eighteenth century offers a parallel in the literature that directly follows the age of Browne and Milton. But though both Dryden and Pope, the dominating figures in this literature, have been credited with many new words, it is evident that what we have called the "experimental" attitude toward language common to the Renaissance has gone forever. Doctor Johnson, whose style admittedly is very largely based on that of Browne, follows his master at a distance in this matter, but does nevertheless introduce an appreciable number of Latinisms on his own account. Smith makes the

[61] Cited by Sir Edmund Gosse in the chapter "Language and Influence" of his *English Men of Letters* volume on Browne. Gosse adversely criticizes the theory of word-creation that they imply; for a view that takes issue with Gosse's, see Lytton Strachey's essay on Browne in *Books and Characters.*

interesting point[62] that authors of the eighteenth and early nine-teenth centuries particularly would seem to have invented (or im-ported) exactly the words most appropriate to their own characteris-tics. Thus *fiddlededee* and *irascibility* are attributed by the *Oxford English Dictionary* to Johnson, *etiquette, friseur,* and *persiflage* to Lord Chesterfield, *bored* and *blasé* to Byron, and *idealism* and *pro-priety* (in their usual modern senses) respectively to Shelley and to Miss Burney. It is likewise fitting, in a somewhat different way, that so much of the modern vocabulary of politics and government—such words as *colonization, diplomacy, electioneering, federalism,* and *municipality*—should be credited to Edmund Burke, one of the few great word-creators of the eighteenth century and, like Johnson and Browne, an exponent of the ornate rather than the simple style of prose. With these creations of Burke's should be compared the con-scious coinages of Jeremy Bentham—words like *minimize, detach-able, deterioration, meliorability, cross-examination,* and *exhaustive.* It is interesting to note that Bentham specifically argued in favor of deliberately creating new words.[63]

In the nineteenth century, English words are created in greatest quantity, in all probability, by two Scotsmen—Sir Walter Scott and Thomas Carlyle. "Creation," perhaps, is scarcely the word to de-scribe Scott's services in this way most accurately, for his most char-acteristic innovations are rather revivals of old words or importa-tions of dialect terms.[64] Thus, there is no record of the literary use of the Shakespearean words *fitful, borderer, thews,* and *arm-gaunt,* and the phrases "towering passion," "coign of vantage," and "yeo-man's service" between Shakespeare's original use and Scott's reintro-duction of them. More important is Scott's turning to the uses of lit-

---

[62] P. 119.
[63] See the note on his attitude by Prof. Graham Wallas, *S.P.E. Tract No. XXXI*, pp. 333-334.
[64] Most of the illustrations in this paragraph are taken from Weekley's article "Walter Scott and the English Language," *Atlantic Monthly* (Vol. 148), November, 1931. A more recent study shows that fully 150 of Scott's reintro-ductions have been used again by later writers. "Many have survived the lit-erature that especially needed them. About thirty have worked down into the language of our newspapers and magazines and into our common speech, so that most of us use frequently words that we would not use if Sir Walter Scott had not written." See Paul Roberts, "Sir Walter Scott's Contributions to the English Vocabulary," *Publications of the Modern Language Association,* Vol. LXVIII, No. 1 (March 1953), pp. 189-210.

erature (in his poems of course as well, but more especially in the *Waverly Novels*) many a word or turn of phrase that, until his use of it, had been confined to the dialect of his native land. These include such splendidly "Romantic" words as *raid, gruesome, uncanny, glamour,* and *grammerye* (the last two, variants of the same word, which we have also in a third form in the now commonplace *grammar*). Revivals that may be from older literature rather than popular dialect are *smouldering, weird* (in the sense of "fate"—Macbeth's "weird sisters"—especially in the phrase "dree one's weird"), and *fiery cross.* It is an odd circumstance that several of Scott's revivals or reintroductions have taken hold particularly in the United States. Mark Twain, we may recall, attributed the blame for the Civil War to the vogue of Scott in the South. However this may be, it is at any rate curious that the special application to political use of *henchman* and *stalwart* is peculiar to America; that *slogan* (war cry) in its advertising significance is much more American than British; and that the modern currency of *blackmail* is due to American practice. Finally, what seem to be innovations of Scott's, in the stricter sense of original creations, are *free-lance, red-handed, passage of arms,* and *Norseman.*

Carlyle's coinages are less romantic than eccentric. Like Scott, he levied upon the Scots tongue for some of his new words: *feckless, lilt* (in the sense of "cadence"), and *outcome* had before him been confined to dialect speech or writing. But far more characteristic of his fantastic audacity in word-creation are such outlandish coinages as *Bedlamism, dandiacal, grumbly,* and *gigmanity.* The genesis of the last is interesting and typical.[65] Like Matthew Arnold's "Wragg is in custody," *gigmanity* was suggested to Carlyle by the proceedings at a trial—one that has left other traces in English literature as well. What had fallen under Carlyle's eye was the report of the examination of a witness testifying as to the character of William Weare, for whose murder John Thurtell was being tried. The dialog between counsel and witness was as follows:

"What sort of a person was Mr. Weare?"
"He was always a respectable person."
"What do you mean by 'respectable'?"
"He kept a gig."

[65] This account of *gigmanity* is indebted to John O'London, *op. cit.,* pp. 44-45.

Thenceforth, as in the perfervid close of *The French Revolution, gigs* were for Carlyle the symbols, and *gigmanity* the sum total of the impulses of a smugly respectable society.

Beyond mere idiosyncrasy, however, Carlyle's innovations in words were of value in restoring to English some little measure of its earlier freedom in compound-making. His compounds were on the German model, and he used the hyphen freely to join words that are not commonly so joined in English, though their German equivalents may be compounds. A great many, like the *"mischief-joy,* which is also a *justice-joy"* referred to by Bradley (the former the equivalent of the German *Schadenfreude*), have seemed mere Teutonisms that are distinctly not English formations, and they have not won other users. A few, like *swansong* (also an adaptation directly from German), have become generally current. He is also given part credit, with Matthew Arnold, for naturalizing the German *Philister* as English *Philistine* (materialist). A few other miscellaneous words— *decadent, environment,* and *self-help*—are coinages of Carlyle's that seem to have no taint of the eccentric. Some of his phrases, too, are still in familiar use: "the unspeakable Turk" and "the dismal science" (economics) have the true Carlylean ring.

Since Carlyle, there has been perhaps no single word-creator whose coinages have added any considerable number of words to the vocabulary. It is conceivable that such a revolt from the usual conventionalities of language as that which James Joyce has fathered, in *Ulysses* and *Finnegans Wake,* will bear fruit of this kind. At present, all that can be said is that the reading public, taken by and large, looks with some distrust at a performance as eccentric as Joyce's. We may very possibly come to the point of being willing to grant to the individual author the right to make for himself a vocabulary that shall be more adequate to the expression of his own thought than the more familiar counters of English can be. Perhaps there will be no quarrel, however, with the statement that so far, the more common reaction to the unconventional treatment of word, punctuation, and sentence by such writers as Joyce, E. E. Cummings, and Gertrude Stein is one of either merriment or scorn.[66]

There is good reason to feel, however, that the revolt against convention in language is, on the whole, a sign of health. Euphuism and Arcadianism, movements of revolt in the Renaissance, were greeted

[66] Cf. Max Eastman, "The Cult of Unintelligibility."

with laughter in some quarters and disdain in others—both of which, at times, they merited—yet the Elizabethan appetite for language of which they were manifestations had its admirable aspects, and we are the richer for it. The revolt against convention in the first half of the twentieth century, then, is by no means novel. And the new *tentatives* which it has produced in word-making and phrase-making may enlarge the resources of the language and help to fill real needs. Logan Pearsall Smith's suggestive article on "Needed Words" [67] catalogs some of the gaps in the English vocabulary, and Roger Fry's addendum lists the specific needs for words in connection with art. Smith's words on what men of letters have done in the past and should do more frequently in our own time may well be quoted; these services, he says, should include "the naturalization or translation of needed foreign words, the creation of new words or the discovery and revival of old ones, the authorization of vivid words of popular creation, the reclamation of old meanings, and the establishment of new discriminations." [68]

How one useful coinage may lead to another is suggested by a remark in the pamphlet just quoted. Smith alludes to Lord Chesterfield's complaint that English possessed no word to express the meaning of the French *mœurs*, since "*manners* said too little and *morals* too much." Chesterfield's suggestion was that English should adopt the Ciceronian word *decorum* to stand for the idea of "propriety of behavior." Smith points out that, as a matter of fact, *decorum* had already been added to the vocabulary when Chesterfield wrote, but that what is still lacking is a word to stand for another sense of the French *mœurs*: "the ways of living, usages, customs, and prejudices of a particular person or class or epoch." He adds in a footnote that the word *folkways* is sometimes used by American anthropologists in this last sense. Surely one can say more than this, for since *Folkways*[69] was used as the title of W. G. Sumner's great book, it has met very wide acceptance by students of sociology, as has also *mores*, another innovation of Sumner's. And *folkways* begets analogical formations. Professor Herbert Shenton—incidentally, a sociologist

[67] *S.P.E. Tract No. XXI.*

[68] The last point is prompted by the article on "Differentiation" in Fowler's *Dictionary of Modern English Usage,* in which the author lists not only discriminations that are in process of being established, but also others that might profitably be worked out in the future.

[69] Ginn, 1907.

primarily—uses the term *speechways*[70] to stand for a similar meaning with reference to language. *Airways,* however different in meaning, is perhaps suggested in form by the same model.

The general attitude toward word-creation has undoubtedly undergone a change since Renaissance times, and perhaps more particularly in the last half-century. One of the original purposes of the Society for Pure English[71] was to encourage authors in an activity that their predecessors have engaged in but that has been increasingly given up in recent times. It was pointed out that most of the new additions to the vocabulary are the deliberate creations of men of science, many of whom are ill-fitted for the task, and that these new additions are but rarely formed out of English material. Men of letters are on the whole more prone than men of science to feel that vocabulary is not a proper field for experimentation; yet, from the very nature of their tastes and their calling, they should be precisely the ones from whom useful and felicitous coinages might be expected. Leon Mead [72] found that many American authors to whom he put the question of what words they had coined repudiated the idea that they had ever been guilty of such a practice, in much the same terms they might have used had they been accused of counterfeiting the currency of the land. That was fifty years ago, it is true, and there have been changes of attitude since. Some authors, however, and many of the scientists who were also consulted, took a quite different attitude, that of pride in their handiwork. The actual words submitted were chiefly compounds of Latin and Greek elements, formed along classical lines; some, like *metropoliarchy* and *deanthropomorphization*—are remarkably awkward and repellent. English elements and English processes of derivation were notably few.

One may regret that the task of coining new words has been so largely abandoned by authors and left so largely to scientists, to the lower order of journalistic humorists, to gossip columnists and radio clowns (whose self-conscious efforts at novelty are often pitifully cheap), and to the usually anonymous creators of popular speech. Nevertheless, a number of neologisms, of known and reputable authorship, have been brought into use within recent years. It may

[70] *International Communication,* p. 46: "This approach to the problem might well be called a study of the speechways of mankind."

[71] See the original prospectus (1913), reprinted after the first World War as part of *Tract I* (1919).

[72] *Word-Coinage,* New York (Crowell), 1902.

be of interest to round out our account of the makers of English by
a miscellaneous list of nineteenth- and twentieth-century word-
creations. To the list already given we may add the names of
Coleridge (*pessimism*), Macaulay (*constituency*), Darwin (*atoll*),
Huxley (*agnostic*), and O. W. Holmes (*anesthesia*). It is more difficult to find creations of authors still alive or recently dead that are
at all well known. No later humorist, for example, seems to have
been able to assume the mantle of Lewis Carroll, in this respect as
well as in others; for not only are the blends *chortle* and *galumphing*
immediately intelligible, but a number of others, of less evident
composition—like *brillig, jabberwock, frabjous*—are almost equally
current coin.

Spoof, an isolated creation of Arthur Roberts's, is even more secure.
Gelett Burgess has contributed a number of novel words like these,
"hot from the depths of necessity"; but though *blurb* has won a firm
place for itself, and *goop* has some currency, others such as *snosh*
(vain talk) and *jujasm* (outburst of sudden joy) died aborning. *Pan-
jandrum*, a nonsense word of an earlier era—invented, it is said, by
the actor Samuel Foote in a passage of similar arbitrary creations
put together to test the word-memory of a fellow-actor—has met a
happier fate. Christopher Morley, among present-day American
writers, typifies an attitude toward word-creation that is no longer
common, even though what seems to be the coinage he is most proud
of—*kinsprit*, a blend of *kindred* and *spirit*—has won very little use.
Many of his innovations—like *infracaninophile* (friend of the under-
dog)—are obviously humorous nonce-words, made "rather for show
than wear"; and this particular word is a Greco-Latin mongrel—
an example, no doubt, of the dog it refers to. In the 1920's, H. L.
Mencken made current—at least among the vanguard of readers
and writers—his scoffing coinages such as *booboisie* (on the pattern
of *bourgeoisie*) and *the Bible belt* (parallel to *corn belt, wheat belt,*
and their kind); but the later reaction of opinion has left them
sounding less trenchant than they did at the time of their creation.
Among the few individual coinages that are at once comparatively
recent and widely known may be listed Bernard Shaw's *superman* (a
hybrid adaptation of the German *Übermensch*, and the inspiration
of other *super-compounds*), Admiral A. T. Mahan's *sea-power*,
Gamaliel Bradford's *psychography*, and W. E. Woodward's *debunk-
ing*. Among words already in existence, which only attained wide

currency when they were used by famous men, may be mentioned *boondoggling* (which President Franklin Roosevelt cast abroad in a new, scornful sense in 1936, though *boondoggle* was actually coined in 1925), and *iron curtain* (to which Winston Churchill gave its present sense in 1946, though the metaphor existed as early as 1904).[73]

Why do authors hesitate to coin words, and when they do coin them, why do others hesitate to take up what seems to be an attractive and useful addition? The answer would appear to be in part that the usual attitude toward the dictionary forbids. An author, when a word suggests itself, looks in the dictionary to see whether it is there, fails to find it—and discards it forthwith in favor of one that enjoys lexicographical sanction. A reader meets a word that is new to him, wonders if it is in the dictionary, does not find it—and silently registers his disapproval of the effrontery of the writer. Yet, as has been well observed by Jespersen, "A word may have been used scores of times without finding its way into any dictionary—and a word may be an excellent one even if it has never been used before by any human being." [74] Suppose the reader is unable to find *somewhen* in a dictionary. Is the effect of the following sentence by Lowes Dickinson in any way damaged?—"You had a faith in the significance of your ideal, somewhere and *somewhen*, though where and when grew more doubtful as you grew older." [75] This is the sort of creation which, on the contrary, ought to be encouraged.

A rather large qualification may perhaps be added to the impression we have given of a general poverty of invention, and a considerable reluctance today—at least at the level of "good usage"—to accept what individual coinages have offered: the field of politics seems to run against this general trend. From the beginning, American political campaigns have produced numbers of phrases, epithets, nicknames, and slogans—indeed, the word *slogan* itself has acquired in America a currency and a sphere of application which it never had in its native Scotland. So plentiful have been the creations and adaptations of this kind that Professor Hans Sperber has compiled

[73] On *boondoggle* see *Notes and Queries*, 188 (May 5, 1945), p. 191, and also *Webster's New Collegiate Dictionary*. On *iron curtain* see Paul Fussell, Jr., in *American Speech*, Vol. XXV, No. 1 (Feb. 1950), p. 40, where the phrase is traced to H. G. Wells's novel *The Food of the Gods*.

[74] *Growth and Structure*, p. 162.

[75] *After Two Thousand Years*, New York (Norton), 1931, p. 115.

for a dictionary of political words and phrases some 2000 entries.[76] In contemplating such a collection one realizes the force of Robert Louis Stevenson's aphorism to the effect that "Man shall not live by bread alone but principally by catchwords." Even in this field, however, not many out-and-out coinages are to be found; usually the trick of arousing enthusiasm or inspiring contempt is accomplished by giving particular application to a phrase that is scarcely a novelty. Cleveland's "innocuous desuetude" shows more inventiveness, perhaps, than Wilson's "new freedom" or Franklin Roosevelt's "new deal" [77] and "forgotten man"—especially in view of the fact that the last is a resurrection of a phrase of W. G. Sumner's. But in general it may be argued that the political leaders who have appealed most persuasively to great masses of people have also been the most accomplished phrase-makers. One thinks of Bryan's "cross of gold," of Theodore Roosevelt's "big stick," "strenuous life," "malefactors of great wealth," of Wilson's "self-determination," "peace without victory," and "safe for democracy," and of Franklin Roosevelt's "nothing to fear but fear itself." Disraeli was on sound ground when he observed that "with words we govern men." [78]

REFERENCES FOR FURTHER READING

Greenough and Kittredge, *Words and Their Ways in English Speech,* New York (Macmillan), 1901.

Groom, Bernard, *A Short History of English Words,* London (Macmillan), 1934.

Krapp, G. P., *Modern English, Its Growth and Present Use,* New York (Scribner's), 1909.

McKnight, G. H., *English Words and Their Background,* New York (Appleton), 1923.

New English Dictionary on Historical Principles, A (the *"Oxford Dictionary"*), 1884-1928; reissued, with supplement, 1933.

Smith, L. P., *The English Language,* New York (Holt), 1912.

Vallins, G. H., *Words in the Making,* London (A. & C. Black), 1935.

[76] *A Dictionary of Political Words and Phrases.*

[77] Roosevelt confessed that "new deal" came from Mark Twain's *Connecticut Yankee.* The connotations of this source must have pleased his opponents.

[78] Prof. I. Willis Russell edits lists of new words which are published semiannually in *American Speech* magazine and annually in the *Encyclopædia Britannica* yearbook.

Chapter 9

Changing Meanings and Values of Words

THE STUDY of meaning in language is called Semasiology or Semantics. The latter term, however, has recently been used widely to refer to what is properly called General Semantics, a study allied more closely to the field of philosophy than to that of linguistics, and which therefore will not be dealt with in this book.[1] The term *Semantics* nevertheless has application within the field of linguistics; there it is limited at present to the description of the meanings which words or other units of language convey, and, when these are seen historically, also to the various types of meaning-change that occur.

But the word "meaning" itself poses difficult problems. What is the meaning of "meaning"? We all recognize that language is a give-and-take of speech-signals, a series of stimuli by speakers and responses by hearers; also that some non-linguistic stimuli produce linguistic responses, and *vice versa.* (Thus a kiss may produce the response "Darling!"—and *vice versa.*) When the hearer of a lin-

[1] The basic books in General Semantics are those of Alfred Korzybski, especially *Science and Sanity*, New York (International Non-Aristotelian Library), 1933, and *General Semantics*, Chicago (Institute of General Semantics), 1940. Another basic (but independent) book is C. K. Ogden and I. A. Richards's *The Meaning of Meaning*, New York (Harcourt, Brace), 1923. Popular treatments include Stuart Chase's *The Tyranny of Words*, New York (Harcourt, Brace), 1938, and Hugh R. Walpole's *Semantics*, New York (Norton), 1941. Semi-popular, and very readable, are the books of S. I. Hayakawa, *Language in Action*, New York (Harcourt), 1941, and *Language in Thought and Action*, New York (Harcourt), 1949. An excellent textbook is Irving J. Lee's *Language Habits in Human Affairs*, New York (Harper), 1941; see also his *The Language of Wisdom and Folly*, New York (Harper), 1949. A treatment with clinical overtones is Wendell Johnson's *People in Quandaries*, New York (Harper), 1946. A recent treatment is that of Anatol Rapaport, *Science and the Goals of Man*, New York (Harper), 1950.

guistic stimulus responds to it in some predictable way, we say, in common parlance, that he has "understood" the speaker. But we are by no means certain—here we must throw ourselves upon the psychologists—what goes on inside the hearer's nervous system between his hearing of the words and his response to them. The student of language therefore limits himself to an investigation of the parts of the process which are clearly accessible, and with which he can deal with some degree of objectivity. Less and less do linguists raise the question of "ideas" or "concepts" in the mind; today they generally define meaning as simply the situation out of which language comes and the response that it elicits.[2]

If this is meaning, how does it change? It is clear that, for speakers of the same language, there must be a large measure of consistency in the response to linguistic signals—otherwise, communication would be impossible. Nevertheless, since no two situations can ever be exactly alike, there is always some area of variation, and over a period of time the increment of slight variations will alter the reference of the linguistic signal. Let us take an example. Since meaning involves both the situation out of which a word comes (which makes the speaker say it) and the hearer's response, every speech situation is complex, with many components. But the relative prominence of these components will not always be the same. When the word *green* is first said it ordinarily brings a response in terms of color; but if the context concerns a fruit, this primary element of color may become associated with a secondary element—unripeness. Repetition may then establish this association until the element of unripeness becomes more prominent than that of color—so much so that it becomes possible to say, without fear of misunderstanding, "Blackberries are red when they are green."

Every new focus of prominence, once established, may beget others: when fruit and young people are associated, the element of unripeness may be paralleled with inexperience, and the latter may then assume primary prominence in such a statement as, "Those freshmen are pretty green." Thus a series of shifts in focus, from one element in a situation to others, will produce shifts in meaning—or "new meanings"—for words. In this example, *green* has acquired two

---

[2] So, for example, Leonard Bloomfield, *Language*, Chap. 9, sec. 1: "We have defined the *meaning* of a linguistic form as the situation in which the speaker utters it and the response which it calls forth in the hearer."

new meanings and lost none; but many a word, after shifting, has lost its first meaning entirely. Indeed, over the centuries meanings grow and decay in a surprising variety of ways, the chief of which we are to examine in this chapter.

Yet before proceeding we must give attention to one more point. Even though it is generally recognized that meanings change, many people still cling, curiously enough, to the quite contradictory notion that words all have "true" meanings, that changes somehow take us away from the "true" meaning, and that the way to find out what a word "really means" is to find out what it once meant. This is particularly true in respect to borrowed words in English, the belief evidently being that the meaning of the word in contemporary English and the meaning of the Latin or Greek word from which the English word is derived must be one and the same. A little reflection should show that an appeal to etymology in order to establish the present meaning of the word is as untrustworthy as an appeal to spelling in order to establish its present pronunciation. And for a reason that is almost exactly parallel: change of *meaning* is likely to have altered the etymological sense, which is thereby rendered archaic or obsolete, just as change of *sound* is likely to be unrecorded in the "antiquarian" spelling that so frequently characterizes Modern English. The study of etymology has great value and interest— a point to which we shall later return—but its usefulness in settling the question of what a word means is subject to considerable qualification.

Let us see what results when one ignores the idea that a word may change its meaning, and appeals to its etymology in order to determine its present meaning. A handbook of only twenty-odd years ago on "correct English" [3] sets forth the following dictum: "*Dilapidated* . . . Said of a building or other structure. But the word is from the Latin *lapis*, a stone, and cannot properly be used of any but a stone structure." One might just as reasonably argue that because *candidate* is related to the Latin *candidus* (white), it cannot properly be used of an aspirant for political office unless he is clothed in a suit

---

[3] *Write It Right*, by Ambrose Bierce, New York (Neale), 1928. The work is well worth investigating as a striking demonstration of what pedantry, combined with ignorance of linguistic processes, will do for one. To much of it, a witty definition of Bierce's own is curiously applicable: "*positive*—mistaken at the top of one's voice."

of white material. More clearly even, one might protest that *holiday* properly describes Christmas or Easter, but should never be used of Independence Day or Labor Day; or that *bonfire* should not be applied except where the combustible material is bone. These arguments are not much more grotesque than some that have been seriously maintained in defense of an etymological crotchet, while ignoring the fact of change of meaning. Indeed, one who argues on this basis is a victim of the "etymological fallacy."

The fact is that what a word once meant is not necessarily what it now means; the etymological meaning has often died out, and a quite new development is the living descendant. This is particularly true of words in common or popular use. Words, after all, are for the most part purely conventional symbols. They mean only what those who are using them agree to make them mean. Exactly the same principles apply to "learned" words, but because their traditional users have generally known the language from which they were borrowed, or of whose elements they were composed, they have tended to preserve the etymological meaning—indeed, it is conventional to use such words with an eye to their source; thus they are less prone to alterations of meaning than are popular words. It is in this way, incidentally, that a cultural tradition holds in check, to some extent, the constant tendency of language to change.[4]

Change of meaning, however, though usually unpredictable, is not utterly arbitrary; as we shall see in a moment, it often proceeds along familiar paths. Furthermore, though it takes place in all languages, it does not proceed at the same rate even in related ones. If we look at cognate words in English and German, for example, which might have been expected to have the same meaning, we often find them widely different, and the difference is most commonly the result of some radical change of sense in the English word. Opposite instances can be found, admittedly, in which the English word has stood still and the German one changed; yet it is usually the latter which is conservative. Examples of this characteristic English shift in meaning are the following: *Schlagen* and *slay* are originally the same word, but the German word retains the general meaning of "smite" or "strike" while the English word has become narrowed

---

[4] Some of this holding in check is unconscious, some conscious; we shall have to postpone to a later chapter the question of the values and judgments upon which conscious attempts to control language are based.

to mean "strike with fatal consequences" or "kill."[5] *Knabe* is the cognate in German of Old English *cnapa* or *cnafa*, and has the same meaning, "boy"; but Modern English *knave* has a radically different one; the German *Tier* means any kind of animal, as did the cognate Old English *deor*, but in Modern English *deer* means one particular kind of animal.

Generalization and Specialization. One very common type of change is that in which the "area" of the meaning is changed. When a word that has referred broadly or inclusively begins instead to refer narrowly or exclusively, this is an example of "specialization" of meaning; the contrary is called "generalization." Interestingly enough, the same word may undergo both processes at different stages of the development of its meaning. *Go*, for example, is a verb of motion that seems as general as possible in meaning, and presumably this is also the basic meaning; early in its history in English, however, it must have specialized, for Old English *gān* sometimes means "walk," and in Middle English *ryde or gon* (ride or walk) is a familiar formula. Although the present meaning is the generalized one, the specialization "walk" was still possible in the late seventeenth century, as we see in these phrases from Bunyan: "I am resolved to run when I can, to go when I cannot run, and to creep when I cannot go."[6]

Borrowed words are quite as likely as native ones to undergo such transformations in meaning. *Virtue*[7] is connected with Latin *vir* (man). Thus, *virtue* first meant "manliness" in general; but its meaning later specialized to stand for the manly quality most in demand in the military state, namely "fortitude" or "warlike prowess"—the meaning familiar in Cæsar's *Commentaries*. But a still later Latin meaning is more comprehensive, and it was this very general meaning that was attached to *virtue* when it was borrowed in English through French. One possible specialization was "power," as in "Virtue had gone out of him," or even "magical power," as in "the virtue of the spell" or Milton's "virtuous ring and glass." More commonly, however, the word in English retained a general sense of "noble quality"—though more and more with reference to moral

---

[5] The Latin word *caedere*, though unrelated to English *slay*, has undergone exactly the same specialization of meaning.

[6] Quoted by Bradley, *The Making of English*, p. 182.

[7] This history is given in greater detail in Greenough and Kittredge, *Words and Their Ways in English Speech*, pp. 241-242.

rather than to mental or physical characteristics. But another specialization limits its application to women; for example, "All the sons were brave, and all the daughters virtuous," where *virtuous* is equivalent to "chaste." "A woman's virtue" will today be interpreted in only the last sense. A curious evolution, indeed, when one recalls that the etymological meaning is "manliness."

The foregoing are particularly striking examples, but hundreds of others could be cited. We find generalization in such everyday words as *picture,* once restricted, as the etymology would suggest (compare: the *Picts,* "painted ones"), to a *painted* representation of something seen, but now applicable to photograph, crayon drawing, and so forth; *butcher,* who once slew one animal only, the goat (French *bouc*); the verb *sail,* which has been transferred to *steam* navigation, just as *drive* has been transferred to self-propelled vehicles; *injury,* which once was limited to "injustice"; *zest,* which meant "bit of lemon-peel"; *chest,* which usually meant "coffin"— "He is now deed and nayled in his cheste";[8] *pen,* which meant "feather," but which is now much more likely to mean a writing implement tipped with metal than a quill; *quarantine,* from which the original meaning of a "forty" days' isolation has quite disappeared; and *companion,* which has likewise lost the etymological sense of "one who (shares) bread with" another.

But generalization of meaning does not always stay within bounds; under some conditions the meaning becomes so broad that, in extreme cases, there is hardly any meaning left. We have a whole set of words, used conversationally when we either do not know, or cannot remember, or perhaps will not take the trouble to search for a more precise term: the *what-you-may-call-it* kind of word— *thingumabob, doohickie, jigger,* and so on.[9] Not so long ago *gadget* was imported into the U.S. from England, and has found a very hearty welcome into this company.

Another type, in which generalization goes even farther, has aroused strong opposition from guardians of literary style, who realize that emptiness and "jargon" result from the indiscriminate use of "words that mean little or nothing, but may stand for almost

[8] Chaucer's clerk, speaking of Petrarch (*Clerk's Prologue,* line 30).

[9] Louise Pound has collected more than 100 such terms now current in popular speech: "American Indefinite Names," *American Speech,* Vol. VI, No. 4 (April 1931), pp. 257-259.

anything":[10] such words are *thing, business, concern, condition, matter, article, circumstance.* As we all recognize at once, these are words that have a fairly exact sense, but which also have acquired the ability to fit into a wide variety of everyday contexts, in which their meaning becomes extremely vague—in fact, almost wholly dependent on the context. The word *deal* is the current American favorite in this group, its gamut of meaning running all the way from perfectly favorable ("Your job sounds like a pretty fine deal") to thoroughly unfavorable ("I won't take part in any of his deals"). This word serves the purpose, and is going through the same general sort of development, that *proposition* did a generation ago.

Even more frequent than generalization, and even more readily illustrated in numberless familiar instances, is the opposite process of specialization. *Steorfan* is an Old English word, cognate with the German *sterben,* which meant "die"; but the standard Modern English meaning ("starve") is a specialized one, namely "die from hunger." Another specialization, "die from cold," is found in certain Modern English dialects: "[he] . . . bid her come . . . sit close by the fire: he was sure she was starved" is from the Yorkshire dialect of *Wuthering Heights* (Chapter XXX). The older meaning of *meat* was "food" in general, as one might suspect from the archaic phrase *meat and drink* and from the compound *sweetmeat.* For the meaning "meat," the older term was *flesh* or *flesh meat.* It is interesting to observe, incidentally, that the German cognate for *flesh, Fleisch,* suggests first of all the specialized sense of "meat"; this is the present meaning, too, of French *viande,* while the English *viands* retains the general sense of "food." *Coast* is a borrowing, through French, from a Latin word for "side" or "rib" (compare Modern English *intercostal*), and once meant "border" or "frontier"—the "coast of Bohemia" was not always an absurdity. But *coast* in present use not only has the usual specialization "seashore"; as employed in the eastern United States, it means specifically "Pacific coast." *Shore,* on the other hand, means, in parts of the east at any rate, "Atlantic shore." [11] In some of the same localities, however, "eastern shore" means what elsewhere would have to be expanded into "eastern shore

[10] Greenough and Kittredge, *op. cit.,* p. 235.

[11] In Philadelphia it is often used in a still more specific sense, "southern New Jersey shore"; it sometimes bears a yet more localized signification: "Atlantic City," which occurs repeatedly in the headlines of Philadelphia newspapers.

of the Chesapeake in Maryland," just as in part of New England "the cape" means definitely "Cape Cod." *Token* formerly had the broad meaning "sign," but was long ago specialized to mean a physical thing that is a sign (of something)—as in *love token,* or the metal tokens used on streetcars or buses.

An *undertaker* once could undertake to do anything; nowadays he only undertakes to manage funerals. So, to people in general, *doctor* stands only for *doctor of medicine. Liquor,* which once was synonymous with *liquid,* is now definitely specialized. *Reek,* like the German *rauchen,* once had the broad meaning "smoke," as it still has in the Scotch dialect; but the standard Modern English use limits it quite definitely to unpleasant exhalations. *Disease* meant "discomfort"—"lack of ease" in general. *Girl* meant "young person (of either sex)." The limitation of *corpse* to *"dead* body" made it necessary to re-borrow the word in its Modern French form *corps* for another possible meaning of "body," and to make occasional use of the original Latin, *corpus,* for still another sense, "complete collection of writings." *Corn,* in general American use, will be immediately understood as "Indian corn" or "maize." But the word itself once meant simply "grain," and so, in other parts of the English-speaking world, it is differently specialized [12]—in Scotland, to mean "oats," and in England "wheat." Keats's allusion to "Ruth amid the alien corn" probably calls up, to many American readers, a very different picture from what the poet had in mind.

What are the factors that account for specialization of meaning? One is, of course, that localities and groups of people have their own specialized associations for words that otherwise may convey a broader meaning. It has been well remarked that "every man is his own specializer." [13] *Pipe,* for example, calls up different ideas in the mind of the smoker, the plumber, and the organist. *Ring* may be thought of in connection with jewelry, opera, politics, or pugilism— even though, in the last connection, the "squared circle" has long since superseded the original truly circular shape. Quite apart from particular or local specializations, however, there are a great many words whose meaning has become specialized for nearly everybody.

[12] In other Germanic languages, the cognate word has still different specializations in various places: "barley" in Sweden, "rye" in north Germany, and "spelt" in south Germany. (Jespersen, *Mankind, Nation, and Individual,* p. 212.)

[13] Quoted by Greenough and Kittredge, *op. cit.,* p. 251.

A second factor that helps to account for both generalization and specialization is the fading of the etymological significance of the word. Thus, to illustrate the one point, *arrive* [<Lat. *ad* (to) + *ripa* (shore)] originally applied to the end of a voyage only, and was used without the preposition, since this was included in the word. Milton's "ere he arrive the happy isle" illustrates a use that is in strict accord with the etymology of the word. When, however, consciousness of the Latin parts that made up the word was weakened, it was no longer used transitively, but in the phrase "arrive at," and with the more generalized application to the end of any journey.

Yet another factor is the competition among synonymous words. The borrowing of the Latin *animal* and the French *beast* meant that, with the native *deer,* English would have possessed three exactly synonymous terms for one idea; it is obviously in the interests of economy that *deer* should have specialized to mean one particular species of animal rather than "animal" in general, and that *beast* should have acquired connotations that limit its sphere. *Bird* and *fowl, dog* and *hound, boy* and *knave, chair* and *stool* are further instances of words that were once synonyms but that have been differentiated in meaning here by the specialization of the second term of each pair.

A further remark about generalization and specialization is suggested by some of the words just alluded to. The degree of specialization which a language exhibits seems to depend on cultural need. In a culture in which the coconut is essential—as in Polynesia—an extremely complex vocabulary is said to have grown up, with different terms for many stages or ripeness of the fruit. So also, the Eskimos have different terms for falling snow, snow on the ground, snow packed hard like ice, slushy snow, wind-driven flying snow, and other kinds.[14] Many similar examples could be cited, for the languages of peoples of undeveloped culture appear to be particularly rich in specialized terms. At one time in the course of the English language it must have seemed desirable to speakers to make verbal distinctions in connection with groups of animals—mostly those of

---

[14] See B. L. Whorf, "Science and Linguistics," *The Technology Review,* Vol. XLII, No. 6 (April 1940), reprinted in *Four Articles on Metalinguistics,* Washington, D.C. (Foreign Service Institute), 1950, p. 6. For further examples see also Jespersen, *Language,* pp. 429-431.

interest to farmers and hunters. An elaborate set of what are called "company terms" was accordingly developed, some (but by no means all) of which survive today. The better known ones include a *herd* or a *drove* of cattle, but of a *flock* of sheep (or birds), a *school* of fish, a *pack* of wolves (or hounds), a *covey* of partridges, and a *swarm* of bees. But there are others far more esoteric,[15] such as *nye* of pheasants, *cete* of badgers, *sord* of mallards, *wisp* of snipe, *doylt* of tame swine, *gaggle* of geese, *harras* of horses, and *kennel* of raches. There is a similar profusion of names for the same animal (*cow, heifer, bull, calf, steer,* and *ox*), the young of various animals (*puppy, kitten, kid, calf, colt, lamb,* and so forth), and the male and female of the same species) *gander* and *goose, drake* and *duck, horse* and *mare, cock* and *hen, dog* and *bitch*).[16] The need for a generic term is of course particularly felt here, and it is supplied, not quite satisfactorily, by the convention of making either the name of the male (*horse* and *dog*) or of the female (*cow, duck,* and *goose*), or even that of the young of the species (*chicken* and *pig*), perform a larger duty.

Elevation and **Degradation.** If generalization and specialization may be said to involve a change in the "area" of meaning, elevation and degradation[17] involve the rising or falling of meaning in a scale of values. Thus a word which once denominated something bad (or at least neutral) but comes to refer to something good, has undergone *elevation* of meaning; the reverse of this process, obviously, represents a *degradation* of meaning.

And here a word of warning: we must not confuse the linguistic signal with the thing it stands for, though that error is too often made. It is not the word as such which is bad or good, or which becomes elevated or degraded, but only the meaning which society chooses to put upon it. As we shall see, society often reverses itself in the course of time, and words which were once disapproved may

[15] These, and many others, are mentioned in an editorial comment in the *New York Times* for November 20, 1930. All but *doylt* are recorded in the *Oxford Dictionary.*

[16] McKnight, *English Words and Their Background,* p. 239, calls attention in greater detail to the lack of generalizing terms in the animal kingdom, and suggests further that the variety of names for sea craft (*sloop, schooner, brig, ship, boat, dinghy, bark,* and so on) is a similar survival of primitive habits of thought.

[17] Elevation is also called *aggradation* or *amelioration,* and degradation is also called *degeneration* or *pejoration.*

become "respectable," while others that had social favor may lose it. This would not be possible if the value were inherent in the word. With this in mind, then, let us illustrate degradation of meaning.

Many terms that are now descriptive of moral depravity were once quite without this suggestion. *Lust*, for example, meant simply "pleasure," as in German; *wanton* was "untaught"; *lewd* was merely "ignorant," "lerned and lewed" being a phrase commonly standing for "clergy and laity"; *immoral* was "not customary"; *vice*, "flaw"; *hussy*, "housewife"; *wench*, "young girl"; and *harlot*, "fellow" (of either sex). In a similar way, words that impute rascality have often been thoroughly innocent labels: *villain*, for example, was "farm laborer"; *counterfeiter*, "imitator" or "copyist"; *pirate* (at least in its earlier Greek sense), "one who adventures or tries"; *buccaneer*, "one who smokes meat"; *ringleader*, simply "leader" (in a good or a neutral sense); *varlet, knave,* and *imp* meant merely "boy"; and *sly, crafty,* and *cunning* all implied the compliment "skilful." A perennial form of humor—the city man's ridicule of the countryman—is witnessed in the degradation of such nouns as *peasant, boor* (compare German *Bauer* and Dutch *Boer*), and *churl,* and in the frequent implication of such adjectives as *bucolic, rural, rustic,* and *provincial.*

When a word may be applied in two possible ways, one favorable or complimentary and the other the reverse, it is extremely likely that it will specialize in the less desirable sense. Thus, *suggestive* is likely to mean only "evilly suggestive," though it *may* still mean "informative" or "illuminating," and though the noun *suggestion* has escaped any such specialization—just as the verb *to harbor* is limited to unworthy or illegal concealment (as in "harboring a criminal" or "harboring thoughts of revenge"), while the noun *harbor* retains the old broad and literal meaning of "haven." *Asylum*, through association with the idea of "refuge for the insane," has followed a course like that of the verb *harbor*. A *libel*, in Middle English and early Modern English, was simply a "brief bit of writing" (from Lat. *libellum*, little book); now it is definitely limited to something malicious or defamatory. *Doom* once meant "judgment"; now it means only "condemnation." *Reek*, as we have seen, can now stand only for unpleasant distillations; *stink* and *stench* have specialized in the same way from a formerly neutral meaning, and *smell* and even *odor* seem likely to follow their lead. A *smirk* was once merely a smile, without the suggestion of affectation. One could formerly *resent* benefits as well as injuries, and *retaliate* for favors as well as slights; compare with the present meanings of these words the ordinary implications of the phrase "get even with" or "get square with."

On the other hand, instances of words that have traveled an opposite path, from the humble to the exalted, or from the base to the refined, are not far to seek. The institution of chivalry brought about the elevation of *knight* (youth) and *squire* (shield-bearer); and *chivalry* itself was invested by the Romantic Revival with a glamor that the word (as we see from its source, Fr. *cheval*, horse) did not originally possess. "Romantic" ideas in the late eighteenth and early nineteenth centuries were similarly responsible for the gain in dignity of such words as *bard*, once a term of contempt like *vagabond; minstrel*, once applicable to juggler and buffoon as well as musician; and *enthusiasm*, in the earlier eighteenth century akin to *fanaticism*. Like *knight*, other terms for rank or position have had the good fortune to take on added prestige when the offices for which they stood changed their character, and when their own etymological meanings were forgotten. Such is the history of *marshal* (originally, "horse-servant"), *chamberlain* (room-attendant), *minister* (servant), *constable* (stable-attendant), *governor* (pilot), and *steward* (sty-guardian). It is true that in a number of these words the extent of the elevation fluctuates: *marshal* is a less dignified title when it is applied to the lone policeman of an American village than when it is applied to the highest ranking officers of the English or the French army; there is a similar variation between the American and the British connotations for *constable*, just as *steward* may suggest a club attendant as well as the Lord High Steward of England, or even the royal dynasty of the *Stewarts* (or *Stuarts*);[18] likewise, *governor* may mean the warden of an English prison or the chief administrative officer of one of our American states. On the whole, however, the fact that any present implication of these words represents a gain in dignity over the etymological one is patent enough. So too it is with a number of political and religious labels: *Tory, Whig, Puritan, Quaker,* and *Methodist* are well-known examples of names that were originally applied in contempt but that have taken on

[18] Greenough and Kittredge, *op. cit.*, p. 296.

dignified associations (though, to some, *Puritan* and perhaps *Tory* still convey a derisive significance). Archbishop Trench long ago pointed out that the influence of Christianity elevated *angel* from merely "messenger," *martyr* from "witness," and *paradise* from "park," through the Biblical application to the abode of our first parents (as in *Paradise Lost* and "*earthly* paradise") to the "blisful waiting-place of faithful departed spirits." [19] Miscellaneous further illustrations of elevation are *pretty* from an early meaning "sly," through "clever," to something approaching "beautiful"; *nice* from an etymological meaning "ignorant," through its earliest English sense "foolish," and later ones like "particular," to its present broad and vague colloquial meaning of "pleasant" or "acceptable"; and *fond* from "foolish" to "affectionate."

The usual view of degradation and elevation has been that the downward path is far the more common. Despite McKnight's protest to the effect that elevation has been less noticed simply because it is less dramatic,[20] there seems to be every reason to agree with the general verdict. Examples of elevation, after all, are far less easy to find than examples of degradation, which indeed meet us at every turn. Besides, most of the words that have been cited as undergoing elevation fall into a few obvious categories, while the types of degradation are extremely various. The truth of the matter would appear to be that degradation has been more noticed not because it is more spectacular but simply because it is omnipresent, as elevation is not. Why should this be so, and why should the use of words be made difficult by a lurking leer, a hint of unpleasant connotation that makes a word that appears to be absolutely right in denotation impossible for a given occasion? It is hard to escape the conclusion that there is a disagreeable commentary on human nature here. How difficult it is for superlatives to retain their superlative force— because the general tendency is to apply them on light occasion and hence to weaken their meaning! So *fair* comes to mean "passable," and indeed is often equivalent to "not good"; and *quite* has passed, in its usual American application at least, from "entirely" or "com-

[19] Archbishop Richard Chevenix Trench, *On the Study of Words,* New York (Armstrong), 20th ed. (no date), p. 114.

[20] *English Words and Their Background,* p. 292; cf. also Janet Aiken, *English Present and Past,* p. 112, and G. A. Van Dongen, *Amelioratives in English.*

pletely" to "moderately." The tendency to procrastinate finds illustration in a whole series of words or phrases—*by and by, presently, anon, immediately, directly,* and *soon* itself—that have "slowed up," changing their meaning from "now" or "at once" to "soon" or "after a time." It is scarcely a far-fetched interpretation to see in the narrowing of *demure* to apply to *mock* modesty, of *genteel* to *spurious* gentility, of *sophistication* to *worldly* wisdom, of *egregious* to notoriety rather than fame, of *sanctimonious* to *pretended* holiness, and of *grandiose* to *tinsel* (itself an example of degradation) grandeur —to see in all these, and dozens of others that might be mentioned, the workings of human motives like suspicion, contempt, and general pessimism.

Euphemism. With degradation is often associated the widespread tendency in language to avoid the direct word by employing a pleasant, neutral, or even meaningless substitute, which is described as its "euphemism" (from Greek words meaning "well" and "speak"). Peoples of all times and places have apparently felt that to pronounce certain holy or ominous words is to tempt Providence. On the other hand, the god, demon, or monster that is feared may be propitiated, if not by silence, at any rate by circumlocution or by deliberately misapplied compliment. Thus the Greeks called the Furies the *Eumenides* (literally, the "well-minded" ones); the Irish peasantry prefer to avoid the term *fairies* and to employ instead *gentry, little people,* or *good people;* and many primitive races have had elaborate verbal taboos that prevent the direct naming of animals that are feared and persons that are either venerated or despised.

Most striking, perhaps, of such reticences and equivocations (in language after language) are the euphemisms for ideas associated with death. Instead of the verb *die,* we substitute *pass away* or *on,*[21] *breathe one's last, succumb, expire, depart this life, be taken* or *called, go to a better world,* or *go west* (the favorite euphemism in the first World War, curiously parallel to the Greek conception of the *Hesperides,* or Western Isles, the abode of the dead). In the second World War, *replacements* was officially changed to *reinforce-*

---

[21] In Old English, *gefaran* and *forþfaran* were used in this way, as in German *fahren* and *vergehen* are used, and in French *passer, trépasser,* and even *partir* or *s'en aller.*

ments, since the former term carried the unpleasant suggestion that somebody had been hurt or killed.[22] The *dead* person is alluded to as the *lost,* the *deceased, departed, defunct,* or the like. Sometimes the idea of the verb is veiled in such jocose phrases as *kick the bucket, push up the daisies,* and *pass in one's checks.* Likewise, *death* itself is more obscurely alluded to by generalized terms like *end, passing, departure,* and *dissolution;* and *kill* is avoided in favor of *settle, do for, remove, destroy,* or (in lower strata of speech) *knock off, bump off, take for a ride, put on the spot,* or the like. Dictators both before and since the second World War have cynically *liquidated* their enemies. (In George Orwell's horribly prophetic novel *1984,* enemies of the régime are *vaporized.*) The superstitious origin of these euphemisms seems evident in the fact that many speakers simply cannot allude to an imminent death by saying, "If he should die. . . ." It is as though merely to pronounce the word would bring about the dreaded possibility. Instead of "If he should die," they say "If he shouldn't recover," "If he shouldn't come back," or— vaguest of all in the words themselves, but nevertheless perfectly clear in the meaning intended—"If anything should happen to him."

One means of veiling the distressing truth is to employ a term that is not immediately intelligible, one that requires, in fact, something like translation. In place of plain words, therefore, we frequently have elaborate—usually borrowed rather than native—synonyms for ideas linked to death and disaster. *Casualty, suicide, mortality, obituary, accident,* and *fatality* have clearly originated in this way. *Cemetery* was once itself a euphemism (literally, "sleeping place"), but it has come to be felt as too direct in its implication of "burial ground"; hence we have *memorial park,* or occasionally *necropolis—* "city of the dead," to be sure, but decently veiled in the Greek equivalents. *Undertaker* was apparently a euphemistic shortening of *funeral undertaker,* but it came to mean what it undertook to conceal; hence *funeral director* was evolved, and more recently *mortician.* The last of course is distinctly American, for this kind of squeamishness (combined, perhaps, with a greater love of the pompous) has gone farther here than in England. So too are *casket* for *coffin,* and *funeral car* for *hearse* distinctively American euphemisms, as are also such elegancies as *mortuary chapel* and *funeral parlors.*

---

[22] This information was kindly furnished by Prof. E. B. Atwood, of the University of Texas.

The ultimate attempt to avoid the discomfort of this subject, however, is surely *funeral home!*

Not that euphemism is always to be ridiculed: on some occasions to soften the brutal reality is surely the part of taste and tact. But the effect of the process is to weaken the force of the euphemistic substitute, and often to lead in turn, as has already been indicated, to the degradation of that word. Thus *insane* (not healthy) begins as a polite evasion of the ugly truth; but it comes to have a direct and unequivocal meaning, so that other euphemisms must be resorted to —*simple, mental case,* and (formerly) *innocent* and *natural* [23]—to make good the loss caused by degradation. Words associated with insanity, it may be observed in passing, afford a peculiarly fertile field for the study of change of meaning in general; not only euphemism, degradation, and specialization, but also irony, metaphor, humor, superstition, and pedantry are to be observed here as active forces. *Sǣlig* in Old English meant "happy" or "blessed" (a sense largely retained by Modern German *selig*) ; but Middle English and Modern English *silly* came, through an ironical application, to mean first "innocent" or "harmless"—the disguised Archimago refers to himself as "silly old man" [24]—and finally "feeble-minded" or "half-witted" (themselves, frequently enough, euphemistic softenings of more accurately descriptive terms). *Crazy* is a jocose metaphor, literally equivalent to "cracked," a word that is itself a slang term for "insane." *Insane,* incidentally, is chronologically before *crazy,* since it is a Renaissance euphemism for earlier terms like *wood* and *mad* (the latter now colloquially transferred to anger rather than insanity, and somewhat stilted in its earlier application). In Old English, the equivalents of modern *dizzy* and *giddy* were the usual adjectives implying a lack of sense; according to Bradley,[25] "the prehistoric meaning of both seems to have been 'possessed by a god.' " *Foolish,* along with *crazy* and *mad,* largely superseded *dizzy* and *giddy* in their Old English meanings; the source of *fool*—a Middle English borrowing of French *fol,* in turn a slangy application of Latin *follis* (windbag)—is also interesting. Other words of this group that may be mentioned are *idiot* (in Greek and in early Mod-

[23] A frequent Shakespearean meaning; it survives in dialect much later. In French, incidentally, *simple* and *innocent* (and in German *einfältig*) have gone exactly the same way.

[24] *Faery Queen,* Book I, Canto I, stanza 30.

[25] *Making of English,* p. 199.

ern English "private person"), in which the application to one mentally deficient seems an unusually far-fetched bit of euphemism; *imbecile*, of unknown origin, but meaning "weak" in general before it meant "weak-minded"; *moron*, a Greek borrowing which literally means "fool"; and *cretin*, from a French word which was originally a dialectal variant of *chrétien* (Christian). The foregoing list, it may be added, by no means exhausts the catalog of terms that betray an effort to gloss over a dreadful fact. Unfortunately there are still many people who seem to believe that to get rid of something undesirable one has only to give it a new name.

Equally interesting, are the distortions in language, sometimes called "minced forms," that result when the human impulse to swear is held in check by religious or social prohibitions. The usual compromise is a word or phrase that suggests rather than states, that at once approaches the forbidden and shies away from it. Thus, *God* becomes *gad*, *damn* becomes *darn*, and *God-damned* [26] becomes *dod-burned*, *goldurned*, and so forth. Further distortions of the sacred name are *goodness*, *gosh*, *gorry*, *Godfrey*, and *golly*; and older oaths like *'Oddsbodkins* (for "God's little body"), *'Sblood* (God's blood), and *Zounds* (God's wounds). *Jesus* is suggested by the Elizabethan *Gis* (now *Jeez*), and by the modern *Geewhiz, Jerusalem*, and "for *Pete's* sake"; *Christ* is alluded to in *Cripes*, "for the love of *Mike*," and the otherwise meaningless "O for *cry*ing out loud"; *Jimminy Crickets* and the more recent *Jeepers Creepers* attempt to combine the two. A curious exhibition indeed, of the human desire to sin combined with want of courage!

A form of euphemism to which passing reference has already been made is that in which the motive is prudery—often accompanied by ostentation. The result is what Mr. Fowler has happily termed the *genteelism*, and defined [27] as "the substituting, for the ordinary natural word that first suggests itself to the mind, of a synonym that is thought to be less soiled by the lips of the common herd, less familiar, less plebeian, less vulgar, less improper, less apt to come unhandsomely between the wind and our nobility." Some of Mr. Fowler's examples are rather British than American—*serviette* for

[26] *God-darned*, put by Galsworthy into the mouth of Hallorsen, the American professor in *Maid in Waiting*, London (Heinemann), 1932, is as unrealistic as the conversation of Americans in British novels so often is. No American ever euphemizes only one syllable of this word.

[27] *Dictionary of Modern English Usage*, p. 212.

napkin, paying guest (still further euphemized to *p.g.*) for *boarder,* and *coal-vase* for *coal-scuttle;* but others are more American than British—*expectorate* for *spit,* particularly. On the whole, indeed, an American must regretfully concede that the tendency both to be mealy-mouthed and to be pompous has gone farther in the United States than in England—though it is probably true that Englishmen are prone to exaggerate the difference.[28] Still, if Mr. Fowler can cite one pompous genteelism like *chiropodist* for *corn-cutter,* an American has no difficulty in citing dozens that are all too familiar to him: for a very few samples, *junior executive* for *clerk, exodontist* for *tooth-puller, custodian* for *janitor, realtor* for *real estate agent,* and *heating engineer* for *plumber.* The American passion for sonorous titles, even when the position in question is not particularly impressive, is further attested by such neologisms as *receptionist, beautician,* and *cosmetician.* H. L. Mencken has recently recorded *stripteuse* and *ecdysiast* as professional euphemisms for *strip-teaser.*

Of a rather different type of genteelism, that in which squeamishness rather than ostentation is the more prominent motive force, a few words may be added. There have always been certain taboos associated with parts of the body and their clothing. Though the Victorian preference for *limb* over *leg* (even when referring to a chicken or a piano) seems to the present generation the height of ridiculous prudery, the tendency to avoid the plain name in speaking of certain other parts of the body is of course still active, and— what may perhaps be illustrated with less offense to the conventions in question—the names for the more personal and intimate garments are likely also to be genteel euphemisms. Thus *shirt* and *drawers* (for women's use) give way to words like *vest* and *panties; petticoat,* a sufficiently innocuous term meaning "little coat," yields to *slip* or to *skirt* (curiously enough, itself a doublet of and evidently a euphemistic substitute for *shirt,* since it is the Scandinavian variant of the Anglo-Saxon word); while *underwear* or *underclothing* as the general term is superseded by the more elegant French borrowing *lingerie* or some such equivalent as *intimate wear.* Moreover, if the

[28] In *Jesting Pilate,* Garden City (Doubleday, Doran), 1926, Aldous Huxley remarks on the "revaluation of values . . . (for the worse)" that has taken place in the United States. This revaluation he finds to be symbolized in the commercialization and degradation of such words as *service,* and the pretentious use of *mortician, casket,* and so forth—all as a result of the "humbug" necessary to maintain the democratic hypothesis that all men are equal.

garments in question have been worn, it is no longer proper to refer to them as *dirty,* and still less, as our distant ancestors would have done without a qualm, as *filthy* or *foul;* no, *dirty clothes* have given way to *soiled linen.* We are not quite so far removed as we may at first suppose from the atmosphere of that period in French society when *shirt* was alluded to by an elaborate circumlocution meaning "the constant companion of the dead and living."

It is true that for a generation or so there has been a cult of calling a spade a spade, and further, as someone has remarked, of inserting as many spades as possible into the conversation—what James Truslow Adams referred to pungently as "the mucker pose." Yet there are conventional limits even to this. Less restraint in speaking plainly of sex and morals is curiously accompanied by a frequent timidity in referring to the ills and unpleasantnesses that flesh is heir to. Thus *halitosis,* the happy discovery of purveyors of mouth-washes, has found a wider usefulness, and *bad breath* is taboo; just as *acute indigestion* some time ago replaced the old-fashioned *belly-ache.* The advertisers would likewise have us suffer from *comedones* instead of *blackheads,* from *conjunctivitis* instead of a *sty* (in the eye), and from *alopecia* instead of *baldness.* Their efforts have been crowned with financial success, for they have not only given dignity to many a homely malady, but the imposing Latin and Greek names play on people's fears associated with the unknown. In modern conversation on the subjects of sex and morals the obscure jargon of Freudian psychoanalysis serves a similar purpose of euphemism, lending at the same time a sense of importance and mystery to the abnormal. Likewise birth, as well as death, is often a subject for euphemistic substitution, *to be born* giving way to *see the light of day, come into the world,* and so forth. The prenatal state is even less likely to be referred to plainly; as in the age of Victoria, a pregnant woman is still too often referred to as being *in the family way* or, with coyest reticence, as *expecting.* Euphemism, in this field as in others, is neither dead nor dying.

Hyperbole. Allied to euphemistic substitution, and likewise springing from dissatisfaction with the plain word, is the use of hyperbole or exaggeration. The most familiar illustrations are the adjectives and adverbs that indicate approval or disapproval. In the one group are terms like *grand, superb, gorgeous, magnificent, perfect,* and *unique* (the last two logically absolute, but nevertheless often qualified by *more* and *most*) ; in the other group are such words as *horrible, dreadful, outrageous, horrid, frightful, awful,* and— *lousy,* the adjective of the moment, the curious result of such incongruous motives as the will to call a spade a spade, the wish to shock by the use of the forbidden, and the desire to be emphatic. The point is, of course, that all the adjectives cited have their own distinctive meanings and serve admirably for exceptional occasions of various sorts; but they are by no means reserved for these exceptional occasions, with the result that their distinctive qualities are inevitably weakened. When the strong word is used on light occasion its strength begins to be dissipated, and when the fitting moment for it actually arrives it will no longer serve; familiarity has bred contempt in the hearer, and one must begin again to find a new "strong word."

One consequence is that the adjective of weakened force is frequently bolstered by an adverb that strives to restore its pristine vigor—but cannot do so long, for hyperbole has entered into *its* employment too. *Very* (truly) has, through overuse, become so weakened that *very good* may easily convey less of praise than an obviously sincere *good*. Expressions like *absolutely unique* and *awfully disgusting* betray a double hyperbole in their very aspect. There is nothing new, incidentally, about the hyperbolic qualifier: phrases like *monstrous agreeable, marvellous fine,* and *vastly pretty* merely anticipate by two or three centuries other phrases like *frightfully agreeable, wonderfully fine,* and *amazingly pretty.* Investigation of other aspects of hyperbole—for example, in terms of courteous address and in titles—would serve to strengthen one's feeling that, like euphemism, its effect upon the vocabulary is a powerful one, in the present as it has been in the past.

Other Changes of Meaning. The types of change of meaning considered so far, let us repeat, are by no means mutually exclusive, nor do they exhaust the possible types. The fundamental conception that should be enforced as to the meaning of the word is that this meaning is unstable. We may think of the first or "etymological" meaning as the nuclear center from which there is radiation or transference of meaning in all directions. Some words, to be sure—and some of the finest and most essential words of language—cannot be so considered: there is every reason to suppose that *father, mother, fire, thunder,* and other such inheritances from the prehistoric past mean in Modern English precisely what their Indo-European equivalents meant thousands of years ago. But they are the exception, and the other state of affairs is the rule. Words on the whole are likely to broaden or narrow their meanings, to go uphill or down in the scale of respectability, and to be subject to the shifts of meaning that figurative uses (irony, metaphor, personification, hyperbole, and so on) promote; and the history of a single word will often illustrate many of these changes. Consider, for example, a few of the various possible meanings of the familiar word *draw*. The root meaning is "pull by force," most clearly preserved in "draw a vehicle." But there are various manners of "pulling," and various effects. "Draw one's breath" and "drawn features" are more literal (though specialization begins to enter the second) ; "draw a lesson" or "draw an audience" are more metaphorical applications. The meaning "obtain" (generalized apparently through metaphor) is present in "He drew his wages" or "What did you draw?" But the last phrase may have a different meaning—not "What did you get?" but "What picture did you make?" For "pulling" a pencil across a paper creates lines that may form the pictorial representation of an object, so that the phrase "Can he draw?" will be understood in this highly specialized sense. This last sense, incidentally, may be metaphorically transferred to a picture in words as well as in lines: "draw a portrait" is to that extent ambiguous. A high degree of specialization, finally, is present in the old phrase *draw and quarter* (remove the entrails), as also in a phrase still occasionally used, "*draw* a chicken," for which, more often, "*clean* a chicken" is euphemistically substituted.

A curious condition that sometimes results from the violent shifts of meaning to which words are subject may be briefly noticed: occasionally, a word will evolve a meaning that quite reverses its original one. Bradley has pointed out[29] the steps by which the meaning of *fast* changed from "immovable" to "rapid in motion." In this instance, the more recent meanings did not entirely supersede the original one; hence it is possible both to "stand fast" and to "go fast." *Fine*, as the same writer notices, may likewise mean both "small" and "large," for the original sense of "highly finished" has been extended in opposite directions: it may express admiration for intricacy and delicacy, or admiration for luxuriant growth. *Phe-*

[29] *Making of English*, pp. 161-162.

nomenal, in present-day journalistic use at least, means "extraordinary"; it was formerly applied not to a wonderful event but to any observed event or process, and hence was more like "ordinary." *Upright* has meant both "erect" and "supine"; the two opposite senses occur in Chaucer. The Chaucerian sense for *reduce,* incidentally, is "add up"; the modern one, "take away" or "lessen." *Demean* was originally "conduct" (the noun *demeanor* still is more likely to be applied in compliment than the reverse), but popular etymology has associated it with *mean* rather than the French *démener,* its real source; so it comes about that the present colloquial, and sometimes the literary, use makes it equivalent to "degrade." A favorite modern sense of *literally* makes it equal to its exact opposite, "metaphorically":[30] "I was literally frozen." *Valetudinarian* includes the root idea of "being well" (Lat. *valere*), but it has gone from "solicitous about health" to "invalid." Further oddities of this sort in which opposite meanings are possible in the present use of the word are *scan,* "scrutinize carefully" or "read carelessly"; *nervous,* "weak" or "strong"; and *distract,* "annoy" or "amuse." [31] Occasionally, it perhaps should be added, opposite meanings are due not to change of meaning in one word, but to the confusion between two words: *let* has meant, in Modern English, both "hinder" and "permit," the one representing Old English *lettan,* and the other Old English *lǣtan*—which have eventually fallen together; *quean* and *queen,* sometimes cited as extreme examples of elevation and degradation of the same word, are really from separate, though related, Old English forms, *cwene* and *cwēn.*

Folk Etymology. We have mentioned in passing, and may now discuss, "folk (or popular) etymology," which often contributes to the unpredictable shifts of meaning that words are heir to. As the term implies, people who do not know the real etymology change the forms of words in accordance with what they fancy them to mean. Thus they convert the unfamiliar into something familiar, even though the connection between the new form and the object it refers to may be curiously far-fetched. A road that runs diagonally across the State of New Jersey appears on the maps as *Provinceline Road.*

[30] Rose Macaulay, "Catchwords and Claptrap," *Hogarth Essays,* Garden City (Doubleday, Doran), 1928, p. 113. This amusing paper discusses a number of examples of "man's deliberate revolt against the rigidity of language."

[31] Cf. John O'London, *Is It Good English?,* pp. 156-158, for these and other "words that have turned their coats."

The etymology is quite clear: it is so called because it formed the original dividing *line* between the old royal *provinces* of East New Jersey and West New Jersey. But the older country people of at least one district through which the road runs call it not *Provinceline* but *Providenceline Road*. The substitution is evidently made because *province* has ceased to have a meaning, while *providence* has one that can be made to serve; the new form does not make very good sense, but it makes more sense than the one it has displaced. Incidentally, there is a glimpse here into the difficulties that beset the science of etymology. If the variant *Providenceline* had come into use earlier, and made its way into general and official use, the clue to the true origin of the word might easily have been lost. The historian might then explain the name as "a line drawn by the hand of Providence," and comment on the piety of the early settlers! Many words are doubtless explained quite as erroneously because popular etymology has obscured their real sources.

Borrowed words are of course particularly likely to be affected by folk etymology. The Old French *crevisse* (cognate with *crab*—compare German *Krebs*) that became Middle English *crevise* has been altered to *crayfish* or *crawfish* quite certainly because the "meaningless" *-vise* could readily be changed to the apparently similar (and not quite irrelevant) native word *fish*. *Simoom* (<Arabic *semūm*) is frequently, and now quite reputably, varied to *simoon*, presumably for a like reason: the obscure feeling that the *moon* has something to do with the weather; probably, also, the pattern of words ending in *-oon* (more common than *-oom*) has had its influence. *Primrose* comes from Old French *primerole*, and meant originally "first little flower (of spring)," but the erroneous association with *rose* has of course distorted the word irrevocably. *Surloin* (from Fr. *sur-*, above) was easily altered to *sirloin* (the change this time affecting only spelling), since *sir* was familiar and *sur-* was not. To "explain" the present orthography of the word, an apocryphal legend has been evolved: it has been said, and sometimes believed, that an English king went to the length of expressing his approbation of a favorite dish by conferring knighthood upon it, using the formula, "Rise, Sir Loin." Miscellaneous further examples of popular etymology affecting the forms and sounds of borrowed words are *buttery*, which is really not connected with *butter* but with *bottles* (M.E. *botery* and *botelrye* <O.F. *boteillerie*); *belfry*, which originally had nothing to

do with *bells*—the Old French *berfrey* (tower) was inevitably distorted in this way, both because of the apparent gain in "meaning" by the introduction of the idea of "bell" and because of the easy transition from *r* to *l; mushroom,* from Old French *mouscheron,* both parts of which have been familiarized in English terms, though the latter—*room*—makes little sense; *penthouse,* from French *appentis* (<Lat. *appendicium*), which has only a fanciful connection with *house; Jerusalem,* in *Jerusalem artichoke* (the latter word also an example of the process we are considering), which is a corruption of the Italian *girasole* (turning with the sun). The American *carry-all* has been explained [32] as an ingenious distortion of French *carriole,* and *petticoat-tales,* a curious name, current in Edinburgh, for "shortbread" as a corruption of French *petits gâteaux.*[33] Translation of foreign words into more familiar terms that are in sound, though not in meaning, approximately equivalent, sometimes achieves almost incredibly grotesque creations in substandard speech: evolutions of this kind include *shoemaker* for *sumac* (tree), *very close* for *varicose* (veins), *high geranium* for *hydrangea, choir practice* for *chiropractic,* and *ruddy Daniel* for *rhododendron.*

Folk etymology is not limited to borrowed words: the original meaning of a native term too can easily be lost sight of, and the word accordingly altered in form (and often eventually in meaning as well) to agree with some imagined etymology. Thus *sand-blind*[34] is a distortion of *samblind,* in which the first element was an Old English prefix, cognate with Latin *semi-,* meaning "half"; the word is likely to be used too as if it meant "totally blind" instead of "partially blind." A *hangnail* is not a nail that *hangs,* but one that is painful (Old English *ang*). *Titmouse* seems a curious name to give a bird until one discovers that its second element had originally nothing to do with "mouse," but comes from Middle English *mose* (<O.E. *māse*), a name for various species of birds. *Shame-faced* is an understandable variant of the older term *shamefast,* which meant rather "confirmed in modesty" than "disconcerted" (i.e., betraying shame in one's face). *Acorn* (O.E. *œcern*) is not really related to *corn, slow-worm* (O.E. *slā-wyrm*) to *slow, bride-groom* (O.E. *brȳd-*

---

[32] Mencken, *American Language,* p. 108. The *Oxford Dictionary* confirms this.
[33] Barfield, Owen, *History in English Words,* p. 57.
[34] Greenough and Kittredge, *op. cit.,* p. 335. Many of these illustrations of folk etymology are suggested either by Chapter XXIII of this book or by Chapter XIII of G. H. McKnight, *English Words and Their Background.*

guma, bride-man) to *groom,* or *hiccough* (an echoic word which has various earlier forms, including *hicket* and *hickup*) to *cough.*

Something a good deal akin to popular etymology may be observed in "learned" and etymologically erroneous spellings which, as we have already seen, have not infrequently replaced earlier spellings that were superior both phonetically and historically. The folk and the scholar have sometimes proceeded in much the same way in distorting a word through some purely fictitious theory of its origin. Sometimes, indeed, it is discovered that what was once thought to be a form established through popular etymology is really the original one, and the rival form is due to the kindred process of learned error. Thus, *country-dance* has been more than once cited [35] as an example of popular etymology, on the assumption that it represented a corruption of *contre* (opposite)-*danse.* According to the *Oxford English Dictionary,* however, the truth is nearly the reverse of this,[36] the real explanation of the rival forms being that *contre-danse* is a mistaken "correction" for *country-dance.* On the other hand, the spelling *rhyme* (for the simpler *rime*) used to be attributed to a learned error in explaining as from Greek *rhythmós* (as in *rhythm*) what was really from Old English *rīm* (measure); however, the earlier theory is now believed to be correct, and *rhyme* is thus scarcely an "absurd spelling" [37] (at least etymologically—though *rime* of course may be preferred on other counts).

Slang. Words altered by popular etymology have often, as most of our illustrations indicate, displaced the original forms and become fully accepted in standard speech. Other types of language created below the standard level may also achieve full sanction—and so it is with slang, to which we now turn. Slang differs in origin from the products of folk etymology in being a conscious substitution (which folk etymology rarely is), and in offering either a new meaning or use for an old word, or a new creation—frequently produced by the deliberate distortion of an existing word.

It is difficult both to define slang and to indicate its relation to

[35] As in McKnight, *op. cit.,* p. 183.

[36] Vendryes (*Language,* trans. by Radin, p. 181) also asserts that "the English *country-dance,* itself borrowed from French, has passed back into that tongue under the term *contre-danse,* which does not make sense."

[37] Greenough and Kittredge, *op. cit.,* p. 333. The spelling *rime* can really be defended etymologically, since, according to the *Oxford Dictionary,* the *immediate* source of the English word is Old French *rime.*

other linguistic types. Popular impressions about it are often erroneous: there is no necessary connection, for example, between the slangy and the vulgar, or between the slangy and the ungrammatical; further, there is nothing new about the phenomenon of slang, nor is it anything peculiarly American. Some of these misconceptions we shall return to. In addition, it may be asserted that entirely competent treatments of slang sometimes take in too much territory. One such treatment, Krapp's discussion in *Modern English*,[38] will serve as our point of departure. Incidentally, it is striking testimony to the ephemeral character of a great deal of slang that Krapp's illustrations, brought together only forty-odd years ago, impress the reader as antiquarian specimens for the most part. Truly, there is nothing so completely dead as last year's slang.

There are, according to Krapp, four chief varieties or sub-species of slang: (1) counter-words, (2) cant phraseology, (3) picturesque metaphor, and (4) picturesque sound. By the first term, "counterword," is meant a word that has so far lost its original, perhaps highly specialized, meaning that it is reduced to a mere counter— hardly more than a plus or minus sign signifying acceptance or rejection, as often as not emotional. The first illustration that comes to mind is, of course, *nice*, in the broad and loose sense of "pleasant"; Krapp aptly compares the present vogue of this word with the Elizabethan fondness for *fair*, and the eighteenth-century liking for *elegant*. But the history of *nice* and the histories of *grand, fine, awful*, and so forth, would merely seem to illustrate the working of factors like generalization, hyperbole, and elevation or degradation. Words of this class resemble slang words only in their tendency to appear in and out of season—for one of the more irritating characteristics of a certain type of slang is that it is used *ad nauseam* (as "O.K." is today constantly substituted for "Yes" or "All right," and as "I'll say" was similarly used a few years ago). "Damnable iteration," nevertheless, is not enough in itself to make the counter-word truly slang. It lacks other characteristic features of slang, as we shall see.

Two of the other categories that have been listed, picturesque metaphor and picturesque sound, must be rejected for another reason: they are not so much distinct types of slang as qualities sought after and often present in slang. As the source of our definition we are therefore left with cant phraseology—indeed, historically, this is

[38] Pp. 199-211.

usually taken as the source, and some go so far as to identify slang with this cant phraseology, or underworld argot. Others, however, classify it with the vocabularies peculiar to various occupations, the "shop-talk" of artisans, students, stockbrokers, and so on;[39] and the less enlightened champions of textbook style proscribe it in the same category with anything colloquial or familiar, without making much distinction among the three.

Yet though hard-and-fast lines cannot be drawn between these types—for they do merge with each other to some extent—they are not indistinguishable. Cant or argot is, true enough, a type of occupational language, for most criminals are professionals too; but cant is deliberately secret, whereas shop-talk in the honest professions, so far as it is secret at all, is so only by the accident that its practitioners are familiar with subjects which outsiders do not understand. Shop-talk, in contrast to slang, is utilitarian; nor does it necessarily have the self-conscious, show-off quality of slang. Perhaps, then, we may define slang as an intentionally, often humorously strained form of speech in which the desire for novelty and for striking expression is paramount; which, though it draws some of its words from the "shop-talk" of various occupations, gives them a currency outside of the limits of the occupation; and which, though not so narrow as cant, betrays its historical relationship to it by showing more than a trace of the desire to be intelligible only to initiates.

A very few examples may be given. The word *scram* (get away fast) was originally part of the cant of criminals, but it became more generally used and known when it entered the sphere of slang. The phrase *to jack up* was part of the shop-talk of garage mechanics and others of similar trades, but it is now a widely known slang expression with change of meaning (to take to task, rebuke). The word *allergy*, and its adjective *allergic*, are recent additions to the technical terminology of medicine, referring to physiological sensitivity, but the adjective, at least, has gone over into slang in a transferred sense: "I'm *allergic* to that girl" meaning "I can't stand her." Thus slang frequently draws on other types of language, giving them its characteristic touch of enlargement, novelty, or surprise, and a greatly increased currency.

One of the interesting aspects of slang is the fact that it not only

---

[39] For different points of view in this matter, see Jespersen, *Mankind, Nation, and Individual,* Chapters VIII and X, and Vendryes, *op. cit.,* pp. 249-250.

exemplifies but exaggerates general linguistic processes. Words and phrases come into being and drop out in ways exactly like those of ordinary speech, but in slang the introduction is more violent and the departure more rapid. We have come more and more to think of the general vocabulary, like other phases of language, as in a continual state of flux; nowhere is this more apparent than in slang, for here the whole cycle of a word's career—introduction, popularization, overuse, senescence, and demise—is often visibly before us in the course of a few years. There is another kind of cycle too which is frequently perceptible within the observation of a single generation: the successive substitution of phrase after phrase to stand for the same thought. Take the retorts connoting cynical or contemptuous disbelief, and notice how the slang fashion alters almost year by year: "Tell it to the marines," "Tell it to Sweeney," "Is zat so?" "Says you," "So's your old man," "Oh, yeah!," "So what?" This list, arranged more or less chronologically, is quite evidently selective and incomplete.

The frequent and quite proper association of slang with youth helps in part to account for such elements in it as contempt for authority, irreverence, high spirits, and freshness. But even the most typical form of slang—that of students—has no absolute consistency, for it alters from school to school and from university to university. Oxford is not at one with Cambridge in this matter, nor Yale with Harvard. A comparison of the slang of colleges[40] even of the same type will show that though a few words are widely spread and apparently well established, the mass of the vocabulary is local and temporary. What persists is the method of formation: the majority of words are produced by clipping, by deliberate distortion of sounds, and by metaphor often more lively than decent.

In the "collegiate era" of the 1920's there was as much extravagance in slang as in other aspects of undergraduate life. But the colleges today are relatively conservative, probably in reaction against imitation of the "collegiate" pose by high-school students—which, of course, spoiled it for the college man and woman. Perhaps the most vigorous student slang is found nowadays at the "teen-age"

---

[40] See, for example, *American Speech*, Vol. XVIII, No. 2 (April 1943), pp. 153-155, "Whitman College Slang"; *ibid.*, Vol. XXI, No. 1 (Feb. 1946), pp. 29-36, "An Aggie Vocabulary of Slang"; *Time*, Vol. LV, No. 16 (April 17, 1950), pp 72-74, "Undergragger Talk: English University Slang."

level. Again, this "jive-talk" or "bop-talk" is deliberately esoteric; it separates the "cool-cats" who know it from the "squares" who do not. It has the other characteristics of slang too, since it changes rapidly, is self-consciously exaggerated, and avails itself of lively metaphor and startling sounds.[41]

There will not be space in which to enlarge upon the special varieties of slang, besides students', that have been developed. As has already been said, slang very often emerges out of the "shop-talk" of various occupations: the ways of speaking peculiar to the theater, the printing-house, the hangar, the garage, the camp, the baseball field, and so on quite without end.[42] But we must turn our attention to the linguistic processes through which the slang word is evolved. Because slang is likely to be created among individuals in groups, a slang word may be substituted for a more formal word and still be understood. The more familiar any word or linguistic formula is, the more rapidly and briefly it may be spoken; so, in the special circle of users of slang, not only phonetic clippings and irregularities, but also semantic novelties may be freely indulged in. Thus we have in slang not merely elisions, syncopations, and losses of syllables, but the use of figures like metonymy, metaphor, and hyperbole as well. Most important of all is metaphor. This is the most characteristic type of creation that slang admits. The metaphorical substitution for the plain, literal word conduces both to a changed meaning for what was once deliberate metaphor, and to a constantly renewed succession of metaphors for a given idea. Let us look at some of the ideas that have had a varied expression in cognate languages because slang has employed a series of metaphors to designate them.

[41] Cf. *Newsweek,* October 8, 1951.

[42] A bibliography for slang would be endless. Mention may perhaps be made of the seven-volume work of Farmer and Henley, *Dictionary of Slang and Its Analogues,* New York (Dutton), 1905—one-volume edition, 1929; and of a few works like Godfrey Irwin, *American Tramp and Underworld Slang,* New York (Oxford), 1931, and Howard N. Rose, *A Thesaurus of Slang,* New York (Macmillan), 1934; Maurice H. Weseen, *Dictionary of American Slang,* New York (Crowell), 1934; Eric Partridge, *A Dictionary of Slang and Unconventional English,* New York (Macmillan), 1937; and Lester V. Berrey and Melvin Van den Bark, *The American Thesaurus of Slang,* New York (Crowell), 1942. The reader will find many articles on the talk of the student, the racketeer, the convict, the soldier, the aviator, and so forth (as well as on contemporary American slang in general) in *Dialect Notes,* the *Publications of the American Dialect Society,* and in *American Speech* magazine.

The parts of the body illustrate this particularly well. Take the concept "head." The ordinary legitimate word is, in English, *head;* in German, *Kopf;* and in French, *tête.* In this instance, it happens that, of the three languages, only English has retained, as the usual term, the older and more respectable word, which, however, does appear in the other two languages in more colorless and less common words, German *Haupt* and French *chef.* English *head,* that is to say, is not cognate with *Kopf* and *tête,* but it *is* cognate with *Haupt* and *chef* (<Lat. *caput*). In German, *Kopf* (related to English *cup*) evidently originated in the same sort of slangy metaphor that accounts for *tête* (< Lat. *testa,* pot, pitcher) ; in both cases, the more vivid slang substitute drove out the more dignified word as the general term.[43] But so far as the slang of popular speech is concerned, the process of course does not stop with one metaphorical substitution, or with change of meaning affecting only the word brought in (and possibly the one that is superseded, which may be given a limited, specialized usefulness such as *chef* and *Haupt* have). Popular slang of course prefers to dip its bucket into the well of metaphor again and again. Thus, though only *head* is possible in formal use, there are metaphors without number in slang—*bean, block, nut, dome, upper story, belfry, coco,*[44] and so on. In French, exactly similar developments are to be observed, *noisette* and *coco* duplicating the metaphors of *nut* and *coco,* and *bobine* (bobbin), *fiole* (little bottle), and so on, providing additional ones.

The number of examples could be greatly multiplied, but one more illustration may serve to bring out the fecundity and variety of slang in this field: English (chiefly American) terms for the idea of "drunk" or "intoxicated." We have, for example, nautical metaphors like *three sheets in the wind* and *half-seas-over;* culinary ones, like *stewed, boiled, fried,* and *pickled;* pathological ones, like *ossified, paralyzed,* and *petrified;* and an endless miscellaneous list that need

---

[43] This process, it may be interesting to note, frequently explains why it is that in French the word for a given idea is not the derivative of the Latin word that would seem its most likely ancestor; *cheval* (horse), for example, does not descend from the classical Latin *equus,* but from a late Latin *caballus,* which apparently had, to begin with, a slangy flavor like that of *nag.*

[44] For *coconut,* which, incidentally, has become the ordinary word for "head" in Beach-la-mar (Jespersen, *op. cit.,* p. 155)—a further striking illustration of the metaphorical substitute superseding the plain word, and changing its own first meaning in the process.

not be further classified, represented by *full, tight, half-shot, canned, lit, loaded, tanked, pie-eyed, shellarked, soused, piffled, pifflicated, blotto, stinko,* and so *ad infinitum.*

One curious result of the use of metaphor in creating slang is that certain expressions that were literal in their original application are metaphorically transferred to general use and then sometimes become so familiar that the metaphor fades out, leaving the word a colorless part of the general vocabulary. This is particularly evident in the vocabulary of sport that has been transferred, by way ot vivid metaphor, to a more common use. *Foul play,* for example, was a term in gambling, but it was extended metaphorically to the game of life. The present use has no tincture of slang about it, though it is a curiously specialized one: when *foul play* is alluded to in the newspapers, it means quite definitely that "murder" is suspected. "To hit the mark" (from archery), "to hit below the belt" (from pugilism), "to run counter" (used of hunting dogs that go in the wrong direction), "it's up to you" (from poker), "to bandy [words]" (from an early species of tennis), "to tilt at" (from the medieval tournament), "to win the palm" (from ancient sport), "to parry" (from fencing), and "to show the white feather" (from cock-fighting)[45] illustrate how what is literal in its original use becomes metaphorical when given a wider application and then sometimes assumes an almost literal cast once more. The slang, of course, appears in the metaphorical use; but it may be said that some of these expressions—"hit the mark," "parry," and "bandy"—have completely lost any odor of slang, while others—"it's up to you," for example—are perhaps in the process of losing it.

In addition to metaphor, figures of speech like metonymy, hyperbole, and irony are freely utilized in the creation of slang. American slang has often been described (like American speech in general) as more characterized by exuberant hyperbole than is British slang, which goes in rather for humorous understatement. To have a *thin time* is a peculiarly British way of referring to a really harrowing experience. On the other hand, to describe a vain person as having a *swelled head,* and then improving upon this by explaining that such a one finds it necessary to use a shoehorn in putting on his hat—this is characteristically American. Metonymy appears in such a term as *skirt* or *frail* (and the older *rib*) for "woman," and, of course, it has

---

[45] Greenough and Kittredge, *op. cit.,* pp. 56-58

a share in many of the metaphors already cited; likewise, irony constantly blends with other figures. Clippings and other phonetic irregularities are perhaps sufficiently obvious. The slang origin of *cab*, *taxi*, and *bus* did not prevent their eventual adoption in standard speech. Student slang is particularly rich in creations of this sort, such as *math, psych, lab, gym*, and so forth. Swift[46] objected to *pozz* as a clipped form of *positively;* today he would feel the same about *natch*.

A final type of slang creation—what has already been alluded to as picturesque sound—may be briefly mentioned here. This often takes the form of a mocking imitation of dignified literary words; such appears to be the explanation of *absquatulate, curmudgeon, discombobulate, rambunctious, rapscallion, sockdolager*, and *snollygoster*.[47] Jespersen quotes a letter of Southey's[48] which gives many illustrations of this kind of coinage in a slang vocabulary peculiar to Mrs. S. T. Coleridge; some specimens, which have apparently found no other user, are *red-raggify, confabulumpatus, toadymidjering, wattlykin, detestabumpus*, and *jabberumpeter*.

Two familiar questions about slang should perhaps be dealt with: Where does it come from, and where does it go? In reference to the former question, there seems no need of differentiating between slang and other aspects of language. It is just as anonymous, for the most part, as the general vocabulary is. Those who exploit it in print very rarely see their individual creations win a wide currency. A list of the ten men who are thought to have done most for current American slang was compiled not so many years ago.[49] But an examination of their actual contributions makes it very clear that in place of the "hundreds" of words they are popularly thought to have put into general circulation, only one or two words (or none at all) make up the sum total of each individual's share. Walter Winchell, for example, is often referred to as a great inventor of American slang. But of creations attributed to him, even *making whoopee*, which once had a considerable vogue, is now virtually dead, and such other punning novelties of his as *infanticipate* for "expect a baby," and *Renovate* for "divorce" are too consciously smart ever to gain very general use

[46] See Chapter 8, p. 204.
[47] McKnight, *op. cit.*, p. 50, and other sources.
[48] *Op. cit.*, p. 154.
[49] By W. J. Funk. See *Time,* Jan. 15, 1934.

The real masters of written slang in our day—of whom the late Ring Lardner was easily first—have but a negligible share in its actual making; their part is rather to give a wide currency to what is already in existence. Like other words, slang terms are usually of obscure and nameless origin. The only essential difference, on this side of the matter, is that they appear in general use, and disappear from it, much more rapidly.

As to the other question, the eventual fate of the slang term, there are obviously three possibilities. The two that everyone recognizes are (1) that what has at first the defiant novelty and the colloquial character typical of slang may lose these attributes through continued and more elevated use, and hence cease to be slang at all; and (2) that what is in vogue today may cease to be in vogue tomorrow, and eventually drop out of use completely. Both courses are generally familiar, and illustration would be superfluous. What is not so commonly understood is the third (of course the rarest) possibility: a slang word or phrase may linger on the outskirts of respectability for decades, even for centuries, and neither drop out of use completely nor be incorporated in the standard vocabulary. A very few years—often indeed only months—usually determine whether an expression is or is not likely to have the sanction of standard use. But occasionally a word—*booze* is a case in point—will for hundreds of years knock vainly at the gate for admission to the reputable vocabulary. For a more recent illustration, it is curious that, among slang phrases standing for an urgent invitation to depart, *beat it* was competing, in the first decade of the present century, with *skidoo* and *twenty-three*, both of which have long since become of historical interest only, while *beat it*, after at least forty years of use, is still with us and somehow seems likely to remain (without becoming reputable) after much younger rivals, like *scram* and *blow,* have been forgotten.

It may be worth noticing that occasionally we have something like a reversal of the process by which slang becomes reputable speech. A word or phrase may fall so completely in dignity that it takes on the associations of the colloquial, and sometimes those of out-and-out slang. Often it is impossible to say whether what appears to us a bit of racy slang (sometimes because it duplicates a current locution) had anything like the same association a century or several centuries ago. We are surely right, in general, in feeling that in Chaucer, for example, the conversation of Pandarus is as utterly natural as it is partly by reason of the colloquialisms and the slang it contains. But has Chaucer's use of *the bones* (for "dice") in the *Pardoner's Tale* (C, 1. 657), directly anticipating a bit of contemporary slang, exactly the same flavor as the word now has? "Slang phrases from Shakespeare" are sometimes compiled; for example, these:[50] "beat it," "done me wrong," "she falls for it," "not in it," "not so hot," "if he falls in, good night," and "let me tell the world."[51] What seems to us slang, however, is by no means necessarily slang to Shakespeare, who sometimes means literally what we take metaphorically, and sometimes, through sheer coincidence, hits upon what has become, in another context, twentieth-century slang. Chaucer and Shakespeare certainly use slang enough, as must any poet who realistically echoes the conversational speech of his day; but their slang is almost never ours.

That slang is a phenomenon of long standing in language surely needs no further demonstration. There is every reason to suppose that the standard language will continue in the future to enrich and invigorate its resources, as it has done in the past, by appropriating a certain modicum of the slang of the moment. To look upon slang, then, as some do, with nothing but horror is to work against the best interests of the language. This need not mean, however, that because slang is useful to language, the more use made of it the better, regardless of the purpose or the occasion. Like any other type of language, slang can easily be overused, used out of place, or used ineptly. Its effective use is difficult—and chiefly because it is so often figurative: to fail with a metaphor is worse than to fail with a prosaic word, simply because the attempt is more ambitious.

The great shortcoming of slang, its ephemerality, has caused it to be used but sparingly in literature. A writer whose stock in trade, so far as his use of conversation goes, is up-to-the-minute slang may achieve temporary success at the cost of quick oblivion. As his language gets out of date, so may he get out of date. This fate now appears to be overtaking O. Henry, and long ago overtook George Ade, and others who entrusted their literary fortunes to a slang that was outmoded a generation after them. It is hard, incidentally, to

[50] Most of these are from a list in the *Golden Book* for April 1932.
[51] Likewise Browning uses "What a man!" (*Protus*, l. 23) and "my weakness" (*Cristina*, l. 5) in a way that may, at first, surprise.

add many names to the list of recent writers of any real significance whom one associates particularly with slang. P. G. Wodehouse and Ring Lardner, perhaps—and if Wodehouse is not a "significant" writer, it is still no small thing, as one of his enthusiasts has put it, to be the most readable of living authors. But for one Ring Lardner, for one first-rate practitioner, there are a dozen inferior imitators; and one should note that Lardner's stories are quite often not in slang but in the "vulgate," as H. L. Mencken calls it—the language of the least literate—which is not at all the same thing as slang. To contemplate what most of those who exploit slang for literary purposes really accomplish with it should not, on the whole, inspire the budding writer with confidence in its possibilities.

British and American. Slang offers so many striking illustrations of general linguistic processes that our discussion of it has been rather lengthy. Before leaving the general subject of vocabulary, however, we must discuss one more topic—touched on before: American vocabulary as compared with British. It has been remarked that the somewhat different contacts to which American English has been exposed—especially the languages of the American Indian and those of the French and Spanish colonizers of the New World—account for the presence in our speech of certain words that are not shared with the speakers of British English. What is to be added here is a comment on characteristics of the American vocabulary that have resulted from the fact that American English has sometimes given new meanings to old words and sometimes retained old meanings for words that have assumed a new value in British English.

When English-speaking colonists came to America in the seventeenth century, it was natural that numerous familiar words should be given a different application when used with reference to the plants, animals, and topographic features of the New World. This is a usual linguistic consequence of colonization. Here, of course, is the explanation why many everyday words like *daisy, robin, corn, creek,* and so forth, convey to an American a different picture from what they convey to an Englishman. Sometimes the fresh application of an older word has given it a new lease of life in American speech; a particularly numerous group of illustrations may be suggested in such representative topographical terms as *branch, fork, divide, snag, cut-off, watershed, gap, tidewater, freshwater,* and so forth.[52] Often the novelty consists in compounding a new word from old elements: *backwoods, cowboy, corncob, hayrack, camp meeting, snowplow, bullfrog,* and *potato-bug* are random examples. Change of meaning in old words and the creating of new compounds from old material are processes that together account for a great many of the terms that are often described as Americanisms.[53] Of equal interest, however, are the survivals in American speech of older English words that have either disappeared or taken on new connotations in England.

H. L. Mencken has carefully and entertainingly documented [54] the growth of the British feeling—less violent today than it used to be—that American habits of speech which vary from British habits are in their nature repugnant. Like all basically emotional attitudes, this feeling has often fallen into absurdities and contradictions. The classical illustration, probably, is that stereotyped mark of the American on the English stage or in the English novel: "I guess." Even when the Englishman, exceptionally, recognizes that the American sense of *guess* meaning "imagine" or "suppose" is not a novelty but a survival, he is still likely to argue that the American and the older English use are to be differentiated in some subtle fashion.[55] But even when the Englishman knows that a word is not a "Yankee invention" but an older English word preserved across the Atlantic, he may shy away from it as if it were somehow irretrievable. The authors of *The King's English* just now alluded to, follow their remarks on "I guess" by this pronouncement as to *fall:*

Fall is better on the merits than *autumn,* in every way: it is short, Saxon (like the other three season names), picturesque; it reveals its derivation to every one who uses it, not to the scholar only, like *autumn;* and we once

---

[52] See the excellent study by George D. McJimsey, *Topographic Terms in Virginia,* New York (Columbia University Press), 1940.

[53] The second group has a better right to be so described. For the origin of the term *Americanism,* and the several meanings that have been attached to it, see M. M. Mathews, *The Beginnings of American English,* Chicago (University of Chicago), 1931, pp. 17 and 31-33.

[54] *The American Language,* Chapter I, and *Supplement One to The American Language,* New York (Knopf), 1945, Chapter I.

[55] Stuart Robertson, "The Chaucerian-American 'I Guess,'" *Modern Language Notes,* Vol. XLVIII, No. 1 (Jan. 1933), pp. 37-40, argues that this belief, as expressed in *The King's English* (3rd ed.), 1930, p. 33, is erroneous.

had as good a right to it as the Americans; but we have chosen to let the right lapse, and to use the word now is no better than larceny.[56]

Guess and *fall* were two of the words that James Russell Lowell selected to illustrate his thesis, in the introduction to the *Biglow Papers* (second series), that the popular speech of New England contained many survivals of words or meanings of words once standard in England but later abandoned. Not merely New England speech but American speech generally has retained these, and others like them, in defiance of British scorn and American Anglomania. That *bug* or *sick* or *bloody* has suffered specialization or degradation of meaning in England is surely no sufficient reason for altering the value that the word has long had in the United States. Moreover, if American speech has kept alive such picturesque and expressive compounds as *clodhopper, greenhorn, loophole,* and *ragamuffin,* and retained such useful older meanings as the ones an American associates with *burly, homely, deft, scant,* and so forth[57]—so much the better for its present state of health!

By way of summarizing impressions derived from a consideration of differences between the British and American vocabularies, two points are to be emphasized: the differences are real enough, and on certain levels of speech, fairly numerous; at the same time, their extent may easily be, and frequently is, grossly exaggerated. Let us look first at the one side of the case. Difference in the choice and use of words, though of course much less than the difference in pronunciation, is still considerable enough to make the realistic imitation of American conversation virtually impossible for the British novelist. Not only do the colloquialisms and the slang of the moment elude him, but even old and well-established differences in inflectional forms and idiom are imperfectly grasped. One small but conspicuous error on the part of the British reporter of American speech may be noted: his conviction that because Americans sometimes use *gotten* where the Britisher would employ *got,* it follows that the past participle for *get* in American speech is always *gotten.* The truth is, of course, that while some Americans use *gotten* in the sense of "become," "acquired," "received," and the like (e.g., "He's gotten better" and "I've gotten my new car"), no American uses *have gotten* in the sense of "possess," "cherish," or "have"; for the latter uses,

[56] Reprinted by permission of the Oxford University Press.
[57] Mencken, *The American Language,* p. 128.

the idiom is either *have got* or *have*. The English writer's failure to appreciate this minor differentiation may be illustrated in the following phrases from "American" conversation in recent English novels: "The kid's the only one who's gotten sense"; "That's what's wrong with Mexico, they've gotten no public spirit"; "we haven't gotten your roots"; "you've lost the spirit of inquiry; or if you've still gotten it. . . ." [58]

Differences in vocabulary and idiom must then be considered to be great enough to prevent an Englishman from reporting American conversation with accuracy. It may be added that these differences are likewise enough to offer a minor difficulty to an Englishman reading an American novel or seeing an American play—though here, of course, it is only slang that is likely to be misinterpreted. In the program notes that furnished a glossary for an American play presented in London, was once observed the following definition (among others equally noteworthy): *"to crack wise* = 'to speak knowingly.' " The Travelers' Library edition of Sinclair Lewis's *Babbitt* contains a glossary for the English reader, in which the following typical misapprehensions are to be found: *to buck* (to defraud, cheat), *flivver* (a cheap motor-car, of delicate build), *heck* (familiar for Hecuba, a New England deity), *Hunky* (Hun), *razz for fair* (heavy censure), *roughneck* (antithesis of highbrow), *roustabout* (revolutionary).

On the other hand, as has already been suggested, it is very easy to make too much of whatever differences in the use of words actually exist, especially since most of these differences are obviously to be found, for the most part, in colloquial and slangy speech only. That is why such a book as Mencken's *American Language*—which has received a very wide circulation—is frequently misleading. For in order to prove his thesis that American English is far more lively, inventive, and expressive than British English, Mencken continually contrasts two quite incompatible levels of language: formal and literary British with colloquial (frequently vulgar) American. In his

[58] The first two quotations are from Rose Macaulay's *Staying with Relations*, the second two from Galsworthy's *Maid in Waiting*. For fuller treatment of this subject, see Stuart Robertson's article in *American Speech*, Vol. VI, No. 4 (April 1931). pp. 314-316. In "American Speech According to Galsworthy"— *ibid.*, Vol. VII, No. 4 (April 1932), pp. 297-301—he has pointed out the same error, together with a number of others, in Galsworthy's imitation of American conversation generally.

original preface,[59] Mencken declared: "I can write English, as in this clause, quite as readily as American, as in this here one"; and throughout successive revisions of the book (though perhaps least in the final edition), there is the same implication that *typical* differences are those between polished·British and guttersnipe American speech. Obviously, this is quite false. The only fair comparison is that between British and American speech on corresponding social or cultural levels.

One must admit at once that it is very easy to compile long lists of paired words in which English and American speakers or writers express, or may express, the same idea differently. But lists of this kind [60] tend to repeat each other in rehearsing certain well-worn examples (*luggage, baggage; shop, store; guard, conductor;* and the like), and to include not only insignificant but decidedly dubious variants (*barber's-shop, barbershop; coals, coal; brakesman, brakeman;* and so forth). The fact is that *luggage, shop,* and *guard* all have a certain vogue in America as well as in England; and it is absurd to imply that there is a clear-cut national differentiation between *return-ticket* and *round-trip-ticket, angry* and *mad, bathrobe* and *dressing-gown, crazy-bone* and *funny-bone,* and so forth. A careful examination of lists of this kind leaves one unimpressed by that sense of a great gulf between two vocabularies that the lists are intended to convey. It is evident, for one thing, that there are only a few departments—shopping and travel, especially—in which there are numerous variations. Further, it is often clear that what have been cited as national differences in the past should no longer be so counted. It may not be altogether admirable, but it is the fact that haberdasher's terms like *great coat, top coat, waistcoat, dressing-gown,* and *boots* (for *shoes*), and a great many miscellaneous ones like *overshoes* (for *rubbers*), *music-hall* (for *vaudeville-theater*), *face-cloth* (for *wash-rag*), *ground floor* (for *first floor*), *agenda* (for *program*), and others like them cited by Mencken have ceased to strike an American as at all exotic.

[59] P. vii, 1st ed. (1919).

[60] E.g., in *The American Language*, 3rd ed., pp. 116-119, and 4th ed., pp. 233-237. Another comparison of the same sort is F. L. Griffin's "Learn English Before You Go," *Atlantic Monthly*, June 1932, pp. 775-776. For criticism of the accuracy of some of Mencken's items (in the fourth edition), see Stuart Robertson. "Notes on *The American Language*," *American Speech*, October 1937, pp. 185-189

Nor has the assimilation been in one direction only. An Englishman discussing the present state of the British vocabulary is perhaps more likely to dilate upon—it may be to lament about—the extent of its Americanization than upon any other feature. Weekley[61] speaks of the "eager adoption" of *underdog, butting in, live wire, third degree, frame-up, gunman,* and the "now indispensable" *bluff, pep, stunt,* and *blurb.* An Englishman writing in an American magazine[62] observes: "You send us *high-hat, hokum, getaway, panties, water-wagon,* and *hangover,* and we send you *swank, spook, click, the wind up, tell off, tick off,* and *up the pole.*" The "Supplement" to the *Oxford English Dictionary* notes among the trends that have been manifest in the half-century which it covers, "the varied development of colloquial idiom and slang, to which the United States of America have made a large contribution. . . ." Though such words as the following are labeled in the "Supplement" as "U.S."— *racketeer, hijacker, hooch, go-getter, jay walker, whoopee, hooey, movie, speak-easy, ride* (*take for a*), *spot* (*put on the*), and so forth —the very fact that they are included is a step in breaking down the appropriateness of the label.

The agencies that cause American and British vocabulary alike to cease to be distinctive are more numerous and more powerful today than they have ever been in the past. Obviously the radio, the movies, the vogue of English novels and English plays in America, and that of American novels and American plays in England provide means of familiarizing the people of the two countries with each other's speech to an extent that has not been previously approached. There seems every reason to conclude that, though "colloquial idiom and slang" continue to develop more vigorously than ever before, and somewhat differently on the two sides of the Atlantic, the differences between American and British English are, through the influence of these agencies of internationalization, destined to diminish rather than increase. Though British films circulate less widely in the United States than American movies do in England, they do play in many of our larger cities and to college audiences, so that the influence is not altogether from the New World to the Old. Nor is the exchange by any means limited to slang or colloquial words; these

---

[61] *The English Language,* pp. 77-80.
[62] Seaman, H. W., "The Awful English of England," *American Mercury,* Vol. XXX, No. 117 (September 1933), pp. 72-82.

are merely more noticeable. A considerable number of words which began as Americanisms have quietly been adopted in British and general use, and their origin is now forgotten: in short, they are no longer Americanisms, but English in the broader sense. Examples of these—a very few—would be *stunt, bifocal, miscegenation, schooner, rifle, rum, torpedo.* The trade in words continues internationally, and those words which prove themselves useful will cross easily in either direction. Only the occasional outburst of emotion about a word or phrase is likely to disturb this interchange.

Complete standardization of vocabulary has of course not been attained, nor is it conceivable, considering the factors involved. And perhaps this is just as well, both as regards vocabulary and pronunciation. The small differences in the meanings or uses of words that one encounters in reading an English book or hearing Britishers talk are generally—like the local variations within our own country—pleasant and interesting rather than irritating; assuming, of course, that the differences, personal, dialectal, or the like, are not so great as to cause unintelligibility. To be specific, in the first page and a half of an English novel [63] opened more or less at random, there occur four words or phrases that are not used, or not used in the same way, in ordinary American English: *city* (financial district), *residential flats* (American "apartments"), *hoarding* (billboard), and *lorries* (trucks). The number, probably, is too great to be typical, but that is not the present point. What is conveyed to the American reader by such Briticisms is the agreeable sense of a different atmosphere, a pleasant awakening of other literary associations—perhaps, in addition, memories of travel abroad. This is accomplished without any suggestion of a barrier against the full understanding of the English writer. Why should we feel that variations between American English and British English are different, except in degree, from variations within the field of American English? Because a New Yorker says *block* where a Philadelphian says *square,* or identifies a street corner by giving the numbered street second, while a Philadelphian puts it first ("Broadway and Fortieth Street," "Sixteenth and Chestnut"), it does not follow that either expression is superior or inferior, as a counter of speech, to the other. It would seem most sensible to feel similarly about the somewhat greater difference between the American and British uses of words: they are merely different and, to

[63] *Big Business,* by A. S. M. Hutchinson, Boston (Little, Brown), 1932.

one interested in words, interestingly different, in the unimportant variations that they display. Both modes of speech have a right to exist, and the variations between them may be discussed without heat or rancor.

Word Origins. If one is at all justified in assuming a general interest in "words and their ways," perhaps space may be found for a comment on a last aspect of this department of our subject. Those who use words and speculate about them are usually given to wondering how individual words have come into being, how they are related to other words, and what their histories in our speech have been. Etymology is a field that has a wide appeal; and though, as we have already suggested,[64] it may be wrongly used, its fascination is surely both legitimate and praiseworthy. Anyone who is capable of being interested in words at all can scarcely fail to be instructed as well as entertained by glancing through the pages of Skeat's or Weekley's etymological dictionaries, or by dipping, even at random, into the infinite riches stored up in the volumes of the *Oxford English Dictionary*.

Perhaps the first query of the man on the street with reference to etymology is this: "How do we know where the word comes from?" It is to be feared that the candid answer, far more often than the questioner realizes, would be, "We don't." Etymology was the first field of linguistics to attract attention; but until comparatively recent times only guesswork was required to establish, to the etymologizer's satisfaction, a historical connection between words that had some chance resemblance in sounds or sense.[65] What the layman does not realize is that a great deal of the etymological information in our dictionaries is, or should be, qualified by "probably," "perhaps," "conjectured to be," or the like. Reckless etymologizing in the past goes far to justify Mark Twain's satirical derivation of *Middletown* from *Moses* by "dropping the -*oses* and adding the -*iddletown*," and the aphorism, attributed to Voltaire,[66] to the effect that in etymology consonants count for very little and vowels for nothing at all. It comes as something of a shock, nevertheless, to find so competent a

[64] See page 1; and Chapter 11.

[65] For illustration of etymological speculation in ancient, medieval, and early modern times, see Pedersen, *Linguistic Science*, pp. 1-8.

[66] Bloomfield points out that this often-quoted saying appears in a work of Max Müller's without a definite citation; he himself has been unable to find it in the works of Voltaire (*Language*, p. 511).

critic as Jespersen observing of modern dictionaries: "It is of course impossible to say how great a proportion of the etymologies given in dictionaries should strictly be classed under each of the following heads: (1) certain, (2) probable, (3) possible, (4) improbable, (5) impossible—but I am afraid that the first two classes would be the least numerous." [67]

To account for the limitations of our etymological knowledge, we may remind ourselves that pure root-creation has rarely been an active process in historic times; that only comparatively seldom can we associate an individual speaker or writer with the first use of a word; and that "phonetic laws" (like Grimm's Law) have a very restricted applicability in establishing etymology—if, indeed, the term *law* itself [68] is not utterly misleading. Analogy is evidently a force that tends to obscure etymology, as when unrelated words that somewhat resemble each other are made formally identical: *corn* (on the foot) and *corn* (the grain), *weeds* (plants) and *weeds* (garments), *let* (allow) and *let* (hinder) are familiar examples of words that are known to be etymologically distinct. Moreover, analogy utilized in the service of folk-etymology has doubtless veiled the true source and history of many other words. The clue to the correct etymology of the word may be lost in many other ways; for example, a mere mistake in its pronunciation—particularly when this results in a simpler combination of sounds—may be spread by imitation and become the standard form. Inadvertent confusion and blending of two words Jespersen believes to be a far more common method of creating new words than is generally recognized.[69] It is entirely conceivable that errors of all sorts, on the part of children as well as adults, have often been perpetuated, so that the word is given a form that either tempts an entirely erroneous etymological theory or suggests none at all. At any rate, there are evidently possibilities enough to explain the prevalence of mistaken or dubious etymologies, and to account for the fact that many very familiar words are of quite unknown origin. To illustrate: *bogus, blizzard, jazz, jitney,* and *sundae* are Americanisms of mysterious derivation; *dog, boy, cut, dodge, fit, fog, fun, girl, jump, job, lad, lass, pull, pun,* and *put* are puzzling

---

[67] *Language,* p. 307.

[68] For a discussion of the various meanings that have been attached to "phonetic law," see Graff, *Language and Languages,* pp. 235-251.

[69] *Language,* p. 312.

monosyllables of (apparently) native English origin; *brave, bronze, baroque, baron, flute, frown, rococo,* and *zinc* are from the Continent, most of them familiar in other European languages also, but all representing unsolved enigmas.

The opportunities for going wrong in etymological guesswork find their classical illustration in the words for "fire" in English, French, and German: *fire, feu,* and *Feuer.* The cross-relationships might be imagined in several ways, but one point would seem to be sure: a common source. This, however, is exactly what cannot be asserted. *Fire* and *Feuer* go back, indeed, to a common Germanic ancestor, which is cognate with Greek *pyr,*[70] the word that we have borrowed as *pyre;* but French *feu,* for all its misleading resemblance in appearance and identity in meaning, is from the unrelated Latin *focus* (hearth). Authors have often laid themselves open to ridicule by asserting or implying an erroneous etymological relationship. The effectiveness of Milton's lines:

> And saw the ravens with their horny beaks
> Food to Elijah bringing even and morn—
> Though ravenous, taught to abstain from what they brought.

is unquestionably weakened by a knowledge that *raven* and *ravenous* are only apparently from a common source: *raven* is from Old English *hræfn,* while *ravenous* is from Old French *ravineux* and is related to *rapine* rather than *raven.* Chaucer was more fortunate in making poetical capital of his (quite correct) etymology for *daisy:* "the 'dayesye' or elles the 'ye of daye' " (*Prologue to the Legend of Good Women,* l. 184). But Carlyle has been derided for his insistence that the "true meaning" of *king* is "man who can." To see an intimate relationship between *king* and *can* (especially in the German forms *König* and *können*) is tempting, but quite mistaken: *king* is really related not to *can* but to *kin* (cognate with Latin *genus*— Grimm's Law again). Thus the *king* is "etymologically" not the "able" man, but the man "of the tribe"—a meaning not at all relevant or helpful to Carlyle's theory of greatness.

Etymology, then, may easily be put to the wrong kind of service; even when correct, it is likely to tell us no more than what the word once meant—not what it means now. It helps not at all to reveal the innermost truth of things, though faith in some such mystical end to

---

[70] As Grimm's Law would suggest.

the study of etymology dies exceedingly hard. Etymologies, often palpably absurd, are constantly being employed to demonstrate some deep verity concealed in a word. The practical usefulness of knowing the derivation of a word must be stated very differently. Such knowledge often serves the more pedestrian purpose of keeping the user of the word from definite mistakes in its pronunciation, spelling, or meaning. Even so, though it helps in one's spelling of *excellent* and *repellent*, and *ignorant* and *dominant* to connect them with the proper Latin conjugations,[71] it may be misleading for pronunciation to recall the compositional elements of *Christmas, handkerchief*, and so on.

Similarly, as remarked before, a sense of the derivation of the word is something of a two-edged weapon when it is a question of its present meaning and use. The meaning of the word we have seen shift its ground continually; to bring it back arbitrarily to its etymological starting point may be thoroughly artificial. Because *endorse* is literally "on the back," shall its application to the *face* of a document be deemed absurd? [72] Because *transpire* (breathe through) is more appropriate, etymologically, to "leak out" or "become known" than to "happen," is there any reason to feel that the popular extension to "happen" may not become standard? [73] It has been argued that Canterbury rather than London is the *metropolis* of England, because *metropolis* (mother city) is properly used only in the original ecclesiastical sense of "chief *cathedral* city." [74] All of which brings us back to the doctrine that usage, not etymology, determines the meaning of words. If enough people "misuse" *awful, aggravate, terrible*, and the like (as in the past they have "misused" *nice, silly,* and *fond*), the etymological meaning is bound to be superseded by one that has hitherto been deemed incorrect. To take the opposite position is to identify one's attitude with that of the writer thus quoted by Brander Matthews:[75] ". . . for twenty-five years or more I have kept my eye on this little word *people* and I have yet to find

[71] And to associate words that are frequently misspelled—*sacrilegious* and *supersede,* for example—with the Latin words that are represented in them.

[72] Krapp, in *Modern English* (1909), p. 282, seems to answer this question affirmatively; in *The Knowledge of English* (1927), p. 140, he answers it negatively.

[73] Cf. Bloomfield, *Language,* p. 442, for a demonstration of *how* this transference of meaning has come about.

[74] Quoted by Fries in *The Teaching of the English Language,* p. 79.

[75] *Parts of Speech,* New York (Scribner), 1901, p. 226.

a single American or English author who does not misuse it."
When one is confident that everyone else is out of step, it is time to
re-examine the grounds for one's own assurance.

Notwithstanding what has just been said, it may still be asserted
that to know the root meanings of words often has a genuine, even
a utilitarian, value. Words, after all, are all too frequently used
loosely rather than precisely, and to be aware of the original force of
the word may save one from what is, both etymologically and by the
standard of the best current use, an out-and-out blunder. Etymology
unmistakably helps one to discriminate among words that are sometimes misapprehended as synonyms. When, during the first World
War, newspaper writers had occasion to refer to a command that had
suffered severe losses, they sometimes varied the expression of the
idea by describing the body of troops in question as being *annihi-
lated,* and again as being *decimated.* The objection, of course, is
that the one word says too much and the other too little. It is difficult
to see how anyone conscious of the *nihil* in the one word and the
decimus in the other could use them so: clearly, the command was
not reduced to "nothing" if there was a single survivor; on the other
hand, a command that lost only every "tenth" man in such an en-
gagement as was described was incredibly fortunate. Likewise, to
understand the source and history of the Greek borrowing *protagonist*—i.e., "first actor (in a play)"—will help to keep one from the
familiar misuse of it as the opposite of *antagonist,* a misuse which
apparently arises from taking *pro-* to mean "for," instead of asso-
ciating it with *proto-* (first). To insist on an "etymological" meaning with a learned word (like *protagonist*) seems more defensible
than to expect the same of such everyday words as *awful, horrid,*
and the like: there is surely a greater obligation to use a learned
word learnedly.

The most important reason for interest in etymology, however, is
not a utilitarian one. It may be admitted at once that the claims for
etymology as "a practical means for insuring correct pronunciation
and spelling, and conducing to a felicitous diction," are often grossly
overstated. What seems much more certain is that, to anyone with a
flair for words, delving into etymology is an end in itself. It may do
little in the way of giving an accurate command of words, but it
can do much in making the meanings of words richer and more picturesque. To know that *ephemeral* is literally "of a day" may help

but little in dissociating it from *transitory, temporary,* and *evanescent* (all of which have their own interesting pictures); but it certainly renders the word more vivid. Even more certainly, to investigate the derivation and cognate relationships of *read, write, pen, style, letter,* and *alphabet,* while not at all necessary as a step in understanding the present use and meaning of the words, is a fascinating occupation in itself. Unexpected and often entertaining stories are again and again revealed in the history of a word; a few random illustrations of such words are *curfew, candidate, neighbor, eliminate,* and *recalcitrant.* Not infrequently, indeed, what the story reveals is a valuable glimpse into some perhaps obscure chapter in the development of human thought or manners. The more human side of what the scientific etymologist has discovered is today, as never before, at the disposal of the mere amateur in words.[76]

James Moncrief

REFERENCES FOR FURTHER READING

The books cited in the present chapter, in footnotes 1 and 76, and:

Bréal, Michel J. A., *La Sémantique,* trans. as, *Semantics: Studies in the Science of Meaning,* New York (Holt), 1900.

Buck, Carl Darling, *A Dictionary of Selected Synonyms in the Principal Indo-European Languages,* Chicago (University of Chicago), 1949.

Krapp, G. P., *Modern English, Its Growth and Present Use,* New York (Scribner's), 1909.

Schreuder, Hindrik, *Pejorative Sense Development in English,* Groningen (Noordhoff), 1929.

Stern, Gustav, *Meaning and Change of Meaning,* Gothenburg (Wettergren and Kerber), 1931.

Van Dongen, G. A., *Amelioratives in English,* Rotterdam (De Vries), 1933.

[76] Of books that deal particularly with the "romance of words," Ernest Weekley's work of that title, New York (Dutton), 1922, may be suggested, as also his *Something About Words,* New York (Dutton), 1936, and similar works. Logan Pearsall Smith's *English Language,* New York (Holt), 1912, and *Words and Idioms,* New York (Houghton, Mifflin), 1925, and Owen Barfield's *History in English Words,* Garden City (Doubleday, Doran), 1926, are also useful, as are the etymological dictionaries of Skeat, 4th ed., Oxford (Clarendon Press) 1910, and Weekley, New York (Dutton), 1924. The best source for etymologies, of course, is the *Oxford Dictionary.* More recently, the byways of word-lore have been explored by Ivor J. C. Brown in several books, of which the best known are *A Word in Your Ear* and *Just Another Word,* published as a single volume, New York (Dutton), 1945, and *Having the Last Word,* London (Cape), 1950.

Chapter 10

Syntax and Usage

W<small>E</small> HAVE BEEN primarily concerned, so far, with the word as an isolated unit, and only incidentally with the combination of words into phrases and sentences. It is now time to come more fully to this latter study—that is, to *syntax*, which examines the ways in which words may be combined, and the relationships that exist between the words in combination. Syntax may conceivably be treated in a number of ways; for example, as prescriptive, historical, or descriptive. Here we shall be concerned only indirectly with the first approach, that which lays down the laws of "correct usage"; and comparatively little space can be spared for the second, which would explain how certain conventions have been established. Our object must rather be to comment, selectively of course, on certain aspects of syntax that are of interest in connection with the present language, as we actually observe it in the speech or writing of today.

What is the function of syntax? Unless one can know in some way how the parts of a sentence are related, one can hardly make sense of it; for some words are always more important, others subordinate; some words chiefly carry meaning, others are structural units. Every language must have some device or devices to show the various relationships among words which its speakers feel it necessary to express. Since Old English, following its inheritance of Indo-European structure, was an inflectional language and largely synthetic, it depended heavily on the variations in the forms of words to show relationships within the sentence: syntax was based on inflection. But, as we have seen,[1] the change from Old English to Middle and Modern English involved a very sweeping reduction of inflection: the very device upon which Old English had depended so heavily to

[1] Especially in Chapter 6.

279

indicate the grammatical categories of number, gender, case, mood, tense, and so on, with their interrelationships, dwindled to a remnant. As a result, some entire categories of distinction ceased to be (for one can hardly speak of dual number, for example, after the distinctive dual forms have disappeared); others were sharply curtailed; still others developed alternatives or substitutes for the lost inflections; and finally, when these new devices had become established, they were used to express grammatical categories which had not been expressed in this way, or at all, in Old English. In a word, the syntactic structure of English, between the earliest times and the present, has been virtually rebuilt, and not only does Modern English have a different range of syntactic distinctions than had Old English, but it possesses new means of expressing them. Let us look at the evidence on these two points.

In respect to the first, we find:

(a) Old English syntactic relationships no longer expressed in Modern English:

— dual number in pronouns, *Ic (I), Wit (we two), We (we)* [OE, OE, OE]
    strong and weak classes in adjectives,
    number, gender, and case in adjectives and articles,
    gender and case in the demonstrative;

(b) Old English syntactic relationships only partly expressed in Modern English:
    case in nouns (only genitive left),
    person in verbs (only 3rd singular present indicative left),
    gender in 3rd personal pronouns (but now "natural" rather than "grammatical"),
    case in pronouns (dative and accusative have fallen together as "objective"),
    number in pronouns (2nd person is the same in singular and plural);

(c) Modern English syntactic relationships expressed by means that did not exist in Old English:
    passive voice (though the analytic passive was in embryo in Old English),
    future, perfect, and progressive tenses (expressed with auxiliaries; in embryo in Old English),
    case-relationships, comparison, etc. (expressed by means of "function words"),[2]
    case-relationships, modification, agreement (expressed by means of word order).

[2] A function-word is one which serves primarily to show grammatical function, rather than to bear meaning. See further below, pp. 283-285.

? Prescription vs. usage ?

In respect to the second point, we find:

(a) Old English inflections were reduced in number, variety, and syntactical scope, though the surviving few are used more widely;
(b) "Function-words" were developed as alternatives to inflections;
(c) Word-order became "fixed" or grammatical, performing some of the functions of lost inflections.

These points must now be examined further.

Inflectional Reduction. If we examine the passage of Old English in Chapter 3 (page 42), we will notice that 56 of the total of 85 words, or 66 per cent, have forms that vary by inflection. In comparison with this, the Modern English translation of the same passage shows that 35 of the 89 words, or only 39 per cent, have forms that vary by inflection. Since this passage has a large number of pronouns, the figures for Modern English are relatively high, but even so, the contrast with the figures for the Old English original suggests well enough how the number of inflections has fallen today.[3] The *variety* of inflections has shrunk still further, for whereas (if we leave out of account the uninflected base) Old English nouns had 9 different inflectional forms, Modern English nouns have only 1; whereas Old English weak verbs had 10 different inflectional forms, Modern English verbs (strong or weak) have only 3; whereas Old English adjectives had 13 different inflectional forms, Modern English adjectives have only 2. And similarly for the other parts of speech. The fact is that there are only six different inflectional morphemes still alive in English—alive in the sense that they may be used with new words entering the language. These survivors are:

-(e)s [s, z, əz]	used for the genitive of nouns and pronouns,
	" " " plural " " " some pronouns,
	" " " 3rd person singular present indicative of verbs,
-ing [ɪŋ]	used for the present participle of verbs,
-(e)d [t, d, əd]	" " " preterit and past participle of weak verbs,
-(e)n [n̩, ən]	used for the past participle of strong verbs,
-(e)r [ɚ]	" " " comparative degree of adjectives,
-(e)st [əst]	" " " superlative " " " .

---

[3] This passage is too short for a satisfactory comparison; these figures must therefore not be considered as proving any more than they are used for here.

Though most of these are vigorously alive, it should be noted that the genitive -(e)s is already limited: it is no longer used, in normal Modern English, with neuter nouns; these generally are put in the "periphrastic genitive": "the top *of the table*" rather than "the *table's* top," the latter not being impossible, of course, though quite unlikely in idiomatic discourse. Nor is this periphrastic genitive the only competitor of the inflected genitive. More and more we find that because genitives are regularly treated as adjectives and put before the noun they modify, and because the same function may be performed by the adnominal noun, the latter is often preferred. Thus instead of the forms just given we hear "the *table* top," and similarly not "*Chicago's* area" or "the area *of Chicago*," but "the *Chicago* area." [4]

The plural -(e)s, and -ing and -(e)d, are in a position to gain ground, since almost every new noun or any irregular noun which becomes regular will use the first, and almost every new verb will use the other two. It is assumed to be not impossible that some new forms may arise in the strong verb pattern (as has happened within modern times), but the drift is all the other way (for strong verbs to go over to the weak pattern) and therefore for -(e)n to be still further reduced. At present it is no more than holding its own. Also holding its own is -(e)s of the third person singular present indicative of verbs, though this ending, be it noted, is virtually without useful function. All other forms of the verb than this depend upon the subject to indicate number, gender, and person; tense, besides, would be just as well indicated in this third person as it is in the other persons without the inflection. Thus -(e)s here is kept up out of tradition, and could disappear at any time without loss to grammar or meaning, though of course it would sound strange for a while if we heard *he come, she walk,* instead of *he comes, she walks,* and so on. This form is probably kept alive by its frequency: it appears so often that we easily learn and keep up the habit of saying it.

The -(e)r and -(e)st of comparison are reduced in use today far below their use in Old English. In the first place, they are avoided

---

[4] These are not exact equivalents, it is true; nor are such substitutions possible with animate referents: *the baby's buggy* and *the baby buggy* are decidedly different. These differences deserve further attention, but there is no room to give it here.

with long words; we will say *quicker, shortest, handiest,* but not *mercifuller* or *kindheartedest*—not, at least, at the standard level. For these longer words we prefer "periphrastic comparison" with *more* and *most*—and, indeed, these two function-words appear to be increasing in use still, for one finds them even with monosyllables: "Nobody could be *more kind* than Joe." Still another reason for the decrease of -(e)r and -(e)st is that though they were quite frequent in adverbial comparison in Old English, they are rarely found nowadays: *more* and *most* are the rule with adverbs. This was not the case even in early Modern English, where one frequently meets with such forms as *straitlier* and *quickliest.* In sum, then, comparison now employs the inflectional method far less than it once did; the device is fully alive, but its range is narrowed and apparently still narrowing.

Finally we must note the reduction in scope of the surviving inflections; for, except for the verbal -(e)s which shows (albeit negatively) person, number, tense, and mood, the other inflections today indicate only one syntactic feature apiece (plurality, case, tense, or degree of comparison). In Old English they would have indicated simultaneously more than one. Thus Old English *stānes* is at the same time genitive, singular, and not-feminine; Modern English [stonz] is either plural or genitive (the context showing which), but if the latter, number is not indicated, since the singular and plural are identical in sound. (Written, of course, they are distinguished by the placement of the apostrophe.) In short, as it descends to Modern English, inflection loses syntactic scope and is also reduced quantitatively.

Function Words. The term "function word" has been defined previously (footnote 2), and examples were given when the "periphrastic genitive" and "periphrastic comparison" were touched upon. Some writers prefer to call these "form words," since they have often taken the place, historically, of inflectional forms; but "function word" seems preferable because it emphasizes the fact that the primary thing about these words is not their meaning—indeed, in many cases they have been virtually drained of any semantic value—but the syntactic function that they perform. Thus the word *of* (which in Old English meant something like "from, concerning, or belonging to") has gradually taken over the function that the inflectional ending of the genitive performed in Old English—has, in effect, become a substitute for -(e)s (and other genitive endings). Thus we may call *of* the "function word" of the genitive; and similarly we may think of *to* and *for* as function-words of the dative: compare "Give *the man* the book", "Do *me* a kindness" (in both of which Old English would have put the indirect object in the dative) with the alternative "Give the book *to the man*", "Do a kindness *for me*." In late Old English, *to* and (much less often) *for* began to be used with these datives, as it seems, to increase the syntactic force of the inflection; then, when in early Middle English the inflections were obscured and many of them were lost, these words took over the whole burden of showing the syntactic function. The so-called "prepositional phrases" of today have developed either directly or by analogy from uses of these and other prepositions with inflected nouns or pronouns; and these prepositional phrases act as modifiers today just as the case-forms of nouns in Old English formed adverbial and adjectival modifiers.[5] It should be noted, once again, that whereas the inflected forms were synthetic in structure, these phrases are analytic. The use of *more* and *most* as the function words of comparison, rather than -(e)r and -(e)st, also represents an increase of analytic structure at the expense of synthetic.

It is in their use with verbs, however, that function words have led to the greatest enlargement in the syntax of Modern English. For what are ordinarily called "auxiliaries" are, in many compound verb forms, no more than the function words identifying the tense, mood, or voice in question. When they are used as full verbs, *be* means "exist," *have* means "possess," *will* means "desire" or "intend," *do* means "make" or "perform." Yet it is obvious that these words have been virtually drained of this kind of meaning in such verbal expressions as "it *was* eaten," "I *have* come," "they *will* remember," "*do* you know"; for these verbs are now function words, and their force is syntactic. By the use of such function words in various combinations with present and past participles, we can express today far more numerous and complex shades of verbal meaning than Old English was capable of. Thus the Old English inflected present tense (e.g., *hē cumeþ*) had to express various presents and also the future; today we have separate combinations for the

unlimited present (*he comes*), the progressive present (*he is coming*), and the future (*he will come*).[6]

In this instance the function-words have not so much displaced inflection as supplemented it. It is true that the inflected subjunctive (or optative) of Old English is now a remnant, and that the meanings it used to express—of possibility, hypothesis, wish, and so on—are now expressed also by such function-words as *can, may, ought*. But it is the addition of a new voice, and a whole array of new tenses, that indicates the success of analytical method in Modern English. It may be noted in passing that French, too, added a whole new future tense; but being more directly under the influence of Latin it made a *synthetic* future: for example, *aurai, auras, aura*, and so on, out of the infinitive *avoir* plus the present tense endings *-ai, -as, -a*. English and German, less directly under Latin influence, made their new futures *analytically*.[7]

Word Order. If reduction in the use of inflection has done much to alter the basic structure of English, the concomitant "fixing" of word order has completed the change. For it is no exaggeration to say that though inflection dominated word order in Old English, today word order dominates inflection. So powerful has it become, indeed, that some features of Modern English syntax have actually been remade under its pressure.

Old English, of course, had word order too; certain patterns were fairly regular, and some firmly established. But because inflection still clearly showed syntactic relationships almost all the time, Old English word order was able to be fairly free, and (as in Latin) words could be moved about for rhetorical purposes. While this is not impossible today, it is much more difficult, because what has always been the common order of words has now become regular—and so much so that there is little room left for variation.

In Old English one could equally well have said *Sē mann bohte þone hlāf, Sē mann þone hlāf bohte, Þone hlāf bohte sē mann*, or *Þone hlāf sē mann bohte*, the only difference lying in the emphasis conferred on particular words by their being put in front position. In

---

[6] Future, of course, may still be expressed as in Old English, with the present tense form; and in other ways as well: see C. C. Fries's "The Expression of the Future," *Language*, Vol. 3 (1927), pp. 87-95.

[7] For a much fuller treatment of function-words, see C. C. Fries's *The Structure of English*, New York (Harcourt, Brace), 1952; esp. Chapter 6.

Modern English we can say only what corresponds to the first of these sentences: *The man bought the loaf,* because subject must come before verb, and object after it, in declarative sentences. And if we wish to emphasize any particular word, we usually have to depend on stress of voice (or, in printing, on italics). Thus in Old English the syntactic relationships of subject and object were expressed by inflection, and changes in the word order did not affect them; today, subject and object are no longer shown by inflection in nouns, and even though pronouns have different forms for subject and object, they dare not violate the established patterns of word order.[8]

Let us look at the word-order patterns of Old English and see how they compare with those of the language today. These patterns are of two different ranks, according as they concern the basic structure of the clause, or the relations of modifiers to words modified within the clause. We shall treat the ranks in this order. Clausal order is usually distinguished into three kinds: *common,*[9] with the Subject before the Verb, and (if there is any) Object or Complement after the verb; *inverted,* when this position of Subject and Verb is reversed; and *transposed,* when the Object is moved up before the Subject and Verb. Since Old English times the common order has increased steadily at the expense of the other two, as certain types of clauses that formerly used inverted or transposed order have gone over to the more regular pattern.

In Old English, for example, in what is a quite frequent type of clause, we find the Object transposed: *Þæt wīf hē onfeng fram hiera ieldrum . . .* (*Chronicle,* 597) (*The woman he received from her parents.*) A similar transposition is still possible today, though unusual; it is found in emphatic situations and exclamations, in which prominence is given to the Object, as, *That I will not believe!* or *The worries I've had!* But except when such emphasis is desired, we use

---

[8] If a foreigner were to say "Him hit I," we would not interpret this as object-verb-subject according to the inflection; we would think he must mean subject-verb-object according to the word order—that what he had meant to say was "He hit me."

[9] This term is borrowed from S. O. Andrew, *Syntax and Style in Old English,* Cambridge (University), 1940. It seems preferable to "Normal," which many writers use, because the latter implies that other orders are somehow abnormal. "Common" should have merely numerical implications, other orders being uncommon or less common.

common order: *He received the woman from her parents, I will not believe that, I've had so many worries!*

What might be called an inverted-transposed order is seen in such a clause as *Fela worda gesprǣc sē engel (Genesis* 271) *(Many words spoke the angel)*; and this is still possible today, though decidedly literary: *Enemies has he none.* Quotations with the phrase following them are often of this same type, e.g., *"No," said he,* for the quotation represents the Object transposed, and the Subject-Verb phrase is inverted. But even this, once common in Modern English, is clearly in decline. Some authors, following spoken practice, refuse to invert the phrase: *"No," he said.* In sum, so long as there is a personal Subject, or a plural Object with a singular Subject, or emphatic stress on the transposed Object—anything, that is, which will prevent the confusion of Subject and Object (or Complement)— we are still able to transpose. But the opportunities are far more restricted than once they were, and the drift is all the other way. The only regular survival of transposed word order comes in relative clauses where the relative is the Object: "the man *whom they want.*"

As for inverted order, its chief use in Old English was for interrogation; and the same is true in Modern English, though with considerable restriction. The auxiliary verbs are the only ones left that can ask questions by simple inversion: *Can he go? Is he here? Need they know?* We can no longer ask, *Walks he? Ride they?* When Robert Browning makes such a line as,

Irks care the crop-full bird? Frets doubt the maw-crammed beast? [10]

he is deliberately seeking an effect of startling grotesqueness, some of which he obtains by the use of inversion in this now abnormal way. In interrogations without simple inversion, the verb *do* has, in effect, become a function word to signal the beginning of a question: *Does he walk? Do they ride?* This method utilizes inversion, of course, since it puts *do* before the Subject; nevertheless, it also leaves the Subject in its regular position before the part of the verb phrase that bears the meaning. The same is true of questions using any other compound verb form: *Will he agree? Are they considering it? Has she decided?* Thus the functional value of inversion is retained, but the sequence of Subject-Verb is, in part at least, pre-

[10] *Rabbi Ben Ezra,* line 24.

served. In short, we see here that the pressure of common word order has reduced the sway of inverted word order, not driving it out, but forcing it to a compromise, so to speak.

Other uses of inversion have fared less well than the interrogative. When two clauses were joined in Old English, the verb at the end of the first appears often to have attracted the verb of the second, drawing it forward and putting the two verbs into a kind of contrast: Thus: *oð þæt ān ongān fyrene fremman, feond on helle: wæs se grimma gæst Grendel haten* (*Beowulf*, 102); or *Æþelheard cyning forþfērde and feng Cūðræd tō Wesseaxna rīce* (*Chronicle*, 741); or *Syððan hē cōm ofer Wætlinge-strǣte, worhton hi þæt mǣste yfel* (*Chronicle*, 1013). Such constructions have passed away completely;[11] we cannot say *Until one began crimes to perform, fiend in hell: was the grim spirit Grendel named*, or *Ethelhard the king passed away and acceded Cuthred to the West-Saxon kingdom*, or *After he came over Watling-street, wrought they the most evil.*

Old English imperatives, unlike the modern, often expressed the Subject, in which case inversion was regular. Thus, *Nim ðū Apolloni, þis gewrit . . .* (*Apollonius of Tyre*)[12] (*Take thou, Apollonius, this writing*). This, as we recognize at once, lasted into Modern English, as in the *Do ye also to them likewise* of the King James Bible (1611, Luke 6.31) and later versions. Today, however, imperatives no longer express the Subject, which makes inversion impossible; and if a word is used in direct address, it is always in some way distinguished by emphasis, e.g., *Open the door, John!* or *You open the door and I'll close the window.* Thus while the imperative situation involves no gain to the common pattern, it represents a loss to inversion.

A similar situation is that in which not a command but a wish is expressed: *Wæs þū Hrōðgār, hāl!* (*Beowulf*, 407) (*Be thou, Hrothgar, in good health!*) This use of inversion is no longer alive, though such a fixed phrase as *Perish the thought!* preserves a trace of it. Other situations involving possibilities but not actualities very frequently relied on inversion in Old English. Some descendants of these today are *Were it possible . . .* , *Had I known . . .* , *Be it for better or for worse.* Such phrases have a rather literary flavor—even a smack of

---

[11] The last two, however, would be normal in Modern German, which is far more traditional than English.

[12] Ed. Julius Zupitza, "Die altenglische Bearbeitung . . . ," *Archiv*, Bd. 97 (1896), p. 30. l. 21.

archaism, for it would be much more natural to use the common order: *If it were possible . . . , If I had known . . . , Whether it be for better or for worse.*

Finally, there were certain adverbs in Old English which frequently were placed at the beginning of the clause, and usually drew the verb after them, producing inverted word order. There were the negatives *ne, næfre,* and such adverbs of time and place as *þā, þær, þonne, nū.* Of some of these we can find modern descendants: *Never have I heard of such a thing, There goes a great man, Now comes the real point;* yet they subsist mainly in formal or literary usage. And so with other adverbs placed ahead for emphasis: *Everywhere stood guards, Willingly would he come,* or with adjectival groups, *How impossibly difficult must that be!* And since each of these has developed a parallel in the common word order, it is evident that they are forms preserved precisely *because* of their irregularity, and for the sake of the stylistic effect which it can produce.

As the position of Subject before Verb was becoming more regular, the other part of the common order was also being established, that of Object or Complement after the Verb. An extremely frequent pattern in Old English placed the Object between Subject and Verb—indeed, Kellner[13] estimated that when the Object was a pronoun, as in *Ic þe þæt secge . . . ,* this sequence was used 80 per cent of the time. But as the nexus between Subject and Verb drew tighter, the Object was more and more relegated to post-verbal position, where (except in transposed order) it must go today. It is impossible to say *I you that tell,* or even *I you tell* or *I that say;* these old sequences are entirely gone from Modern English, casualties of the establishment of common word order.

One more consequence of the "fixing" of word order in Modern English must be noted. Just as *to* became the function-word that superseded dative inflections, as with the Indirect Object, so one particular word-order pattern has grown up to serve the same purpose. In Old English the Indirect Object could come in almost any position in the clause. Today, except when it is a relative pronoun, the Indirect Object without *to* must come between the Verb and the Direct Object.[14] Thus, for the Old English *Sē hlāford him geaf*

[13] *Historical Outlines of English Syntax,* page 292.

[14] With two pronouns, the order of the objects after the verb may be reversed: *Give it him.* This is usual in Britain, at least, though hardly known in the United States.

þæt gold, we may say *The lord gave the gold to him,* or *The lord gave him the gold.* This is another instance, then, of a pattern of word order taking over the syntactic function of a lost inflection.

The illustrations adduced so far have used only single words as Subjects or Objects, but common order applies equally to combinations of words: compound, appositional, phrasal, or clausal Subjects and Objects. Thus we find: *John and I gave Mary and Jane handkerchiefs and gloves; Dr. Jones, the history professor, likes baseball, our national game; To know is to be free; Whatever he says proves that you are wrong.* These furnish further evidence, if any were needed, that word order in Modern English is the foundation of every clause, and this abstract framework is firm enough to hold quite complex groups of words in proper syntactic relationship to each other without confusion.

We may now come to the second rank of word order, that pertaining to modifiers. In Old English, adjectival modifiers normally came before their noun, as they do today, but there were some that came after, notably the adjectives of quantity, and ordinal numbers used as cardinals. The latter we still prefer: *Chapter Five, page seven;* but the former have virtually yielded to the regular pattern. Kipling's *Soldiers Three* is certainly exceptional, and though we can still say *space enough, the time being, the money needed,* such phrases are few. Parallel to these are a small number of phrases borrowed or translated from French, such as *malice aforethought, Knights Templars, body politic;* and the trace of French word order may be seen in some of our place-names, such as *Lake Superior, River Rouge.* So, too, during and since World War II, such phrases as *Operation Sledgehammer, Operation Bootstraps,* have come into vogue—another testimony to the order of French modifiers, which is opposite to that of English.[15] The words *something, everything, nothing, anything,* which coalesced during the Middle English period, also have their adjectives following; we can still say *some good thing,* but *something good* is more frequent. *Somebody, everyone,* and other such pronouns, take the adjective afterwards; the other pronouns can hardly be modified, but such a phrase as *Poor me!* uses the regular adjective pattern.

With the exceptions listed, then—and they are numerically very

[15] The significance of these phrases is well brought home in M. M. Byrant's *Modern English and Its Heritage,* New York (Macmillan), 1948, pp. 249-250.

small—all simple adjectival modifiers today must come before their nouns. Phrases and clauses, on the other hand, usually come after, particularly when they are long: *The men, living and dead, who fought here. . . .* But even quite long modifying groups may precede the noun when the sentence is not too complicated: *a certainly not very patriotic motive, a hardly to be overestimated factor, his take-it-or-leave-it attitude.*

But though the place of noun modifiers has become more firmly fixed than it was in Old English, the verb modifiers have preserved freedom of movement—greater freedom, indeed, than any other member of the clause—for they can come before or after their verb, or (as we have seen) can be moved forward for emphasis to beginning position. Thus we may equally well say, *Quickly he followed the man, He quickly followed the man,* or *He followed the man quickly.* The position of these modifiers with regard to the Object depends on the Object itself; if it is single, as in this illustration, the verbal modifier follows. If, however, the Object has modifiers of its own, the adverb tends to remain close to its verb: *He followed the man who was wearing a brown hat and chasing a cat quickly* carries *quickly* too far from its verb, making its reference ambiguous. Therefore for clarity we prefer *He quickly followed the man who . . .* , and so on. Nevertheless, of all parts of speech, the verbal modifier is least subject to the limitations of word order that rule the Modern English sentence.[16]

Effects of Word Order. We are now ready to examine the changes which have come to English syntax as a result of the establishment of grammatical word order. For, paradoxically enough, despite the popular admission that vocabulary and spelling and the sounds of words change in the course of time, there is still somehow the feeling that "grammar" is changeless. Somehow the categories of grammar are identified in many people's minds with "logic," or the very modes of thought of the human mind. Numerous grammarians of the past have held this view, consciously or unconsciously—indeed, some write of "logical" word order. But the more we see of language and languages throughout the world, the clearer it becomes that what seems logical to one man is exactly the contrary of what

---

[16] More could be said about the word order of more than one adjective modifying a noun, and of adverbs modifying adjectives, but limitations of space forbid.

seems so to another. In English, adjectives are put before nouns; in French they are put after. Which language is illogical?

The fact is that there is a world of variety in the structural devices which mankind has utilized in language; to talk about "logic" in this connection, therefore, is beside the point. The real question is, in any given language, what devices *are* used at a given time for a given purpose; and if we study that language historically, what changes come about as it develops? For we must recognize the principle that, though syntax is more stable than pronunciation or vocabulary, it, too, changes. And even if we admit the logician's definition of what is or is not logical, we will find that admittedly "correct" usage contains a number of illogicalities which everyone accepts—indeed, of which the majority of people are entirely unaware.

As our first example we may take one of the newest acquisitions of the English language—one hardly to be paralleled in other European tongues—such a construction as *He was awarded the prize*. Now according to traditional syntax this is grossly illogical. We may say, in the active voice, *They awarded him the prize;* converting this to the passive voice, we make the Direct Object into the Subject, and say *The prize was awarded (to) him,* and so the Indirect Object remains Objective. There is no precedent, however, for converting the Indirect Object into the Subject, and the purist must look upon this as no less than a barbarism.[17] And yet in Modern English it is no barbarism, but, in plain fact, a fully accepted construction, constantly in use by good writers and speakers. What has happened? Evidently something like this. In Old English and Middle English one would have said *Him was awarded the prize,* keeping the Indirect Object in the oblique case but moving it forward in the sentence for emphasis' sake. But in common word order the noun or pronoun that comes before the Verb is felt to be the Subject, because it is in "Subject position." When nouns were moved forward in this way (compare *John was awarded the prize*) no necessary change of form was involved as between Object and Subject; but when the pronoun was moved forward, it had to be changed to suit the feeling for word order—hence *him* became *he.*

[17] E.g.: *"Given.* 'The soldier was given a rifle.' What was given is the rifle, not the soldier. 'The house was given a coat (coating) of paint.' Nothing can be 'given' anything." (Ambrose Bierce, *Write It Right,* p. 31.)

For another illustration, let us observe the history of the phrase that is now either *It is I* or *It is me* (usually in the form *It's me*) —a differentiation to which we shall return. In Old English, the corresponding idiom (like the Modern German "Ich bin es" except for the order) was *Ic hit eom*. In Middle English, this alters to *Hit am I;* but it proves impossible, eventually, to maintain *I* as Subject when it follows the Verb, for the Verb seems to belong to the word preceding it—that is, the word in "Subject position." The Verb is therefore altered to *is,* and the phrase becomes *It is I*. But in this new phrase, as early as the sixteenth century, *me* is competing with *I*, obviously because the Object form is expected in the position following the predicate. The point that we would emphasize here is the thoroughgoing way in which the syntax of the phrase has been shifted.

The rival phrases that have just been alluded to form one of the battlegrounds in current discussions of "correct English." It seems worth while, therefore, to go somewhat more deeply into the implications of divided usage in *It is I (me)* and kindred phrases. First, just how is usage divided? There can be no doubt that the frequent condemnation of *It is me* as "ungrammatical" is absurd in view of the actual facts of the case. Even a better-informed view, such as that of Professor Curme[18]—"the predicate pronoun should be in the nominative and in choice language usually is, but in popular and loose colloquial speech there has persisted . . . a tendency to employ here the accusative of personal pronouns as the predicate complement after the copula"—overstates the case for *It is I (he, they,* and so on). It seems more accurate to distinguish, not between "choice" and "loose colloquial" speaking or writing, but between more and less formal occasions for both speaking and writing. Here, as always, the spoken language sets the pace; and in the spoken language, especially of the less formal (but not necessarily the "loose") type, only *It is me* is in natural, idiomatic use.[19] Writers employing dialog in the printed page sometimes hesitate to use this phrase, out of deference to a tradition that condemns it; or if they use it, they do so either apologetically or defiantly, in such a way as

[18] *Syntax,* New York (Heath), 1931, page 41.
[19] This includes, of course, the spoken language realistically rendered in literature. See the many examples, chiefly from contemporary British practice, of the literary use of "It is me" cited by G. H. McKnight in *Modern English in the Making,* pages 532-533.

to indicate that they recognize that they are violating a generally accepted grammatical rule. The quotations which follow illustrate these attitudes.

> His eye was so dim,
> So wasted each limb,
> That, heedless of grammar, they all cried *That's him.*
> (Ingoldsby, *The Jackdaw of Rheims*)[20]

"That's *him* [italics]," said Ann Veronica, in sound idiomatic English. (H. G. Wells, *Ann Veronica*, Chap. VI)[21]

"He may be any of the passengers who sit with me at table."

"He may be me," said Father Brown, with cheerful contempt for grammar. (G. K. Chesterton, *The Incredulity of Father Brown*, p. 145)

The true status of the two expressions actually seems such that *It is I* rather than *It is me* is now on the defensive. This reversal of attitudes that have obtained in the past is illustrated in a characterization of *It is I* as "suburban English." [22] The implication is of course that the phrase is overcorrect, artificial, and stilted. A contemporary American novelist, Robert Nathan, touches this distinction very neatly when he has a character, speaking naturally, say, ". . . it's me she's married to, not him, and I won't stand for it" (*There Is Another Heaven*,[23] p. 124) ; a little later (p. 128), the same character, in a formal, almost a bombastic tone, gives utterance to these words: "It was I with whom she lay in bed; it was I she consoled." The difference in the atmosphere of the two speeches, be it noted further, is suggested also by the stilted "with whom she lay in bed," as contrasted with the colloquial "she's married to." Contemporary English, in other words, discriminates between *It is I* and *It's me* by employing the one phrase in formal, literary style and the other in informal, colloquial expression; and it may well be argued that the language is the richer for the distinction.

How can we account for the drift to *It's me?* The chief reason is, quite certainly, that the sense of case has become so weakened in Modern English, and the force of word order so dominant, that the latter overrides the former. Furthermore, the objectives of the per-

---

[20] New York (Houghton, Mifflin), 1919.

[21] Quoted by McKnight, *supra*.

[22] By William Ellery Leonard in "Concerning the Leonard Study," *American Speech*, Vol. VIII, No. 3 (October 1933), p. 58. See also Wallace Rice's article "Who's There?—Me," *ibid.*, pages 58-63.

[23] New York (Bobbs-Merrill), 1929.

sonal pronouns have been gaining at the expense of the nominatives, which tend more and more to be used only when they are immediately followed by a predicate. We feel, in some obscure fashion, that the objectives are both the more normal and the more emphatic words. The classical illustration of this emphatic use of *me* is in the passage from Shelley's *Ode to the West Wind,*

> Be thou, spirit fierce,
> My spirit! Be thou me, impetuous one!

This is indeed the triumph of poetry over grammar. And how feeble, how grotesque would *I* have been! Another illustration of the greater force of the objective pronominal forms is thus cited by Havelock Ellis:[24] "The Frenchman, when asked who is there, does not reply, 'Je!' But the would-be purist in English is supposed to be reduced to replying, 'I!' Royal Cleopatra asks the Messenger: 'Is she as tall as me?' The would-be purist no doubt transmutes this as he reads into: 'Is she as tall as I?' We need not envy him." Shakespeare of course lived before the establishment of the "rules" by grammarians of the eighteenth and nineteenth centuries; the freer syntax that his works display—where not "corrected" in modern school editions—often anticipates developments that are only now being given academic sanction. As to the "corrections," the First Folio reading of a familiar passage in *Macbeth* is

> lay on, Macduff,
> And damned be him that first cries, "Hold, enough!"

but a weaker *he* too often silently replaces *him* in our school texts.

It's me is undoubtedly in a stronger position than *It's them, It's him,* or *It's her.* Many of us, without being able to give very sound reasons for doing so, would agree with Professor Weekley's practice: "Personally I say 'That's me,' hesitate at 'That's him (or her)' . . ."[25] *Current English Usage* likewise lists *It is me* as "established," but finds that *If it had been us . . .* is on the border-line, while *I'll swear that was him, I suppose that's him, I am older than*

---

[24] *The Dance of Life,* New York (Houghton, Mifflin), 1929, Chapter IV. The whole argument for the "psychological necessity" of ". . . a double use of 'me' in English" is worthy of consideration.

[25] *Cruelty to Words,* New York (Dutton), 1931, p. 79. And of course others who condone "It is me" will condemn "It's him" or "It's them" more emphatically. C. T. Onions (*An Advanced English Syntax,* p. 34) takes this stand: the one is "used even by educated speakers," the others are "generally regarded as vulgar or dialectal."

him, and *It seems to be them* are all "disputable." [26] Nevertheless, good contemporary speech and writing often employs the objective forms of other pronouns than the first personal (singular) in analogous ways. A former Prime Minister, Ramsay MacDonald, used these words in his speech opening the naval conference of January, 1930: "The way of Great Britain is on the sea, for it is a small island. . . . Its defence and its high-road have been the sea. . . . Our navy is no mere superfluity to us: it *is* us." Though the *us* was widely criticized, would not *we* have been both flat and absurd? Aldous Huxley uses a similar *us* in this phrase: "A movement whose consummation is *us* [italicized] must be progressive." [27]

A few years ago,[28] Winston Churchill, visiting the United States and making a special recording of his voice, addressed the workers of the Soundscriber Corporation factory as follows, "This is me, Winston Churchill, speaking himself to you. . . ." This seemingly innocent remark created a considerable flutter for some weeks. An editor of the *New York Times* commented with obvious disapproval that this was a "remarkable sentence," and when *Time* reported the incident, letters from readers berated the Prime Minister for his "bad grammar," the most extreme of all seeing in such language a general reflection of the decay of the British Empire, and a consequent threat to the United States if we ally ourselves to Britain. Least stirred by the incident were those who were best informed, the professors at Columbia University whom *Time* consulted. They agreed unanimously that Churchill was using perfectly acceptable informal English.

In the light of usages like these, it would seem that the traditional textbook statements on the use of the personal pronouns need revision. (Some revisions there have been, it is true, but by no means enough.) What is really happening to pronouns in general has been summed up thus by Jespersen: "On the whole, the natural tendency in English has been towards a state in which the nominative of pronouns is used only where it is clearly the subject, and where this is shown by close proximity to (generally position immediately before)

---

[26] It should, perhaps, be added that "You are older than me" is also "disputable." For the meaning of "established" and "disputable," see p. 99 of this study.

[27] "One God or Many," *Harper's,* No. 952 (September 1929), p. 401.

[28] Cf. *Time,* Vol. 47, No. 13 (April 1, 1946), p. 66.

a verb, while the objective is used everywhere else." [29] This tendency, more marked as we have shown it to be in colloquial than in literary style, has as yet won but little recognition in the grammars and handbooks of writing and in our schools. When it is admitted that there is a drift in current English that takes more account of the position of pronouns in the sentence than of the traditional meaning of their case forms, the drift is all too likely to be noted as resulting in "incorrect" syntax.

Jespersen's way of putting the matter is certainly more suggestive than Curme's. The latter speaks of "the plain drift of our language . . . to use the accusative of personal pronouns as the common case form for the nominative and accusative relations; just as in nouns there is here no formal distinction," [30] and continues by citing examples—all, however, from dialectal or substandard speech—in which *me* replaces *I* immediately before a predicate. There would seem, however, to be no indications of a tendency in this direction in good colloquial speech, in which *me* has superseded *I* only after the verb or where used without a verb (as in *Dear me!, Unhappy me!*, and so forth). The drift, then, is not really a tendency for accusatives to replace nominatives in all positions, but rather for the separate forms to be interpreted and used in a new way, one dictated by word-order.

Who and Whom. The principle applies too to other than personal pronouns, especially to the interrogative *who*. What we notice here is a strong tendency to use the traditionally nominative form *who*, rather than the accusative *whom*, whenever the word comes first in the sentence, no matter whether it is subject or object. The inverted order used in a question will therefore result, in natural, unpedantic speech, in sentences like these: *Who did you see? Who is the message from? Who did you call on?* Thus there is no real incongruity between the drift to *me* in *It is me* and that to *who* in *Who did you see?* The circumstance that in the one instance it means the replacing of a form traditionally nominative with one traditionally accusative, and that in the other it works in the opposite way, merely makes the general principle the more obvious.

[29] *Essentials of English Grammar,* p. 136. This statement applies better to personal pronouns than it does to relatives and interrogatives.
[30] *Syntax,* p. 43.

There is, however, a further point to be made about the present use of *who* and *whom* (both interrogative and relative). The general leveling of inflections in English provides a powerful impetus to substitute a caseless and generalized *who* even where traditional syntax calls for *whom*. After all, many people get through life without ever saying *whom;* if they are aware of its existence at all, they regard it as a luxury of speech beyond their simple needs. George Ade once described in these illuminating terms a man obviously not of the folk: "He wore horn-rimmed spectacles and said 'whom.'" The situation, then, is not quite parallel with the one that we have discussed with reference to the first and third personal pronouns, singular and plural; it is clear that even the most illiterate do not simply discard *I* in favor of *me*, or *they* in favor of *them*. What we are here concerned with is the drift, making its way upward from the lower levels of speech, to replace *whom* with *who* in *every* position in the sentence. The interrogative *who* coming first in the sentence is the entering wedge of a more general movement to eliminate *whom* completely. Still, to find an eminent student of language like Jespersen making the following statement doubtless comes as something of a shock to many minds: "Grammarians have been so severe in blaming this [*Who did you meet there?* and so forth] that now many people feel proud when they remember writing *whom* and even try to use that form in speech."[31]

This way of putting the matter, surely, is sound and salutary doctrine, even if a trifle sweeping. Nevertheless, exception may be taken to a qualification that Jespersen gives to his remarks about *who* and *whom*: ". . . the only places in which *whom* is still naturally used are those in which it comes immediately before the subject of the following verb: *than whom* and sentences like the following: 'Ferdinand, whom they supposed is drowned' (Shakespeare) ; 'I met a man whom I thought was a lunatic' (E. F. Benson) ; 'Let Gilbert's wife be whom she might' (G. Eliot)." Here the objection is to Jespersen's use of the word *naturally*. *Than whom* is a phrase that has scarcely a place in colloquial English at all; it belongs essentially to formal, literary style. The other illustrations of the "natural" use of *whom*— sentences of the type of *We feed children whom we think are hungry,*

---

[31] *Op. cit.*, p. 137. The notation under *whom* in the *Oxford Dictionary*—"no longer current in natural colloquial speech"—is perhaps less extreme in its implication.

which Jespersen elsewhere[32] has defended most elaborately—must be discussed more fully.

Most grammars of course dismiss the *whom* in *We feed children whom we think are hungry* as a gross error, though it is curious that Fowler, in observing ". . . probably no grammarian would have a word to say for it," [33] should have overlooked the fact that one of the greatest of modern grammarians, Jespersen, has had many words to say for it. One may, however, be convinced by the cogency of Jespersen's reasoning, and feel with him that the attacks on the construction are based on at least two false premises,[34] without feeling that at present the *whom* in such sentences is in *natural* use. It seems far more likely to be a product of "overcorrection." The psychology would seem to be that the writer is too conscious of the existence of *whom* in the language; as a consequence of the fear of being thought ignorant of "correct" syntax, he uses *whom* in and out of season— surely the exact opposite of a *natural* use of it. Present-day writers who use *whom* in such a construction thus afford an additional and a very striking illustration of the fact that *whom* lacks any real vitality in contemporary English, since one of the best exhibitions of the decadence of a form is its use contrary to the plain drift of the language—in this instance, the generalized and caseless use of *who*.

Collections of contemporary uses of *whom* in the constructions under consideration have several times been made,[35] and we shall not repeat them here. However, the reader may be referred to a recent note by Professor Kemp Malone[36] which conveniently summarizes the question. As he points out, the whole matter of *who* and *whom* has really become a stylistic one today. Is one seeking an unstudied style? Then *"Who will you take?"* and *"Who are you writing to?"* are the only acceptable forms for the interrogative, and "The man *(that)* you speak of isn't here," for the relative. Is one

---

[32] *Philosophy of Grammar*, pp. 349-351, and *Modern English Grammar*, Part III, 10.7₃ ff.

[33] *Modern English Usage*, p. 724. *Current English Usage*, though its trend has been widely criticized as ultraliberal, likewise classifies this construction as "illiterate"—"definitely among uncultivated usages" (p. 110).

[34] Namely, that a subject *must* be in the nominative, and that the insertion of the words "we think" does not change the relation between the relative pronoun and its verb.

[35] E.g., Fowler, *op. cit.*, pp. 724-725; Weekley, *Cruelty to Words*, pp. 23-27; and Jespersen, *Modern English Grammar*, *loc. cit.*

[36] "Whom," *College English*, Vol. X, No. 1 (October 1948), pp. 37-38.

seeking a studied style? Then *"Whom* will you take?" and *"To whom* are you writing?" are the only acceptable forms for the interrogative, and "The man *of whom* you speak is not present," for the relative. We should note also that when interrogative *whom* is used with a preposition, the latter must precede; such a question as *"Whom* are you writing *to?"* mixes the styles, and is neither clearly studied nor unstudied. Also, relative *who* and *whom* are possible solely in studied style: in the unstudied the only relative in natural use is *that,* but as often as not it is omitted.

Whom, today, then, is still strong in only one position: as the immediate object of a preposition—and that only in studied style. The force of this feeling, that after a preposition *whom* is right, is strong enough, in fact, to lead to another overcorrection, when *whom* (or *whomever*) is the subject (or the "predicate nominative") of a verb in a clause introduced by a preposition as in the following sentences: "And you heard nothing as to whom it might be?" [37] and "All the whatnots that a man collects and insists on showing to whomever enters his house." [38] These are not quite as bad as the "Whom are you?" with which the night-school pupil is said to have triumphantly greeted people after finishing his series of grammar lessons. Nevertheless, they clearly indicate that *whom* has fallen into the confusions that always accompany decay, and that one of the few remaining strongholds of case-form in Modern English is considerably less solid than is commonly supposed.

The Split Infinitive. We may turn next to the "split infinitive," another crux of contemporary usage, and one which illustrates the importance of word-order in Modern English where no question of case is involved. The split that is objected to, of course, is that caused by the insertion usually of an adverb between *to* and the verb form. Yet, in favor of this position for the adverb, it should be recalled that modifying words in Modern English generally come immediately before the words they modify. Moreover, a very familiar sentence pattern consisting of subject, adverbial modifier, predicate, and object tends to be followed even where the adverb does not logically refer to the verb: "He only had one" is an order objected to by purists but nevertheless persisted in by a very great

[37] Eden Phillpotts, *Found Drowned,* London (Macmillan), 1931, p. 95.
[38] Lord Dunsany, *Don Rodriguez,* London (Putnam), 1922, p. 105.

majority of speakers. There is a strong impulse, therefore, to put the adverbial modifier of the infinitive immediately before the infinitive and after its "sign," the preposition *to*. This order has apparently been developed also through the influence of many parallel phrases: *to sincerely regret,* after all, is not very different from *he sincerely regrets, that he should sincerely regret, of sincerely regretting,* and so forth. There seems no good reason why the infinitive should not be "split"—really a misnomer,[39] since *to* is not historically or necessarily a part of the infinitive—just as there can scarcely be hesitation about "splitting" the predication *he regrets* or the participial phrase *of regretting.* Nevertheless, there is a powerful convention that forbids, and it is this that is in conflict with the feeling for word-order that leads to the splitting.

To understand the convention, it is necessary to be aware that the infinitive with *to* was originally a substantival phrase, in which a noun in the dative case was governed by, and of course immediately preceded by, the preposition *to,* which formerly meant "toward." As early as the fourteenth century, however, *to* ceased to be felt as a preposition; hence the way was open for the insertion of adverbs between *to* and the infinitive. But the opportunity for greater precision of expression which the split infinitive affords has been made use of only occasionally by many writers, and some have sedulously striven to avoid it altogether. Grammarians of the eighteenth and nineteenth centuries condemned it so severely and so successfully that even now only a few writers employ it freely, and it is one of the favorite taboos of those teachers—unfortunately, no inconsiderable number—who are unaware that there has been any development in language since the days of Queen Anne. As a matter of record, however, the split infinitive has had the sanction of at least occasional use by many good writers for at least three centuries,[40] and there are signs today that the unreasonable prejudice against it as vulgar or uncultured is beginning to abate. Certainly, the literary

[39] Jespersen points out that *"to* is no more a part of the infinitive than the definite or indefinite article is part of a noun." *Society for Pure English Tract No. LIV,* Oxford (Clarendon), 1940, p. 153.

[40] Jespersen gives examples *(ibid.,* pp. 154-155) trom Wilde, Butler, Stevenson. Hardy, Shaw, Meredith, Kipling, Galsworthy, Wells, Arnold, Dickens, Walpole, and other British authors; and from American authors, including Dreiser, Norris, Lewis, and Bromfield.

precedent for it and the solid advantages to expressiveness that it may possess have been pointed out by students of language in our day as never before.[41]

Too free a use of the split infinitive, of course, may not gain a writer praise for independence, but censure for his "ignorance of rhetorical conventions." There is wisdom—or at least caution—in a certain conservatism. Yet the writer or speaker who blindly bows to the taboo runs other and possibly worse risks: he is quite likely to create something that is either ambiguous or awkward (or both). Let us look first at the possibility of ambiguity. When the adverb precedes the *to*, it is often not clear whether it refers to what goes before or to what follows:

> Such writers as Hemingway, Dreiser . . . have not failed heartily to abet the leaders.[42]

Here there is the momentary suggestion of the absurdity "hearty failure."

> A young woman with a figure whose perfection her ill-fitted . . . clothes failed altogether to conceal.[43]

> Von Hern performed the introduction with a reluctance which he failed wholly to conceal.[44]

In both these instances, it is presumably not "total failure," as is at first suggested, but "failure at total concealment"—that is, *partial* failure—that is really intended.

Apart from the risk of such ambiguities, however, there is a downright clumsiness of expression which the split-infinitive phobia engenders. It is curious to find even so militant a critic as George Jean Nathan betraying an excessive timidity in the face of a split infinitive as the following excerpts from a single article betray:

> I allow myself the honor seriously to doubt . . . ; If the gentlemen in Downing Street were determined deliberately to spread subtle propaganda . . . ; Who makes it a business closely to follow their activities . . . ; Seriously to review such garbage. . . .[45]

[41] For an older defense, see T. R. Lounsbury, *The Standard of Usage in English,* New York (Harper), 1908, pp. 240-268; for more recent favorable views of it, see the witty article by Fowler, *op. cit.,* pp. 558-561, the excellent treatment by Curme, *op. cit.,* pp. 458-467, and Jespersen's tract just cited.

[42] *Saturday Review of Literature,* Vol. VIII, No. 42, May 7, 1932.

[43] E. P. Oppenheim, *Clowns and Criminals,* Boston (Little, Brown), 1931, p. 5.

[44] *Ibid.,* p. 462.

[45] *Vanity Fair,* May, 1931.

And a few more examples from other writers:

This appeared greatly to cheer the *Times* reviewer.[46]

That acquaintance with Southey, . . . which was deeply to color the next few years of his life.[47]

There was a fine chance for a Senator with character and brains effectively to unload his mind.[48]

As Fowler comments justly, "It does not add to a writer's readableness if readers are pulled up now and again to wonder—why this distortion? Ah, to be sure, a non-split die-hard!"

That such diehards exist also outside the ranks of the writers is borne out by the story told of the late Secretary of the Interior, Harold Ickes, who is said to have refused to sign any document that contained a split infinitive. On one occasion a large group of settlers, ready to leave for Alaska, were delayed for some weeks while the enabling document, in which Ickes had found an offending "split," was being rewritten before he would affix his name to it.

Possibly, however, the most grotesque result of the fear of the split infinitive is the fact that it not infrequently causes a writer to take elaborate precautions to avoid offending against a convention that does not exist. "To severely criticize" is a split infinitive, but "to be severely criticized" or "to have severely criticized" is not. "Successfully to have mined or torpedoed the ship would have required considerable and expensive equipment and a good many hands" [49] is decidedly an awkward way of expressing the idea "to have successfully mined . . ."—to say nothing of the fact that the present infinitive would be still more desirable. "They appear rapidly to have assimilated . . . ," [50] with its irrelevant suggestion of "a rapid appearance," likewise betrays the extreme solicitude of the "non-split die-hard." More remote ramifications of apparently the same trend are to be noticed in an occasional distorted word-order that seems dictated by the writer's anxiety to get the adverb disposed of as soon as possible lest he should commit the unpardonable sin—even though he is not always quite clear as to what the sin is. "Nobody solicit-

[46] "Solomon Eagle" [J. C. Squire], *Books in General,* 2nd series, New York (Knopf), 1920, p. 152.

[47] *Cambridge History of English Literature,* Vol. XI, p. 130.

[48] *New Republic,* Vol. LXVI, No. 851, March 25, 1931.

[49] Walter Millis, *The Martial Spirit,* New York (Houghton, Mifflin), 1931, p. 128.

[50] H. C. Wyld, *The Growth of English,* p. 116.

ously is trying to save science for the simple reason that in its own sphere science is saving us." [51] Here it would seem that the writer feared that even between *is* and *trying* the adverb would be too near the infinitive, and so inserted it in the strange position that it now occupies.

The sensible conclusion would seem to be that while deference to a not very reasonable convention makes it wise to avoid the construction ordinarily, and certainly makes it unwise to take the opportunity to split every possible infinitive, the occasional use of a split infinitive is entirely permissible. One may well agree with Mr. Fowler's conclusion that a split infinitive is preferable to real ambiguity or patent artificiality. Reason is all on the side of the splitter: note, for example, that there is no objection, in any quarter, to a construction like this—"It is the virtue of Cummings' poems to capture and accurately preserve the color of moments like this";[52] and the fact that there is no other equally unambiguous and straightforward way of expressing such an idea as this—"He ended a string of abuse with a vigorous back-hander, which I failed to entirely avoid." [53] But in matters of convention there are other things than reason to consider. To a really astonishing degree the authority of an older generation of grammarians has been strong enough to hold in check such powerful forces as analogy, the demands of clarity, and the usual trend in word order.

Logic and Usage. We have already made the comment that "logic," as it is usually thought of, is not necessarily in agreement with "correct grammar." Correctness is a matter of acceptance and acceptability: if a majority of people of cultivation—literary men, educators, editors, linguists, and others who have a professional knowledge of language—approve and use any locution, it is, by that very fact, good usage. Furthermore, strict logic has its limitations, since it offers no way out of some of the dilemmas that arise in language.

To mention only the most striking of these we may cite the fact that outside of religious and poetic contexts, the second person singular pronouns *thou, thy, thee,* and *thine* are dead, and the plural forms

---

[51] H. E. Fosdick, "What Is Religion?" *Harper's,* Vol. 158, March 1929.

[52] *New Republic,* Vol. XLIX, No. 895, Jan. 27, 1932.

[53] A. Conan Doyle, *The Return of Sherlock Holmes,* London (McClure, Phillips), 1905, p. 106.

have taken their place; and so it has been for fully three hundred years. Since the distinction between singular and plural is, in general, very much alive in English (though many other languages in the world do not indicate it grammatically) this is a surprising development. Verbs depend on their subjects almost entirely to show number, yet in one verb the plural form has gone over to singular (*you are*), following this "illogical" use of the pronoun. The feeling that this loss was illogical came soon after the change, or while the singular forms were in their last throes, for we find George Fox, in his "A Battle-Door for Teachers and Professors to Learn Singular and Plural," (1660) writing:

Do they not speak false English, false Latine, false Greek . . . and false to the other Tongues . . . that doth not speak *thou* to *one*, what ever he be, Father, Mother, King, or Judge; is he not a Novice and Unmannerly, and an Ideot and a Fool, that speaks *You* to *one*, which is not to be spoken to a *singular*, but to *many?* O Vulgar Professors and Teachers, that speaks Plural when they should Singular. . . . Come you Priests and Professors, have you not learnt your Accidence? [54]

The want of distinctive forms for number has been felt so strongly in our linguistic consciousness (or unconsciousness) that at least three tentative attempts have been made to supply it by the invention of new plurals—*you-uns, youse,* and *you-all*—to go with the new singular *you.*[55] None of these has gained or is likely to gain general acceptance—yet they would actually make the system more logical than it is at present.

Again, we hear children and other linguistic innocents saying *hisself* and *theirselves,* instead of the correct forms *himself* and *themselves.* Yet are not these unorthodox pronouns made on a sound analogy? For *myself, thyself, yourself, yourselves* are correct, and all begin with possessive forms. The fact is, however, that the change-over of this set of pronouns was arrested half way, and the very words which would complete it and make the whole set consistent and logical in structure—*hisself* and *theirselves*—are condemned as illiterate and inacceptable.

These are morphological matters, but similar developments also occur in the realm of syntax. Let us look first at agreement in num-

---

[54] Quoted from C. C. Fries, *The Teaching of the English Language,* New York (Nelson), 1927, p. 6.
[55] See Chapter 6, p. 126.

ber between subject and verb. There is, to begin with, little if any advantage to expressiveness in the retention of this syntactical convention. As Jespersen puts it, ". . . singular and plural in verbs have nothing to do with the verbal idea: when we say 'birds sing' with the plural form of *sing* . . . this does not denote several acts of singing, but is only a meaningless grammatical contrivance showing the dependence of the verb on its subject." [56] There is every reason to feel that English has gained much and lost very little through the inflectional leveling that has left only the ending -*s* to stand for difference in number in verbs. Indeed, as has been pointed out before, this -*s* itself could be disposed of without any real loss.

Early Modern English usage permitted a great deal more liberty of choice between singular and plural forms of verbs than is at present allowable, at least in theory. It is of course quite generally admitted that collective nouns may take either a singular or a plural verb, according to whether the thought stresses the body or the parts that make up the body; thus, "the senate was in session" and "the senate were debating" are both admissible. A parallel situation is that in which a compound subject, plural according to conventional grammar, is used with a singular verb. This usage has been found from Old English times forward, and is particularly common in early Modern English where the singular verb *precedes* a number of subjects, as in the Biblical "Now abideth faith, hope, and charity, these three," "Out of the same mouth proceedeth blessing and cursing," "To comprehend what is the breadth, and length, and depth, and height," and "Thine is the kingdom, and the power, and the glory." It also occurs when the compound subject precedes, as in "Where moth and rust doth corrupt," "Hostility and civil tumult reigns" (Shakespeare, *King John*, IV. ii. 247), and "Our faith and knowledge thrives by exercise" (Milton, *Areopagitica*). What these quotations show, of course, is that the way in which a writer or speaker thinks of his subject is more important than the strictly logical rule: he feels a unity or closeness of association between the parts of the compound subject which justifies his choice of the singular verb.

Good contemporary prose is less bound by the rule of concord, theoretically made rigid since the eighteenth century, than is generally realized. Grammarians sometimes allow as a legitimate exception the construction in which two nouns that together make up an

[56] *Essentials of English Grammar*, p. 216.

idea are followed by a singular verb, as in "the long and short of the matter (or, the sum and substance) is. . . ." However, not every use of singular verb with plural subject that is to be found even in formal, literary style can be defended on this basis. Here are a few miscellaneous examples of the construction:

The office had been in abeyance for many years, and its revival and bestowal at this time *was* indeed a remarkable sign of the royal favor.[57]

It is when that action and reaction *is* vivid enough that there start forth . . . visions chiseled in words.[58]

But the assault and robbery *is* at least equally likely to have been a reason for his voluntary resignation.[59]

This act has an intensity and an impetus that *carries* one through, without a moment's let-down, from the opening to the end.[60]

In some of the foregoing quotations the singular verb doubtless seems more natural and more necessary than in others; taken together, however, they serve to demonstrate that the rule-of-thumb application of the principle of "concord" to this point of syntax has its limitations, even for present-day English.

As a final bit of evidence on this point we may examine two successive sentences written by one of the most skilful of modern writers, G. Lowes Dickinson:

For such nobility, as all history and experience clearly shows, if we interrogate it honestly, is the product of a class-consciousness. Personal initiative, personal force, a freedom from sordid cares, a sense of hereditary obligation based on hereditary privilege, the consciousness of being set apart for high purposes, of being one's own master and the master of others, all that and much more goes to the building up of the gentleman; and all that is impossible in a socialistic state.[61]

That a subject may have an essential unity though it happens to be expressed in two words connected by *and* is a principle that will help to explain why "all history and experience" (i.e., "all the experience

---

[57] Lytton Strachey, *Elizabeth and Essex,* New York (Blue Ribbon Books), 1933, p. 161.

[58] John Galsworthy, "Literature and Life," *Candelabra,* New York (Scribner), 1933, p. 4.

[59] F. N. Robinson, *Complete Works of Geoffrey Chaucer,* New York (Houghton, Mifflin), 1933, p. xix.

[60] Edmund Wilson, *Europe Without Baedeker,* New York (Doubleday), 1947, pp. 221-222.

[61] *A Modern Symposium,* New York (Doubleday, Doran), 1905, p. 139. Reprinted by permission

of history") is followed by *shows,* and "all that and much more" by *goes.* But there is probably a better, though a subtler, reason. If, in the first sentence, *show* had been used, it would have been necessary to refer to the obviously plural subject by *them* rather than *it;* these plurals would somehow have been less harmonious with the singular *is* of the main clause that is resumed after the two parentheses. Even more clearly, in the second sentence, there is not only greater force and intensity in the singular *goes* than there would have been in the plural *go,* but the antithesis between *goes* and *is* would have been weakened if the parallelism in number had been destroyed by the opposition of *is* to *go.* In both sentences, to follow the rule of "concord" would have been to obtrude syntax and make it conspicuous; and that is precisely what Modern English when well handled does *not* do.

The Group Genitive. A somewhat similar story is that of the interesting phenomenon, peculiar to Modern English, known as the "group-genitive." When we say "the chairman of the board's opinion" it is clear that the opinion referred to is not that of the board, but that of its chairman; in other words, the phrase "chairman of the board" is inflected as a unit, and the ending *-'s* is attached to the end of the phrase, not added to the noun to which it syntactically belongs. Thus we say, "the mayor of Philadelphia's house," "the man in the street's attitude," and "my brother-in-law's car," just as we habitually add the possessive ending to only the second of a pair of personal names that together form a partnership: "the King of England's influence" is thus akin to "Beaumont and Fletcher's plays," "Gilbert and Sullivan's works," and so on. The locution "the King of England's influence," however, has established itself only gradually, and within the Modern English period; Malory, for example, used instead such a construction as "Sir Marhaus, the king's son of Ireland." In colloquial English today, the group-genitive is used extensively, and in an extreme fashion. Bradley[62] notes that a phrase like "That was the man I met at Birmingham's idea" is not at all uncommon in speech, though rather unlikely in writing, unless it is imitating speech. The colloquial turn that the construction gives to the following sentence admirably suggests that what we have is a reproduction of a man's thoughts: "He thought he'd go after them; he could take the little girl with the hair ribbon's other hand, and

[62] *The Making of English,* p. 61.

walk with them, two grown-up people and one little girl." [63] Incidentally, the writer just quoted furnishes, this time in dialog, a different
and a very extreme example of group inflection—the superlative ending -*est* attached to a long phrase, "hand-in-glove with God Al-
mighty": "He was the hand-in-glove with God Almightiest man you
ever see." [64]

One group-genitive, "someone else's," has established itself beyond
any cavil in both colloquial and literary style; yet some of our school
texts, and of the people who administer them to unfortunate pupils,
continue to insist on "someone's else." It is a melancholy observation
to put on record, but for the purpose of the present chapter a significant one, that while more than half the linguists who were consulted
for the preparation of *Current English Usage* classified *everybody's
else affairs* as illiterate or at best semiliterate,[65] the teachers of English would place it among "established" usages. There are indications, however, that this opinion is rapidly yielding to the force of
fact.

Prescriptive Rules and Actual Usage. What has just been suggested is that the brand of "grammar" taught in our schools tends to
be not only prescriptive but proscriptive. Far from regarding English as a living language susceptible of change and development, it
considers that syntax has been definitively codified and is now fixed
and unalterable. To defend this point of view it is necessary to outlaw any locution or construction that is at variance with theories
originally laid down by grammarians now long dead. A remarkable
illustration of the discrepancy between theory and practice, and the
resulting necessity (from the point of view of the kind of teacher
referred to) of preaching against firmly rooted habits of speech, is
the present status of our future auxiliaries *shall* and *will*. The elaborate code of distinctions that has been built up by theorists is of
course simply ignored in general present-day—and more specifically
present American—usage. To the folk, *shall* is almost as unknown as
whom. But what is its use in cultivated speech?

A foreign student of language, illustrating the point that the dia-

[63] Robert Nathan, *There Is Another Heaven,* New York (Mathews), 1932,
pp. 138-139.
[64] Robert Nathan, *The Woodcutter's House,* Indianapolis (Bobbs-Merrill),
1927, p. 85.
[65] "Not English—a pseudo-correction by the semiliterate for *everybody
else's*" was one comment.

lect of a colony tends to do away with certain subtle distinctions of the language of the home-country, has this to say of our present topic: "The difference between *I shall* and *I will* no longer exists in the English spoken in America: *I will* alone is used for the future." [66] At first blush, this strikes an American as a gross exaggeration, but a little reflection makes it evident that the statement is not, after all, very wide of the mark. Most educated Americans would *write,* "I *shall* be glad to come," but they would *say,* "*I'll* be glad to come." Now *I'll* must be, phonetically, the contraction of *I will,* not of *I shall,*[67] so that the phrases commonly used in American speech ("I'll be there," "I'll be glad to serve") do, in a sense, level the distinction between *I shall* and *I will.* At the same time, a differentiation between *I shall* and *I will* is unquestionably preserved in writing of any degree of "correctness" or formality.

Incidentally, with reference to *I'll,* there seems to be something decidedly misleading about statements like these: "The contracted forms *'ll, 'd* . . . [are] . . . never contractions of *shall, should:* 'I'll go, we'll go, I'd go.' . . . The written forms *I shall, we shall* are often in rapid speech pronounced *Ishl, weeshl.*" [68] These last contractions are surely, so far as American conversation goes, theoretical rather than realistic. In opposition to Curme's opinion, Krapp's observations may be quoted: "*I'll, you'll, he'll* may as well stand for *I will,* etc., as for *I shall,* etc." [69] ". . . as this abbreviation [*'ll*] may stand for either *shall* or *will,* there is no way of telling whether *I'll, you'll, he'll* contains the one or the other of these forms . . ." [70] The upshot of the matter would appear to be that Jespersen and Curme, while of course correct in assuming *I'll* to be developed from *I will* and not from *I shall,* are wrong in implying that in its present-day use *I'll* always and necessarily represents *I will* as opposed to *I shall.* In its American use, at any rate, *I'll* is simply a generalized form, which is often used, indeed, partly because it does not imply *either* "I will" or "I shall." To be sure, the less cultivated speaker in using it does not realize that he is avoiding a difficulty, but the more

[66] Vendryes, *Language,* p. 353.

[67] Cf. Jespersen, *Modern English Grammar,* Part III, 15.2 (1).

[68] Curme, *Syntax,* p. 362.

[69] *Modern English,* p. 295. C. C. Fries, in an elaborate discussion of *shall* and *will* in Modern English, *P.M.L.A.,* Vol. XL, No. 4 (December 1925), pp. 963-1024, takes issue with this way of putting it.

[70] *Comprehensive Guide to Good English,* p. 533.

speech-conscious person is, perhaps subconsciously, grateful for the opportunity of dodging a choice that is largely artificial.

That American speech is far from being in accord with the "rules" for *shall* and *will* is even more evident when *I'll* cannot serve to dodge the difficulty. Admittedly there is a neat and useful differentiation in meaning between "Shall you be there?" (an inquiry) and "Will you be there?" (an invitation); but in natural, unaffected speech, this differentiation simply is not made. "Shall you?" to American ears sounds "stilted, tony." [71] The rules of our textbooks are here in line with a distinction that in England is in perfectly natural and unforced use but that is not followed in the United States —or in Ireland or Scotland. Some years ago, this quotation from another periodical was reprinted in *Punch:* "Before traveling in France I think that I will have to study French." Underneath it appeared the following comment: "We think that the writer shall have to study English first." Would the sentence "I think that I will have to study French" have appeared to an American editor as worthy of mocking quotation? And would his American readers have got the point of it if it had?

Space cannot be spared here even for a summary of the "rules" for *shall* and *will*—especially since the exposition of these rules varies most remarkably in different grammars and dictionaries. Surely, however, an American is justified in looking with some distrust at this way of putting one of the most cherished of the rules: "In the first person, *shall* has, from the early Middle English period, been the normal auxiliary for expressing mere futurity. . . . To use *will* in all these cases is now a mark of Scottish, Irish, provincial, or extra-British idiom" (*Oxford English Dictionary*). If Scots, Irishmen, Americans, and other "extra-British" speakers do not use the "normal" auxiliary it is a little difficult for one who is not a Southern Englishman to understand how it can continue to be "normal." Again, Professor C. C. Fries has amply demonstrated [72] not only that actual usage has been quite different from what the rules would imply, but also that the rules themselves were compiled in defiance of existing practices. It is somewhat startling to discover that the

[71] *Current English Usage,* p. 115.

[72] In the article on *shall* and *will, op. cit.,* and also in "The Rules of Common School Grammars," *P.M.L.A.,* Vol. XLII, No. 1 (March 1927), pp. 221-237. See also Leonard, S. A., *The Doctrine of Correctness in English Usage, 1700-1800,* Madison, Wisconsin (University of Wisconsin), 1929.

complete scheme of conventional rules, which was formulated in the eighteenth century and repeated with more conviction through the nineteenth, unmistakably had its origin in the typical eighteenth-century purpose of "correcting" the practice of English speakers and writers by means of these very rules. These precepts were based on "reason," not usage; indeed they explicitly repudiated even the practice of "the most approved authors."

Perhaps all that can safely be said of contemporary trends with reference to *shall* and *will* is that there is a general drift, more marked in American than in English practice, away from *shall* and toward *will* in almost every category. Deference to the artificial and arbitrarily formulated rules is less common, even in formal writing, than it once was. At the same time, it is quite clearly unwise to assume that *shall* is always pedantic or affected; in a question with the first personal pronoun, for example, *shall* is almost always preferred in general American (though not Scots or Irish) practice. The popular drift to *will* has, of course, been opposed by the conservative tradition of the schools as well as the survival of an older attitude toward "rules" in our grammars; and the opposition has been successful enough to make it expedient for anyone who desires to conform to generally accepted standards to pay some deference to it. However, to use only *will* as the sign of the pure future in all three persons would certainly be an improvement over the confused and confusing distinctions that are still recommended. The popular tendency, then, is one that should be encouraged rather than combated; it may be observed that the best of recent grammarians (for example, Poutsma, Curme, and Jespersen) on the whole incline to this attitude. For teachers of English, often completely ignorant of both the history and the dubious validity of the "rules" they advocate, to insist that their pupils must conform to the fantastic code of discriminations between *shall* and *will* and *should* and *would* (a code that Jespersen takes 118 pages to outline) is an act of folly.

Another point in which a traditional rule of syntax is more often followed in English than in American practice, but in which nevertheless American teaching usually insists on strict conformity, is the convention as to the "generic" personal pronoun *one*. Several observations suggest themselves with regard to this form and its use in the sentence. In the first place, it is not quite analogous to the French *on* or the German *man*, for *one* is used much less freely; there is no English parallel, for example, for *on dit* or *man sagt*. The best we can manage seems to be *They say,* or (much more formally) *It is said*. Again, English writers have employed what Fowler has termed the "false first-personal use of *one*" more commonly (and doubtless more naturally) than have American writers. Viscountess Rhondda, telling of her experience on the *Lusitania,* used the *I* that seems natural for vivid first-hand narrative until the *one* construction suddenly suggested itself—with this result: *"One's* lifebelt held *one* up in a comfortable sitting position with *one's* head rather back, as if *one* were in a hammock. *One* was a little vague and rather stupid."* To most Americans, it is safe to say, this seems a peculiarly stilted and artificial jargon. Nevertheless, it occasionally obtrudes itself in American writing of the more mannered variety: *"One* has no reproaches for the people who get headaches at movies: *one* can only be sorry for them. *One* has, indeed, no reproach for the people who honestly do not enjoy them. *One's* only reproach is for the people who have pre-judged them. . . ."* [73]

What most Americans feel to be the chief awkwardness about *one* is of course the theoretical necessity of referring to it by itself, or by *one's* or *oneself* (or *one's self*). In early Modern English, *one* might be continued by *his, him,* and *himself* (*oneself* indeed is unknown in Shakespeare). American, and other "extra-British," usage often perpetuates this older practice; but the schools are likely to insist on the alien nicety of "When one employs *one,* one is obliged to continue *one* to the end of one's sentence." It is fair to add, however, that a flouting of the "rule" in American speech and writing of the more formal sort is probably less common than the practice of avoiding like the plague any construction that requires the application of the rule. The alternatives to *one* usually resorted to in such a sentence as *One has to think of oneself,* are *a man, a person,* or *you,* followed by *himself* or *yourself.* Or one may take refuge in the plural: *We have to think of ourselves, People have to think of themselves.* To avoid the necessity of using *one* (or another form of the same pronoun) more than once, or at most twice, in the sentence is thus the practical compromise between deference to a convention and defiance of it.

The -ly Words. Perhaps one of the most curious examples of divided usage today is the hesitation between adjective and adverb

[73] K. F. Gerould. "What, Then, Is Culture?" *Harper's,* Vol. 154, January, 1927.

(or between two forms of the adverb, one with and the other without the *-ly* suffix) that frequently occurs when the qualifier follows the predicate. Should one say, for example, *I feel bad* or *I feel badly*? This one question brings into focus what is really a much larger matter, the value of *-ly* and of the forms with and without it, adjectives and adverbs—a matter so complex, indeed, that even the best informed may be excused if they sometimes feel uncertainty about one or another particular usage. The popular belief, very widespread, that "*-ly* is used to form adverbs," gives very little help, since it is a gross oversimplification and leads as often as not to overcorrection or absurdity. A look at the facts, historical and descriptive, should help to clear up the confusion.

Let us begin at the beginning. During the Old English period the majority[74] of adjectives could easily be distinguished from adverbs because the latter ended in *-e*. Thus there were the pairs (adjective and adverb) *heard, hearde; lang, lange; fæst, fæste; strang, strange; wāc, wāce; wīd, wīde;* and many more. In the Middle English period, however, when the final *-e* lost its distinctive value, all of these became identical in form, so that today we have *hard, long, fast, strong, weak, wide, full, high, thick, soft,* most of which preserve both adjective and adverb forms: *a hard hit, hit him hard; a long wait, don't wait long; a fast runner, she ran fast;* and so on.

Secondly, in Old English the word *like* was added to nouns or adjectives to form other adjectives and adverbs, the form *-līc* being used for adjectives, and *-līce* for adverbs—which, of course, paralleled the general distinction of form between these two parts of speech. Thus we find such adjectives as *mannlīc, frēondlīc, godlīc* based on nouns, as also the adverbs *mannlīce, frēondlīce, godlīce;* so too we find such adjectives as *clǣnlīc, wāclīc, cyndelīc* and many others based on adjectives, as also the adverbs *clǣnlīce, wāclīce, cyndelīce,* and so on. The two forms *-līc* and *-līce,* distinguished also only by the final *-e* (or the lack of it), were reduced in Middle English to the *-ly* of Modern English, and we have survivors still of most of the types of formations just listed: the adjectives *manly, timely, friendly, godly, cleanly* [klɛnlɪ], *weakly* (dialectal today), *kindly;* and the adverbs *cleanly* [klinlɪ], *weakly, kindly.* Two groups, how-

---

[74] Some, however, had identical forms: without *-e,* as *full* (adjective and adverb), *heah* (adjective and adverb); or with *-e,* as *þicce* (adjective and adverb), *sōfte* (adjective and adverb).

ever, have been greatly diminished: the adjectives based on other adjectives (*a goodly portion, a kindly appearance*), and the adverbs based on nouns, which are now found only in substandard English (*he treated me friendly*). The two remaining groups are very much alive, however: adjectives based on nouns, and adverbs based on adjectives, both formed by the addition of *-ly*. The latter pattern is so much the strongest of all that it has furnished the basis of the popular misconception mentioned above.

The group that has suffered most, in the course of this complicated development, is that of the old adverbs without *-ly;* for, understandably enough, the more *-ly* has become the mark of an adverb, the harder is it for adverbs without *-ly* not to be taken as adjectives. Thus, though in *go slow* we have a true adverb, people often mistake it for the adjective *slow,* and insist on the form *slowly.* In this particular case, considerable opposition to the shorter form has arisen, though to any sound ear it is far more suggestive of a warning than *go slowly.* Many similar phrases that are deep-rooted in English idiom would be utterly spoiled were they treated to the same kind of regularization: *easy come, easy go; mighty kind; clean through; sure enough; wide apart; going strong; full well; straight from the shoulder; think hard; fly high; sleep late; rest quiet; lie soft;* and so on. Nevertheless, people who are uncertain of themselves take refuge in the "rule," feeling that it is safer to add *-ly* than to risk leaving it off. And so we get overcorrections such as the oft-heard gem *an awfully lot.* The reasoning about this, clearly enough, goes somewhat in this fashion: "I know that *awful bad* is not correct; what I ought to say is *awfully bad.* Therefore I ought also to say *an awfully lot.*" Of course the analogy is wrong and the "cure" both ungrammatical and ridiculous.

But the actual history of the forms with and without *-ly* does not by itself explain the confusion that attends their use. A great part of it is due to the effect of certain particular verbs, which sometimes require an adjective, sometimes an adverb. The copula, or linking verb, of which the best example is *to be,* calls for an adjective after the verb: *He is strong, This train is slow.* If the other linking verbs were like *to be* in requiring for their completion an adjective (such as *strong*) which describes their subject (*he*), there would be no confusion. However, most of these linking verbs have other meanings and functions as well, and before we can know whether to use

an adjective or an adverb with them, we have to find out how they
are being employed. One group of them in particular is the source
of much annoyance: the verbs referring to the senses. We can use
them as linking verbs (followed by adjectives) as in *He feels weak,
He smells bad, It tastes sharp, It looks pretty;* and there are other
verbs of similar meaning which also are followed by adjectives modifying their subjects: *I kept clean, It worked loose, It became tangled,
It got mixed, It stayed steady, It held firm, It remained fixed, It
seemed large, It appeared small,* and so on. But these same verbs, in
their other senses, do not link subject and adjective, but are often
modified by adverbs: *He feels deeply, smells sharply, tastes cautiously, looks clearly, sees well, hears poorly.* This is the place where
an adverb without *-ly* can be mistaken for an adjective (*They
marched slow, grew thick, shouted loud, worked hard, climbed high*)
—and where, therefore, by analogy, some adjectives are ungram-
matically used (*He sees good, hears poor, talks stupid*).

The only way out of the difficulty presented by these verbs is
through their meaning. Are they, we must ask, functioning as copulas
or not? If they are, they take adjectives; if not, they take adverbs.
And so we return to the two phrases with which the discussion of
-ly began: *I feel bad,* and *I feel badly*—and, one might add, *I feel
well.* It is true that *bad* is only an adjective; therefore it can be used
only with the copula: *I feel bad,* meaning that my health at the
moment (or possibly my moral intention) is not of the best. But
both *badly* and *well* may be either adjective or adverb, therefore
may be used with either linking or non-linking verbs: *I feel badly*
(linking verb and adjective, meaning "in poor health"), *I feel well*
(linking verb and adjective—cp. *a well man*—meaning "in good
health"); *I feel badly, I feel well* (non-linking verb and adverb,
meaning "my sense of touch is not—or is—good"). Into such ramifications has the historical development of the forms with and without
-ly led us! It is no wonder that the oversimplified popular "rule"
brings confusion upon its users.

How are we to summarize the situation? Briefly, thus. Though *-ly*
is most often added to adjectives to form adverbs, every word ending
in *-ly* is not an adverb, nor do all adverbs end in *-ly.* A number of
the older adverbs without *-ly* are identical in form with adjectives,
but the formation of new adverbs by the addition of *-ly* to these
adjectives does not render the old adverbs wrong—indeed, they are

often idiomatically preferable to the new ones. There is no doubt, too, that esthetic considerations often have a part in deciding usage. Why, for example, should the same person say "I feel bad," but "I feel very badly about the matter"? For the same reason, very likely, that accounts for "go slow" by the side of "he went slowly down the street." Euphony and rhythm, that is to say, sometimes take precedence over mere syntax. They have probably aided in preserving the older adverb despite the competition of the newer one with -*ly* (e.g., "How slow he climbs!" "Please read very slow" and "Sing as slow as you can").[75] The analogy of *go fast* perhaps helps to explain how it is that *go slow* has maintained itself and now serves as a foothold for resisting the encroachments of *slowly* in other phrases.

Still another factor to notice is that of language level, since forms, though they may weaken in standard spoken usage, often remain strong in dialect or in literature. In any case, it should be evident that an uninformed use of "unidiomatic -*ly*," as Fowler calls it, will lead as often as not to overcorrection, awkwardness, and other blunders. We leave this subject with two final examples. In a particularly dignified announcement of one of our leading actresses in a new role, this unfortunate statement was made: "The curtain will rise at 8:15 sharply." Now *sharp* is not, perhaps, the most formal of adverbs—it is somewhat colloquial in tone—but it *is* an adverb, and it means "precisely." *Sharply* means nothing of the sort. In the pseudo-Biblical diction of *The Good Earth*,[76] use is made of this phrase: "to rest easily in the grave." The authentic idiom is of course "to rest easy," which means rather "to be easy" (or "at ease") than "to rest without difficulty" (the irrelevant suggestion of the other phrase).

To return to examples of that type of divided usage in which the teaching of the schools is not strictly followed in wide and sometimes in good practice. A construction that is sternly prohibited in the grammar of the schools is that in which *and who* or *and which* (or *but who* or *but which*) is used without a preceding relative clause introduced similarly. The corresponding idiom is regularly used in French, but academic opposition to its use in English has been strong enough to cause it to be regarded, quite generally, as an error. Jesper-

---

[75] Cf. Fowler, *Dictionary of Modern English Usage*, p. 542. But the differentiation in *Current English Usage*, pp. 131-132, seems more plausible.

[76] John Day, 1932.

sen says of it:[77] "It is, however, frequently heard in colloquial English, and is by no means rare in literature, though not so much used now as in the 18th century." That its use is by no means confined to colloquial speech or to the literature of the eighteenth century or earlier is attested by the following quotations from three leading (nineteenth-century) exponents of that most carefully written prose form, the familiar essay:

> The sweetest names, and which carry a perfume in the mention, are Kit Marlowe, Drayton. . . . (Charles Lamb, "Detached Thoughts on Books and Reading")
>
> . . . others of a less extravagant character, and that excite and repay interest by a greater nicety of detail. . . . (William Hazlitt, "On the Pleasure of Hating")
>
> Montaigne . . . —the creator of a distinct literary form, and to whom even down to our own day . . . every essayist has been more or less indebted. (Alexander Smith, "On the Writing of Essays")

Professor Jespersen, incidentally, is true to his own conviction as to the usefulness of the idiom when he writes, "The method I recommend and which I think I am the first to use consistently . . ." (*Language*, p. 418), and ". . . a question beset with considerable difficulties and which need not detain us here" (*Growth and Structure*, p. 63). Finally, the use of the construction in literary English of our own time may be illustrated in these excerpts:

> . . . a spinster cousin of the family, always present, always silent and whose lips never ceased moving.[78]
>
> . . . a free intelligence playing over the problems of our time, without prejudice or passion, and which has won for itself a commanding position in the life of the nation.[79]

In the light of citations like these, it is clear that the familiar statement of the school rhetorics that the *and which* (*who*) construction is *never* employed in good writing is decidedly an overstatement of the facts.

The Final Preposition. A last illustration, and a more inexcusable one, of pedantic prohibition in the face of widespread and thoroughly idiomatic usage, may be added: the "rule," now happily less dwelt

[77] *Modern English Grammar*, Part III, 4.12.
[78] Thornton Wilder, *The Cabala*, New York (Modern Library), 1929, p. 94.
[79] J. T. Adams, *Saturday Review of Literature*, Vol. 7, No. 29, February 7, 1931.

upon than formerly, that a sentence must not end with a preposition. As is well-known, it is largely to John Dryden that we owe this absurd principle. Dryden's sudden realization that in Latin the preposition never comes last in the sentence moved him to recast the English sentences of his prefaces in order to eliminate what he had come to feel as barbarous. His influence has been amazingly powerful; school grammar after school grammar has repeated the warning against the prepositional ending, in spite of its continued use in the best speech and writing. A wrong use of etymology has even been drawn in to further the movement that Dryden began; the literal implication of *preposition* has often been invoked to prove that a preposition should not come last. The better texts of our own time of course no longer include the warning; but every college instructor in English knows how firmly intrenched the tradition still remains in the teaching of English in our lower schools. Freshmen come to college, generation after generation of them, knowing pitifully little, to be sure, about their native tongue, but with a few deeply rooted ideas on grammar and rhetoric. What they know, if it is not too cynical to put it thus, consists quite largely of things that are not so; and among these scraps of misinformation, almost as the cardinal tenet, is the notion that a sentence should not end with a preposition. To illustrate: two college freshmen were endeavoring to recall this sentence from the *Religio Medici*—"For the world, I count it not an inn, but an hospital; and a place not to live, but to die in." It is surely not inexplicable that the students should have independently set down, as their idea of how Sir Thomas Browne should have worded it, this paraphrase: "I count the world not an inn but a hospital, and not a place in which to live but a place in which to die." The stumbling clumsiness of such a sentence—forced upon the student by a hidebound rule—could never have been perpetrated by Sir Thomas Browne. But fortunately this rule is beginning to be laughed at, and perhaps the awkwardness it leads to may be avoided in the future. A radio announcer recently remarked, on a baseball broadcast, "Rain again! Some more of the kind of weather up with which the Yankees have had to put!"

Space cannot be taken to exemplify further the cleavage to be observed between theory and practice in current English syntax. What the illustrations already cited seem to imply must, however, be set forth more completely. There are, it may be maintained, two extreme and opposite attitudes toward grammar and syntax, and they are related, at least in part, through cause and effect. The one is the traditional school attitude that stems directly from the eighteenth-century grammarians. This attitude makes for the rejection of actual usage and for the retention of the outmoded conventions that clutter up the rhetorics. What it stresses is prohibition, and what it neglects is observation. Teaching of this sort insists that sentences shall *not* begin with *and* or *but,* and shall *not* end with *to* or *in.* It insists upon *It is I* for all occasions, upon the strict application of the rule as to *one,* and upon an impossibly complicated (and variously interpreted) set of distinctions between *shall* and *will.* It is particularly severe with such usages as the split infinitive, and with locutions current in popular colloquial speech like *and which, like he does, these kind of apples,* and *those sort of people*[80]—for it avoids the difficult task of differentiating among the several purposes and planes of discourse.[81] It even outlaws such completely established idioms as *none are, someone else's* and *had rather.*

That an attitude exactly opposite to the one just outlined should exist need occasion no surprise. It requires very little observation of the actual customs of speech and writing to see that there is a discrepancy between such precept and authentic practice. The schoolboy, consciously or unconsciously recognizing that the language foisted upon him in the classroom has no real existence elsewhere, very sensibly rejects it for other than classroom purposes. Perceiving that what is taught him is artificial, bookish, and pedantic, he comes to feel that "grammar" as a whole is to be rejected. This then is the attitude that is at once the consequence and the antithesis of the ultraconservative approach to language characterized above. It adopts the comfortable, albeit unfortunate, theory that the study of grammar is a case of much ado about nothing, or, at best, about very little indeed. This point of view once found expression in a letter congratulating a newspaper columnist on his admirable ignorance of English grammar. The communication is so illuminating in its frankness that it will be quoted:

[80] Jespersen (*Essentials of English Grammar,* p. 202) says, ". . . we may look upon *kind* and *sort* as unchanged plurals. . . ."
[81] On this matter, see the excellent (and salutary) article of Prof. J. S. Kenyon, "Cultural Levels and Functional Varieties of English," *College English,* Vol. X, No. 1 (October 1948), pp. 31-36.

If you are really as ignorant of English grammar as you profess to be, you are to be congratulated, for there isn't any such animile. English is practically a grammarless tongue. What is found in books called "English Grammar" that children are obliged to study in their so-called education is a lot of stuff faked up by self-styled grammarians, whose object is to make the English language seem to be like languages that have a grammar, when, in fact, it is totally unlike them. For instance, the only forms of the verb "to be" in our language today are "be" and "been." There is no nominative case in English, so, of course, it cannot agree with any verb. And so on through all the "conjugations" and "declensions" and "syntax" that the grammatical fakirs have invented. Keep on writing English "as she is spoke" by fairly intelligent Americans, and your column will be above reproach on the score of its grammar.

These ideas, violently exaggerated and not particularly well-informed as they are, yet contain a certain grain of truth. What is more to the point for the present purpose, this repudiation of grammarians as fakirs and of English grammar as a fraud is obviously due to the fact that the writer has encountered the wrong kind of grammar and grammar-teaching. The attitude that holds that there is no such thing as English grammar is an entirely natural reaction to the attitude that takes no account of the drift from emphasis on form to emphasis on word position, admits no difference between colloquial and literary style, and, finally, has never understood the fundamental concept of syntax being subject to change by usage.

These opposite attitudes, reactionary and anarchistic, were brought clearly into the light some years ago in the curiously varied reception accorded *Current English Usage*, by Sterling A. Leonard and his associates, a pioneering study that investigated competent opinions as to the "correctness" of a number of disputed expressions. While the ultraliberal element rejoiced to find their own convictions as to the "correctness" of many a popular locution apparently upheld by this cross section of the "actual practice of the educated world," the conservative-minded were profoundly shocked. To them it seemed that liberty of choice in matters of syntax had degenerated into mere license, and that popular "errors" were being given the approval of academic sanction. Neither extreme opinion is of course well justified. The usage of the majority—perhaps even a majority of the "educated," unless that term is more strictly interpreted than it generally is—does not necessarily constitute good usage. On the other hand, to observe that many educated speakers consider certain

colloquial phrases thoroughly established—for colloquial purposes—
should cause distress only to those who are deaf to the actual ca-
dences of spoken English, and who are ignorant not only of the
existence of different levels in language, but also of the fact of change
through usage.

The attitude of newspapers on questions like these is particularly
interesting. With certain noteworthy exceptions, such as the *New
York Times,* whose many editorial comments on linguistic matters
are consistently well-informed and enlightened, our newspapers are
ordinarily given to heavy-handed humor or solemn protestations
against tampering with the sacred "grammar" of the language. The
sort of thing that is commented on, and the typical comment, may
be briefly illustrated by this excerpt from an editorial:

> The President has written a letter to Speaker Rainey, announcing that
> he would veto the Bonus Bill if it were passed, adding, "I don't care who
> you tell this to." Teachers of English who are justifying errors in grammar
> on the ground of usage may tell us that this form of words is correct. . . .
> There seems to be a difference between official English and the English of
> the grammars.[82]

Comment on this is perhaps superfluous, but it would be interesting to know what grammars the editor had in mind.[83] He was not
acquainted, it may be conjectured, with any really authoritative
recent treatment of the *"who* and *whom"* question. Nor does it seem
possible to express a more wrong-headed view on the larger question
of the relation between syntax and usage than is done in these words:
"justifying errors in grammar on the ground of usage." How can an
error, it may be asked, remain an error if it is justified by usage?
What is of course implied is the familiar delusion that "grammar"
has been codified, once and for all, and that the particular school
text used by the individual years ago, with its tenth-hand repetition
of the "logic" of eighteenth-century grammarians, summed up the
final truth on the subject.

Our survey of some of the questions of syntactical usage in present-day English has necessarily been cursory. Perhaps, however,
enough has been said to indicate that syntax is to be regarded, like

[82] Philadelphia *Evening Ledger,* Feb. 28, 1934.
[83] Presumably not Jespersen's *Essentials of English Grammar,* for one. It
would be extremely salutary for the editor to ponder these words in its first
chapter (p. 17): "Grammatical expressions have been formed in the course of
centuries by innumerable generations of illiterate speakers. . . ."

spelling, pronunciation, and meaning, as a department of language in which a shifting of standards is incidental to, indeed an essential condition of, the life and change that are the very soul of speech. The question of what, at a given time and for a particular purpose, constitutes good English will always be a difficult one. But the realistic approach to it is evidently through observation of the changing contours of language in actual, present-day use. Let us, by way of conclusion, look at some of the factors in this most important and most perplexing of all the problems that confront the individual in the use of language.

Good English is not merely correct English; it is something at once greater and different. But even the lesser question of what is correct is not always easy. By what authority is correctness to be determined? Standards of various sorts have been proposed and appealed to in settling a particular question of usage. Perhaps Jespersen's formulation of these standards is the most satisfactory that has been compiled: the standard of authority, the geographical standard, the literary, the aristocratic, the democratic, the logical, and the esthetic.[84] Yet each one of these in turn proves to be questionable and, for the purpose of settling every doubtful case that arises, clearly inadequate. One is too rigid, another too nebulous; one too loose, another too tight. And it is decidedly a makeshift to turn from one to another, as all of us to some extent do, in grappling with difficult problems.

The approach to a solution comes only with the realization that there is no such thing as absolute correctness—for all persons, all places, and all purposes. Our search for what is correct is transformed into a quest for what is desirable, appropriate—hence "good" —when we come to understand that the world of language, even the English-speaking section of it, is too vast and too variable for absolute standards to apply. The individual speaker is a member of a much smaller linguistic community, even though he may have difficulty in setting limits to this community. The only kind of correctness that is demanded is compliance with the conventions of this community. But compliance is not the highest goal. Compliance suggests something merely negative: absence of faults, rather than

---

[84] From the chapter "Standards of Correctness," in *Mankind, Nation, and Individual from a Linguistic Point of View.* To this and the following chapter, "Correct and Good Language," the present remarks are greatly indebted.

positive merit. Good English must be more than merely free from error. It must also be more than simply intelligible—a still lower goal than correctness. The individual strives, not only to speak clearly and, according to certain conventional standards, "correctly," but also to express himself with force and with grace. It is just here that he has a certain liberty of choice. After all, he is not merely a member of a community, but an individual: he not only adopts, but helps to make, the customs of his community. His influence can be both detrimental and beneficial. It is detrimental not only when it is exerted to keep alive such excrescences, the very "dry rot of syntax," as lead to obscurity rather than clarity, but also when it lends its weight to perpetuate those more labored and more formal manners of speech that the community still theoretically approves even after they have been discarded in good practice. It is beneficial when he as an individual follows those customs that he conceives to be healthful developments in contemporary speech, and even perhaps when he introduces rebellious innovations of his own. There is thus, as Jespersen has put it, "a constant tug-of-war between individual and community, an eternal surging backwards and forwards between freedom and linguistic constraint." These forces, one leading to regimentation, the other to anarchy, are the centripetal and centrifugal impulses in language. The individual at one moment defers, at the next rebels; through his unique compromise between conformity and liberty, he forges for himself an individual style.

A single and, in great measure, an unanswerable question remains. What guides shall the individual take to assist him in his choice in matters of divided usage and in his personal experimentation with language? There are, alas, no formulas for tact and taste. Perhaps all that can be said is that acquaintance with the past of the language offers a certain measure of protection against the dogmatism that is born of ignorance: no one who acquaints himself, even cursorily, with the history of English is in danger of supposing that a speech that has undergone such radical changes is likely to be standing still now. Nor will such a one be apt to suppose that there is available a tangible external standard, one that will offer infallible counsel in all linguistic perplexities. The value of the best of these guides should not be depreciated. Any adverse criticism of school texts, such as the present chapter contains, does not of course extend to the great grammars of such men as Luick, Jespersen, Poutsma,

Kruisinga, and Curme and Kurath. The National Council of Teachers of English also has begun work upon a *Dictionary of Current American Usage*, which promises us a sound and full study based, in part at least, on fresh, up-to-date materials. Such guidance of course is infinitely to be preferred to the varied sources—antiquated school rhetorics, ipse dixits by publicity-seeking lexicographers, newspaper departments on "How's Your Grammar?," magazine quizzes on "What's Wrong with These Sentences?," and the courses in "English in Six Easy Lessons" that are advertised so lavishly—from which the man in the street may glean miscellaneous bits of dubious information on the nature and use of his speech. What must be here insisted upon, however, is that even the most enlightened of guides have a limited usefulness. The individual's growth in good English is naturally to be assisted by recourse to them. But, in the last analysis, mastery of English comes back to a feeling for idiom on the part of the individual, and, however supplemented by external guides, depends finally upon his own taste, and his own observation of and sensitiveness to good practice.

References for Further Reading

Aiken, Janet R., *A New Plan of English Grammar*, New York (Holt), 1934.

——, *Commonsense Grammar*, New York (Crowell), 1936.

Curme, G. O., "Are Our Teachers of English Adequately Prepared?" *Publications of the Modern Language Association of America*, Supplement for 1931.

Fowler, H. W., *A Dictionary of Modern English Usage*, Oxford (Clarendon), 1926.

Fries, C. C., *The Teaching of the English Language*, New York (Nelson), 1927.

Jespersen, Otto, *The Philosophy of Grammar*, New York (Holt), 1924.

Kellner, Leon, *Historical Outlines of English Syntax*, London, 1892.

Kennedy, A. G., *Current English*, Boston (Ginn), 1935.

Krapp, G. P., *Comprehensive Guide to Good English*, Chicago (Rand, McNally), 1927.

Kruisinga, E., *A Handbook of Present-Day English*, Part II, "English Accidence and Syntax," Groningen (Noordhoff), 5th ed., 1931, 1932.

Leonard, S. A. (and others), *Current English Usage*, Chicago (Inland Press), 1932.

Marckwardt, A. H., *Introduction to the English Language*, New York (Oxford), 1942.

Onions, C. T., *An Advanced English Syntax*, London (Kegan Paul, Trench, Trubner), 4th ed., 1927.

Poutsma, H. A., *A Grammar of Late Modern English*, Groningen (Noord-hoff), 2nd ed., 1928.

Wyld, H. C., *The Growth of English*, London (J. Murray), 1907 and later editions.

Chapter 11

The Modern Period—Dictionaries, Spelling

DEVELOPMENT in language, as in other things human, goes irregularly, with periods of rapid change or expansion when new elements are added or old rejected, followed by periods of consolidation when the new become fully established—for a time, at least. In the preceding chapters of this book we have seen something of the process by which the English language, as we know it, was born; how, after the Germanic dialects had achieved some literary distinction in the eighth and ninth centuries, the literary progress of the language was interrupted for several centuries and an alien tongue introduced in its stead; and finally, how, in the fourteenth and fifteenth centuries, a literary language was again evolved from popular dialects that had meantime undergone sweeping changes, and a standard stamp was set upon it by such men as Chaucer and Wiclif, Caxton and Malory. After this time, though alternate consolidation and expansion of the language continues, it is less violent, less revolutionary. One obvious reason is that never again was England subjected to foreign conquest. Nevertheless, in one sense something like this did happen: in the sixteenth century, the republic of letters was conquered by the humanistic movement, the revival of learning that put the study of Latin on a new basis and introduced the study of Greek.

Thus the Modern English period began on a phase of expansion which continued until close to the end of the seventeenth century; and the nineteenth and twentieth centuries represent another period of expansion, that of the Industrial Age. Between these two lies the eighteenth century, a time of consolidation and relative stability. In our two remaining chapters, then, we shall take up the Early Modern period, including the years between 1500 and about 1700, and the

Late Modern period, coming down to the present time. We shall try to summarize the developments that came about in various departments of the English language in regard to style,[1] spelling, pronunciation, and grammar, as the language has reflected alterations in the social structure during these four and a half centuries.

The general effect of the Renaissance in the progress of the English language was twofold: a temporary neglect of the vernacular by those whose classical studies made them almost contemptuous of modern tongues, but a later recognition of the possibility of giving to modern languages something of the grace and the sonorous quality that scholars found in the classics. In addition, the developing of nationalistic feeling under the later Tudors gave a new incentive to the literary use of the vernacular. The great tradition of Biblical translation, from Wiclif and Purvey in the fourteenth century, through Tindale and Coverdale in the sixteenth, to the King James version of 1611, is likewise to be mentioned as one of the channels through which literary Modern English took form and exerted a powerful and widespread influence.

What is perhaps most striking in the attitude of scholars and writers toward the English language in the early Modern English period is a tendency to divide into two opposing camps: those who held that English should be "improved" by free importations from without, particularly by borrowings from Latin; and those who believed that the language should rather develop its own resources, and that an admixture of other languages meant not improvement but corruption. These points of view are, of course, signs of the opposite beliefs about vocabulary that have always existed and, to some extent, will always exist; but conservative and radical tendencies in this field have seldom been so consciously and definitely opposed as they were in the late sixteenth century. We have already seen how these two influences affected the development of the vocabulary, and will recall that the eventual victory was with the radical camp, and that in the Renaissance there was established, once and for all—though there are, to be sure, later qualifications— the principle of liberal word-borrowing as a permanent policy of the language. Not every aspect of this victory, however, is to be regarded

---

[1] Style, it is true, is "metalinguistic"—not properly within the sphere of linguistics. Since, however, stylistic ideals and practices constantly involve grammar, vocabulary, and other aspects of language, it cannot be ignored.

as admirable. Free borrowing from Latin was accompanied by an aping of Latin rhetoric, and more than that, a deliberate striving to give English prose certain ornaments and decorations that would lend it dignity and an aloofness from ordinary speech comparable to that of verse. The Euphuism of John Lyly and the Arcadianism of Sir Philip Sidney are merely two particularly conspicuous examples of the general tendency to cultivate a highly self-conscious and thoroughly artificial language. The promise of Malory's beautifully simple manner, based upon French, was set aside in favor of the new manner based upon Latin. Despite noteworthy exceptions (the outstanding one being the simplicity of diction of the King James Bible), the all but universal trend of literary prose is toward the rhetorical and the ornate until the Restoration and the early eighteenth century see the establishment of quite opposite ideals.

Abraham Cowley's *Several Discourses, by Way of Essays, in Prose and Verse* and John Dryden's *Of Dramatic Poesy* both were published in 1668. These two works are sometimes thought of as marking the first appearance of a truly modern prose in English literature —a language that is to all intents identical, in syntax and in structure as well as in vocabulary, with the English of our own day. The long separation between an elevated and ornamental diction for literary purposes and a plain, terse vocabulary for conversation begins to draw to a close. Throughout the eighteenth century, beginning with the work of men like Swift, Steele, and Addison, the striving is for simplicity and directness. The vocabulary is no longer looked upon as susceptible of change and addition. The Elizabethan exuberance, the joy in language as in a new toy, is gone. Gone too are the long, rolling periods, the Latinized diction of Milton, Sir Thomas Browne, and Jeremy Taylor. What takes their place (for the French influence is visibly at work once more) is conciseness and simplicity—a desire for clarity and accuracy. The tendency is toward "purification" and refinement; to make the best use of the language we have but to suffer no innovations. Swift protests against the borrowing of foreign words, and, later in the century, Samuel Johnson believes that his dictionary will forever "fix the English language." [2] On the whole, this more conservative attitude toward language is to

---

[2] The phrase is from the *Plan* of the Dictionary addressed to Lord Chesterfield. Johnson, however, experienced a change of heart, as the *Preface* to the Dictionary indicates.

be regarded as a salutary reaction from earlier radicalism; in language too, it is "our indispensable eighteenth century."

With the dawn of Romanticism toward the end of the century, a freer and a more liberal atmosphere becomes evident, in language as in other matters. Sir Walter Scott, for example, takes delight in reviving obsolete words and in introducing dialect terms, particularly from the balladry of the Scottish border but also directly from the living language of the peasantry. It is, however, not merely the language of literature that is renovated in the nineteenth century. The colonial expansion of England and the great advances in scientific thought are both accompanied by a changing and freely developing vocabulary. As in the spacious days of Elizabeth, though to be sure with somewhat more restraint, original writers like Carlyle create words and phrases for their individual purposes, colonizers and travelers borrow exotic words from the languages of foreign peoples, and men of science coin the terms to describe the new ideas and new discoveries that they have contributed to the world's knowledge.

Just as much, then, in the history of the language as in literary history, is the eighteenth century, with its precursor, the age of the Restoration, to be regarded as a conservative interlude set between two epochs of far greater liberalism. We shall see later that in certain respects the conservative spirit then triumphant established conventions and ideals that have not been easy to overthrow in later periods. Particularly is this true of the attempts to set up rules[3] for spelling, pronunciation, and syntax—to bring about conformity, if not uniformity—a movement to which dictionaries, grammars, and the printing houses lent their powerful support. In the preceding chapter the syntactical aspects of this movement were dealt with; we must now treat of pronunciation and spelling.

Spelling. English spelling has had many vicissitudes during its history. The earliest remains in Old English are written in the Runic alphabet—the one common to all the Germanic peoples. This was an adaptation, probably, of the Latin alphabet,[4] itself the most important offshoot of the Greek alphabet;[5] but after the Christianization of the Anglo-Saxons—that is, beginning about 600—these runes

---

[3] We are not here finding fault with rules as such. Rules there must be. But they ought not to be so rigid that they cease to reflect actual changes in a language. This subject will be discussed more fully later.

[4] Cf. Chapter 5, p. 89.

[5] Cf. Chapter 1, p. 11.

were for the most part rapidly superseded by the Latin letters. Since, however, Latin did not have the sounds [θ] and [ð], and therefore no characters to spell them, the Old English carried over into the newly adopted Latin alphabet the runic þ; and somewhat later, ð was also developed for the same use. But here came one of the first failures of English orthography, for, there being two sounds and two symbols, it would have been manifestly sensible to attach one value to each symbol. Yet this was never clearly done; þ and ð were used interchangeably for either [θ] or [ð]; nor do we yet distinguish these sounds in spelling, since *th* serves for both. Another runic character, ρ ("wen"), was used for the sound of [w], but modern editors of Old English usually transliterate it to *w*. Two ligatures (later dropped) were used for vowel sounds by the Anglo-Saxons: æ, for a sound familiar through the whole history of English, and represented in modern phonetic alphabets by a similar symbol, though eventually discarded in conventional spelling in favor of simple *a;* and œ, for a sound like German *ö*, and soon discarded for *e*. The vowel *y* and the digraphs *ea* and *eo* also correspond to symbols of the Runic alphabet. Thus the earliest spelling of English in Latin characters was not greatly different from that of Modern English in respect to the symbols that it employed. Apart from the few preservations of runic characters, the principal differences are the absence of *j*, *q*, *v*, and *z*, and the rare (usually late) use of *k*. Although there were irregularities in the spelling of Old English, and although it was not perfectly phonetic, it nevertheless represented a much nearer approach to correspondence between symbol and sound than does that of Modern English.

Why, then, has our spelling today so far lost touch with pronunciation as to be relatively unphonetic? Easily the foremost cause is that pronunciation itself has changed so often and so radically that spelling has never been able to keep up with it. The fact that considerable dialectal differences existed within the language, particularly during the Middle English period, also tended to prevent spelling from changing as pronunciation changed. But even when spelling was changed, the alteration did not necessarily bring it closer to the desired correspondence, and the result was too often a further dislocation. Earliest among the larger factors that have brought confusion into English spelling was the influence of Norman French. New letters, *j* and *q*, were introduced, or at any rate first given wide use; new phonetic values were attached to the old symbols, or the old symbols were used in new combinations; e.g., *c* was written for *s*, *o* for *u*, and *ou* for *ū*. On the favorable side one must add that from French came *v* (about 1200) and *z* (about a century later) to spell sounds which had existed in Old English but for which there had been no separate characters.[6] French influence did not cease with the centuries following the Conquest. To it, to give only a few illustrations, we owe such spellings as *tongue* for what would more sensibly be *tung* (like *lung;* compare the German cognate *Zunge*) ; *guess* for what Chaucer spelled *gesse;* and such other anomalies as *programme, catalogue,* and *quartette,* now fortunately being simplified.[7] But spelling was still, until late Middle English times, quite largely a field in which the individual might display whatever eccentricity he pleased. Orm, whose *Ormulum* appeared soon after 1200, is one of the first of spelling reformers; his contribution was to double the consonant after short vowels, and thus, after a fashion, to indicate pronunciation somewhat more accurately.

The invention of the printing press, however, marks the second great event in the history of English spelling, and the remote beginning of modern standardization. It was a kind of standardization, curiously, that made whatever confusion existed before appear unimportant. In the bitter words of Lounsbury, "Upon the introduction of printing, indeed, English orthography entered into that realm of Chaos and old Night in which it has ever since been floundering; it then began to put on the shape it at present bears, 'if shape it may be called that shape has none.' "[8]

Several reasons may be advanced to account for the unfortunate effect that the early printing press had upon spelling. One was the circumstance that most of the earliest printers came from Holland.

[6] Different characters were not really necessary in Old English, since [v] and [z] were only positional variants of [f] and [s], and constituted with them but two phonemes. When these variants gained phonemic status, *v* and *z* were borrowed to indicate them.

[7] Of course, the French today—unlike the Normans—cannot be blamed for our irregularities of spelling, since they do not prevent us from respelling the words we borrow from them. But when we attach "prestige value" to foreign spellings, imputing culture to those who can pronounce them in the foreign way, they naturally tend to remain unadapted. One British writer has boldly offered "orderve" for *hors d'oeuvres*—a rather good rendering; but our tendency seems to be to leave such words in all the un-English complexities of their foreign spelling.

[8] *English Spelling and Spelling Reform,* p. 272.

These men followed certain Dutch analogies, and introduced absurdities like *ghost, gherkin; ghospel, ghossip; ghess, ghest.* The illustrations have been given in three groups, to suggest the three different lines of development that these *gh* words later took: the first pair retained the unnecessary *h;* the second pair dropped it and restored the Old English *g;* the third pair was later "Gallicized" by the substitution of *gu* for *gh.* Probably of more importance than such arbitrary respellings of individual words was the setting up, by different printing houses, of separate and inconsistent rules for spelling in general—a practice inherited in some measure by their modern successors. Moreover, the first printers were not only aliens, unfamiliar with English pronunciation; quite certainly, they were in general men of less education than their predecessors, the copyists of medieval manuscripts. Medieval authors sometimes complained of the incompetence and carelessness of their scribes—Chaucer's humorous exasperation with "Adam, his owne scriveyn" is a well-known instance—but undoubtedly these scribes were as a class far superior in knowledge and culture to the early printers. Spelling fell increasingly into the hands of semi-literate men; authors were frequently, as they have been ever since, misrepresented by the typesetter.

The full burden of blame, nevertheless, cannot fairly be loaded upon the printers, for we must remember that at the very time when printing was coming in, the pronunciation of many vowels—of all the tense vowels and some of the lax ones—was itself changing: the great vowel shift which forced English out of orthographic line with other European languages and with its own past, was in progress. Even had the printers been scholars—which they decidedly were not —they would have been hard put to it to adapt spelling at such a time to the actual sounds of speech.

Furthermore, while Orm had sought to reform spelling by a phonetic principle so that it would more clearly reflect the actualities of pronunciation, later attempts at reform sometimes followed other principles, perhaps quite false. The least defensible of these—an unfortunate by-product of the humanistic movement—was an etymological principle, according to which scholars and writers began to respell English words to make them conform to Latin or Greek analogies. Often this was done with words that, though originally Latin, had been borrowed not from Latin but from French, with the changes in spelling and in pronunciation that had taken place in Vulgar Latin and Old French. Thus *debt* was respelled to indicate its remote ancestor, the Latin *debitum;* and *doubt* similarly to show a connection with Latin *dubitum;* the Middle and early Modern English spellings *dette, det, doute,* and *dout,* better both phonetically and etymologically, were discarded. In these words, the *b* has never been pronounced. The *p* in *receipt* has a similar history: Elizabethan scholars changed the earlier *receit* or *receyt,* as they did also *conceit* and *deceit* (though here with less permanent results). Sometimes, the changed spelling has in turn affected the pronunciation, as when *perfect* (for Chaucer's *parfit*) was made to look like its Latin grandfather rather than its French father.

This zeal for etymology becomes amusing as well as deplorable when the etymology is utterly mistaken. A poor defense can be made, on the ground of remote relationship, for the *b* of *debt,* the *c* of *perfect,* and the *p* of *receipt;* but even this limited excuse does not serve to justify the *s* of *island* (not even remotely from Latin *insula* or French *isle,* but from an Old English *igland,* which became *iland* in Middle English and early Modern English), or the *g* in *foreign* or *sovereign.* The last two words are particularly instructive. *Sovereign* comes from Old French *sovrain,* in turn derived from the Latin *superanus* [<*super* (above)]. It was erroneously associated with *reign* [<Lat. *regnare* (rule)], and the mistaken analogy not only affected *sovran* (so spelled by Milton), but accounts for the spelling of *foreign* as well. *Foreign* is really from Old French *forein* [from Vulgar Lat. *foraneus,* eventually from Lat. *foras* (out of doors)]. Thus even those with some pretensions to scholarship wrongheadedly took English spelling, in hundreds of words, still farther away from pronunciation. Many of their innovations were adopted by the printers and are preserved to this day.

Nevertheless, through the sixteenth and seventeenth centuries, a degree of uniformity in spelling—however irrational with respect to etymology or pronunciation—was increasingly approached by the printing houses, which drew gradually closer together in their practices. Ironically, such agreements as they did arrive at were upon spellings that had long since ceased to represent pronunciation. Thus many Renaissance spellings, standing often for still older prounciations, were permanently fastened upon the language. From early

Modern English times the gulf has rapidly widened, pronunciation changing freely and spelling remaining relatively static. Here are the seeds for the growth of two distinct branches of the language— spoken and written. Whatever may be thought of the result, it can scarcely be denied that something like this is the present state of affairs: We possess a language that appears, on the printed page, in a form so different from the way in which it is spoken that the only adequate way for the dictionary to indicate the pronunciation of Modern English words is to respell them in a phonetic alphabet. One should not let familiarity with this situation conceal its oddity.

There still remained one more step to be taken, however, toward the present fixation of spelling. The system itself, as we have seen, was much more the creation of printers than of authors. But the stamp of approval set upon it by the dictionaries of the middle and late eighteenth century was very far-reaching indeed. It was this that made the approximate uniformity that had been achieved by printers up to the eighteenth century very nearly absolute. Indeed, dictionaries have had so powerful an influence upon Modern English that we must not proceed without at least brief notice of their development.

Dictionaries. The approach to the modern English dictionaries was by way of Latin-English glossaries, of which many appeared in the Middle Ages and the Renaissance. Just which of their successors deserves the title of first English dictionary is a point on which opinion is divided. John Bullokar's *English Expositour* (1616) is the earliest claimant;[9] but it is soon followed by Minsheu's *Ductor in Linguas, or Guide into the Tongues* (1617), the first of etymological dictionaries; and by Henry Cockeram's *English Dictionarie*[10] (1623), the first in which the word *dictionary* is used in the sense in which we now understand it. The full titles of Bullokar's and Cockeram's compilations suggest the early conception of a dictionary as limited to *difficult* words only: the one reads *An English Expositour: Teaching the Interpretation of the hardest Words used in our Language, with sundry Explications, Descriptions and Discourses*

[9] *A Table Alphabeticall,* published in 1604 by Robert Cawdrey, should perhaps be mentioned; though according to its full title, it is intended to be limited to *borrowed* words, and to importations from Hebrew, Greek, Latin, and French exclusively, it does in fact include archaic native words.

[10] Referred to above, Chapter 7, p. 175.

(incidentally implying also the early affiliation between dictionary and encyclopedia) ; the other, *The English Dictionarie: or, An Interpreter of hard English Words.*

Later dictionaries, with greater pretensions to completeness, are that of Milton's nephew, Edward Phillips—*New World of Words, or a General English Dictionary* (1658)—and that of Nathaniel Bailey, the direct predecessor of Johnson—*Universal Etymological English Dictionary* (1721). Weekley[11] points out that it is only just before Bailey's work is published—in the seventh edition (1720) of Phillips's dictionary, to be explicit—that the familiar word *dog* makes its appearance. Bailey's volume seems, on the whole, to be the best candidate for the position of first complete dictionary. It was Bailey, too, who began the practice of marking the accent of words, in which he was followed by Samuel Johnson in his epoch-making dictionary of 1755. Johnson, however, did not give the full pronunciation, because, as he observed to Boswell, it was impossible to model this "after the example of the best company because they differ so much among themselves." He had come to believe, in other words, that even if he could "fix" the spelling and signification of words he could not fix their pronunciation.[12] Not until after Johnson, therefore, was the final step taken in indicating the pronunciation of words: the vowel sounds were indicated, for the first time in a general dictionary, by William Kenrich in the *New Dictionary,* which he published in 1773.[13] This precedent was immediately followed by other British lexicographers of the late eighteenth century, and by the Americans, Webster and Worcester, in the early nineteenth.

It has been more than once remarked that there is a certain poetic justice in the history of dictionary-making since Johnson, in that the two nations he particularly abhorred, the Scots and the Americans,

[11] "On Dictionaries," *Atlantic Monthly,* Vol. 133, No. 6 (June 1924), p. 786.
[12] For a fuller statement, see the chapter "Johnson's Dictionary" in McKnight, G. H., *Modern English in the Making,* pages 351-376; and the more recent study by Allen, Harold B., *Samuel Johnson and the Authoritarian Principle in Linguistic Criticism,* 1940 (available in University Microfilms, No. 381, Ann Arbor, Michigan).
[13] Two Scotsmen had in the meantime published pronouncing dictionaries. These were James Buchanan and William Johnston, whose works appeared respectively in 1757 and 1764. For a treatment of Buchanan's work, see Burt Emsley, "James Buchanan and the Eighteenth-Century Regulation of English Usage," *P.M.L.A.,* Vol. XLVIII, No. 4 (December 1933), pp. 1154-1166.

have taken the lead in the production of English dictionaries. Noah Webster's *Compendious Dictionary of the English Language* (1806), in its various revisions,[14] was the leading authority during the greater part of the nineteenth century, and its chief rivals at the close of the century were two other American works, the *Century* and the *Standard*. The greatest of all dictionaries, the *New English* or *Oxford*, the first volumes of which were published in 1884 and the last in 1928, was begun under the editorial supervision of one Scotsman, Sir James Murray, and finished under that of another, Sir William Craigie.

And what of the authority of the dictionaries, their influence upon the speakers and writers of the language in the three centuries that had elapsed since Bullokar and Cockeram? The authority of dictionaries arose out of at least two forces present in the seventeenth and eighteenth centuries, one artistic, the other social. As to the first: with the end of the Middle Ages it became evident in Europe that Latin could no longer continue to dominate all fields of scholarship and art. Thus, while it kept its primacy in the schools, and while writers continued to use it to some extent, in each land they worked also in the vernaculars—sometimes in more than one. Chaucer's contemporary, John Gower, wrote in Latin, French, and English. In Italy, Dante sought to prove his native Tuscan fit for the highest literature; and Milton, though he wrote also in both Latin and Italian, was animated by the same ideal as Dante's, hoping to leave in his beloved English language something so written "that the world would not willingly let it die."

With the rise of the vernaculars for scholarly and artistic use, came the foundation of academies through which it was intended to undertake the purification and control of these languages. In Turin, in 1592, the Accademia della Crusca was founded, and the Académie Française in Paris in 1635. Attempts to set up an English counterpart, however, failed. Nevertheless, if there was no Academy to produce an authoritative dictionary, the need remained, and Johnson's

---

[14] The elaborate two-volume revision published in 1828 was suggestively called *An American Dictionary of the English Language*. This work is termed by Krapp "the most significant contribution to English lexicography between Dr. Johnson and the appearance of the first volume of the *New English Dictionary*," *The English Language in America*, Vol. I, p. 362. Its later forms, particularly the first edition to be designated *Unabridged* (1864), were successive improvements over the earlier.

great dictionary, when it appeared in 1755, was accepted as satisfying that need.

The second force which led to the authority of dictionaries—the social one—came with the rise of the middle class to social prominence, and the development of middle-class anxiety about "correctness" in speech.[15] As more and more people rose in the world, they sought some way of assuring themselves that their use of the language (among other appurtenances of social acceptability) should be "right." These, then, were the impulsions under which dictionaries (and grammars, which increased in numbers and prestige at about the same time and in a parallel way) took on the character that to many minds they still possess: that of being the final arbiters of speech. The general veneration of "rules" in the early and middle eighteenth century—implicit, to take a single example, in the doctrine of Pope's *Essay on Criticism* that literature is to be both produced and judged according to a formula—naturally lends its weight to the treatment of language as something that must be adjudged, once and for all, as either "correct" or "incorrect."[16]

Dr. Johnson's dictionary purported to give the correct meaning, spelling, and accent of all words then existing in accepted usage—and what he approved of, Johnson conceived to be generally desirable. The extent to which even the most cultivated spirits of the age were willing to submit themselves, accepting dictation in the interest (as they hoped) of refining the language, is hardly to be better suggested than by a quotation from Lord Chesterfield's letter "On Johnson's Dictionary":

I had long lamented that we had no lawful standard of our language set up, for those to repair to, who might chuse to speak and write it grammatically and correctly. . . .

The time for discrimination seems to be now come. Toleration, adoption and naturalization have run their lengths. Good order and authority are now necessary. But where shall we find them, and at the same time, the obedience due to them? We must have recourse to the old Roman expedient in time of confusion, and chuse a dictator. Upon this principle I give my vote for Mr. Johnson to fill that great and arduous post. And I hereby declare, that I make a total surrender of all my rights and privileges in the

[15] Cf. Wyld, H. C., *A History of Modern Colloquial English*, New York (Dutton), 3rd ed., 1937, pp. 18-20.

[16] C. C. Fries has an excellent chapter on the part that grammars have played: "The Rules as Measures," *The Teaching of the English Language*, pp. 1-31. Cf. also McKnight's *Modern English in the Making*.

English language to the said Mr. Johnson, during the term of his dictator-ship. . . .[17]

Since Dr. Johnson was the first really authoritative lexicographer, and by all odds the most influential figure of the time, we may glance for a moment at the man and his work. There is no question that he was unabashedly authoritative by nature; he had no false modesty and played the pundit willingly—and on the whole well, if at times heavy-handedly. Nevertheless, Johnson was too intelligent and experienced to be rigid, and he was fully aware that rules must be adjusted to circumstances. Many of the procrustean formulas which have been associated with his name were really the inventions of lesser men, the like of whom he might well have repudiated had he been alive. Despite its undoubted faults, Johnson's dictionary—produced in a mere eight years with very little help and under manifold difficulties—is one of the splendors of English lexicography.

It was no part of Johnson's purpose to establish new and radical principles in English spelling. The almost contemporary dictionary of the French Academy (1762) reformed the spellings of something like five thousand words—more than a quarter of the whole number it included; but Johnson's dictionary of 1755 sets out, in more conservative fashion, to bring order out of the chaos of English spelling by ironing out existing inconsistencies rather than by innovations. It is significant of his attitude that he specifically asserted that he preferred, in the few changes he had made, to go back to old models:

I have attempted few alterations, and among these few, perhaps the greater part is from the modern to the ancient practice; and I hope I may be allowed to recommend to those whose thoughts have been, perhaps, employed too anxiously in verbal singularities, not to disturb, upon narrow views, or for minute propriety, the orthography of their fathers.

Johnson's aim, then, as he set out to "ascertain" English spelling, was primarily to make it consistent and uniform, and preferably by conformity with long-established custom. As he sought to control irregularity by applying the principle of analogy, he was often forced to compromise with the latter purpose. That he was very frequently unsuccessful even in the limited endeavor to be consistent is well known. It may be of interest to rehearse a few of the amusing in-

[17] In *The World,* Nov. 8. 1754. Quoted from Allen. *op. cit.*

consistencies he fell into, some of which seem now to be fastened all but irrevocably upon the language. These may be shown by indicating pairs of words in which inconsistent spellings have been used: *moveable, immovable; downhil, uphill; distil, instill; sliness, slyly; deceit, receipt; deign, disdain; install, reinstal; anteriour, posterior; interiour, exterior.*

From the time of Johnson on, the dictionary has been a conservative and a standardizing agency for the spelling of the language as well as for its other aspects. Some of Johnson's mistakes and inconsistencies were corrected by later lexicographers, but others, such as *deign* (by the side of *disdain*) and *receipt* (by the side of *deceit*), were not. Though no single lexicographer of later times has enjoyed the prestige of Johnson in his era, there can be no doubt that dictionaries as a whole have, since his day, occupied a position of authority that gives unquestioned weight to their decisions on spelling. The belief that, with but the rarest exceptions, there can be but a single correct spelling for one word, and the premium placed on "correct" spelling as one of the readiest indications of the individual's education and culture, were both firmly established by the end of the eighteenth century. Spelling is no longer commonly regarded as a proper field for individuality or experimentation. This is not to imply that later lexicographers have been as ill-equipped for the task of regulating spelling as was Samuel Johnson, or that their attitudes necessarily resemble his in conservatism. On the contrary, dictionaries have often given aid and comfort to spelling reform; the early work of Noah Webster and the whole policy of the *Standard* are striking instances. It remains true, nevertheless, that the public's (particularly the American public's) ready acceptance of the authority of dictionaries, in spelling as in other matters, is a force that on the whole works for both conservatism and standardization. As a result, changes manifestly necessary are not made, if at all, until they are long overdue, and, as we shall see later, even the best movements toward spelling reform have foundered upon this conservative attitude.

Returning then to Johnson we may point out briefly one more direction in which his influence—albeit a reflection of the ideals of his age—has worked undoubted harm. For though ideally his judgments in regard to the value of words should have been objective, actually he let creep into many of them a flavor of personal prejudice. His prejudiced definitions, though few, have become well known, and for them everyone should make due discount. But the judgments which have had great and continuing influence are those rating words according to their relative elegance or vulgarity. A recent study[18] has shown that whereas the two largest dictionaries before Johnson's —Phillips's and Bailey's—made a number of linguistic judgments, "the increase [in Johnson's dictionary] is actually eleven or twelve times the total in Phillips and nearly twice that in Bailey. Johnson, then, although he is not the first English lexicographer to use his verbal likes and dislikes to direct the reader's choice of words, is the first to indulge himself in the practice. . . ." [19] If the word "indulge" is a trifle too strong, there is no denying that grammarians and dictionary-makers after Johnson, who had not his knowledge nor the same right to authority, were heartened by his expression of prejudices into committing many extravagances and inventing many taboos in language which had scant basis in fact.

This eighteenth-century attitude toward language, and toward the dictionary as the final authority on language, has been inherited in more recent times by both the users and makers of dictionaries (despite the latter's frequent protestation to the contrary) to an astonishing degree. Recent dictionaries, it is true, maintain that they do not profess, like Dr. Johnson's, to tell what the standard of language should be; they merely record in tangible form the standard already set by usage. In theory their attitude is much less dogmatic and conservative than the eighteenth-century one; in practice, many of them fall far short of it. New spellings are recorded with great reluctance, new words sometimes knock long at the gates for admittance, and the indication of a change in pronunciation in many cases lags far behind the actual usage of good speakers.

Grammars. But the further development of this subject must be postponed until we have dealt with the second agency by which the

---

[18] Allen, *op. cit.*

[19] Johnson, too, by using verbal labels rather than mere typographical signs as his predecessors had done, made his judgments of words far more articulate. For example, he used such labels as *proper, improper,* and their adverbs, 300 times; *low* 217 times; *corrupt, corruption,* and the like, 94 times; as well as *cant, barbarous, ludicrous, erroneous, wrong, mistaken, false, elegant, inelegant, vitious, vulgar,* and many others. See Allen, *op. cit.,* pp. 170 and following.

eighteenth-century authoritarian attitude was expressed and enforced—the grammars of that time.[20] Sterling A. Leonard has
pointed out impressively the extent to which the interest in grammar
grew:

> Whereas fewer than fifty writings on grammar, rhetoric, criticism and
> linguistic theory have been listed for the first half of the eighteenth century,
> and still fewer for all the period before 1600, the publications in the period
> 1750-1800 exceeded two hundred titles. And most of these were concerned
> in whole or in part with solecisms, barbarisms, improprieties, and questions
> of precision in the use of English.[21]

Not all of these were authoritarian, it is true, but the large
majority were dedicated to remolding the language completely in
the attempt to "correct, improve, and fix" usage, following the "principles of reason." This clearly reflects the subscription of that period
to the concept of "universal grammar," which held that language
(except as it was debased) was an entity reflecting immutable laws
of thought founded in nature. The trouble was, of course, that the
discovery of these "laws" and of how they were to be applied depended largely upon the individual interpreter and such authority as
he could arrogate to himself. Against this "entity theory" of language some voices were raised, insisting (and as we know today,
insisting rightly) that language has no mystical archetypal "genius,"
but that it is a collection of symbols having meaning only through
the agreement of its users to use them meaningfully. In Leonard's
words, language is a "vastly complicated and often haphazard
growth of habits stubbornly rooted, the product of great variation in
social soil and climate, not more readily changed by fiat into clipped
and formal garden pattern than is any vast area of swamp and
jungle and timber-line vegetation." [22]

It is true that a few writers—notably Joseph Priestley[23]—went
farther than merely to repeat with approbation the words of Horace,
Quintilian, and other authorities to the effect that the true deter-

---

[20] The best book on this subject is still Sterling A. Leonard's *The Doctrine
of Correctness in English Usage, 1700-1800*, Madison (University of Wisconsin
Studies in Language and Literature, No. 25), 1929, to which the following remarks are much indebted.

[21] Leonard, *op. cit.*, p. 12.

[22] *Ibid.*, p. 13.

[23] *The Rudiments of English Grammar,* 1768.

miner of correctness is usage. The majority, having nominally accepted this principle, actually flouted it in practice, seeking to "correct" usage. They were apparently unaware of the paradox in such a statement as that of Buchanan—by no means an unusual one—that "considering the many grammatical Improprieties to be found in our best Writers, such as Swift, Addison, Pope, etc. *A Systematical English Syntax* is not beneath the Notice of the Learned themselves." [24]

The writers who, after Dr. Johnson, took up the cudgels and led the attack, were, chiefly, Bishop Robert Lowth in *A Short Introducduction to English Grammar* (1762), Anselm Bayly in *The English Accidence* (1771), James Harris in his *Philological Inquiries* (1781), and Lindley Murray in his *English Grammar* (1795), which last, for its combination of conservatism and eclecticism, proved for years extremely popular and extremely influential. The principles upon which these men and others of their mind based their work were those of logic; of the analogy of the classical languages, particularly Latin; of the appeal to etymology; and of the appeal to "what sounds best." Under this last head might be included anything from considerations of euphony to far vaguer matters in which they displayed likes and dislikes which, though purely personal, were yet presented as if they had some objective reality.

As we have seen above,[25] "logic," as a criterion of correctness, has its limitations. Usage does not always or necessarily consult logic, and many a "more logical" locution today would be simply incorrect English. This, the first argument, is of very uncertain value, then; nor are the others less open to objection. To the theorists of the eighteenth century, who knew few languages and to whom Latin had come early with all the prestige of tradition behind it, it seemed only good sense to set up Latin as a model, to consider English as far decayed from it, and to try to return English to Latin, so far as possible, as if to a Platonic ideal. Indeed, knowing Latin best, they tended to equate its grammar with the "universal grammar" of which they dreamed. The notion that each language develops—and has a right to develop—its own structure, and that it can be judged only in terms of its own structure, though latent in a few writers, was

---

[24] From the preface to his *A Regular English Syntax*, 1767, p. ix.
[25] Chapter 10, pp. 291-292, 304-308.

overborne by the authoritarian attitude. The scientific approach to language had to await a far wider knowledge of actual languages.

Related to this, of course, was the appeal to etymology at a time when etymology was largely guesswork. We have already seen what the application of this criterion did to spelling in the Renaissance, introducing many false forms on the ground that they were "closer to their Latin originals," when actually they had come to English through French, with simplifications of form. As with spelling, so with grammatical forms: the derivations offered were frequently quite erroneous. And in regard to meaning, the "etymological fallacy" flourished; for as we know, meanings change—sometimes out of all relation to their source; the correctness of a meaning is not to be decided by what a word may have meant in the language of origin. Thus, even when etymologies were correct, they were often used for false proofs.

It was in the category of "what sounds best," or what is "within the genius of the language," however, that the self-appointed authorities, naturally enough, clashed most among themselves. With so vague a criterion they could hardly have done otherwise. As Leonard writes,

So long as a belief in a "genius and right nature of English" prevails, every one is altogether free to set up any criterion he pleases of this essential form, and none can disprove his contention. He can be met only by counter-assertion, and downed by nothing less than superior weight of authority.[26]

Present-Day Attitude. The authoritarian attitude thus established in the grammars and dictionaries of the eighteenth century has been surprisingly tenacious. As a result, the attitude of even well-educated persons toward dictionaries is often curiously naive. When any problem regarding the sound or form or meaning arises, the usual question is, "What does the dictionary say?" The implication, of course, is that there is only one verdict to be found in any dictionary, and that dictionaries, of any kind and any date, are all equally valuable. No thought is given to the possibility of consulting the wrong dictionary,[27] or to the discrepancy between dictionaries, or to that between

[26] *Op. cit.*, p. 32.
[27] Wrong, for example, because of insufficient authority, because of date, or because of national or sectional bias.

dictionaries and good usage. No, "the dictionary," however that authority is conceived, is all-sufficient; to question its omniscience is
heresy. In the conservative attitude of the dictionaries and in the
docile acceptance of their authority by the great majority of their
users we have a most important influence upon the development of
the modern language. It is clear that when dictionaries, grammars,
and handbooks of usage are widely circulated and uncritically accepted as the final word, their judgments that disagree with actual
usage may confuse the users, shake their confidence, or invite them
to employ stilted or unnatural ways of speech.

Americans seem to inherit the eighteenth-century attitude, or the
middle-class veneration of authority, to a greater extent than Englishmen of equal education and culture. The educated Englishman
is more prone to consider that his own observation of what constitutes good practice in speech takes precedence over any written
guide. Much more than the educated American, he is likely to think
of dictionaries and grammars as being primarily for those whose
background and upbringing have not brought them in contact with
the best tendencies in English. For himself, he quite frequently
scorns their use very much as he would scorn to follow, in other
aspects of social intercourse, the dictates of a book of etiquette. The
following observation of a traveled and cultured Englishman illustrates this point of view: "When I came to America nothing struck
me more forcibly than the respect paid to the dictionary, and the
disposition to fly hotfoot to it when any question arose." [28] If we
have rejected the eighteenth-century dogma that dictionaries make
usage, we still seem reluctant to accept, in all its implications, the
converse of the proposition.

Yet actually, there is no such thing as "the dictionary"; there are
many dictionaries, of varying degrees of reliability and usefulness.
There is, particularly, a very considerable diversity in the matter of
pronunciations recorded. We may very easily, that is to say, "look
it up" in the wrong dictionary. It comes as a shock to an American
using the *Oxford*, for example, to find that the preferred pronunciation of *ate* is [ɛt]. The best of all dictionaries for such questions as
etymology may thus be a most inadequate index to accepted Ameri-

[28] Letter to "Contributors' Column" of *The Atlantic Monthly*, January
1931, p. 30.

can pronunciation.[29] The *Shorter Oxford* (1933), indeed, specifically disclaims making allowance "as a rule, for dialectal, colonial, or American varieties [of pronunciation]." [30] Nor is this difficulty completely removed if we grant merely that differences in national standards do exist, and therefore confine our choice, for questions of pronunciation, to American dictionaries only. It is still a far from remote possibility that the pronunciation one finds will be a sectional rather than a broader or national one.

The sectional bias of the leading American dictionaries, particularly Webster's, takes the form of frequently preferring the New England to other widespread regional variants, in words that have no one nationally accepted pronunciation. The realistic method of dealing with such words would certainly seem to be to indicate multiple pronunciations for those words in which differences do in fact exist in the cultivated speech of the main regions. Only in this way could the dictionary approach a real record of divided usage as it actually exists. Moreover, only in this way could the dictionary keep abreast of the present state of knowledge as to American pronunciation. If it be objected that this solution is a counsel of perfection, that to attempt it would be an impracticable extension of the present scope of our dictionaries, it is still possible to reply that the solution adopted—not to be sure in theory, but frequently in practice—is decidedly not the best one. For if one section has a better right than the others to be considered as approximating national status in its pronunciation, it is obviously that which differs least strikingly from the others, and is used more widely and uniformly than the others—and this is not the New England region. Though the second (1934) edition of the *New International* is less subject to criticism of this sort than its predecessors, it still gives *à*—that is, [a]—as the vowel of such words as *ask, chance, grass, path,* in spite of the fact that *ǎ* [æ], in Professor Kenyon's excellent preface on pronunciation, is described as the vowel used in these words (in the United States and Canada) by "a large majority of speakers—probably not

---

[29] Of H. C. Wyld's excellent *Universal Dictionary* (New York, Dutton, 1932), Professor Kemp Malone remarks, *Modern Language Notes,* Vol. XLVIII, No. 6 (June 1933), p. 379: ". . . the American reader must be on his guard, for Mr. Wyld makes a curious distinction between sounds and meanings: in dealing with the former he ignores American usage, whereas in dealing with the latter he is careful to record everything American that comes his way."

[30] Introduction, p. ix.

less than a hundred million." The real status of the sounds in question is that [a] is likely to be artificial or pedantic, that [ɑ] is virtually limited to Eastern New England and Eastern Virginia,[31] and that [æ] is in every other respect the one sound in national use. To the ordinary user of the dictionary, who does not trouble to investigate the careful qualifications of the preface, the recording of [a] for these words (and [ɑ] *or* [a] for *aunt, calf, half, laugh,* and so forth) surely implies that the "hundred million" who use the [æ] are vulgar speakers—in other words, that the general national practice is wrong.

This preference for New England usage, perhaps less marked in our other leading dictionaries than in Webster's but still all too generally familiar, can be explained only as the survival of a former deference, outmoded now in most other matters, to New England as the center of our national culture, and to Boston as the "hub of the universe." It is coupled perhaps with another and a more ancient survival: the Colonial attitude of subservience to English tradition and authority. Since, in matters of pronunciation, the usage of Eastern New England and that of Southern England are frequently at one, both influences affect our dictionaries in the same way, and both operate to disqualify them as reliable guides to American pronunciation. Professor Kurath has stated the result forcibly, but not extravagantly:

Why should the dictionaries deliberately ignore this divergence [that of the West, the East, and the South]? Why should they take it upon themselves to force the standard of one area on the entire country? How fruitless their efforts have been! If it be the aim of scientific investigation to find out the facts and to make them known, should we not expect our better dictionaries to record faithfully how the educated classes actually speak, instead of indulging in their make-believe? [32]

The first cause of dissatisfaction with the result of "looking it up in the dictionary" is thus the very real possibility of discovering either a non-American or a sectional pronunciation. It might be added that the mere factor of time militates against the accuracy of

---

[31] Even here it would seem that usage is sharply divided between [æ] and [ɑ]. See Krapp, *op. cit.,* Vol. I, p. 39, and his reference to Primer, *Pronunciation of Fredericksburg, Va.* Linguistic atlas collections show that [ɑ] is not general in eastern Virginia, but its prestige as an upper class feature is apparently increasing its use.

[32] *Op. cit.,* p. 281. Reprinted by permission.

dictionaries. Not only will an early edition of a standard dictionary occasionally, and quite inevitably, record a pronunciation that has been superseded, but even the latest edition must necessarily be behind actual speech. Even if dictionaries were less conservative than they are one might still argue that, by the very nature of the task, every dictionary is out of date as soon as it is issued. Living speech is an ever-flowing stream that is continually passing by the stationary and unchanging record of its course that the dictionaries preserve for us. The record is of great value, to be sure, but it must not be mistaken for the thing which it records.

A second general reason for feeling that dictionaries give but inadequate guidance on pronunciation is the fact, honorable as it is to dictionary-makers, that there is no consensus of dictionary opinion as to what is the best pronunciation of many words. Both Webster's *New International* and Funk and Wagnalls's *Standard* include, in their unabridged editions, long lists of words for which the leading dictionaries give differing pronunciations. Nor should it be supposed that differences of this sort occur only in unessential details or in uncommon words. One who has thought of the advice on pronunciation given by "the dictionary" as being available, unchanged, in any dictionary, will be astonished by the variety of the preferences exhibited in several different dictionaries. To test the matter (and limiting the search to a few familiar words beginning in *a*), let the reader investigate, in four or five of the best dictionaries, the pronunciation of *adult, advertisement, aerial, again, alkali, aristocrat, associate,* and *asthma.*

Not only do our leading dictionaries disagree among themselves, but as a group they fail—some more, some less—to give the full record of the obscuring of unaccented vowels and the blurring of consonantal combinations that are phonetically difficult—both of which, as we have seen, take place on a large scale in actual speech, cultured as well as uncultured. The dictionaries are all too ready, in a word, to recommend spelling-pronunciations, with the result that what the dictionaries present is not current usage, but rather the sounds of a former day that are embalmed in an archaic spelling. Richard Grant White observed that "it is in the delicate but firm utterance of the unaccented vowels with correct sound that the cultured person is most surely distinguished from the uncultured," and something very like this was the standard still recommended, at least by implication, by F. H. Vizetelly, editor-in-chief of the *Standard,* when he wrote: "Unfortunately, we have with us a large class of persons who speak without thinking how our words are spelled, and who, therefore, squeeze all the juice out of our speech by refusing to enunciate carefully all the niceties of sound that the words contain." [33] As the necessary antidote to this, let the reader note the words of H. C. Wyld condemning such an attitude ". . . a rigid appeal to the spelling—the very worst and most unreliable court for the purpose." [34]

The full consequences of connecting spelling and pronunciation, as most of our leading dictionaries do, have not yet been suggested. Almost inevitably, inaccurate or merely theoretical [35] pronunciations are constantly being presented, especially when the effort is made to indicate pronunciation without respelling. The Websterian diacritical markings, which are, unfortunately, the one code at all generally familiar in our schools, continually suggest quite untrue relationships between the written aspect and the sound of the word. Their use can only be deplored. Would anyone suspect, for example, that the second vowels of *novĕl* and *finăl* (so marked) are in present practice actually one and the same—an [ə] so thoroughly obscured that it tends to be lost in [1]? Or that *carat,* keyed as "kăr'ăt" and *carrot,* keyed as "kăr'ŭt" are in fact pronounced identically? The other vowel that prevails in unaccented syllables is of course [ɪ]; but in the Websterian code it appears as *ê* in *êvent* and as *ĭ* in *ĭmmense.*

One of the unfortunate results of the dictionaries' weakness for spelling-pronunciations is that teachers are likely to accept them and to insist that their pupils use them. Professor Kenyon[36] tells of

[33] Preface to *A Desk-Book of 25,000 Words Frequently Mispronounced,* New York (Funk and Wagnalls), 4th ed., 1929, p. viii.

[34] *A History of Modern Colloquial English,* New York (Dutton), 2nd ed., 1936, p. 18.

[35] Even the *Oxford* is not beyond reproach in this matter. In its latest form, the *Shorter Oxford* (3rd ed., 1937), there is an introductory explanation (p. ix) to the effect that twelve vowel sounds, which are given with a separate symbol for each, occur in certain words only as "primary or ideal" values, "as in rhetorical utterance, in singing, and in cases of deliberate or affected precision"; otherwise, and "in normal speech," the value of each one is [ə]. Yet these twelve variants, which are further described as occurring only in "the historical and ideal pronunciations" of the words in question, are the only ones that are given when these words are pronounced in their alphabetical order in the dictionary. Surely this is misleading: the average user of the dictionary, who in nine cases out of ten will not have read the introduction, naturally assumes that he is being given pronunciations that are not "historical" or "ideal" but current and realistic.

[36] *Op. cit.,* p. 4.

a teacher who carefully drilled her pupils to pronounce the noun *subject* with the "full sound of *e* as in *let*," and then, passing to another topic, observed that she would change the ['sʌbdʒɪkt]. This is, one may be sure, an all too typical consequence of depending on the spelling. Not, of course, that dictionaries are always to blame. Theoretically, they recognize that spelling follows pronunciation, not pronunciation spelling. They do not advocate, for example, that such words as *busy, colonel, debt, does, English, knife, said, two,* and *women* be pronounced as the spelling might suggest. That other teacher, referred to by Professor Fries,[37] who instructed her pupils to pronounce *laughter* like *slaughter* and *daughter* (i.e.,['lɔtɚ]), because it was similarly spelled, could not blame the dictionary for her mistake. In a less extreme way, however, pronunciations suggested by the spelling rather than by usage are not uncommon in dictionaries. A few random illustrations are the unstressed syllables of these words: *carpet, engage, fidget, goodness, preface, mistress, necklace,* and *useless.* The usual dictionary tendency is to represent the unstressed vowel by a symbol—*ĕ* or *ă,* for example—adapted from the conventional spelling of the word, rather than to indicate the [ɪ] or the [ə] that is actually heard in speech.[38]

It will be recognized that at least part of the remedy for this failure of the dictionary is plain. If the system of indicating pronunciation without respelling leads to inaccuracies, the obvious improvement is to employ a phonetic alphabet and respell all words phonetically.[39] That this is what ought to be done is scarcely to be doubted, but there are more serious practical obstacles than perhaps appear at first sight. For Webster's *New International* in its next edition to change its entire system of indicating pronunciation would be, for one thing, an enormously expensive undertaking. Even apart from considerations of this sort, there is grave doubt as to whether the great mass of the users of the dictionary would want their familiar, though unscientific, symbols done away with. Our leading American dictionaries are, after all, primarily commercial enter-

---

[37] *The Teaching of the English Language,* New York (Nelson), 1927, p. 59.

[38] The *Thorndike-Century, American College,* and *Thorndike-Barnhart* dictionaries have at last moved forward at least one step by introducing the symbol [ə]. Perhaps others will follow.

[39] Only the Kenyon-Knott *Pronouncing Dictionary of American English* (Springfield, Merriam, 1944), does this, but it is a work specifically devoted to pronunciation.

prises that cater to a public whose habits and prejudices must be considered. Webster's chief American rival, the *Standard,* while using a second and a phonetic alphabet—not, unfortunately, a very close approximation to the International Phonetic Alphabet—still retains the Websterian symbols, doubtless as a concession to the deeply rooted habits of its patrons.[40]

To return to our catalog of the shortcomings of "the dictionary." More can be said than that individual dictionaries fail as a guide to present-day, national pronunciation; that dictionaries as a group vary among themselves; and that most of them record inadequately the obscuration of unstressed vowels. Besides all this, the user of the dictionary should be aware that, in the very nature of the task, the record of the dictionary is that of individual, isolated words—not of words in their ordinary groupings. The pronunciation of the word does, in practice, vary with its setting in the phrase or the sentence. Spoken language is made up rather of phrase-groups than of separate words. It therefore follows that a single word may very well have two (or more) pronunciations, which vary with the amount of emphasis given to the word in different contexts. Dictionaries show differences of this kind only very rarely: to distinguish two *the*'s ([ði] and [ðə]), as most dictionaries do, is to apply this principle; but such an instance is very exceptional. Yet a parallel variation in the pronunciation of other words is very common indeed in natural, colloquial speech. Professor Kenyon lists[41] a group of very familiar words that have, in good pronunciation, two or more variants. These variations are sometimes the result of the stressed or unstressed character of the word in the phrase, but sometimes also the result of its immediate phonetic environment. Thus, *that* will be either [ðət] or [ðæt] according to whether it is the unstressed conjunction or the stressed demonstrative. Observe how the pronunciation varies in the phrase, "He said that that was correct." A contemporary novelist,[42]

---

[40] Wyld's *Universal Dictionary* has adopted a similar policy. One cannot forbear quoting Professor Malone's comment (*op. cit.,* p. 379) that this is ". . . a phonetic respelling for the literate, preceded by a makeshift Websterian respelling for the illiterate. . . . Although we may be sceptical of the value, commercial or otherwise, of the makeshift respellings, we must be grateful for the presence, alongside them, of phonetic spellings which the hapless editor can look at without shame, and the student can use with safety."

[41] *Op. cit.,* pp. 102-108.

[42] V. Sackville-West, in *Family History,* New York (Doubleday, Doran), 1932

by the way, attempts to make the spelling record these pronunciations, by employing *that* for the conjunction and *thatt* for the demonstrative. The other type of variation, that caused by the immediate phonetic environment, is illustrated in Kenyon's citation of seven possible pronunciations for *and:* the stressed forms [ænd] and [æn] in, respectively, "and, indeed, I should" and "both Jane and James"; and the unstressed forms [ənd], [ən], [nd], [n], and [ŋ] in "snow and ice," "cup and saucer," "head and arm," "rod and gun," and "Jack and Kate." When variation exists to this extent in good usage, it is not difficult to understand that the dictionaries, with their rigorous limits of space, must necessarily fail to echo the real accents of speech.

Dictionaries, in spite of their protestations to the contrary, not infrequently yield to the temptation to tell what the pronunciation of a word should be, rather than what it is. The spelling of the word, or its etymology, or an analogy which is suggested with other words —all of these are possible factors in the dictionaries' occasional recommendation of a pronunciation that is simply at variance not only with wide usage but even with good usage. There undoubtedly is such a thing, in other words, as a "dictionary pronunciation." In such terms one may perhaps describe the dictionaries' preference for the accent on the first syllable of *arbutus, frontier,* and *peremptory,* for the accent on the second of *abdomen,* for the sounding of the first *c* [k] in *Arctic,* for [e] rather than [ɑ] as the accented vowel in *armada,* for the [g] rather than the [dʒ] in *oleomargarine,* and for *oboe* as ['oboɪ, 'oboe, or 'obɔɪ]. It is only fair to add, however, that the actually more frequent pronunciation is sometimes grudgingly admitted—occasionally prefaced by "often *mispronounced* as." As a final illustration of this attitude of the lexicographer, with its implication that his dictum takes precedence over usage, let the reader ponder these words on *interesting:* "The word is never correctly pronounced as if consisting of three syllables. *No dictionary* or work on pronunciation *indicates any such pronunciation* as in'-tristing." [43]

In summary, then, it may be said that modern dictionaries do not altogether deserve the uncritical respect in which they are so widely held. In some ways it is impossible for them to live up to people's

---

[43] The italics are ours. The quotation is from F. H. Vizetelly, *How to Use English,* New York (Funk and Wagnalls), 1932, p. 378.

expectations: by their very nature they cannot keep abreast of changes in the language; they must necessarily treat words out of context, yet pronunciation varies with context; and they must work under stringent limitations imposed by cost, for to produce a good dictionary is a most costly undertaking, and there is simply not the space to include everything that might be put in yet keep the cost within bounds. Nevertheless it does seem that dictionaries might not be so pusillanimous as some are in submitting to conservative prejudice, and that they might seek more actively to bring to the public the advances of linguistic knowledge and method. They might more truly carry out their avowed purpose of reflecting actual usage by making new and better studies of this matter, avoiding sectional bias or prescriptive judgments. Some steps in the right direction have been taken in recent years, and it is to be hoped that more will follow.

Spelling Today. The subject of dictionaries was introduced, earlier in this chapter, in connection with spelling, since it was the rising authority of dictionaries that finally served to establish the spellings arrived at mostly by convention of the printers. The contact between spelling and pronunciation had to a great extent been lost, and it was this unphonetic spelling that the dictionaries canonized and have in large measure traditionally preserved to this day. This development has not taken place without opposition, however. In the modern period there have been many noteworthy attempts to simplify in the direction of a closer bond between spelling and pronunciation. One of the earliest to state the principle of purism in vocabulary was Sir John Cheke, the first Regius Professor of Greek at Cambridge. Consistently enough, he advocated reform in spelling as well as in the choice of words,[44] giving preference, in both departments, to the Anglo-Saxon as opposed to the classical. Cheke's friend and Cambridge associate (like him, too, a secretary of state), Sir Thomas Smith, worked out a more systematic scheme of spelling reform, in the shape of a Latin treatise (1568) advocating the adoption of an alphabet with additional letters as well as the use of diacritical marks. John Hart (1569) and William Bullokar (1580) also published treatises on orthography—the latter a scheme, like Smith's, of a new alphabet, consisting of thirty-seven letters. In the seventeenth

---

[44] His best-known statement with regard to the English language (1557) is quoted in McKnight, *op. cit.*, pp. 118-119.

century, Doctor Gill (1619) and Bishop Wilkins (1633) put forth similar proposals for a reconstructed alphabet. None of these more ambitious proposals bore much practical fruit;[45] but simplifications, often widely adopted, in the spelling of individual words were sometimes made by writers and scholars. Such were many of the recommendations of James Howell's *Grammar* (1662), including the replacing of *logique* with *logic, warre* with *war, sinne* with *sin, witt* with *wit*, and so on.

We have already glanced at Samuel Johnson's zeal for etymology. In his case, as so often in our own day, as well as in the eighteenth century, this meant more particularly the desire to make English spelling conform to Latin and Greek analogies: "etymology" was almost equivalent to "classical etymology," for the scientific study of the Germanic languages had yet to be born. When Johnson does recommend a "Saxon" spelling it is more than likely to be a mistaken one, historically. Thus, he insists on the final *k* in such words as *critick, historick, musick,* and *prosaick* on the ground that the truly English spelling should "always have the Saxon *k* added to the *c*." As Lounsbury remarks,[46] "The 'Saxon *k*' was the lexicographer's personal contribution to the original English alphabet." If such an elementary fact in the history of English orthography could be unfamiliar to him, it is no wonder that Johnson's enthusiasm for etymology should have had curious results upon the spellings he advocated. Since he preferred to recommend spellings that had already been in vogue, this meant all too frequently that he threw his authority upon the side of artificial respellings, based upon real or imaginary classical analogies, that had been perpetrated by Renaissance scholars.

The rigidity of English spelling from the eighteenth century on, and its general failure to record the many changes in pronunciation that have since occurred are thus in large measure to be laid at the door of Samuel Johnson. Not that there has been an utter lack of individuals and groups of people who have felt that it is more important to have spelling indicate the sounds of words than their "etymology." An eighteenth-century protestant against the *status*

---

[45] A nineteenth-century analog to such schemes is that of Isaac Pitman, the creator of phonographic shorthand. Pitman's proposal, worked out in its final form in 1843, was an alphabet of forty letters, including sixteen new symbols.

[46] *Op. cit.*, p. 292.

quo in spelling was Benjamin Franklin, who found time among his multifarious activities to compile, in 1768, a "Scheme for a New Alphabet and Reformed Mode of Spelling." Franklin's purpose differed from that of his contemporaries who were publishing spelling and pronouncing dictionaries in that he proposed, not to make pronunciation follow spelling, but rather, by means of a phonetic alphabet, to alter the spelling to suit the prevailing pronunciation. This radical reform, however, proved abortive, for Franklin felt "too old to pursue the plan," and his proposals were never published. It was left for another American to make the first effective move against the system largely inherited from Johnson. This was Noah Webster, the most important lexicographer since Johnson. His advocacy of simplified spelling has been chiefly responsible for the accepted differences between British and American spelling. Some of his activities may repay more detailed attention.

In early life Webster was strongly influenced by Benjamin Franklin, though not to the extent of adopting the phonetic system which Franklin attempted to have him carry through. The extreme nationalism prevalent in many American circles in the last decades of the eighteenth century is voiced in Webster's *American Spelling Book*, 1783: "For America in her infancy to adopt the present maxims of the old world, would be to stamp the wrinkle of decrepit age upon the bloom of youth, and to plant the seed of decay in a vigorous constitution." With increasing age, however, and—perhaps it may be added—with the increasing prospect of appealing to a British as well as an American public, Webster's patriotism became less flamboyant. Nevertheless, though in his great dictionary, the first edition of which came out in 1828, he recognized the fact that "the body of the language is the same as in England," he recommended many spellings that deviated from British practice. Later editions of the dictionary and later editions of the spelling book (the latter also an enormously influential work, for more than fifty million copies were sold) are alike much more conservative than the early ones. From a reformer *of* orthography Webster had become content to be a reformer *in* orthography.[47] Still, the milder type of reformation was sufficient to cause violent protests, and Webster (and his later editors) often receded before the storm. Some of the simplifications that were retained and that are now no longer questioned in

[47] The terms are Lounsbury's (p. 240).

American usage are the -*or* rather than the -*our* ending in such words as *honor, labor,* and the like; the -*er* rather than the -*re* in *center, meter,* and so forth; and the single *l* (or other consonant) in such words as *traveled, traveling,* and so on.

Webster's simplifications were not necessarily phonetic simplifications. Two other motives took precedence, indeed, over any attempt at phonetic shortening: the desire for etymological correctness, and the desire for uniformity. Distrusting the etymological lore of his predecessors as worthless, he evolved a new theory of the relationship of languages for himself and quite largely, in Sir James Murray's words, "out of his inner consciousness." The results, of course discarded in later editions of the dictionary that bears his name, were quite naturally devoid of value, and where, as was frequently the case, they affected the spellings recommended, they could only be deplored. Orthographic changes that he introduced with the idea of consistency and uniformity in mind (as opposed to etymological theory) must be somewhat differently regarded. Changes of this kind frequently removed such absurdities as those in which Doctor Johnson's dictionary abounded, and a number of them have fortunately met with favor in later usage.

On the whole, however, it must be said that the spelling reform achieved by Noah Webster was not on a great scale. Webster lacked, after all, the firmer basis for both phonetic and etymological simplification that the work of later generations of linguistic scholars was to supply. It was not until the last decades of the nineteenth century that the science of linguistics achieved anything like its present status. It is from scholars trained in this newer school that recent and contemporary movements aiming at spelling reform have come.

Modern Spelling Reform. If the eighteenth century saw the culmination of the belief that language could be "fixed," and a consequent attempt by its literary and learned men, according to their lights, to fix it; and if the nineteenth and twentieth centuries, with the growth of linguistic science, have seen the increasing recognition that language is by its nature changing, that it is a culture-phenomenon, and that it must and will adapt itself to social changes, we may perhaps hope before too long to see some fruition in such adaptive changes. The language steadily continues to grow with the words brought in by new inventions, new technics, new attitudes. Literary style reflects obviously the quickened pace of contemporary life, and the ideals of brevity, directness, and simplicity which are necessitated by the huge quantity of printed material that the present-day reader absorbs. The same ideals carry over into the spheres of grammar and diction and will inevitably affect the survival of many constructions, idioms, and words.

As we shall see in the next chapter, the spread of English over the world, and the present position of the English-speaking nations, make this language the most likely contender for international use as a "second" or auxiliary language. The greatest obstacle in the way of English, if it were to play such a role, is its spelling-system —so antiquated, and in a number of ways irrational, therefore forbidding to learn. If in this century the spelling-system of English could be brought into effective phonetic relation with the sounds of the language—or if, at least, some of the worst anomalies could be eliminated—this would be an enormous gain. Yet the hopes for such a consummation, it must be admitted, are anything but bright. A sketch of the fortunes and misfortunes of the movement for spelling reform within the past 70 to 80 years will bring out the reasons for this.

The activities of Isaac Pitman and A. J. Ellis just before the middle of the century[48] were a forerunner and a symptom of the temper of the scholarly world on spelling;[49] but the first concerted step was the action of the American Philological Association in 1875 in appointing a committee to consider the whole matter of spelling reform. From this, and similar action on the part of the Philological Society (of England), sprang the Spelling Reform Association and the British Spelling Reform Association. In 1906, the Simplified Spelling Board was organized to conduct the more active propaganda financed by Andrew Carnegie,[50] and in 1908 the Simplified Spelling Society was formed in England. Of these three societies—Spelling Reform Association, Simplified Spelling Board, and Simplified Spelling Society—only the last is still in existence. However, since for

[48] See *Handbook of Simplified Spelling*, Part I, pp. 9-12.
[49] W. D. Whitney published in 1867 several articles advocating a thorough reform in spelling.
[50] This financing ceased upon Carnegie's death in 1919. Since then the activities of the Board have dwindled to almost nothing, though it appears to keep up a nominal existence at Lake Placid, New York, under the name of the Simplified Spelling Association.

many years they worked more or less concertedly, it may be of interest to review briefly their aims and achievements.

The somewhat different tactics that underlie the proposals of the three organizations are succinctly stated in the periodical *Spelling*,[51] which was issued by them jointly. Briefly, the Simplified Spelling Board believed that progress might best be achieved by seeking, as the first step, the widest possible adoption of a very limited number of new spellings, on the theory that a campaign of gradual education is necessary before new spellings so numerous as to transform the appearance of the printed page can conceivably be accepted by the general public. The Simplified Spelling Society would go further: while keeping the present alphabet of twenty-six letters, it recommends for a teaching device in elementary schools an entirely new and consistent scheme of using the existing symbols, with no additional letters or diacritics. (It apparently recognized a distinction between a revised spelling as a method in general education and a revised spelling for general use; for the latter, it went along with the comparatively small changes which the Simplified Spelling Board proposed.) The Spelling Reform Association, on the other hand, accepted no compromise with the ideal goal: it stood for thoroughgoing renovation, as opposed to merely partial simplification; accordingly it advocated a complete phonetic alphabet, with such new letters as a minimum-precision, one-sign-one-sound alphabet may require.[52] It is of course quite possible for one individual to sympathize with all three of these purposes—to accept the first as a practical initial stage, the second as an educational measure, and the third as the ultimate objective.

Not only were the three principal organizations for spelling reform in England and America in large measure united for a common purpose; more than this, they joined in welcoming a new recruit to the cause of English spelling reform. This was the Swedish project known as "Anglic," primarily a scheme to make English more adaptable for world-wide use by renovating its spelling. Anglic spelling is

[51] Vol. I, No. 1 (March 1925), and Vol. 2, No. 5 (March 1931).

[52] In 1928, the Spelling Reform Association proposed a phonetic alphabet "for immediate use in the teaching of English, particularly in the elementary grades, and as a practical working basis for eventual phonetic spelling reform of English for general use." It was adopted also by the Simplified Spelling Board "for immediate use as a phonetic key alphabet for English wherever respelling to indicate pronunciation is required." (Pamphlet of May 1928.)

not phonetic, nor does it add new letters to the alphabet. It aims to bring order out of the general chaos of conventional spelling by "generalizing the most common or serviceable of the existing spelling variants, introducing at the same time a few new digraphs (*uu, dh,* and *zh*), which have to do the duty of new letters." [53] Though Anglic obviously runs counter in important particulars to the purposes of the older organizations, it was nevertheless endorsed by representatives of all three of them (and of the International Phonetic Association as well) at the World English conference held in London in June, 1930. The conferees agreed "to give the Anglic movement their full support and coöperation . . . both as an international auxiliary language and as a basis for reform of English spelling for the English-speaking world." [54] It should be added, however, that the Simplified Spelling Society, whose program was more directly in rivalry with that of Anglic, was perhaps less enthusiastic about Anglic than were the other two organizations. Sir G. B. Hunter, chairman of its committee, states that the committee "have considered, but do not advocate, Professor Zachrisson's Anglic as an improvement of our spelling; though some of the most eminent members of the committee approve and are willing to adopt Anglic." [55]

For the sake of brevity we must limit our attention chiefly to the activities of one organization, the American Simplified Spelling Board. It has already been indicated that in England the Simplified Spelling Society has not been quiescent. For example, in June, 1932 it offered to the British Board of Education a petition, bearing the signatures of some seven hundred members of the faculties of British universities, for an inquiry into the simplification of English spelling. The plea was based on the conviction that the increasing world-wide use of English is chiefly hindered by "its inconsistent and difficult spelling." And since 1939, when it inherited a large sum of money from its late chairman, Sir G. B. Hunter, it has been enabled to continue its work with renewed vigor. Nevertheless, the most con-

---

[53] Pamphlet published by the Anglic Fund, Uppsala, Sweden. 1931. For a fuller statement, see the larger booklet, *Anglic, a New Agreed Simplified English Spelling,* also published by the fund (1930). Discussions of Anglic are contained in the various numbers of *Spelling* for 1931; in *American Speech,* Vol. VI, No. 5 (June 1931), pp. 378-380; and in the *Bookman,* February 1931 ("Or Shall We Go Anglic?" by Mrs. Aiken).

[54] *Spelling,* Vol. II, No. 5 (March 1931), p. 7.

[55] *Ibid.,* No. 6 (June 1931), p. 19.

spicuous activity in spelling reform during the present century undoubtedly has been that which followed the formation of the Simplified Spelling Board in 1906. To that activity we now return.

The very title of the new organization implied that the strategy of the campaign against the conventional spelling had been modified. It was no longer to be "reform," but "simplification"—obviously a concession to the strength of popular prejudice and conservatism. But even the policy of "cutting off the dog's tail an inch at a time instead of all at once" [56] did not disarm hostile criticism on the part of public and press. And when President Theodore Roosevelt, with characteristic impetuosity, officially announced his conversion to the cause by ordering the Public Printer to use in Government documents the new spelling of certain words, a most amazing storm broke. Congress threatened to withhold the appropriation for the printing of executive department publications if the order was not countermanded. The President was forced to limit his reform to White House correspondence. On the whole, the controversy that ensued probably did the cause of simplified spelling more harm than good. The movement had more publicity than it has had before or since, in the memory of those now alive, but it was publicity of an unfortunate kind.[57] Simplified spelling, if not exactly considered a mere foible of Roosevelt's, was all too generally regarded as the creation of a few misguided cranks. Newspapers ordinarily dealt with it only to misrepresent and ridicule it. An unusually witty reference to it was the famous single-word editorial of the New York *Sun* on the occasion of President Taft's inauguration in March, 1909; glancing not at the new but at the old president, the editor was able to cram an astonishing amount of malicious satisfaction into the four letters: "Thru."

In the years that have followed the first campaigns of the Simplified Spelling Board, progress has been very slow. Dictionaries, especially the *Standard*, have given aid; but the public acceptance of dictionary permission has been somewhat surprisingly hesitant.

---

[56] *Handbook of Simplified Spelling*, Part II, p. 39. In this policy, all adherents of spelling reform, quite naturally, did not, and do not, concur. Sir G. B. Hunter not long ago used this very phrase in a derogatory sense, *Spelling*, Vol. II, No. 4 (December 1931), p. 59; he concluded, "Save us from trusting to gradual improvement."

[57] A lively account of the controversy will be found in Mark Sullivan's *Our Times*, Vol. III.

Newspapers, though some have lent partial sanction to the proposal of the Board, have on the whole maintained their original attitude of contemptuous, and frequently thoroughly ignorant, criticism. Only a few weekly or monthly periodicals adopted a real measure of simplification in their own columns, and the most important of these, the *Literary Digest*, ceased to exist in 1938.[58] Many educators have given complete or partial assent to the program outlined by the Board, but many more are ultraconservative, to the extent of refusing to accept from their pupils even the milder deviations from spelling orthodoxy. The National Education Association in 1907 and again in 1916 adopted certain of the Board's recommendations, but in 1921 withdrew a large measure of this sanction. Last, but perhaps most important, the man on the street has in large measure inherited an attitude of complacent and ill-informed ridicule of the whole project, an attitude which the newspapers of the last forty years have done a great deal to foster. A dispassionate observer must be struck, in retrospect, with the spectacle of small results achieved by great and valiant efforts.

The spelling-reform movement in the United States, then, suffered two severe blows: first the ill-timed backing of Theodore Roosevelt, which made a political football of something that should have remained outside the partisan field; and second, the failure of Andrew Carnegie to provide financially for its continuance after his death. The post-war weariness of 1920 and the many uncertainties of the following years led to its further neglect; such interest as survived has been largely unorganized: a great many individuals have worked out systems of their own, some acceptable, others remarkably forbidding; but none has come to anything, nor is any likely to do so without powerful backing of some sort.[59]

As one turns from the history of spelling reform to the arguments for and against it, the first impulse is to assert that almost everything can be said for it, and exceedingly little against it. Yet it is

---

[58] The Chicago *Tribune* entered the movement in 1931 with the adoption of a list of some 80 simplified spellings, which list by additions and subtractions it has since repeatedly revised under pressure of public protest or according to the whim of its editors. Its practice is unsystematic—for example, it uses *frate* for *freight*, but rejects *wate* for *weight*. Any "progress" it makes, therefore, is not toward order, but toward a new chaos, presumably more "modern." See Mencken, *American Language*, p. 406, and *Supplement Two*, pp. 294-295.

[59] An excellent summary of individual schemes coming down to 1948 may be found in Mencken's *Supplement Two*, pp. 287-316.

Whitney — Century Dictionary

clear that the somewhat less tangible and certainly less logical objections that have commonly been urged against it seem nevertheless
very powerful to many people: only thus can its small measure of
success be accounted for. The program that was outlined by the
Simplified Spelling Board and recommended for immediate adoption
rested on the following four principles:[60]

1. *When current usage offers a choice of spellings, to adopt the shortest
and simplest.* EXAMPLES: *catalog,* not *catalogue; center,* not *centre; gage,*
not *gauge; honor,* not *honour; maneuver,* not *manoeuvre; mold,* not *mould;
quartet,* not *quartette; rime,* not *rhyme; tho,* not *though; traveler,* not
traveller.

2. *Whenever practicable, to omit silent letters.* EXAMPLES: *activ,* not
active; anser, not *answer; definit,* not *definite; det,* not *debt; frend,* not
friend; hart, not *heart; scool,* not *school; shal,* not *shall; thru,* not *through;
yu,* not *you.*

3. *To follow the simpler rather than the more complex of existing analogies.* EXAMPLES: *aker,* not *acre; buro,* not *bureau; deciet,* not *deceit; enuf,*
not *enough; spritely,* not *sprightly; telefone,* not *telephone; wize,* not *wise.*

4. *Keeping in view that the logical goal of the movement is the eventual
restoration of English spelling to the phonetic basis from which in the course
of centuries and through various causes it has widely departed, to propose
no changes that are inconsistent with that ideal.* [No examples of the last
principle are given. It may, however, be illustrated through the fact that
elsewhere in the *Handbook*[61] the Board deprecates such spellings as *fite,
lite,* and *nite* (for *fight, light,* and *night*) on the ground that, though shortenings, they are unphonetic shortenings and would perpetuate a wrong
principle of notation: the use of final silent *e* to indicate the quality of the
preceding vowel. On the other hand, to restore *delite* and *spritely* is a somewhat different matter; these spellings are recommended not as innovations
but as older and better spellings than the present ones.]

It is necessary to add that the arguments advanced by the Board
refer not only to the minor changes recommended for immediate
adoption, but also to the completely phonetic spellings that are
sought as the eventual goal. Some of the chief claims made for simplified spelling, then, are as follows: it will save much time and expense in elementary education, and in writing, typewriting, and

---

[60] *Handbook of Simplified Spelling,* Part I, pp. 18-19, with the omission of
some of the examples. Here, as elsewhere in the chapter (when matter in reformed spelling has been quoted), the spelling is altered to conform to that
used in this book generally. It is, however, an indication of the small extent of
the changes recommended for immediate adoption that, of seventy-eight words
quoted, only three (*fonetic, thru,* and *ar*) have had to be changed.
[61] Part II, pp. 5-6.

printing; it will improve and tend to standardize pronunciation; it will remove the greatest barrier to the Americanization of our foreign population and to the use of English as an international language.[62] These three propositions will be considered separately and in the light of other arguments growing out of them.

The practical gain in time and money would doubtless be enormous. Dr. Godfrey Dewey, secretary of the Board, computed that the present conventional spelling (as compared, in this instance, with a single one-sound-one-symbol phonetic alphabet) wastes at least a billion dollars a year,[63] and consumes a full year of the school life of every English-speaking child. As to the latter point, it is arguable that even worse than the loss in time is the needless distraction and "atrophy of logical faculties" experienced by the child. Many another father has echoed these sentiments of the great sociologist, W. G. Sumner:

> I have two boys who are learning to spell. They often try to spell by analogy, thus using their brains and learning to think. Then I have to arrest them, turning them back from a rational procedure, and impose tradition and authority. They ask me, "Why?" I answer, "Because your father and others who have lived before you have never had the courage and energy to correct a ridiculous old abuse, and you are now inheriting it with all the intellectual injury, loss of time, and wasted labor which it occasions. I am ashamed that it should be so." [64]

The new spelling, which would certainly be more easily learned than the old, would be an infinitely better index to pronunciation. If it be objected that spelling that followed pronunciation would vary as pronunciation varies, the retort is of course obvious: that the ideal of uniform "correct" spelling is an utterly false one. A variation between any system of spelling and the many existing varieties of pronunciation is inevitable in any case. On the other hand, it is plausibly maintained that variation in pronunciation would be lessened as the corresponding variation in spelling made it more conspicuous. The effect of a more phonetic spelling would quite conceivably be to

[62] Most of the eight "reasons for simplified spelling" as advanced in the Board's pamphlet "Rules and Reasons" (1919) and elaborated in the *Handbook*, Part II, are here summarized.

[63] The unsympathetic may feel that the *reductio ad absurdum* of this type of argument is the statement of Zachrisson that to English spelling are due "increased unemployment and the going down of trade not only in England and the United States but in the whole world" (*Anglic*, p. 18).

[64] *Spelling*. Vol I. No. 1 (May 1887), p. 16.

center attention on pronunciation in a new way, to promote discussion of the variants in current use, and to work toward a greater standardization after the pattern of the most approved, or the already most widely established, models. Complete standardization of pronunciation would never take place, nor does it seem desirable that it should.

If these arguments have any great measure of truth, what can possibly be said on the other side? What *is* most commonly urged is undoubtedly what the Board, perhaps justifiably, refers to as the "etymological bugaboo." This is the notion prevalent among amateur defenders of the status quo in spelling that to change it would be to "destroy etymology"; what they really mean is that it would obscure the derivation of words. No scholar of repute any longer holds this point of view. It is necessary, indeed, to go back to Archbishop Trench's *English Past and Present* (1855) to find a presentation of it by any competent writer; and Sir James Murray expressed, in 1880, the opinion that Trench himself "if leisure had been given him to keep pace with the progress of science, . . . would now have been second to no one as a spelling reformer." The belief voiced by Trench (and to quote it is to voice the argument in its most nearly respectable form) is that to retain the etymological spellings of words is to help a large class of readers—but neither the grossly ignorant nor the accomplished scholars—because to keep these spellings is to enable such readers "to recognize the words which they are using, whence they came, to what words in other languages they are nearly related, and what is their properest and strictest meaning." We cannot take the space to examine all the fallacies stated or implied in such a dictum, but since the belief is still widely held it may be worth while to indicate some of them.

The existing spelling, in the first place, is a most unreliable index to the derivation of the word. Indeed, to simplify the present spelling would very frequently restore an earlier and a more nearly etymological, as well as a more nearly phonetic, spelling. Further, the help afforded by the present spelling (even if *etymologically* defensible) is useful only to those acquainted with the languages from which the words are derived. Trench was thinking of those readers—proportionately a much smaller group now—whose knowledge of Latin and Greek would be useful for their understanding of English. On this basis, spelling is to be kept safe for only a very limited fraction of

our democracy. But if as further prerequisites for the full appreciation of our present spelling we add acquaintance with such other
important studies as Old English and Old French, it is evident that
the minority has dwindled very much more. Yet, how can anyone
defend a spelling on the ground of its being etymologically correct
and etymologically revealing unless he knows the etymology involved? The advertising slogan "Patronize your naborhood store"
may be objected to on other grounds, but does *nabor* really *mean*
less than *neighbor* unless one knows that *neighbor* literally is "nigh-
dwell-er"? The chances are that a negligible fraction of objectors to
this spelling have this information. The "etymological bugaboo," on
the whole, has very little indeed to commend it. Skeat, the editor of
the best of etymological dictionaries, has appropriately disposed of
it in the observation: "In the interest of etymology we ought to spell
as we pronounce. To spell words as they used to be pronounced is
not etymological, but antiquarian."

More weight may justly be given to a second objection to spelling
reform: the fact that many homophones would no longer be differentiated on the printed page. Bradley, by no means an opponent of
spelling reform, has pointed out how very commonly "difference of
spelling, once phonetically significant, has become a mere ideographic device." [65] The useful distinction (to the *eye*) between such
pairs of words as *night, knight; son, sun;* and *bare, bear* would be
lost. It is true that there would be a certain compensation for this in
the visual differentiation of words now spelled alike but pronounced
differently, such as the present and past tenses of *read; bow* meaning
"knot" and "fore part of boat," *tear* meaning "to rend" and "water
from the eye," and so on. At the same time, it is evident that this
second list is much shorter than the other. The proponents of spelling
reform are perhaps in general too prone to neglect the gulf that simply must be recognized as existing between spoken and written English. As Bradley further points out, a great many words one encounters on the printed page are but rarely pronounced; the first, and
almost the sole, function of their spellings is to convey meaning to
the eye and mind of the reader. This they do without calling up the
question of pronunciation at all. There is some reason, therefore, to
feel that frequently more would be lost than gained if words now
spelled differently, though pronounced alike, were made identical in

[65] *On the Relations Between Spoken and Written Language,* p. 11.

appearance. It should not be forgotten, however, that these homophones normally appear in contexts which, even if they were spelled identically, would in almost every case make it clear which of them was meant. The ambiguity of "the bright [sʌn]," "the slow [naɪt]," "the girl's [bo]," "a low [baʊ]" and others of the same kind would be quickly resolved once they were put in context.

A kindred objection is that a phonetic spelling would obscure the connection between words related in meaning. Vowel sounds are almost invariably altered when the accent shifts from one syllable to another: observe what happens to all three vowels of *photograph* when the word is made into *photographer.* Yet it is a practical convenience that the two words should *look* alike and be recorded together in dictionaries, as should also *history* and *historical, injury* and *injurious,* and so on. Sometimes the pronunciation is altered even by an ending that does not shift the primary stress of the word: *conspire* and *conspiracy, nature* and *natural, zeal* and *zealous.* To use different symbols for the vowels in cases like these would confuse children and foreigners learning the language. There is a good deal to be said (apart from strictly "etymological" considerations) for a spelling that makes words that are alike in meaning *look* alike even though they have developed widely different sounds. So far as that goes, there is something even in the "etymological" argument of the anti-reformers—especially if it is limited to words that appear only on the printed page and that carry their meaning to the eye of the educated reader, who alone is concerned with such words. R. W. Chapman has well pointed out how much would be sacrificed by a phonetic spelling of such words as *adolescent, chryselephantine, hypotenuse,* and *ichthyophagous.*[66]

Still, there is danger that the plea for the retention of familiar spellings on the ground that they are familiar (and even, in one way or another, logical) may blend into the less defensible position that they should be retained because they are beautiful. One aspect of our prejudice in favor of things familiar is our conviction that there is a superior beauty and appropriateness in such labels as are already established. Saintsbury takes dangerous ground in his well-known

---

[66] In his essay, "Thoughts on Spelling Reform," in *The Portrait of a Scholar,* pp. 89-108. He reinforces many of Bradley's points, and is, like him, not unsympathetic with a certain measure of reform.

outburst of exasperation, "If the pestilent folk who call themselves Spelling Reformers or Simplifiers ever thought of the beauty of words—which, I believe, they honestly profess either to know nothing about or to disregard entirely—it would be worth while offering them a *crux* or two in the department of proper names." [67] Yet, even in the department of proper names—which the spelling reformers leave studiously alone—it is clear that many of Saintsbury's preferences are purely subjective. As he is quite aware, his dislike of "Ann" and admiration for "Anne" are not shared by everyone; and, as he himself admits, Thackeray liked "Anny," which Saintsbury thinks hideous (though he thinks "Annie" quite pretty). This finding of beauty and ugliness, particularly the former, in the mere outward forms (or even the sounds) of words is often a most curious delusion. At least, it is a wholly personal matter, on which there is no objective ground of agreement among men. As an antidote to Saintsbury, one should read Max Beerbohm's delightful essay on "The Naming of Streets." [68] No demonstration of the position that "what you take to be beauty or ugliness of sound is indeed nothing but beauty or ugliness of meaning" could possibly be more convincing than his calling attention to the "beauty" of *ermine, manor house, gondola*— and then exhibiting the "ugliness" of *vermin, warehouse, scrofula!* To be sure, Beerbohm is not primarily concerned in this essay with spelling, but many are undoubtedly convinced that the *appearance* of the first group is as beautiful as the *sound* is. Obviously, it is the meanings and associations of these words—not their form—that makes them seem beautiful or ugly. To one who heard them without knowing what they meant, the last three might be quite as melodious and pleasing as the first. A most instructive illustration of this point is the fun that Aldous Huxley has, in *Chrome Yellow*, with the word *carminative.*

In considering the "esthetic" argument against spelling reform we have turned from the logical to the illogical form of objection. At the same time, this delusion that the familiar is appropriate and beautiful and the unfamiliar ugly (or at least comical) is clearly very deeply rooted and extremely influential. Many of those who dislike simplified spelling do so for no better reason than that it "looks

---

[67] In his *Last Scrap Book*, New York (Macmillan), 1924.
[68] *Yet Again*, London (Heinemann), 1930, pp. 193-207.

queer" and is therefore distasteful to them. To the objection, "I don't like it," the Spelling Board admitted its inability to reply.[69] Frequently too, this type of opposition is reinforced by mere inertia. Some who might overcome their distaste for the queer appearance of reformed spelling are kept by both conventional and lazy habits of mind from doing so. After all, they reason, the benefits of the reform would be for the succeeding generations, not for ours. Why should we make matters smoother for our children than we have found them—particularly as it would entail our living in an era of readjustment and distracting change? To this unheroic but exceedingly human mental attitude would seem to be due in large part the slow progress of spelling reform—precisely the same factor that prevents speedy progress in other fields. And finally, inertia and distrust of change are easily rationalized as a wise caution. The English language, we are told (and by voices of considerable weight) has got along for centuries with reasonable success; its admittedly bad spelling has not prevented other nations from learning it—it has spread over the world despite this handicap. Perhaps, they say, as English is a mixed language, the spelling could not be reformed without great dislocation: better, then, not to tamper with it.[70] This kind of rationalization, of course, becomes one more obstacle to rational improvement.

To sum up. It has been contended that the logic of the case is chiefly (but not quite exclusively) on the side of the advocates of systematic spelling reform. Not, however, that they are altogether the children of light, and their opponents the children of darkness. There is a good deal of Samuel Johnson's characteristic common sense in his observation that, "Some have endeavored to accommodate orthography better to pronunciation, without considering that this is to measure it by a shadow, to take that for a model which is changing while they apply it." Amplified, this is a just and permanent argument against a thoroughly phonetic spelling. We have questioned, particularly, the reformers' assumption that spelling exists *solely* to indicate pronunciation; and we have found support for our contention in the temperate yet incisive comments of Henry Bradley and R. W. Chapman. Further, it seems fair to say that

---

[69] *Handbook,* Part II, p. 38.

[70] Craigie, Sir William, in *S.P.E. Tract No. LXIII* (1944) makes the point concerning the mixed nature of English (p. 57).

there has sometimes been an excess of zeal in the terms used by the reformers to describe the absurdities and anomalies of conventional spelling. Sir William Craigie points out in the preface to his *English Spelling, Its Rules and Reason* that the impression that "English spelling is a hopeless chaos" is one that can and should be corrected; yet the enthusiastic reformer would find that description of it unsatisfactory only because he thought it too mild. The late Professor Joseph Wright, successor to Max Müller in the chair of comparative philology at Oxford, likewise observed that "our English orthography . . . far from being devoid of law and order . . . is considerably more systematic than would appear at first sight," and that the "ordinary general reader" is mistaken in thinking of it as "a thing born of ignorance, grown up haphazard, and existing by pure convention without rhyme or reason for its being, or method in its madness." [71] These quotations have been included in order to indicate that at least some highly qualified students of the language have felt that the ill opinion of our spelling familiar to the ordinary user of it (and still more to most scholars) is very frequently exaggerated. The final evidence that the orthodox spelling is not quite hopeless would seem to be the fact that Anglic, described as achieving "most of the practical advantages of complete and exact spelling reform," can still leave unchanged "sixty to seventy-five per cent of the words on an average printed page." [72]

The foregoing remarks are being altogether misinterpreted, however, if the reader takes them to assert that the case for spelling reform is weaker than the case against it. On the contrary, what has been said to modify the position of the spelling reformers and to reinforce *some* of the objections of their opponents has been said simply because the latter position is so evidently the weaker. Spelling reform—as we have seen it, for example, in the program of the Simplified Spelling Board—appears to be a cause amply fortified by reason; the fact that it has had only slight success is due much more to ignorant prejudice and sheer inertia than to any serious weakness of its own.

One more question remains: What can the individual writer who believes in the advantages promised by spelling reform do to promote

[71] Preface to Wright, Joseph and E. M., *An Elementary Historical New English Grammar*, London (Oxford), 1924.
[72] Pamphlet published by the Anglic Fund, *op. cit.*

its cause? It is a curious commentary on the whole matter that some of the most zealous of spelling reformers have confined themselves to preaching, and have practiced what they preached not at all. Says Bradley, ". . . even Professor Skeat, one of the most impassioned advocates of reformed spelling, seems never, in his published writings, to have ventured to spell any single word otherwise than in the conventional fashion, nor, if I may judge from his many letters to me, did he do so in his correspondence." [73] Similarly, one of the most militant of our American reformers, Lounsbury, accused himself in these terms: "Were I not myself inconsistent and lazy and several other disreputable adjectives, I should write *fonetic* instead of *phonetic*. This I cheerfully admit." [74] If "impassioned advocates" of the cause thus hesitate to practice what they preach, even in the smallest and least questionable changes, need they be surprised at the small response to their exhortations? For the man in the street has even more cause than the scholar to hesitate: coming from him, "reformed" spellings would be interpreted (as they would not, coming from Lounsbury or Skeat) not as advanced, but merely as illiterate.

Granting that reform must come gradually, how many and what sort of innovations can the individual use without subjecting himself to violent criticism? It is to be admitted at once that the principle of changing first what most needs changing will scarcely apply. Proper names are, from the point of view of the reformer, among the least satisfactory, orthographically, of all classes of words. Yet even the extreme proposals of the Simplified Spelling Society stop short of meddling with their spellings. Surnames like *Jonson, Johnson, More, Moore, Spencer,* and *Spenser* are (in this instance, in the history of English literature) identifying labels in their present spellings; to change these spellings would be to confuse the identities they represent. Geographical names likewise have a traditional background that it seems, even to the reformer, inexpedient to disturb. No, the principle of first attacking the worst offenders cannot well be adopted; it would seem preferable to begin with those changes that are least conspicuous and hence least disturbing.

This policy is admittedly not an easy one to follow. Let us see

[73] *Op. cit.,* p. 33.
[74] *Op. cit.,* p. 287.

how it applies to the four general proposals of the Board that have already been quoted. In doing this, we shall be outlining an attitude toward reformed spelling that compromises with the compromises of the Board. The first principle, to use the shortest and simplest of any variants sanctioned by current usage, is one that can hardly be questioned except by the confessedly reactionary. Even here, however, there is occasionally some doubt as to just what choice current usage does permit. Still, it is clear that no one need hesitate to employ *center, check, gram, honor, license, maneuver, plow, quartet,* or *traveler*. To use any of these spellings is merely to adopt what has long since become, in American practice at least, the better orthography. There is surely something suspiciously like Anglomania in an American's use of *centre, cheque* (or *checque*), *gramme, honour,*[75] *quartette*, and so forth. But unfortunately, actual usage does not permit the rule to be simply generalized, for *theater* has not quite the standing of *center*, nor *cigaret* that of *quartet*. There is considerable objection, too, to *catalog* rather than *catalogue*, and *rime* rather than *rhyme*. On the whole, however, the illustrations which the Board provided for its first principle give few qualms even to the conservative-minded. It is no very bitter dose to swallow even *tho,* the least generally used, perhaps, of the spellings included in this group, but still one that is unquestionably sanctioned by the test of present usage.

The second and third principles,[76] however, put us upon different ground. If we use the spellings recommended under these heads, we are not merely progressive: we need to be pioneers, active crusaders. Perhaps only *thru*, of all the examples given in the two lists, will pass muster—that is, by its being in fairly widespread use, and therefore not unduly disturbing. To many, *thru* (like *tho*) is something of a shibboleth. It is theoretically better than *through*, and sufficiently sanctioned in practice; yet it requires a positive effort to use it. As to the other words, human inconsistency and the common lack of even a small measure of courageous enterprise are all too clearly exemplified in the general rejection of spellings that are both simpler and

---

[75] For a most elaborate discussion of the often misstated issues involved in words of this type, see Lounsbury's chapter "The Question of Honor" (*op. cit.,* pp. 194-237).

[76] See above, p. 362.

historically preferable like *det* and *tung* and those that involve such an apparently innocuous simplification as the dropping of the silent, and completely misleading, *e* of suffixes like *ite* and *ive* (e.g., *definit, favorit, activ, positiv*). A beginning has been made with *iodin* and one or two more, but the list of the unaffected is long.

Of the third principle, to follow the simpler rather than the more complex of existing analogies, perhaps a specific example should be commented on in some detail. Let us consider the recommendation to substitute *f* for *ph*. The words affected are all of ultimately Greek derivation and the "etymological" spelling would hence be *ph*. But this *ph* has been superseded by *f* in a few English spellings that are unquestionably standard, such as *fancy* and *fantasy* (from the same Greek source, *phantasia*). There is therefore good precedent for making the corresponding simplification in many other words of Graeco-Latin descent, as is done indeed in a language like Italian, with a more phonetic orthography, in which *filosofia* corresponds to English *philosophy*. Nevertheless the "simpler analogy" has been invoked in vain, save in rare instances. *Fantom* has a certain vogue, and so, in scientific work especially, has *sulfur*, but that is about all. The same writer who uses *sulfur* would hesitate at *fosforous*, where the *f* appears twice and, through its use as initial symbol especially, is more conspicuous. Again it would appear that the *conspicuous* changes are the difficult ones. Lounsbury, as we have seen, was apologetic about his failure to write *fonetic* for *phonetic*. Small wonder, then, that a spelling that changes both initial and final symbols, lige *fonograf* or *fotograf*, appears to the ordinary writer quite unthinkable. One can only regret that the second and third proposals have met with so much resistance, and, because of their very nature, have been so little accepted.

The fourth and last general recommendation of the Board is a negative one: in brief, the caution that new spellings should not be mere simplifications, but simplifications that are consistent with the eventual purpose of restoring spelling to a *phonetic* basis. It is a caution that is necessary and useful. Amateur enthusiasts for spelling reform frequently seem to prefer the unauthorized to the authorized innovations. They indulge, for example, in such questionable novelties as *lite* for *light*, *nite* for *night*, or (still worse) *thot* for *thought*. The common-sense warning is very evident: If you wish to be progressive in spelling, be sure that the new forms you use have a really authoritative basis. Look them up, for example, in the *Standard* dictionary, which includes the recommendations of the Simplified Spelling Board (sometimes as alternatives, equally recommended, to the conventional spellings), or study them in the *Handbook* of the Board. Even so, you will not be free from suspicion; and if you escape the imputation of ignorance, your motives, in all probability, will not be clear to every reader: indeed, you will probably be charged with a desire to be conspicuous or, at least, "different." Finally, if you are writing for publication, you will often be challenged by the printer. In the end it is quite likely that you will be thwarted in all but the most minor items in your program.

There may be some small grain of hope to be picked up, however, from one or two current tendencies. Though slowed to a trickle, spelling reform does continue. It has recently been calculated [77] that, of the list of three hundred spellings which Theodore Roosevelt tried to have accepted in 1906, more than half are now preferred, and only forty-four are not listed in the Webster *Collegiate* dictionary. And if the source of most people's objection to spelling-change is that it makes words look odd or queer, then the numerous unconventional spellings of trade-names, many of which are phonetic, may gradually familiarize the public with spelling by sound, and so to a small degree at least break down their resistance. Scores of products today spell "nu" for *new*, "rite" for *right* or *write*, "kool" for *cool*, "tru" for *true*, "sho" for *show*, "mor" for *more*. Granted that these spellings are recognized as unconventionalities, that their use is unsystematic, and that their connotations are highly commercial, nevertheless, like word-puzzles they take one's attention, and the more familiar they become, the less inacceptable must other changes seem. If at present even some scholars fall back into a defense of the status quo, it is still clear that at work within the language are some forces tending toward change. If and when, at some time in the future, the movement for spelling reform is revived, the way will have been prepared somewhat by the efforts of individuals, and by the increment of small alterations that are made ineluctably from day to day.

[77] W. L. Werner, "English for the World!" *The Saturday Review*, Vol. XXXV, No. 40 (October 4, 1952), p. 46.

REFERENCES FOR FURTHER READING

Bradley, Henry, *On the Relations between Spoken and Written Language, with Special Reference to English*, London (Oxford), 1919.

Chapman, R. W., "Thoughts on Spelling Reform," *The Portrait of a Scholar*, London (Oxford), 1922.

Craigie, Sir W. A., *English Spelling, Its Rules and Reasons*, New York (Crofts), 1927.

———, "Problems of Spelling Reform," *S.P.E. Tract No. LXIII*, 1944

———, "Some Anomalies of Spelling," *S.P.E. Tract No. LIX*, 1942.

Handbook of Simplified Spelling, New York (Simplified Spelling Board), 1920.

Lounsbury, T. R., *English Spelling and Spelling Reform*, New York (Harper's), 1909.

Mathews, Mitford M., *A Survey of English Dictionaries*, London (Oxford), 1933.

Mencken, H. L., *The American Language*, New York (Knopf), 4th ed., 1936, Chapter VIII. Cf. also the additions in *Supplement One*, and *Supplement Two*.

Spelling (1887-94), official organ of the Spelling Reform Association.

Spelling (1925 and 1931), pub. jointly by the Simplified Spelling Society, the Simplified Spelling Board, and the Spelling Reform Association.

Starnes, D. T., and Noyes, G. E., *The English Dictionary from Cawdrey to Johnson, 1604-1755*, Chapel Hill (University of North Carolina), 1946.

Warfel, Harry R., *Noah Webster, Schoolmaster to America*, New York (Macmillan), 1936.

Chapter 12

The Modern Period—Pronunciation,
Variations and Standards

THE EIGHTEENTH century, as we have seen, was a time of consolidation between two periods of change. As we move into the nineteenth century we find the English language spreading and expanding as never before: its stage becomes rapidly as wide as the whole world, and it adapts itself in a variety of ways to the new industrial society which it must serve. Unless we admit the powerful inter-effects of language and society, it is impossible to see the recent past and the future clearly. Language is the most important tool of human society; as the structure of society is altered, the tool loses some former uses and is adapted to new ones. And *vice versa:* the society itself may be altered by new applications of the tool, by the discovery or development of additional capacities in it.[1] Something of this we must touch on in this final chapter.

Both the geographic and the social changes just alluded to began, of course, much earlier than the nineteenth century; but it has taken time for their effects to become manifest, and to make it evident that we must readjust our focus. It is at last generally admitted, for example, that British standards of pronunciation and usage are not the only possible ones, the only "right" ones. Until near the end of the eighteenth century, the English-speaking world may have had only one pole; today it is obviously bi-polar. The independence of the United States—for better or for worse—is an undeniable fact, and if H. L. Mencken's thesis that British English is now following American, reversing the historical order of things, may not be con-

[1] Consider, for example, the relationships of language to the new forces of popular education, propaganda, advertising, and so on, so powerful today. See also Estrich and Sperber, *Three Keys to Language,* New York (Rinehart), 1952.

sidered as proved, the fact that such a thesis can be proposed at all is sufficiently significant. When we consider the English language today, raising questions of practices and standards, we cannot speak of the language of the mother country alone. Let us compare, then, the two poles of this language—the one British, the other American —to see in what respects they differ, what elements they preserve in common, and how far apart they now are. From such a comparison we may then go on to questions of standards, and possibly to some consideration of what the future may hold.

It may be well to begin with the matter of terms, already tacitly raised. Shall we discuss "American English" or, as some would have it, "the American language"? It is curious that two of the first books produced when attention, long overdue, began to be paid to American speech some thirty-odd years ago, indicate in their very titles these opposing points of view: Gilbert M. Tucker's *American English* and H. L. Mencken's *The American Language*.[2] The divergence of opinion, of course, is absolute: American speech is either conceived of as a special section of a larger whole, or it is thought to have departed so widely from its seventeenth-century point of contact with the English of England as to deserve to be considered an entirely separate entity. Before attempting to decide for either position, it may be interesting to glance at the opinions that Americans have held, from Colonial times forward, about the relationship of their speech to British English.

The usual Colonial attitude was quite naturally one that accepted the language of southern England without cavil as the standard for the English-speaking world, and deprecated such departures from it as appeared in the language of the Colonists. Parenthetically it may be observed that this provincial and apologetic attitude lasted until very recently. Richard Grant White, *arbiter elegantiarum* in the middle nineteenth century, was still convinced that American English can be good only in so far as it is identical with British English.[3] Even in the twentieth century, particularly in New England, this

---

[2] Sir William A. Craigie has already made this observation ("An American Language," *Saturday Review of Literature,* Vol. VII, No. 31, Feb. 21, 1931, p. 614); he further points out that Krapp avoids definite issue by using as the title of his most elaborate survey of the field, *The English Language in America.*

[3] "In language, everything distinctly American is bad" (*Atlantic Monthly,* Vol. XLI, p. 495), quoted in Emerson, p. 106.

feeling occasionally persists, in scarcely diluted form. "It is a safe rule to require every perceptible departure from English usage to justify itself"—so runs the general advice given in a rhetoric published not very long ago and widely used in American colleges.[4] This attitude, of course, hardly enters into the dispute between American English and the American language, for it amounts almost to a denial that either has a right to exist.

After the Revolution, there was a sharp reaction from the general unquestioning acceptance of British authority, in language as in other matters; indeed, a demand for a "genuine American language" is to be heard. This seems even to have gone to the grotesque length of demanding that an entirely different language—Greek or Hebrew, for choice—be substituted for English.[5] Among the more realistically minded, however, such schemes had no place; nevertheless, the conception that the English language as spoken in America would in time be widely different from the English language as spoken in England and might eventually become a separate dialect was not uncommon. Whether such a development should be helped or hindered was, of course, the bone of contention. Several leading men of the new republic—most notably, Thomas Jefferson[6]—felt that it should be helped.

The leanings of Noah Webster were undoubtedly, and more particularly in his earlier work, toward an American language. He conceived that the American language of the future would be "as different from the future language of England, as the modern Dutch, Danish, and Swedish are from the German, or from one another." [7] "Let us," he said, "seize the present moment and establish a national language as well as a national government." [8] But Webster was forced to recede from this extreme position, as the title of his chief work, *An American Dictionary of the English Language* (1828), significantly indicates. The more conservative and more British

[4] Greenough, C. N., and Hersey, F. W. C., *English Composition,* New York (Macmillan), 1917, p. 353. The attitude still flourishes among teachers of speech in many parts of the country.

[5] Just how serious such suggestions were is a little dubious; cf. Mencken, *American Language,* 4th ed., p. 79, and *Cambridge History of American Literature,* Vol. I, p. vi.

[6] Cf. Mencken, *op. cit.,* p. 11, and Krapp, *English Language in America,* Vol. I, p. 9.

[7] *Dissertations* (1789), p. 22 (quoted by Krapp, p. 9).

[8] Quoted by Mencken, *op. cit.,* 3rd ed., p. 45.

character of the work of his great rival, J. E. Worcester, the first form of whose dictionary was published in 1830, is obviously one reason for the moderating of Webster's patriotic ardor. Worcester, indeed, was long preferred by the Tories in language.[9]

Through the nineteenth century and in the twentieth century, the debate between conservative and radical, on this question as on other linguistic matters, has continued. Men of letters and professed students of language have been more inclined to the conservative tradition; they have sought to emphasize the likeness of our speech to that of England, rather than its differences. Until quite recently, only works deliberately couched in dialectal speech—Lowell's *Biglow Papers*, Holmes's *Autocrat*, Harris's "Uncle Remus" stories, Twain's *Huckleberry Finn*, and so on—have ordinarily striven for a distinctly American idiom. Occasionally, however, it is to be noted that an American writer has protested against the blind following of British tradition; the most famous protest is perhaps that of Lowell in his preface to the second series of *Biglow Papers*. William Dean Howells[10] and Mark Twain[11] have also joined their voices to Lowell's. Walt Whitman, too, who has been called by Louis Untermeyer "the father of the American language," [12] is to be remembered for his conviction that America both needed and would have a distinctive speech, and for his experimentation to that end: "The new world, the new times, the new peoples, the new vistas, need a tongue according—yes, what is more will have such a tongue—will not be satisfied until it is evolved." [13]

So much for hopes and projects: what of actualities? For the hard fact is that a language is a most difficult thing to influence; it is a set of complex and deeply rooted habits, mostly unconscious, which responds very slowly to conscious attempts to control it. Thus even while the projectors have been expressing their hopes for one or another kind of American language, the language itself has been in

[9] "As late as the last decade of the nineteenth century Harvard University, in its English entrance requirements, specified Worcester's dictionary as the authority in spelling," McKnight, *op. cit.*, p. 490.

[10] Cf. "The Editor's Study," *Harper's Magazine*, January 1886.

[11] As in "Concerning the American Language," in the volume *Tom Sawyer Abroad, etc.*

[12] As quoted by Mencken, *op. cit.*, 3rd ed., p. 90.

[13] As quoted by Horace Traubel in the preface to *An American Primer*. For an account of this, see Leon Howard, "Walt Whitman and the American Language," *American Speech*, Vol. V, No. 6 (August 1930), pp. 441-451.

existence, growing and changing in response to the developing society in which it was being used. The question of whether we are to speak of an "American language" or of "American English," then, can be answered only by a factual comparison of the English language in Britain with its offshoot in the United States.

Furthermore, this rather academic question is less important in itself than in respect to another question: that of standards. If English has expanded in the past century and a half, has this expansion involved so wide a divergence that there is no longer any common standard possible for all parts of the English-speaking world? No one can well deny that, with the greatly increased interdependence of nations today, it would be a real advantage if some degree of uniformity were obtainable in the English language—and not only for the sake of the English-speaking peoples, but also, as many suggest, because English seems on the way to becoming a second or auxiliary language for international use. Is there, then, some standard now in existence which the whole English-speaking world accepts; and if not, can one be set up? Or must we consider the alternative of two or more coexisting standards? The bipolarity already spoken of does not necessarily prejudice our answer, since the existence of a standard never does away with other forms of a language, but merely means that one form is recognized as pre-eminent. Let us come at once, then, to the comparison of the English of Britain and the United States.[14]

American and British English. First, then, it will be quite commonly agreed that American speech is far more uniform than British. We have no dialects, in the sense in which they exist in England; the local speech of any part of America is almost wholly intelligible to a visitor from any other part. Numerous local variants there are in words, and some differences in pronunciation (as we shall see later), but even the most extremely contrasting types do not differ enough to prevent communication. Further, in the United States there is no geographical standard that stamps a special value upon the speech

---

[14] If the comparison is to be fair, we must compare similar things—in this case, language of relatively the same level of cultivation in the two lands. We shall hope to escape what is the flaw in an otherwise splendid book—Mencken's *American Language:* that its author particularly in the earlier editions, repeatedly puts vulgar American into comparison with cultivated British usage—which may tickle Mr. Mencken's humor, but which also misleads the unwary or heartens the prejudiced reader.

of a particular city or state: our ideal is unquestionably national, rather than local or sectional, usage. And third, the gulf that separates the speech of the most highly educated from that of the average citizen is considerably less than the corresponding one in England.

A familiar misconception of the relation between American speech and English is that which describes our language as relatively nearer the English of Shakespeare's day. This is a confusion of the part with the whole, for of course it does not apply to American speech generally. There are, it is true, a number of words and expressions, archaic by British standards, that continue in living use in some isolated communities—and not only those mountain communities of Kentucky and Tennessee which are usually offered as illustrations, but also the much older Atlantic seaboard settlements of Maine and New Hampshire, along Chesapeake Bay, and on the coast of North Carolina. Krapp has aptly pointed out that "the speech of these communities is archaic . . . not because it is transplanted speech but because the communities in their general social life have had few social contacts. Thus the speech of Iceland is archaic as compared with that of Norway." [15] The "arrest of development," in other words, is due not to the fact that the language was transplanted, but rather that the regions to which it was transplanted have been largely untouched by outside influence. It is a fallacy to suppose that such a condition applies in most of America, or that American English has not altered as thoroughly as British English from their seventeenth-century point of separation.

As to the general vocabulary, it is fair to say that popular belief exaggerates the number of words that are peculiar to American English or have a different meaning here. A partial explanation, perhaps, is that in a group of words with which the American visitor to England must come in contact—the vocabulary of travel—the differences are unusually great, no doubt because railroad travel developed in the two countries *after* the separation. The same would apply to the automobile, airplane, telephone, and so on. At any rate, the differences here[16] are far from being typical. The proof of the

[15] *The English Language in America,* New York (Century), 1925, Vol. I, p. 51.

[16] Some of them, for example, are listed by Mencken, *op. cit.,* 4th ed., pp. 238-239, and by Greenough and Kittredge, *Words and Their Ways in English Speech,* p. 271. The large number of Americanisms printed in such works as the *Dictionary of American English* and the *Dictionary of Americanisms* is

essential identity of the two vocabularies is simply the fact that no American has the slightest difficulty in reading a book by an Englishman and printed in England, or an Englishman with a book by an American and printed in America—unless, perchance, the book is unusually full of either British or American slang, localisms, or technical trade jargon. Nor is the fact that an occasional word is spelled differently in the two countries enough of an obstacle to be worthy of the name. American practice has been a trifle more hospitable to spelling reform than British, but the divergence, on the whole, is small and unimportant. It is not to be denied, on the other hand, that an American does sometimes experience difficulty in listening to an English lecturer, and an Englishman in understanding an American speaker. But what difficulty there is comes rather from different habits of pronunciation than from different vocabularies.

And what are these different habits of pronunciation? As satisfactory a generalization as any, so far as the less admirable but unfortunately more conspicuous aspects of pronunciation are concerned, is George Arliss's dictum:[17] "The chief fault in speech in America is sloppiness and the outstanding defect in England is snippiness." It may also very possibly be true, as Americans are often told by Englishmen, that our speech is harsher and more nasal than theirs; indeed, from the eighteenth century on, American speech (especially that of rural New England) has been labeled by both British and native observers as characterized by a "drawl" and a "twang." The "drawl" evidently refers to the generally slower tempo, or to the prolongation of stressed vowels. Perhaps it is also intended to reflect the fact that in general there is a great deal less variation in the pitch-patterns of Middle-Western American than of British speech. The former is relatively monotonous, with little variation in the level of the voice; the latter goes up and down with an effect that, to many Americans, suggests excitement. American speech is generally less precise than British in the enunciation, so that though the American may syllabify more fully where the Englishman elides, he also slurs more.

---

somewhat misleading, since it includes a great number of localisms, obsolete words and meanings, and others whose use was or is retricted in some way. The number of Americanisms in *general current* use is very much smaller. It should also be remembered that many words which began as Americanisms are now a part of English in the broader sense, wherever it is used.

[17] "Mr. Arliss Makes a Speech," *Atlantic Monthly*, February 1931.

What is meant by "twang," in all probability, is the quality of nasality that often associates itself, more frequently in the rural districts (both of New England and the Middle West) than in the cities, with the "drawl." "The word 'twang,' " Krapp points out, "often means nothing more than merely 'flavor.' " [18] It is in fact, we may add, confused with "tang." Nevertheless, the term "nasal twang" undoubtedly has a real meaning, and describes an ingredient in American speech that once was more conspicuous and more general than it is now. Of course, the habit of nasalizing vowels is no more of indigenous growth in America than are other distinguishing features of American speech. It once flourished in England (and to some extent still does), as Krapp indicates, and was satirized as a Puritan failing in *Hudibras* and elsewhere.[19]

Connected with the "drawl" rather than the "twang" is a further conspicuous difference between American speech and British. It is manifestly untrue of Southern speech, and probably going too far to say of American speech in general, as has recently been said, "The stresses are levelled out and all syllables have almost the same value. . . ." [20] But if this is exaggeration, it is the exaggeration of a real truth. The point is that British English has more and more tended to emphasize the heavy stress accent characteristic of the Germanic languages in general; it has obscured, and often telescoped, unaccented vowels. Many varieties of American English have, in many classes of words, done this to a less degree; all have preserved distinctive vowel qualities through a habit of secondary accent that has been largely discarded in British English. This is particularly noticeable in polysyllables ending in -*ary*, -*ery*, and -*ory*. These are Middle English borrowings, for the most part, of Old French words that are ultimately Latin. The main accent in Old French was ordinarily on what is now the penultimate syllable, but in Middle English it shifted to the fourth syllable from the end rather than the second, as native words were commonly accented on the first syllable if this

---

[18] *Op. cit.*, Vol. II, pp. 14, 23; and compare his reference to Ripman, *Sounds of Spoken English*, p. 14.

[19] For references to dramatic satire directed against the Puritans' habit of speaking "i' th' nose," see A. M. Myers, *Representation and Misrepresentation of the Puritan in Elizabethan Drama*, Philadelphia (University of Pennsylvania), 1931, pp. 20, 36, and 85.

[20] Larsen and Walker, *Pronunciation: A Practical Guide to American Standards*, New York (Oxford), 1930, p. 13.

syllable was a root. However, a secondary accent remained on the penultimate syllable, and this secondary stress is preserved in general American practice though it has been lost, probably within the last century and a half, in British speech.[21] Our ultra-refined radio announcers who stress only the first syllable of words like *dictionary*, *ordinary*, *secretary*, *laboratory*, and *cemetery*, and telescope the rest are presumably either ignorant of this law or convinced of the plausibility of a "Received Standard" for the whole of the English-speaking world.

The contrary tendency, however, is not lacking in American speech, since in some other words the stress is so strongly on the first syllable that the ending becomes reduced—as it would not be in British pronunciation. The best example is the group of adjectives —also ultimately from Latin—ending in *-ile*, such as *puerile*, *febrile*, *sterile*, *versatile*, *volatile*, and others. Americans tend to pronounce these [ɪl] or simply [l] in British pronunciation they are [aɪl]). The well-known lines of Ogden Nash,

> I find it clever of the turtle
> In such a case to be so fertile

could have been rimed so only by an American!

If the "drawl," so called, is a point against American pronunciation, surely the greater intelligibility that results from the secondary stress somewhat compensates for it. The frequent testimony of foreigners, even those who have learned their English in England, that they can understand an American's English more easily than an Englishman's seems most plausibly explained through the slower tempo of American speech, and particularly, its habit of secondary stress. This habit, it may be added, affects certain other words besides those in *-ary*, *-ery*, and *-ory* already referred to. A footnote in Nicklin's *Standard English Pronunciation* in regard to *circumstances* is somewhat amusing to an American: "Some speakers seem to have let themselves be influenced by Gilbert's rhyming of this word with *chances* and *dances*, without observing that such rhymes no more pretend to guide us to the Standard pronunciation than the rhyme with *folly* suggests that we should remove the emphasis from the

---

[21] Kenyon, *American Pronunciation*, Ann Arbor (Wahr), 6th ed., 1935, pp. 82-85, has a fuller account of the matter, with lists of words in which American and British practice vary.

first syllable of *melancholy*." [22] As to the latter point, it is interesting
that the rime *folly* and *melancholy* that seemed good to Milton
(*Il Penseroso*, ll. 61-62) is still equally good in American speech,
though the Englishman prefers ['mɛlənkəlɪ]. But to suggest that any
British deviation from the practice of accenting *circumstances* on the
first syllable only is due to a lyric in *The Mikado* is surely to exaggerate the influence of the rimes of comic opera librettos. If
Gilbert has contaminated British taste on this point, is he also responsible for *gal* (in place of *girl*), which, in an equally familiar lyric
in *Iolanthe*, he rimes with *liberal?*

Here, however, a word of caution: although it is true that in certain groups of words American pronunciation retains a secondary
stress that British pronunciation discards, it nevertheless fully shares
in the general trend of Modern English speech toward obscuring unstressed vowels. Indeed, the rule which Nicklin formulates for British
pronunciation applies pretty closely also to American: "It is hardly
too much to say that in nearly every word of more than one syllable
all the vowels except those on which the principal stress accent falls
are now sounded either as [ə] or as *i* in *fit*, and this however the
word is spelt." [23] Failure to observe this principle leads to many
pedantic "spelling-pronunciations," not a few of which, unfortunately, are dignified by the authority of dictionaries. For heavy
stress, followed by relaxed and obscured pronunciation, has been a
phonetic fact in the language from Old English times forward; it
took part, as we have seen, in the inflectional reductions that produced Middle and Modern English; had it not existed, we might still
be saying *hlāfweard* rather than *lord*, and *dægesēage* rather than
daisy. And if we can recognize the fact in the past, why should it be
difficult to accept it in the present? Yet there are people who would
pronounce a *p* in *raspberry*, or a *t* in *Christmas*. Actually these relaxed pronunciations are very common indeed and in perfectly reputable practice—*towards* as a monosyllable, *forehead* as [farɪd], and
cupboard as [kʌbɚd] are a few random illustrations. The [ɪ] of the
unstressed syllable of such a word as *forehead* is a sound of wide
occurrence in contemporary pronunciation; it occurs in the best
speech, for example, in *cabbage, lettuce, senate,* and *subject,* despite
the spelling and despite some opposition of dictionaries.

[22] P. 72. Reprinted by permission of the Oxford University Press.
[23] *Ibid.,* p. 71.

Most prevalent, of course, is the neutral [ə] just mentioned: it is almost safe to assume that *every* unstressed vowel approximates [ə] or [ɪ]. To put it differently, it is almost a necessity to have either secondary stress or distributed stress if other vowel sounds than [ə] or [ɪ] are to be preserved. Thus in the more rapid British pronunciation of *registrar* and *bursar,* the [ɑ] sound is lost in the final syllables, which thus have the vowel of *sir;* but the usual American practice is to preserve the [ɑ] through secondary stress in one case, and through distributed or hovering stress in the other. British and American pronunciation are both, however, subject to this type of change, though the words affected are often different. Thus *medicine* and *venison* have lost their middle vowels in British practice but not in American; American *diamond* and *auxiliary,* on the other hand, have lost their middle vowels, though the British retain them; *business* has become dissyllabic on both sides.

So much for general differences; the differences in individual sounds, the vowels and consonants of present-day American and British, remain to be discussed. It is impossible in this book to go into great detail; we shall therefore limit ourselves in two respects: first, the standard pronunciation of the London area (discussed below under the name of "Received Standard") will be the type of British speech taken for comparison; and second, the chief American regional variants will be compared with this and with each other. It may also be appropriate at this point to make a historical comment. We all know, of course, that the language was brought to America from England in the first place. Why, then, does the pronunciation of the United States differ from that of England? Are its characteristics of native development? Or are they survivals from older speech habits in the English language? This query may be answered in the words of the scholar who was first to make noteworthy contributions in this field, George Philip Krapp:

If one did not fear to affirm a universal positive, one might say that in every case the distinctive features of American pronunciation have been but survivals from older usages which were, and in some instances still are, to be found in some dialect or other of the speech of England.[24]

The colonists of both New England and Virginia were chiefly from London and the adjoining Midland and Southern counties, and

[24] *Op. cit.,* Vol. II, p. 28.

though, in the course of time, their speech has come to differ in many details, both groups unquestionably spoke some more or less dialectal variant of Southern English. New England, more subject to influences from both England and other parts of America, has retained fewer seventeenth- or eighteenth-century peculiarities than has Virginia; but in a number of ways—most conspicuously in its treatment of r—Southern American speech is still associated with that of Eastern New England in its resemblance to the speech of Southern England.[25] In contrast, later colonizers of other parts of America, coming from other parts of the British Isles than London and the adjacent territory, have been influential in transplanting a speech more like that of the North than that of the South of England, and this inland speech has spread not only westward with the frontier, as everybody realizes, but southward too.

Linguistic Geography. Before entering farther upon details, however, we must describe briefly the chief method by which the study of present-day pronunciation is made to serve our better understanding of the regional differences in a language—specifically, of the English language in America. Written records, as we have seen,[26] are all that remain to us from the past; and since they reveal but few of the details that we should like to have, we must perforce be satisfied with a rather broad reconstruction of the sounds of former times. But contemporary pronunciation flourishes all around us; we have only to listen, to train our ears, to go to those places where variant types exist, to record the wealth of detail, and to work out the existing patterns of difference, correlating them with historical and social facts. The branch of science which undertakes this task is linguistic geography.

Everybody is aware that differences both geographic and social exist in our language. Even those of us who have not traveled, or who have lived in a limited area, will have had this fact thrust upon us by comic strips, movies, radio, and television—usually, it is true, in a form distorted and conventionalized for humorous effect, but once in a while more truthfully represented.[27] Thus we are made

[25] For a recent study of part of this matter, see Raven I. McDavid, Jr., "Postvocalic /-r/ in South Carolina: a Social Analysis," *American Speech,* Vol. XXIII, part 3 (1948), pp. 195-204.

[26] Chapter 4, p. 52.

[27] An example of a sound handling of such matters was the radio program "Where Are You From?" given in 1940 by Dr. Henry Lee Smith. Dr. Smith

conscious of "hillbilly talk," "cowboy talk," "Brooklynese," "gangster talk," and so on. And each of us has surely made for himself certain connections between particular parts of the country and the more striking varieties of pronunciation and vocabulary found in those localities. The linguistic geographer seeks to make such correlations systematically, and when he has done his work in any area he is able to draw maps showing the distribution of the significant variations, and thus, in effect, setting off the regional subdivisions of the language.

Linguistic geography began in Germany in the nineteenth century with the work of Georg Wenker, who sent out to over 44,000 village schoolmasters a list of forty sentences containing words and sounds known to vary locally. He asked them to translate these into the form of pronunciation used in their part of the country. Unfortunately they were not trained for accurate listening or recording of small differences, so the experiment was not wholly successful. The first successful full-scale linguistic atlas of a whole country was produced in France by Jules Gilliéron and Edmond Edmont (1902-9), the evidence on 2000 items being gathered at first hand by Edmont in 600 localities throughout the area. Further improvements in method were made by Karl Jaberg and Jakob Jud in their atlas of Italy and southern Switzerland, and still others have been added in the work of the *Linguistic Atlas of the United States and Canada*, still in progress.[28]

The linguistic geographer today first studies the settlement-history of the area he is to work in. Upon this basis, guided often by some preliminary sampling of the area's speech habits, he chooses a number of communities which, in aggregate, will represent the whole area.

---

asked members of his audience to say certain words and phrases; then from their pronunciation he worked out, on the spot, with a high degree of accuracy, the place of their birth and sometimes other places where they had lived. Dr. Smith was a student of linguistic geography.

[28] Wenker's work was published as *Sprachatlas des deutschen Reiches* (1877-) ; Gilliéron and Edmont's as *L'Atlas linguistique de la France*; Jaberg and Jud's as *Sprach- und Sachatlas Italiens und der Südschweiz* (1928-40) ; the first part of the American work is the *Linguistic Atlas of New England*, produced under the editorship of Hans Kurath. Out of the Atlas collections in the Atlantic states have also come Kurath's *A Word Geography of the Eastern United States*, Ann Arbor (University of Michigan), 1949, and E. Bagby Atwood's *Survey of Verb Forms in the Eastern United States*, Ann Arbor (University of Michigan), 1953. For the most recent survey of linguistic geography, see Sever Pop, *La Dialectologie*, Louvain (Université de Louvain), 1950-.

Some of these must be rural, some urban; some must be long-established, others relatively new; some must be along the routes of
population movement, others isolated; they must also represent
proportionally the national or ethnic backgrounds of the population.
Next, in these communities he seeks people who have been there all
their lives (and their forbears too if possible, though in recently
settled areas of the United States, the latter is obviously impossible) ;
they must also be of various generations, occupations, and degrees of
education. To all of these people the investigator puts the same series
of questions. The sum of their answers (which he records in careful
phonetic transcription) allows him to compare for local variations,
and since he knows the appropriate facts about each of the answerers
(or "informants"), he is in a position to correlate the differences of
language with geography, education, and social status. Furthermore,
by a comparison of the generations he can judge the direction of
change—what things are old-fashioned or new-fangled. Ultimately
he can set off on the map what are called "focal areas" (those which
are being imitated, and whose influence is therefore spreading), "relic
areas" (those which conserve language forms longer than others do),
and "transition areas" (those in which outside influences are more
striking than local characteristics).

Though pronunciation is decidedly the best criterion, since it is
the aspect of speech of which people are least aware and with which
they tamper least, the linguistic geographer does not study sounds
alone. Words too, and grammatical usages, fall into geographic
patterns and help him to draw his "isoglosses" or lines of demarcation. The questions asked of the informants therefore concern the
kinds of words which are most likely to be traditional, least subject
to imposed influences—words concerned with the ordinary activities
of most people—among others, food, clothing, weather, time-telling,
home life, family relationships, community attitudes, and the basic
activities of housekeeping and farming. The accompanying map[29]
showing the loss or retention of r in New England is an example of
what a linguistic atlas can tell us about pronunciation. The Connecticut River, clearly enough, forms a striking physical boundary
whose effect is reflected in a vertical division of the area into an

[29] From the *Handbook of the Linguistic Geography of New England,* by
Hans Kurath *et al.,* Providence (Brown University), 1939. Acknowledgment is
hereby made to the American Council of Learned Societies.

Eastern part, where *r* is generally lost, and a Western part, where it is generally retained. Relic areas are those (Martha's Vineyard, Marblehead, Cape Ann) where *r* hangs on within the area of general loss.

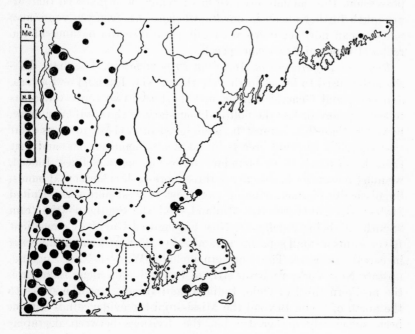

PRECONSONANTAL AND FINAL *R*

An r *preceding a vowel, as in* road, borrow, far out, *is pronounced in all parts of New England. But before consonants and finally, as in* hard, how far?, *usage is regional: in Western New England and in New Brunswick the* r *is regularly pronounced, in most of Eastern New England it is dropped, while the Conn. Valley is mixed and unstable in practice.*

*Martha's Vineyard, Marblehead and Cape Ann, all secluded communities, appear as "*r *islands" in Eastern New England, where this* r *is still losing ground. On the other hand, the* r *is gaining ground in the Conn. Valley.*

The largest circles indicate regular use of this r, *the smallest ones sporadic use, and the two intermediate sizes rather evenly divided usage.*

The *Linguistic Atlas of New England* comprises 734 maps displaying the information on distribution of words and sounds, and giving us therefore a valid basis for the study of local variations in American speech within the area covered. Similar information has now been gathered through almost all of the Atlantic coast states and in the Great Lakes region, and is being gathered in the northern plains states, Rocky Mountain states, California, and the Deep South. Twenty years hence, perhaps, the entire story may be in our possession. But enough advance has already been made so that we are much farther ahead in our knowledge than even ten years ago, and we can now set down with fair assurance the outlines of the regional types of American speech.

Regional Differences in American Pronunciation. The main divisions that used to be set forth were three: New England or Eastern, Southern, and General American,[30] the latter two conceived of as reflecting more or less the political boundary of the Civil War. Now, however, these labels must be abandoned or revised, for it is clear that the New England area is by no means homogeneous, and that there is no north-south boundary following political lines. Indeed, we must recognize that there are three more-or-less horizontal bands, linguistically distinct, running from east to west across the United States: the Northern, the Midland, and the Southern (the term "Southern" being redefined). New England east of the Connecticut River forms a small separate area allied to the northern but differing in certain respects. The Northern includes Western New England, upstate New York, a narrow strip of Pennsylvania along Lake Erie, the northern third of Ohio, Indiana, and Illinois, and the states to the north of them. Beyond the Mississippi the evidence has not yet been sufficiently gathered [31] but the divisions between the areas appear to run generally westward, with regional boundaries becoming less sharply defined as one approaches the Rocky Mountains and the Pacific coast.[32]

[30] The application of the label "General American" to the largest part of the North raised considerable objection, as it seemed to imply that the rest of the country was somehow less American. Nevertheless, nobody could offer a more satisfactory term, and it gained wide use.

[31] However, Prof. Harold B. Allen (University of Minnesota) has nearly completed the collecting in Minnesota, Iowa, the Dakotas, and Nebraska. Work has also been begun in the Maritime Provinces of Canada (Prof. Henry Alexander), in Colorado, New Mexico, and Montana (Prof. Marjorie Kimmerle), in Texas (Prof. Bagby Atwood), in Louisiana (Prof. Sumner Ives), in California (Dr. David Reed), and in Washington (Dr. Carroll Reed).

[32] In other words, some Northern features have spread southward (as Prof. C. K. Thomas, of Cornell University, showed in his paper before the American Dialect Society in New York City, 1950), some Midland features have spread northward (as Prof. Allen has discovered in his study of Minnesota and

Returning to the Atlantic, the Southern area (redefined) includes the coastal plain east of the Blue Ridge; therefore southern Delaware and the eastern parts of Maryland, Virginia, the Carolinas, and Georgia; thereafter it appears still to follow the southern coast westward through Alabama, Mississippi, and Louisiana into eastern Texas, but here the *Atlas* investigation has not yet been made. The Midland area begins in eastern Pennsylvania, and spreads west and southward to the west of the Blue Ridge. It therefore includes most of New Jersey and Pennsylvania; all of West Virginia, Kentucky and Tennessee; the mountains of Virginia, the Carolinas, and Georgia; northern Alabama and Mississippi; and the southern two-thirds of Ohio, Indiana, and Illinois. Beyond the Mississippi River it appears to continue southwesterly to the Mexican border and the Pacific coast.

What, then, are the features of pronunciation that distinguish these three large areas and the smaller one of Eastern New England? There is space in this book only to summarize them broadly. The only striking consonantal variation is in the loss in some areas of final and pre-consonantal *r*. This, and the phenomena attending the loss, have been described before,[33] so only the distribution need be noted here. Through almost all of the Northern region—that is, excepting Eastern New England and the area of New York City—the *r* quality is present: *farm* [fɑrm], *fur* [fɝ] or [fʌr], *fear* [fiɚ]. The Southern region is more like Eastern New England in this respect than any other, for in it, too, *r* shows a widespread loss.[34] Midland, on the other hand, agrees with Northern in generally retaining it, and there are, again, signs of pressure from the Midland upon the South, so that on the Southern border with the Midland the *r* is very often retained. In short, only the Eastern and Southern coastal fringe of the United States drops the *r* (and not all of that, since the Philadelphia area retains it); elsewhere this *r* is a distinctively American feature—one that comes into striking contrast with

---

the Dakotas), and sometimes speech forms illustrate the junction of routes of migration from the North and the South (see M. M. Kimmerle, R. I. and V. G. McDavid, "Problems of Linguistic Geography in the Rocky Mountain Area," *Western Humanities Review*, Vol. V (1951), pp. 249-264.

[33] Chapter 4, pp. 68-69.

[34] In the South Atlantic states, however, the loss of *r* is less a regional than a social feature; that is, it is lost chiefly in the speech of upper-class people. See McDavid, *op. cit.* ("Postvocalic /-r/ . . .").

southern British pronunciation. Americans not of the Atlantic seaboard sometimes feel that the dropping of the *r* shows affectation, Eastern schooling, or imitation of the British. The *Chicago Tribune*, in its constant attacks upon Franklin Roosevelt, cartooned him as dropping his *r*'s, thus appealing to the sturdy Anglophobia of the Midwest—a device of propaganda which, in the East, would have fallen flat.

In areas where *r* is lost, the phonetic situation is appropriate for intrusive *r*, as in *idear, lawr*. This is regularly present in British standard and Eastern New England speech, and can be heard in New York City (though less often) and in the south coastal cities (though rarely). But it is not coextensive with the loss of *r* itself. Where *r* is lost, it either lengthens the preceding vowel or leaves some diphthongal element attached to it (particularly when the vowel is high). Thus *door* is [doɚ] in the Midland and North generally, [doə] in Eastern New England and the South, and frequently [doː] in the South. In New England and the South one frequently hears the diphthong broken under heavy stress into two syllables: ['dowə].

Other differences in consonants are relatively minor, but the use of [hw] (or [ʍ]) in *when, whistle, what*, and so on, should be noticed. In British standard pronunciation this is regularly reduced to [w], with the result that *which* and *witch*, or *whales* and *Wales*, are pronounced identically. In the Eastern United States the same is widespread in natural pronunciation between Albany and Baltimore, less common in other parts of the Atlantic seaboard. Elsewhere in the United States [hw] is more common, and since the distinction between this and [w] is widely taught in the schools, it is not likely soon to disappear. Since [hw] or [ʍ] is kept up in Northern Britain, Scotland, and Ireland, this is another feature linking American pronunciation rather with the northern than the southern types of British speech.[35]

When we come to the vowels, however, we find many geographically varying patterns. A feature already mentioned[36] will do well to begin with: the sound in *ask, laugh, class*, and so on. The well-nigh universal American sound here is [æ], the so-called "flat a"; only in Eastern New England and the coastal fringe of Virginia do we find

[35] See the article by R. I. and V. G. McDavid, "*h* Before Semivowels in the United States," *Language*, Vol. XXVIII, No. 1 (Jan.–March 1952), pp. 41-62.
[36] For a full enumeration, see Kenyon, *American Pronunciation*, pp. 174-175.

the "broad a," [ɑ].[37] This feature, therefore, ties Eastern New England more closely to "Received Standard" than does any other—yet the rest of America differs. Interestingly enough, there has been a complete reversal in opinions about these sounds in the past two hundred years. In early Modern English the [ɑ] in such words was dialectal, and until the mid-eighteenth century it was generally regarded as vulgar, while [æ] was considered the polite sound.[38] But by the last decades of the nineteenth century the broad *a* had become the educated usage of England and was firmly established in New England; and since New England's standards were then dominant in education and culture, broad *a* was striven after elsewhere in the United States. Even as recently as 1917 some of its proponents, still under the New England cultural tradition, and perhaps slightly touched with Anglomania, write of it:

The broad *a* seems likely to come in. Some New Englanders, as we have seen, overdo it; but unquestionably, *aunt, laugh, last, past,* and *fast,* as pronounced in New England, have the weight of authority so distinctly on their side that *laff* and *ant* are fast becoming provincial.[39]

Time has proven this a bad guess, for though the preference for [ɑ] lingers on in the very restricted territory already indicated— and occasionally in young ladies' seminaries and in schools of elocution outside—there is no longer any doubt that [æ] is the normal American sound. Even within New England, and in England itself, [ɑ] is losing ground. A very practical reason for not making the attempt to cultivate it may be given to any not to the manner born who seek to acquire it: It will surely be used in the wrong places. Even if they avoid the most grotesque error—that of dropping [æ] altogether, and making *hat* and *cat,* for example, almost if not quite

[37] It is true that one finds [a] in both areas, but usually as an allophone of either [æ] or [ɑ]. However, see Chap. 4, footnote 36. Use of [ɑ] rather than [æ] in the South Atlantic states is an "upper class" feature.
[38] H. M. Ayres has pointed out that this distinction still persists in the English of Bermuda: [æ] is the polite, and [ɑ] the low-class pronunciation. See his article "Bermudian English," *American Speech*, Vol. VIII, No. 1 (February 1933), pp. 3-10.
[39] Greenough and Hersey, *op. cit.,* pp. 354-355. But alas for human hopes! In 1932 it evidently seems to the same writers less certain that the broad *a* will "come in"; for, in their revision of this book, now called *Writing Well,* they have reduced this statement to the innocuous (if meaningless) advice: "Care should be taken in pronouncing *have, aunt, laugh, last, past,* and *fast.*" (P. 451.)

identical with *hot* and *cot*—how can they possibly remember that *class, pass,* and *grass* have the [ɑ], but not *mass* and *gas;* that *dance* is different from *askance* and *entrance, example* and *sample* from *lamp* and *amble,* and *plastic* from *plaster?* They may recall that *vast* and *mass* have different vowels, but what will keep them from the all too revealing [væst] [mɑs], instead of the "correct" [vɑst] [mæs]? To put it on the lowest ground, that of expediency, it is an attempt that had better not be made.[40]

Another case in point is what happens with the word *aunt.* Many schoolteachers—perhaps recalling such recommendations as that last cited—try very hard to prevent this word from being pronounced like *ant.* This is a dubious investment of effort, to say the least, since in the natural speech of most Americans the words are homonymous. Nevertheless, the attack on [æ] in *aunt* has led individuals to substitute a vowel farther back, and in striving for an "elegant" [ɑ] they fall into overcorrections: [ɒ] or even [ɔ]. Perhaps they would be wiser to heed Mark Twain's complaint: "When I say *ass* with a broad *a,* I feel like an ass with a flat *a.*"[41]

The other feature in which Eastern New England differs strikingly from the rest of the country is in the sound of historical [ɑ] before *r.* For in the parts of New England where *r* is lost—in such words as *barn, march, farm, hard*—the [ɑ] tends to shift forward to [a], and becomes a distinctive regional feature. This same [ɑ], in many other parts of the country, and regardless whether *r* is lost or retained, tends to shift in the opposite direction, backward and upward to [ɒ] or even [ɔ] (thus in the New York City area, in parts of the Ohio valley and of Texas, and elsewhere); and though these are usually allophonic variations, [ɑ] sometimes appears to fall in with the [ɔ] phoneme. Nevertheless, over the greater part of the United States, [ɑ] is the usual sound in this position.

One feature that differs decidedly as between Britain and America is the development of the "short *o*" of Middle English, found in such

[40] The story of [ɑ] and [æ] is further complicated by the attempt of early nineteenth-century grammarians and lexicographers, in both England and America, to introduce a compromise vowel [a]. It is curious to remember that this was at first advocated as an alternative to a more vulgar [ɑ], if one was not willing to go the whole way and say [æ]. In the later nineteenth century, [a] was advocated in just the other way—as an alternative to a more vulgar [æ], if one was not willing to go the whole way and say [ɑ]!

[41] I owe this to Prof. Miles Hanley.

words as *stop, hot, lock, rob, rod, log, long, cough, bother,* and many
more. The British sound is consistently lip-rounded and short, made
in low-back position: [ɒ], or somewhat higher [ɔ]. The American
sound varies all the way from low-central [ɑ] to lower-mid-back
[ɔ], the former unrounded, the latter rounded and normally longer
than the British sound. Of these variants, obviously, the one that
differs most strikingly from the British is the unrounded sound [ɑ]
—"typically American" to an English ear. Yet (recalling the words
of Krapp) it is nothing but the accomplishment of a tendency that
has existed in the language since at least early Modern English times.
As Wyld has pointed out,[42] Queen Elizabeth herself wrote *stap* for
stop, and Shakespeare rimed *dally* with *folly.* This pronunciation,
then, which was probably common in the sixteenth century, and
which by the seventeenth century had even reached the point of
being fashionable,[43] has since been dropped from standard usage in
England—but not before it had been transplanted to the New World,
where it has flourished mightily.

It varies in the United States (as was just said) from [ɑ] through
[ɒ] to [ɔ]. Such humorous spellings as *dawg, cawfee, Gawd* represent exaggerations of the third variant; the second is the intermediate sound, closest to the British, but not so short. The distribution
of these forms in the United States is not fully known, and appears
to be changing. Furthermore, the variations are to some extent tied
to the phonetic environment of the vowel, yet sometimes they vary
from word to word.[44] In broad summary it may nevertheless be said,
first, that Eastern New England stands apart by having [ɔ] in all
phonetic categories (thereby agreeing with British Standard pronunciation), and second, that the rest of the United States is divided
phonetically and regionally as follows:

1. Before *p, t, k, b, d,* [ɑ] is normal almost everywhere (the chief
exception being the Pittsburgh area);
2. Before *g* or spirants, and in the word *on,* [ɑ] is normal in the

---

[42] *A Short History of English,* p. 162.

[43] See Prof. A. H. Marckwardt's article, "Middle English ŏ in American
English of the Great Lakes Area," *Papers of the Michigan Academy,* Vol.
XXVI, 1940, p. 561.

[44] Prof. Marckwardt has shown that in the Great Lakes area a *rounded* vowel
appears more often in monosyllables than in polysyllables. It is most common
before the voiceless spirants [f], [θ], [s], [tʃ]; fairly common also before [r], [ŋ], [g];
least common before front nasals, voiceless stops, and voiced spirants.

North, [ɔ] in most of the Midland and a large part of the South (but on the other hand the word *dog* has [ɔ] almost everywhere, and *log* has [ɔ] more often than do other words in the group, except *dog*);

3. Before *ng*, [ɔ] is normal almost everywhere (the chief exception being Eastern Virginia).

(The "New England short *o*" mentioned on page 93 is not the same as this, being historically a shortening of Middle English [ɔ:].)

Another feature in which the behavior of individual words cuts across broad geographic patterning is the Middle English [o:], reflected in such words as *roof, coop, room, root, soot*. As we have seen (pages 102-103), the general line of development in Modern English has been from [o:] to [u] to [ʊ] to [ʌ], and various words have taken up positions along this line (e.g., *food, foot, blood*) where they have become stabilized in general usage. Others, however, are still unsettled; considerable variation in them may still be noted. *Coop* and *Cooper* are pretty clearly regional, with [u] Northern and North-Midland, and [ʊ] Southern and South-Midland (British standard being [u]). *Soot* divides somewhat differently: [ʊ] is general and increasing in the North and North-Midland (though [ʌ] is still common among older people), and [ʌ] is general in the South and South-Midland, though [ʊ] is coming in, especially in cultured speech. In all regions, [u] also occurs sporadically. (British standard again agrees with the North in having [ʊ].) It is in certain very common words where the vowel comes before front consonants—as in *room, root,* and *roof*—that the usage is strikingly divided, even within the speech of individuals. About the only generalization that may be made at present is that the more conservative [u] is still the established pronunciation in most of the South, the South-Midland, and the inland North (though the New York City area also favors it); and that the more recent [ʊ] is best established in coastal New England and the Virginia Piedmont. It appears to be on the increase in both Northern and Southern regions; on the other hand, there is evidence of an increase of [u] in metropolitan centers.[45] In British

[45] Thus in *room* the older [u] is still pretty solid in the Midland and the inland North, but [ʊ] has become fully established in Northeastern New England and the Virginia Piedmont, and is coming in generally in the North and the Charleston area. In *root* [u] is the established Southern and Midland pronunciation, [ʊ] the Northern; [u] is found in parts of the North, but [ʊ] never in the South and rarely in the Midland. In *roof* the division is less sharp: [u] is predominant in the South and South-Midland, [ʊ] favored in the

standard, *root* and *roof* have [u]; *room* has had [ʊ], but [u] is reported to be increasing rapidly.[46] Thus British and American tendencies seem here to be at least partially opposed. But the variations
are so complex that it would be rash to predict what will have come
of it all fifty years hence.

Turning from the vowels to the diphthongs, we find in the United
States some striking geographic distributions. The Middle English
[u:], which became diphthongized in such words as *out, house, now,*
probably acquired many variant sounds as the first element of the
diphthong. Reflections of these are to be found today: British standard [aʊ], with which Eastern New England generally agrees, while
the rest of the North has [ɑʊ], and the South and Midland generally
[æʊ]. Interestingly enough, in the focal area of the Virginia Piedmont and the coastal strip of South Carolina and Georgia [ʌʊ] is
still heard before voiceless consonants, but [aʊ] or [æʊ] before
voiced consonants—which agrees with the common usage in Canada.[47]

The diphthong [aɪ] (British standard), as in *cry, fine, ice,* and so
on, predominates in the United States except in the Northern region,
where [ɑɪ] is general; along the Southern coast one may also hear
[ʌɪ] before voiceless consonants, as in *knife* [nʌɪf], but with the
plural [naɪvz]. British standard [ɔɪ] as in *oyster, choice, boy,* is also
the common United States pronunciation, though the second element
tends to be reduced (sometimes almost out of existence) in the South
and South-Midland, while the first element is lengthened. It has been
mentioned more than once that [o] and [e] are generally diphthongized to [oʊ] and [eɪ] in British standard and to some extent in the
United States, chiefly in the East. We may add that these often become "ingliding" diphthongs along the South Carolina and Georgia
coast, [oə] and [eə].

Only one other diphthong need be mentioned: the [ɪu] (now
rather old-fashioned) or [ju] which is very often reduced to [u]
in such words as *new, due, Tuesday.* Words in which the preceding

North. For further details on part of the problem, see R. I. McDavid, Jr.,
"Derivatives of Middle English [oː] in the South Atlantic Area," *Quarterly
Journal of Speech,* Vol. XXXV, part 4 (December 1949), pp. 496-504.

[46] Daniel Jones, *English Pronouncing Dictionary.*

[47] See Guy S. Lowman, Jr., "The Treatment of aʊ in Virginia," *Proceedings
of the Second International Congress of Phonetic Sciences,* Cambridge (Cambridge University Press), 1936, pp. 122-125.

consonant is a labial (or [k] or [h]) give no difficulty: *pew, beauty, music, few, view, cute,* and *huge* are pronounced only with the [ju]. Normally *l* and *r* are followed by the simple vowel, in England as well as in America; *lucid, lure, grew, true,* and *rule* are typical instances. This is probably more generally true, however, in respect to British pronunciation, for *r* than for *l.* But Nicklin[48] observes that ". . . in *lute,* the more careful pronunciation is the rarer, and the majority of speakers confuse the word with *loot.*" To an American, the "more careful" actor's pronunciation of this line in the opening soliloquy of *Richard III:* "Capering to the lascivious lute" sounds decidedly stagey. It may be added that there is no doubt about the [u] when *l* is preceded by another consonant: *blue, clue, flute,* and *glue* are examples. Words of the group in which British and General American usage are sharply divided are those in which the stressed vowel is preceded by *s, z, sh, t, d, th,* or *n.* Even here, however, a further discrimination may be made. After the first three consonants just mentioned, it would appear that [u] is gaining ground, in England as well as in America. To quote Nicklin again (page 29): "Thus, while the stage until quite lately persisted in speaking of *Syew'-zən* (*Susan*), modern English has abandoned the painful attempt and says quite frankly *Soo'-zən.*" For the word *suit,* [sjut] was John Barrymore's pronunciation in:

> Nor customary suits of solemn black,

but it was, to an American ear, decidedly artificial. For these words as a group, American usage almost always favors [u], and British usage may have begun to follow suit.

The real cleavage is in those words in which the stressed vowel follows *t, d, th,* or *n.* Typical words are *stew, tune, tube, due, duke, duty, enthusiasm, thews, new, nude,* and *nuisance.* British usage recognizes only [ju] for all these and similar words. This is also the usual prescription of dictionaries and schools in America, and radio broadcasters are painfully taught it. There can be no doubt, however, that [u] is in far more general use in actual practice in the North and North-Midland, and that it is gaining ground. This is so even in New England, where once [ju] was more prevalent—so very prevalent, indeed, that [ju] lingers on in rural New England even where [u] is the only sound in cultivated speech; *to* and *two,* for

---

[48] *Op. cit.,* p. 29.

example, are sometimes made [tju], and *do, due,* and *dew* given alike the pronunciation [dju]. Only in the South and South-Midland does [ju] remain in general natural use, alike in rude and in polished speech.

The fact that [u] is the usual American pronunciation, and that it is undoubtedly winning wider and wider acceptance in cultivated speech, would seem to be sufficient proof that it cannot be rejected as characteristic only of vulgar speakers. And the fact that a different practice obtains in England surely does not make it necessary for Americans to abandon [u] and studiously cultivate [ju]. Some Americans do, of course—and frequently with as ludicrous results as when they substitute [ɑ] for their native [æ]. If the appeal to individual authority carries more weight with such people than does the force of general (including good) usage, let them consider that W. D. Whitney, perhaps the greatest student of language that America has yet produced, went on record with the observation that in his pronunciation the vowel of *tube, new,* and so forth, was "frankly and unmistakably" identical with that of *food.*

It would be a matter of great interest if we could map the linguistic differences in Britain today as we are beginning to be able to map those of the United States, but unfortunately, linguistic geography has not been taken up in England as vigorously as elsewhere. The great *English Dialect Dictionary* of Joseph and Mary Wright does, it is true, present us with a large collection of facts about local differences, but since the collection is unsystematic, comparison is difficult. Quite apart from the light which would be thrown upon the language of Britain itself by a linguistic atlas, such a study would greatly aid American scholars in connecting transatlantic with cisatlantic features.[49]

With the evidence before us of the main differences between British English and American, it should now be possible to answer our original question—the matter of terminology: whether the term "the American language" is justified. The answer is, clearly, that it is not. One cannot speak of a different language until—as in the case of French and Spanish, for example—forms diverge decidedly in all or

[49] There are hopes for the future. Prof. Harold Orton (University of Leeds) is preparing for a survey in England, and Prof. Angus McIntosh (University of Edinburgh) launched the Dialect Survey of Scotland in 1951 and has published the first monograph: *An Introduction to a Survey of Scottish Dialects,* Edinburgh (Nelson), 1952.

most respects: this is certainly not true of American and British English. Though there are noticeable divergences between the pronunciations of a couple of consonants and half a dozen vowels and diphthongs, all the rest of the sounds are virtually the same. Differences in grammar and in vocabulary, similarly, at the standard level, are not numerous. The farther one gets away from the usage of educated people, of course, the wider becomes the gap—but so it would be even *within* either of the broad national types. Thus while any two speakers, one using standard British and the other using standard American from any of the main regions, will differ in many details, they will have no real trouble in understanding each other. And what of Mencken's title, *The American Language?* Our conclusion must be that, however flattering to national chauvinism,[50] it is not justified linguistically. If it were, one would have to speak equally—or even more—of "the Scottish language" for that type of English spoken north of the Tweed. Mencken, of course, was grinding an ax—and, as has been pointed out, he exaggerated the differences between American and British English (one can hardly believe that it was unwitting) by emphasizing the non-standard parts of the language. The fact is, however, that despite all the very numerous differences of detail that exist, and which Mencken has documented fully in *The American Language* and its two *Supplements,* the similarities are vastly greater in importance.

The Question of Standards. We may now return to our second main question—that of standards. Can there be one type of speech, admittedly pre-eminent, that all speakers of English may strive after? As regards the language of books, the answer has virtually been given already: while there is no single standard for Britain and America, actual variances in spelling and vocabulary are not enough to cause any real difficulty to Englishmen or Americans reading each other's books. Here, in other words, two national standards differ so little that they coexist easily. If spelling were to be reformed, this might bring the two standards even closer to unanimity. And so long as the two nations continue literary contact at the present level, divergences are not likely to increase.

But in the matter of pronunciation, as we have seen, not only are

---

[50] Chauvinism, and its commercial value, would appear to be more important sometimes than linguistic accuracy, if we may judge by the title of the *New World Dictionary of the American Language,* Cleveland, 1953.

there a number of striking disagreements between British and American, but also regional variations within the latter. If any single standard is possible, where is it to be sought? To depend on "the dictionary," as we saw in the preceding chapter, is no solution, since there is no such single work as the phrase implies, and actual dictionaries differ among themselves—as, indeed, they must in some respects if they are to give us an accurate record of facts.

What, then, of the type of pronunciation which is already the "Received Standard" of Britain, and which to many people seems the best contender as a standard for all the English-speaking world? This is conceived of as a peculiarly desirable type of pronunciation used, in its purest form, by educated residents of southern England. Scholars whose pronunciation it is, by birth or by acquisition, write of it (naturally enough) with special enthusiasm. Professor Daniel Jones's definition of it has already been quoted, but may well be repeated here in another and fuller form: "that most usually heard in everyday speech in the families of Southern English persons whose men-folk have been educated at the great public boarding schools." [51] Jones, that is to say, conceives of "Received Standard" as a geographical as well as a class dialect.

Another eminent English phonetician, Professor H. C. Wyld—to whom, indeed, we owe the term "Received Standard"—formulates the idea somewhat differently: ". . . it is not confined to any locality, nor associated in any one's mind with any special geographic area. . . . Received Standard is spoken, within certain social boundaries, with an extraordinary degree of uniformity, all over the country." [52] To Wyld, then, the essence of "Received Standard" is that it is exclusively a class dialect—not, as those who follow Jones believe, a class dialect spoken within a geographically limited territory.

The two definitions cannot of course be wholly reconciled, though Wyld too believes that "perhaps the main factor in this singular degree of uniformity is the custom of sending youths from certain social strata to the great public schools. If we were to say that Re-

---

[51] *Op. cit.* (1924), p. vii. In the 1937 revision the last part is altered to "well educated families of the South of England."

[52] *History of Modern Colloquial English*, p. 2. In the 1934 edition of Jones's *Outline of English Phonetics* and in the 1937 revision of his *Dictionary* he has substituted the phrase "Received Pronunciation" for what was formerly "Standard English Pronunciation."

ceived English at the present day is *Public School English,* we should
not be far wrong." [53] Both definitions have been quoted in order to
indicate two somewhat different (and almost equally authoritative)
English conceptions of what is meant by "Standard English." Yet,
although the term "Received Standard" is Wyld's, Jones's definition
probably comes closer to the truth: that this form of speech is not
only a class dialect, but that it is geographically limited as well—
almost entirely, indeed, to London and what are known as the "Home
Counties." This does not mean that it might not be fitter than some
other types of English to be received as a standard; indeed, its use
by the leaders of what is the mother-country of the language itself,
with its long tradition of literary excellence, makes it the strong contender it is for general acceptance. But against these things must be
set the hard fact that pronunciation elsewhere in the British Isles, in
the colonies and dominions, and in the United States is for the most
part derived independently. Besides—and of far more importance—
dominance in language, as has been noted more than once, is the by-
product of political, social, economic, and intellectual dominance.
Were it possible for London to exert such power it might impose the
"Received Standard" everywhere. But even the other British lands
hold it as an ideal more honored than observed, while the United
States has no compelling reason for desiring it. Thus it is too much
to expect the standard of Southern England to be "received" very
widely outside of its own geographical and social limits. It is far
more likely that existing differences in Australia, Canada, New Zealand, and South Africa, like those in the United States, should become established as regional standards—a natural consequence of
political maturity and self-dependence. Nor would this inevitably
lead to *increasing* divergence, but only to the continued coexistence
of somewhat different forms whose cores, through continued inter-
communication, would remain much the same.

There are some, it is true, who either do not see or who refuse to
admit the facts of the case, and who consequently hold that there
really are *no* differences as between British and American pronunciation—that, in short, "Received Standard" is already accepted
everywhere. One such statement is to be found in Palmer, Martin,
and Blandford's *Dictionary of English Pronunciation with American
Variants.* The authors take Wyld's description of "Received Stand-

[53] *Op. cit.,* p. 3.

ard" and insert, in parentheses, their own running remarks, extending the description as Wyld himself would never have done:

It is not any more the English of London, as it is sometimes mistakenly maintained, than it is of York (or we might add: *New* York), or Exeter, or Cirencester, or Oxford, or Chester, or Leicester (we might add: Harvard, or Chicago, or New Orleans, or San Francisco). In each and all of these places, and in many others throughout the length and breadth of England (we might replace "England" by "the English-speaking world"), Received Standard is spoken among the same kind of people, and it is spoken everywhere, allowing for individual idiosyncrasies, to all intents and purposes, in precisely the same way.[54]

Now this, to put it bluntly, is sheer nonsense. Either these authors are quite ignorant of American pronunciation, or else they look upon any admitted differences as unfortunate strayings, wilful or unwitting. But this is as false historically as it is actually. For as we have seen, the pronunciation of the United States today, insofar as one can generalize about it, has demonstrably far more in common with the speech of Northern England (and the contiguous lowlands of Scotland) than with that of Southern England—and so more than one scholar has observed.[55] The affiliations of "Received Standard" are with a restricted area, that of the Atlantic seaboard, particularly of Eastern New England and the southern coastal cities. The most obvious connecting link between Northern British and general American pronunciation is undoubtedly their common preservation of final and preconsonantal *r;* by contrast, these *r*'s are vocalized or lost in "Received Standard" and in the greater part of Atlantic coast and Southern United States speech. The speech of the Northern Englishman further resembles that of the average American in its use of [æ] or [a] as the vowel of such words as *ask, laugh,* and *class;* the Londoner and the Eastern New Englander alike use [ɑ].[56] In other

---

[54] "Introductory," p. xvii. Reprinted by permission of the D. Appleton-Century Co.

[55] For an illustration of this, see the three versions of the fable "Wind and Sun" as given in the pamphlet "The Principles of the International Phonetic Association," pp. 20-22 (a supplement to *Maître Phonetique,* Sept.–Oct., 1912). These are phonetic transcriptions of Southern British English, Northern British English, and American English pronunciation. The transcriptions are also reproduced in Krapp, *Pronunciation of Standard English in America,* pp. 208-211, and in Ripman, *op. cit.,* pp. 135-138.

[56] On the other hand, Southern British and American English sometimes agree on [æ] where Northern British uses [a] or [ɑ]; this is true, for example, in the transcriptions cited above, for the words *traveler* and *wrapt.*

points of differences[57] between London and Northern English—for example the greater tendency in Southern English to make vowels such as [e] and [o] into diphthongs—it is again clear that the characteristic American pronunciation is considerably nearer to that of the North of England than to that of the metropolis.

These differences are, of course, explained by the history of the settlement of the American colonies, and the subsequent migrations of the population.[58] Yet another very important point is that, so far as the speech of any "class" has been concerned in the establishment of standard types, England has (at least theoretically) received and accepted an upper-class speech, whereas the United States has elevated through education and (mostly unconscious) selection what came to the American colonies as a middle-class speech. Furthermore, at the time of the American Revolution, "Received Standard" was certainly both less influential and less uniform than it is now. Any general influence that this British ideal may have had in America must have been subsequent to the establishment of what has become the main body of American speech.

Educated American speech, then, is historically neither a form of nor a departure from British "Received Standard." This would not make it impossible, even so, for the latter to be received throughout the world—but that such a thing should come to pass is most unlikely. Even within the United States no single standard of pronunciation is now accepted; speakers of the main regions pronounce in their own way, and nobody expects the cultivated Chicagoan to adopt the speech of Charleston, nor the cultivated Charlestonian to imitate Boston or Philadelphia. The differences in no way deter communication; therefore several regional standards coexist comfortably —adding, in fact, a pleasant variety which standardization, if it could be achieved, would only destroy.[59] The same holds true as between the two main poles of pronunciation within the English-speaking world: there is as little likelihood that the Chicagoan would

[57] Many of these are pointed to by R. E. Zachrisson in his paper "Northern English or London English as the Standard Pronunciation," *Anglia*, Vol. XXXVIII (1914), pp. 405-432.

[58] For a condensed treatment, see Kurath, *Word Geography*, pp. 1-7.

[59] A present-day American "standard" for radio announcers—actually an arbitrary compromise—may be seen in such a book as the *NBC Handbook of Pronunciation*, by James F. Bender, New York (Crowell), 1943 and 1951.

want to submit himself to the standard of London as that the Londoner would accept the standard of Chicago.

Time, however, will surely reduce the divergences in English spoken everywhere. In the words of the eminent British lexicographer who was chief editor of the *Dictionary of American English,*

A distinct American language, clearly marked off from other forms of English, in the same way as one Germanic or Romanic language is from another, is less likely to arise than seemed possible a century ago. . . . The new American Language . . . is . . . impossible, for the reason that it can no longer develop by itself, but must keep in touch with that wider English which concerns the world at large.[60]

Indeed, increased communication and easy travel have begun to reduce divergences already. The stationing of thousands of American troops in Britain, Ireland, Australia, and elsewhere during the second World War may have left no great trace behind: American slang words already familiar through the movies may have been given even more currency; and in return American soldiers may have brought back such words and phrases as *scrounge, browned off, you've had it;* these are sufficiently trivial matters. What is vastly more important, though perhaps less tangible, is that the ears of each, British and Americans, became somewhat more accustomed to hearing the sounds spoken by the others—not always sympathetically, it is true; for sometimes the contact merely served to enforce existing prejudice. But there undoubtedly was some movement of rapprochement. Certainly the leaders of the two nations were heard with mutual respect: the British listened with hope to the voice of Franklin Roosevelt—and understood it; the Americans listened with admiration to the voice of Winston Churchill—and understood it.

Not only does radio work as a means toward the rapprochement— nor only in time of war—but also the moving pictures. American productions have been in great popular demand in Britain, even to the embarrassment of the British film industry. But that industry has also sought, with some success, to win a market in America. The commercial necessity of intelligibility in motion pictures has led to a deliberate effort on both sides toward clarity. To mention one small but indicative item, the word *again* is now pronounced [ə'gɛn] rather than [ə'geɪn] in British films: in other words, of the alternatives

[60] Sir William Craigie, *op. cit.,* p. 615.

current in Britain, the one that agrees with American usage is chosen. The fact that American stage speech—which to a lesser degree affects the movies—is partly modeled on British pronunciation helps further. By such compromises as these, the gap is gradually lessened.

Leaving pronunciation, it should be hardly necessary to comment that there is a lively interchange of literary works—a new thing in one respect, since a century ago the direction of flow was almost entirely westward. But in this century American novelists and playwrights have been increasingly attended to in Britain, and though some writers' works have been rather invidiously accompanied with a glossary to explain the Americanisms, this is becoming less necessary today. Certainly the interest is no longer one-sided. And if the acceptance or imposition of a single standard is at present out of the question, and we must content ourselves with the actuality of several coexisting standards, we may at least feel confident that the future is likely to bring not more divergence, but less.

One further point may be raised before we leave the matter of standards. Are we certain that standardization in language, in any absolute sense, can ever be achieved anywhere? Does language, in its nature, permit of such a thing? The question has been well commented on by Lounsbury:

Where exists that perfect standard which all orthoëpists assert or imply that they have furnished, but in the representation of which in numerous particulars no two of them concur?

From what quarter are we to look for the coming of this infallible guide for whose arrival we are all longing? It seems never to have occurred to any of the compilers of dictionaries, and to but few of those who consult them, that the simple solution of the whole difficulty is that in the matter of pronunciation there is no standard of authority at all. Nor, as things are, can there be. Pronunciation must and will vary widely among persons of equal intelligence and cultivation. A dictionary which sets out to establish on a solid base an authoritative standard is bound to take into account the practice of the whole body of educated men the world over who are entitled to consideration. How is that to be ascertained? The mere statement of the fact shows its physical impossibility. It is a task beyond the power of any one person or any number of persons to accomplish.

Even this is not the worst. If everybody worth consulting could be consulted, we should still be left in precisely the same state of uncertainty as before. . . .

Still this belief in the existence of a standard authority is one that will die hard even with the educated class. With the semi-educated class it will never die at all. . . .[61]

In short, the desire for the absolute authority exists and perennially keeps alive the hope that one may be found or established—but it is a futile hope, for language is far too fluid a thing to be cabined, cribbed, confined into any fixed or absolute form.

If one had to choose between the two opposite conceptions—a standard of pronunciation that is extremely limited, and no standard at all—the second would probably have more to commend it. Nevertheless, many feel that there is such a thing as a standard of pronunciation based upon good usage, yet elastic enough to allow for sectional and even individual variations. Further, such a standard cannot be one and the same for all purposes: good usage varies with the more or less formal character of the occasion. Thus it is just as inappropriate to be too formal on some occasions as to be too informal on others. A greater number of "relaxed" pronunciations and of elisions and syncopations will naturally be admitted into ordinary conversation than would be appropriate for platform speech. Yet good usage is perfectly possible in familiar situations: herein lies the error of those who make the word "colloquial" a label of automatic condemnation. The "colloquial" word or the "colloquial" pronunciation of the word is quite as much in place in informal conversation of the educated—"the language of well-bred ease" it has been called —as the "formal" word or the "formal" pronunciation would be out of place. Standard pronunciation—whatever the occasion—is determined by the practice of good speakers, of cultivated people, all over the English-speaking world; by and large, these are the people who hold positions of leadership in their various nations and regions, and what they as a group do—and the kind of language they use—determines the standard. In this sense, "standard" is evidently not equivalent to "uniform," for clearly enough it must include divergences not only as between British and American usage, but regional ones within the United States, and those of Canada, Australia, New Zealand, South Africa, and so on.

How then is the individual to determine what is prescribed as the pronunciation for individual words and phrases by this somewhat elastic international standard? In the last analysis, the method must

[61] *The Standard of Pronunciation in English*, pp. 212-216. Reprinted by permission of Harper and Brothers.

be the individual's own observation of what constitutes good practice in his section of the English-speaking world. Clearly it will not do to restrict the application of "section" very narrowly: *sectional* must not be identified with *local*. The danger in that direction is that the sectional become the parochial or the provincial. Yet even this danger is to be preferred to that threatened by the opposite course, that of accepting a rigid and uniform and (from the general American point of view) alien standard. Here lies the way to artificiality, to affectation, and to pedantry.

One word more, to qualify and also to safeguard the position just set forth. Because the observation of the individual is necessarily circumscribed, he should avail himself of whatever help is afforded by reputable dictionaries and handbooks of usage. Only, as we have insisted perhaps to weariness, he should do this always with a full realization that the usefulness and the reliability of such guidance is limited. Direct observation of the spoken tongue as employed in good practice must ever be paramount. To supplement this observation is the proper function of the guides we have mentioned. If this version of good pronunciation and the method of arriving at it has any validity, it follows that the grossest possible error is to reverse the positions of the primary sanction and its supplement. A pronunciation is not "correct" because it may be found in a dictionary; rather, it may (or should) be found in a dictionary because good usage has already determined that it is "correct."

World English? If the English language in the past century or so has entered a new phase of growth to suit it to the rapidly developing democratic-industrial society of today, a phase in which it necessarily breaks free of the eighteenth century's static ideals, and gradually becomes adapted to the needs of a more dynamic age, we must realize that it does not throw over all tradition or historical continuity—indeed, with language that would be suicidal. The chief patterns of the language, in its modern stage, remain firm: what proves good in past usage, and what proves good of new acquisition, continues. Just as the stylists of the Restoration laid aside the Latinized brocade, splendid as it was, of Sir Thomas Browne, and put on the plain English broadcloth of Defoe and Dryden, so the writer of today weaves a new fabric of his own, experimenting in many types. The prose of today (if any generalization can be made about so various a thing) is less formal, more rapid and practical; it travels light, throwing off the weight of convention, decoration, or structural complexity. At its worst this makes it seem harried, mean, flaccid, or flat; but at its best it can be pungent, sinewy, clear, and direct. Mass-produced it is like any other such product—less finely wrought, but achieving an art of its own, reaching a larger number of minds, and supporting a larger number of artisans than has been possible in former ages. Mass-production, in its early stages, scorns art—but once established, it returns to art. This explains why it can be said with some measure of truth that more people are using the language better today than ever before. It is also true, no doubt, that there is a larger audience for cheap, inartistic, stupid, and vulgar uses of language than ever before. The Elizabethan broadsides and chapbooks have their innumerable, and equally ephemeral, modern counterparts. If language is mechanized, like everything else it is dehumanized and dies; but the forces of renewal are perpetually at work, and whatever is really vital survives. The English language is changing and will change still, but it is in no serious danger of decay.

Meantime, as we have remarked before, one of the most important considerations for the future of the language is that English, in the past three centuries, has spread all over the world. Its use as an international language is constantly increasing. That some general medium of expression is really to be desired we have the experience of history to testify. In the Middle Ages, Latin occupied this position, and in modern times French has approximated it, especially as the language of international diplomatic relations. Is English, possibly, in line for the succession? Before examining the claims of English as a world auxiliary language, however, we must first consider whether a natural language or an artificial one—such as Esperanto—holds out the best hope of effective use and general acceptance.

The ideal of an artificial speech, scientifically constructed so as to combine the merits of some of the leading naturally developed languages and at the same time embody none of their defects, is by no means a new thing. Some of the projected artificial languages do not, it is true, fulfil the first of these conditions; that is, they are based not on one or more existing languages, but are purely a priori schemes. None of these, however, is seriously advocated at present;

it is quite generally recognized that a universal language must be founded on one or more of the vernaculars of the world. To go into the many variations of the project[62]—such as Volapük, Ido, "Latino sine flexione," Novial—would take us too far afield. A few words must nevertheless be said about Esperanto, the claimant favored by the majority of the advocates of a universal language.

Esperanto has Latin, as the most nearly international and neutral of elements, as the chief basis of its vocabulary; its grammar is exceedingly simple and its spelling is phonetic. That it has won a real, though necessarily limited, measure of successful adoption, is indicated by the support given it after the first World War by the League of Nations, the International Telegraphic Union (1925), and the Union Internationale de Radiophonie (1927).[63] The second World War, of course, set the movement back considerably, and the United Nations has been less hospitable to Esperanto than was the League: it has five official languages—English and French as "working languages" and in addition Chinese, Russian, and Spanish. The Esperantists have resumed activity, however, as witness their thirty-fifth annual conference, which met in Paris in 1950, with 2500 delegates from 34 countries. Nevertheless, they can lay claim to only one and a half million people who use Esperanto daily, which is less than the number who speak even a minor natural language, and is utterly dwarfed by the daily users of any major one. No more than five thousand daily users are claimed for the United States—yet a dozen natural foreign languages are spoken by more people than that in the United States. Thus even the most successful of the artificial languages, after more than sixty years of existence, has achieved very little actual acceptance, and not even the acceptance of all who favor an artificial auxiliary language.

Furthermore, the arguments that have been urged against Esperanto in the past[64] are still valid. The uniformity claimed for it all over the world is partly vitiated by its different pronunciation in various countries. And while its grammatical system is simple by European standards, it is still very difficult for speakers of non-

---

[62] Cf. particularly L. Couturat and L. Leau, *Histoire de la langue universelle,* Paris (Hachette), 1903, and Jespersen, *An International Language.*

[63] *Encyclopaedia Britannica,* article *s.v.* "Universal Language" (14th ed., Vol. 22, p. 861).

[64] Those, for example, of Krapp, *Modern English,* New York (Scribner), 1909, pp. 40-43.

European languages. A recent Esperantist publication[65] makes much of the international misunderstandings that have resulted through mistranslation from one natural language to another (French, English, Russian). The implication is that the use of Esperanto would remove all such difficulties. But of course this is quite without foundation, since the various languages would themselves have to be translated into Esperanto words, and the possibilities for misunderstanding would be just as great.

If, then, the project of an artificially constructed universal language has so far met with only a very limited measure of success, what claims may be advanced for English as an international language? It seems more and more certain that if any living speech attains this position, it will be English.[66] In our own day, English has come to rival French in the field of diplomacy, and since the second World War, has virtually replaced French as the "second" language —the language most useful for the traveler—all over Europe.[67] In other parts of the world, its prestige and usefulness are still more commanding. Though India gained independence in 1950 and might have been expected to set up one of its native languages as a national standard, the rivalry existing among them, combined with the fact that English was already known everywhere among educated people, has led to the retention of English. As someone has said, the Indians, in coming together to throw off the British yoke, found it necessary to communicate with each other in the language of the British.

Beach-la-Mar or Sandalwood-English, spoken and understood all over the Western Pacific, and Pidgin-English, known in China and to some extent in Japan and in California, are the most conspicuous examples of corrupt forms of English that have been evolved from

[65] Compiled by G. A. and D. T. Connor, W. Solzbacher, and J. B. S-T. Kao, *Esperanto, The World Interlanguage,* New York (Beechhurst), 1948. See especially pp. 4-5.

[66] A middle position between those who support the claims of an artificial language like Esperanto and those who support the claims of English is taken by those who advocate the artificially simplified form of English known as "Basic English." See C. K. Ogden, *Basic English,* London (Kegan Paul), 1930, and *The System of Basic English,* New York (Harcourt, Brace), 1934. For some discussion see Chad Walsh, "The Verb System of Basic English," *American Speech,* Vol. XVII, No. 3 (Oct. 1942), pp. 137-143, and the reply in the following issue by I. A. Richards.

[67] It is now the first foreign language taught in the schools in France, Holland, Norway, and other countries.

the contact with exotic tongues[68] and spread over large areas. It is said, incidentally, that the American share in these trade languages is becoming larger than the British.[69] But it is not, of course, merely in such corrupt jargons that Modern English has gained a world-wide ascendancy; in its more standard British and American forms, it is, especially since the first World War, more and more dominating the civilized, and a large part of the uncivilized, world.

This leadership among the languages of the world has been achieved well within the Modern English period. In the Renaissance, and probably as late as the period of the Restoration, the speakers of English were fewer than the speakers of at least four other European languages—German, French, Spanish, and Italian. Even in the eighteenth century, English was still, for a time, outdistanced in numbers of speakers by four other European languages, since, if Italian had been left behind, a new rival, Russian, had asserted itself. In the nineteenth century, however, English came rapidly to the front, largely as a result of the swift increase in the population of the United States and of the British colonies. Probably by the middle of the century it had outdistanced its competitors. Estimates, in millions of speakers, made at several times since then, are as follows:[70]

	English	German	Russian	French	Spanish
1868	60	52	45	45	40
1890	111	75+	75	51+	42+
1900	116(123)	75(80)	70(85)	45(52)	44(58)
1912	150	90	106	47	52
1921	170	87½	120½	45	65
1936	191	85	90	—	100
1952	225	—	180	—	110

[68] For a description of these and similar jargons, see the section "Pidgin and Congeners" in Jespersen's *Language* (pp. 216-236). *Pidgin,* as Jespersen explains, is derived from the Chinese distortion of *business.*

[69] Cf. Mencken, *op. cit.,* p. 597. He also quotes (p. 598) a striking testimony to the use of English as a world language in the account of an English traveler who observed Chinese mandarins speaking English not only in conversation with German ship's officers and Japanese travelers but even with one another. Since they came from various provinces of China, they found English a more convenient medium than their less standardized native tongues.

[70] The following sources have been used: for 1868 and 1900, the figures quoted by Mencken, *op. cit.,* 3rd ed., pp. 383-384; for 1936, his 4th ed., pp. 592-593; for 1900 (minimum and maximum) and 1912, those quoted by Jespersen, *Growth and Structure,* p. 252; for 1921 the estimate of L. Tesnier in Meillet, *Langues,* as quoted by Bloomfield, *Language,* p. 44; for 1952, Werner, *op. cit.,* p. 16.

The figures, necessarily only approximations, have at least the merit of coming from a number of different sources and representing various points of view. Their testimony to the recent and rapid increase in the number of those speaking English is perhaps for this very reason the more impressive. It is evident, of course, that they do not tell the whole story as to the languages of the world; but China's 450 millions speak dialects that are mutually unintelligible[71] and that, besides, scarcely spread beyond her borders; and a similar situation holds for those who speak cognate varieties of Indic—the Indo-European languages of India—perhaps 325 millions. Clearly, any rivalry for the position of a world language must come from the tongues of Europe; and the figures that have been quoted are a striking evidence of the way in which English has outdistanced its European competitors. In numbers of native speakers, English is rivalled only by North Chinese; in numbers of native *and foreign* speakers, it is quite unrivalled by any language in the world. The fact that English has gained the ascendancy is not to be disputed. There may be difference of opinion, however, as to *why* it has done so.

The reason for the spread of English is probably quite unconnected with the language as such, or with any intrinsic virtues over other languages which it may be thought to have: England's rise as a world power, beginning in the days of Elizabeth, is accompanied, step by step, by the ascendancy of English as a world language. The political union of England and Scotland under James I in 1603, followed by the formation of the United Kingdom of Great Britain and Ireland, helped to make it certain that English would be used, and in a form substantially the same, throughout the islands and in the newly founded Colonies. In the New World, the fall of New Amsterdam in 1664 and that of Quebec in 1759 assured the triumph of English over two important rivals, Dutch and French; and the expansion of the United States brought it about that Spanish, the only remaining competitor of English on the North American continent, was reduced to a decidedly subordinate position. In the latter half of the eighteenth century and throughout the nineteenth century, the English language was established in every corner of the earth through conquest, colonization, and the commercial ascendancy of

[71] Though one of them, North Chinese, in all probability has more native speakers than even English, and another, Cantonese, is not very far behind.

the English-speaking peoples. It may even be conjectured, as Krapp suggests,[72] that the tenacity with which the British and the Americans hold to their own language and their own ways has been a real factor in spreading the English language; for if the English-speaking people would not learn a foreign language, it is evident that foreigners, to trade with them, had to learn English. The contrast has been observed, for example, in the far greater readiness of the Germans, as compared both with the English and with the Americans, to learn the Spanish language and adapt themselves to Latin ways, when engaged in commerce with South America. Doubtless, the more complacent Anglo-Saxon attitude is bad for trade, when better linguists, like the Germans, are competitors; but, just as evidently, it has proved in the past to be an appreciable factor in the world-wide use of English.

Having, by the middle-nineteenth century, won first place among the languages of the world, English has been favored by more recent developments so that its primacy is less and less questioned. Inventions that make communication between nations easier have inevitably lent themselves to the spread of English. So we may regard the telephone, the telegraph, the radio, the movies, and no doubt, once its range is increased, television. Here too, it may be said, it is often the American brand of English that is spread abroad, frequently to the chagrin of the British. The second World War, particularly, took great numbers of Americans into places where they had never been before; and airplane travel takes tourists, businessmen, and many others in increasing numbers almost everywhere. The fact that since the close of the war only Americans have been in the economic position to travel much beyond their national borders has made English even more the language that goes abroad.

But what of the intrinsic merits of English? Is it on the whole well- or ill-fitted for the role of auxiliary world speech? Has it not spread, in part, because it is a better language than its competitors? This is a dangerous question! In the first place, linguists nowadays are agreed that there is no real evidence to prove any one language better than any other *as a language*. That is, though languages compared will certainly be found to differ in structure and resource, the "advantages" of one sort in any language will generally be offset

[72] *Modern English*, p. 39.

by its "disadvantages" of another sort. The structure of "primitive" languages is no less complex, and no different in potentiality, than that of "cultivated" languages. To make value-judgments about them, therefore, is not a matter for the linguist. But the greatest danger in such questions comes from the fact that our emotions are so deeply and secretly involved with our native language that it is almost impossible to be objective. The best medicine, in such a case, is to read Edward Sapir's excellent tenth chapter of *Language*, "Language, Race, and Culture."

Once alert to the dangers of subjectivity, however, we may note with some interest what has been said about the values of English by competent observers. One foreign scholar who has studied English and other languages intensively, and who can more dispassionately assess merits and shortcomings, Otto Jespersen, has written, "The English language is a methodical, energetic, businesslike, and sober language";[73] and again (with particular reference to its increasing use as a world language),[74] "It must be a source of gratification to mankind that the tongue spoken by two of the greatest powers of the world is so noble, so rich, so pliant, so expressive and so interesting. . . ." In still another place, he states his view of English as compared with other languages in these terms: ". . . it seems to me positively and expressly *masculine*, it is the language of a grown-up man and has very little childish or feminine about it." [75]

The foregoing terms represent, with entire adequacy, the usual favorable view of Modern English. It is most frequently praised for its businesslike simplicity—in sound-system, in grammar, and in at least the more frequently used core of its vocabulary. This simplicity, it is commonly thought, makes it easy for a foreigner to learn, and hence makes it particularly adaptable for use as a world tongue. To modify this judgment, however, we have such an admission as the following, from the pen of an enthusiastic defender of this very quality of simplicity: "The foreigner essaying it, indeed, finds his chief difficulty, not in mastering its forms, but in grasping its lack of forms." [76] More subtly, and from a different angle, the apparent simplicity of English has been declared to be a delusion and a snare:

---

[73] *Growth and Structure,* p. 17.
[74] *Ibid.,* p. 252.
[75] *Ibid.,* p. 2.
[76] Mencken, *op. cit.,* 3rd ed., p. 387.

The fact that a beginner in English has not many paradigms to learn gives him a feeling of absence of difficulty, but he soon learns to his cost that this is only a feeling. . . . The simplicity of English in its formal aspect is . . . really a pseudo-simplicity or a masked complexity. . . . He [the foreigner] may well feel that the apparent simplicity of English is purchased at the price of a bewildering obscurity.[77]

Granting that there is some truth in these strictures and that the superficial impression of simplicity that English gives is somewhat ambiguous, one may still feel that its forms, its words, and its sounds compare favorably, in the ease with which at least approximate mastery of them can be attained, with those of other languages. Its vocabulary has the enormous advantage of being compounded almost equally of Germanic and Romanic elements, so that a good part of it is already familiar to the speakers of many other European languages. Its morphology is so inconsiderable that the language has been called "the grammarless tongue"—which is, of course, inaccurate, since what it lacks in morphological complexity is fully counterbalanced by syntactical complexity; yet the phrase does emphasize its simplicity in one respect. In inflections and word order, as we have seen, the modern speech has greatly simplified and regularized the practices of Old English. (On the other hand, it has acquired a complex array of phrase-groupings, using function-words, which are no less difficult than the inflections of Old English.)

The greatest stumbling-block in the way of the foreigner who would acquire English is, as will be granted on all sides, the spelling —"that pseudo-historical and anti-educational abomination."[78] On the subject of English as a world speech it is perhaps worth recalling that long ago the great German linguist Jacob Grimm congratulated other Europeans that the English had not yet discovered that only one thing prevented the universality of English from being completely apparent: its "whimsical, antiquated orthography." Today, with the English language perceptibly nearer the indicated goal, the same handicap remains. If it could be removed, or at least reduced,

---

[77] Edward Sapir, "Wanted: A World Language," *American Mercury,* Vol. XXII, No. 86 (February 1931), pp. 202-209. Reprinted by permission of author and publisher. These excerpts cannot do justice to the keenness of the writer's analysis of the deficiencies of English as an international language. Sapir presents this point of view also in his contribution to *International Communication,* a symposium by H. N. Shenton, Sapir, and Jespersen, London (Paul, Trench, Trubner), 1931.

[78] Jespersen. *Growth and Structure,* p. 250.

that might bring English still nearer to acceptability as a world language. Even with this handicap, English can perhaps qualify on its merits—insofar as these can be judged. But it is worth remarking that the point will be decided in the future, however it goes, not on linguistic grounds, but on grounds of the continued rise in world influence—or the fall—of those whose language is now English.

REFERENCES FOR FURTHER READING

The histories of the English language referred to on page 34 and page 51, the books by Jones, Wyld, Kruisinga, and Jespersen listed on pages 86 and 108, and, in addition:

Barrows, Sarah T., and Hall, Alta B., *An American Phonetic Reader*, Boston (Expression), 1936.

Burbank, John, *What Is Standard English Speech?* Tokyo (Shijo Shobo), 1934.

Grandgent, C. H., *Old and New*, Cambridge, Mass. (Harvard), 1920, including "Fashion and the Broad A" (pp. 25-30), "The Dog's Letter" (pp. 31-56), and "New England Pronunciation" (pp. 121-149).

Grant, William, *The Pronunciation of English in Scotland*, Cambridge, Eng. (Cambridge University), 1913.

Guérard, A. L., *Short History of the International Language Movement*, New York (Liveright), 1921.

Jespersen, Otto, *An International Language*, New York (Norton), 1929.

Kenyon, J. S., and Knott, T. A., *A Pronouncing Dictionary of American English*, Springfield (Merriam), 1948.

Krapp, G. P., *Pronunciation of Standard English in America*, New York (Oxford), 1919.

Kurath, H., "American Pronunciation," Society for Pure English, Tract No. XXX, London (Oxford), 1928.

Lloyd, R. J., *Northern English*, Leipsig (Teubner), 2nd ed., 1908.

Lounsbury, T. R., *The Standard of Pronunciation in English*, New York (Harper's), 1904.

Moore, J. L., *Tudor-Stuart Views of the Growth, Status, and Destiny of the English Language*, Halle (Niemeyer), 1910.

Nicklin, T., *Standard English Pronunciation*, London (Oxford), 1925.

Palmer, H. E., Martin, J. Victor, and Blandford, F. G., *A Dictionary of English Pronunciation with American Variants*, Cambridge, Eng. (Heffer), rev. ed., 1935.

Pyles, Thomas, *Words and Ways of American English*, New York (Random House), 1952.

Shenton, Herbert, *Cosmopolitan Conversation: The Language Problems of International Conferences*, New York (Columbia University), 1933.

Shenton, Herbert N., Sapir, Edward, Jespersen, Otto, *International Communication: A Symposium on the Language Problem*, London (Kegan Paul), 1931.

Society for Pure English, Tract No. XXXIV, London (Oxford), 1930, containing "Interlanguage," by T. C. Macaulay, and "Artificial Languages," by J. A. Smith.

Thomas, C. K., "Pronunciation in Upstate New York," *American Speech*, April, 1935–April, 1937.

——, *An Introduction to the Phonetics of American English*, New York (Ronald), 1947.

Tucker, Gilbert M., *American English*, New York (Knopf), 1921.

Phonetic Symbols, with Key Words

(as in Northern American pronunciation, except where
otherwise indicated)

Vowels

[i] *bead, feet*
[ɪ] *bid, fit*
[e] *bait, fade*
[ɛ] *bed, bet*
[æ] *bad, fat*
[ə] *about, villa*
[ɚ] *forgive, giver*
[ɝ] *bird, hurt*
[ɜ] New England
     bird, hurt
[ʌ] *but, bud*
[a] Scotch *man*
[u] *boot, food*
[ʊ] *book, foot*
[o] *boat, note*
[ɔ] *autumn, law*
[ɑ] *father, fodder*

Diphthongs

[ɑɪ] *bide, buy*
[ɑʊ] *loud, lout*
[ɔɪ] *boil, boy*
[ju] *muse, feud*

Voiced-Voiceless Pairs of Consonants

[b] *bad, cub*
[v] *vast, prove*
[ð] *thy, either*
[d] *dug, sad*
[z] *zest, is*
[ʒ] *azure, measure*
[dʒ] *jam, edge*
[g] *game, rag*

[p] *pad, cup*
[f] *fast, proof*
[θ] *thigh, ether*
[t] *tug, sat*
[s] *sit, nets*
[ʃ] *shoot, hush*
[tʃ] *chair, rich*
[k] *came, rack*

Other Consonants

[m] *mist, chasm*
[n] *noon, rotten*
[ŋ] *sing, song*
[l] *look, battle*
[r] *road, throw*
[j] *ye, ewe*
[w] *witch, weather*
[ʍ] *which, whether*
[h] *high, who*

The symbols [ə, ɚ] are used only in unstressed syllables.
"   "   [ɜ, ɝ, ʌ] "   "   "   " stressed   "   .

419

Glossary of Linguistic Terms

NOTE: Certain terms, particularly those that are specifically defined in the body of the book (on the page on which the term is first used), are not listed here and should be sought in the Index.

Ablaut. Series of variations of the radical vowel, in the different forms of a group of related words.

Acronym. A word formed from the initial letters or syllables of the words in a phrase.

Affix. Additional sound or group of sounds that, when added to the radical element, changes the meaning of the word or makes a new word. See *Infix, Prefix, Suffix.*

Affricate. A combination of stop and homorganic fricative, especially [tʃ] and [dʒ].

Agglutination. Process of adding affixes to the roots of words, with the result of changing their meaning or use. (*See* p. 24.)

Allophone. Any member of the class of sounds constituting a phoneme.

Alveolar. Speech sound articulated with the point or blade of the tongue in contact with the upper gums.

Analogy. The influence exerted by certain formations that have come to be regarded as normal and typical and hence are used as a pattern—a tendency making for standardization and uniformity.

Analysis. The tendency in certain languages to make the simple root-form the unit of expression, with the result that ideas are conveyed by relatively many, but by short and unvaried words; the trend opposite to synthesis.

Aspirate. The puff of air, represented phonetically by [h], that distinguishes, for example, *hall* from *all* and *high* from *I.*

Assimilation. The phonetic process by which a sound is changed to conform to a neighboring sound.

Back (of the tongue). The rear part of the tongue, that opposite the velum when the tongue is in the position of rest.

Back-formation. A new word formed, by a mistaken assumption, from a previously existing word which is taken to be its derivative. (*See* pp. 202-204.)

Bilabial. The type of consonant in the formation of which both lips are active.

420

Blade. The part of the tongue that includes the point and the region immediately behind it; that part which is opposite the front gums when the tongue is in the position of rest.

Breath. Sound produced by the breath stream passing through the open glottis—that is, without the vibration of the vocal cords.

Close vowel. A vowel made with a relatively small opening of the mouth— i.e., made with part of the tongue in proximity to the hard palate or to the velum.

Closed syllable. A syllable ending in a consonant.

Cognate. A word related to another by being descended from the same original or root; also used of languages having common ancestry.

Colloquialism. An expression characteristic of and appropriate to the informal, spoken language rather than the formal, literary language.

Composition. The process of forming a compound.

Compound. A combination of two words, or of a word and an affix, that constitutes a new word.

Conjugation. The inflection of a verb; or a class of verbs (e.g., *strong* or *weak*) having the same type of inflection.

Consonant. A sound characterized by contact or narrowing of parts of the resonance chamber.

Declension. The inflection of a noun, adjective, or pronoun; or a class of nouns, and so forth, having the same type of inflection.

Dental. A consonant articulated with the tongue in contact with the upper teeth; in a looser sense, the term is sometimes applied to alveolars like [t] and [s] as well as to true dentals (or pre-dentals) like [θ].

Derivation. The formation of a new word by an addition to the radical element or by a change in this element.

Derivative. A word developed from an older or primary form.

Devoicing. The change of a voiced into a voiceless sound.

Diachronic. Going through time: the historical method of studying language not at one point of time only. See *Synchronic.*

Dialect. The local or sectional form of a language, often as compared with a standard or literary form.

Digraph. A combination of two letters—e.g., *th*—that represents only one sound.

Diphthong. A continuously gliding vowel sound, which begins with one position and ends with another within one syllable.

Dissimilation. The phonetic process by which two neighboring sounds that were once identical are made unlike.

Doublet. One of a pair of words, in a single language, differently derived from the same origin. (*See* pp. 148, 156.)

Dual. A third number, in addition to singular and plural, that in some languages is given separate forms in various parts of speech.

Echoism. Formation of a word by imitating a sound made in nature. Same as *Onomatopoeia.*

Etymology. The branch of linguistics that deals with the origin or derivation of words. \ᔕᑫ\,

Explosive. A consonant articulated with a puff of air after closure or stoppage.

Flection (or *Flexion*). Same as *Inflection.*

Folk etymology. The process by which an unfamiliar (usually foreign) word or phrase is changed in popular use to give it a more familiar or meaningful form.

Fricative. A consonant produced by air forced through a narrowed passage.

Front (of tongue). The part of the tongue opposite the hard palate when the tongue is in the position of rest.

Fronting. Change in vowel or consonant that involves a position farther front in the mouth.

Germanic. One of the branches of Indo-European; in this sense, synonymous with *Teutonic.*

Glide. A transition sound that leads up to, or away from, a definite speech sound.

Glottis. The opening between the vocal cords.

Gradation. Same as *Ablaut.*

Guttural. A back consonant, preferably called *Velar.*

High vowel. Same as *Close vowel.*

Homonym. A word that is phonetically identical, or virtually so, with another word of different meaning.

Homophone. A word, or part of a word, that duplicates in sound another word, or part of a word.

Hyperurbanism. A language error resulting from an attempt to be urbane that goes too far. Same as *Overcorrection.*

Ideogram. A pre-alphabetical symbol, originally pictorial, that represents the meaning rather than the sounds.

Idiom. A syntactical pattern peculiar to a certain language and hence often untranslatable, in literal equivalents, into another.

Incorporation. The process of joining derivative elements to the radical of a word, with the result that the several parts of a sentence are virtually fused into a single word.

Infix. An affix inserted within a word.

Instrumental. A declensional case, the distinctive endings of which are partly preserved in Old English, that expresses such concepts as agency or means.

Intervocalic. Said of a consonant between voiced sounds: e.g., the *d* of *medial.*

Isogloss. In linguistic geography, the line showing the farthest extent of the area in which a linguistic feature is used.

Isolating language. A language that consists of invariable and usually monosyllabic roots, and in which therefore the relation of the words in a sentence depends more upon position than upon form.

Labial. A consonant in the formation of which the lips are active.

Labio-dental. A lip-tooth consonant; one articulated with the lips, or one lip, in contact with the teeth.

Larynx. The voice-box, or enlargement of the upper end of the windpipe, that contains the vocal cords.

Lateral. A consonant in the formation of which the current of air is divided or diverted by the tongue in contact with the palate or gums.

Lax vowel. A vowel articulated with relatively little tension in the tongue and associated muscles.

Liquid. A vowel-like consonant, especially the lateral and trilled or rolled sounds, but sometimes including all the semi-vowels.

Low vowel. Same as *Open vowel.*

Medial. Position within a word, as distinguished from initial and final.

Meliorative change. Same as *Elevation of meaning.* (*See* Index.)

Metaphor. A figure of speech in which a word suggests or symbolizes an idea by the use of comparison or analogy, rather than by directly or literally stating the idea.

Metonymy. A figure of speech in which an object or idea is named by something frequently associated with it.

Monophthong. A vowel that is pronounced without change of position and, hence, that remains constant in quality throughout its articulation.

Morpheme. A simple linguistic form which differs phonetically or semantically (or both) from all others in the language, and is therefore a minimal formal unit. Examples: *bear, bare, pre-, -er.*

Morphology. The department of linguistic study that deals with forms, especially inflections and derivational forms.

Mutation. Same as *Umlaut.*

Mute. Said of a "silent" letter, one that does not represent a sound; also formerly used to designate what are now preferably called the stop consonants.

Nasal. A sound in the production of which the nasal passages are open; the nasal consonants are [m, n, ŋ].

Nasalization. A modification of the quality of a vowel brought about by using the nasal passage as a resonator.

Neologism. A newly coined word not yet a part of the recognized vocabulary.

Neutral. Said of an unstressed vowel of colorless quality, especially [ə].

Oblique. Any case-form other than the nominative or subject-form is said to be an oblique case.

Onomatopoeia. The naming of a thing or action by an attempted reproduction of the sound associated with it. (*See* pp. 6, 186.) Same as *Echoism.*

Open syllable. A syllable ending in a vowel.

Open vowel. A low vowel, that type made with the tongue depressed and the jaws relatively wide.

Orthography. That phase of linguistic study which treats of spelling.

Overcorrection. An incorrect pronunciation or grammatical usage that results from trying too hard to be correct.

Palatal. A sound in which the tongue arches toward the hard palate; the term is sometimes applied to the blade as well as the front consonants.

Palatalization. The approach or approximation to a blade sound; for example, the shift from [k] to [tʃ] in O.E. *cirice*, Mn.E. *church*.

Pejorative change. Same as *Degradation of meaning.* (*See* Index.)

Person. One of three relationships—called respectively first, second, and third—that represent the speaker, the one addressed, and the person or thing spoken of; or one of the pronominal or verbal forms that indicate these relationships.

Personification. The metaphorical attribution of human qualities to animals or things.

Pharynx. The part of the alimentary canal between the oral cavity and the esophagus.

Philology. The study of thought and culture as embodied in literary monuments; in a narrower sense, the study of language (but for this sense, the term linguistics is now preferred).

Phoneme. The minimal significant structural unit in the sound-system of any language. It is therefore not a single sound but a *class* of sounds (called *allophones*) which do not appear in structurally contrasting positions, and whose differences from each other within the class (usually due to phonetic environment) do not alter the meaning of the word in which they may appear.

Phonetics. The department of linguistics that deals with the sounds of speech.

Phonogram. A symbol that represents a sound or a group of sounds.

Phonology. The study of speech sounds; but the term is often differentiated from *phonetics* by applying it only to the sound system of a particular language, dialect, or period.

Pictogram. Same as *Ideogram.*

Pitch. Difference in musical sound that is brought about by varying the frequency of the vibrations producing it.

Plosive. See *Explosive.*

Point. The tip of the tongue; a *point-consonant* is one in the production of which the tongue-tip is in contact with the upper teeth, the gums, or the hard palate.

Popular etymology. Same as *Folk etymology.*

Pre-dental. See *Dental.*

Prefix. An affix placed before the radical element in a word.

Preterit-present. The type of verb that is a preterit in form (and older use) but is now functionally a present. (*See* pp. 140-141.)

Quantity. Length or duration of sounds.

Raising. That type of phonetic change in which the tongue assumes a higher position.

Reduplication. The process by which one of the sounds in a word is repeated as part of an additional syllable.

Referent. A term used in semantics to designate the object or situation, in the real world, for which the word serves as label

Resonance. The vibrating quality of a voice sound.

Resonance chamber. A general term for the cavity of the mouth and the nose.

Retroflex r. The type of *r* made with the tongue tip raised and bent back.

Rhotacism. The tendency to change *s(z)* to *r*.

Root. The central part or basic element of a word, and the unit common to all cognate words in related languages.

Rounded sounds. Sounds articulated with rounding of the lips; the term applied to such vowels as [u], [o], and [ɔ] and to the consonants [w] and [ʍ].

Runes. Characters of the alphabet used by the Teutonic peoples from about the third century A.D. (*See* p. 89.)

Sandhi. A phonetic modification that many words assume in familiar syntactic patterns; thus the articles *a* and *the* are usually given the sandhi-forms [ə] and [ðə] rather than the absolute forms [e] and [ði].

Semantics. That branch of linguistics that deals with the theory of meaning and with the growth and change that the meanings of words undergo; these two divisions of the field have been called "static" and "dynamic" semantics.

Semasiology. Same as *Semantics*.

Semi-vowel. A term sometimes applied to the glides [r, w, j] because they most nearly balance vocalic resonance and consonantal narrowing.

Short. A term used of vowels of brief duration, and of some syllables which contain one of these vowels.

Sibilant. One of the "hissing" sounds: [s, z, ʃ, ʒ, tʃ, dʒ].

Slack. Same as *Lax*.

Sonorant. That type of consonant that most nearly approximates vocalic sonority and hence is often syllabic.

Sonority. Degree of audibility.

Speech. The spoken, as opposed to the written, language. *Speech* and *language*, however, are sometimes differentiated in other ways (cf. references on page 14); and recently *speech* tends to be used of the art of vocal expression, with particular reference to pronunciation.

Spelling-pronunciation. A pronunciation which differs from the usual pronunciation through following an unphonetic spelling.

Spirant. Same as *Fricative*.

Stem. The base or theme of an inflected word; the stem is sometimes the same as the root, but is more often distinguished from it by the addition of a formative suffix.

Stop. Same as *Explosive*.

Stress. Emphasis or dynamic accent.

Strong noun or adjective. A noun or adjective, in the Germanic languages, that once had a stem ending in a vowel.

Strong verb. That type of Germanic verb that forms its preterit and past participle by ablaut gradation rather than by the addition of a dental suffix.

Suffix. An affix added to the end of a word.

Syllable. A unit of utterance, or division of a word, with its own "center" (usually a vowel) that forms its most audible peak, or point of greatest sonority.

Syllabic consonant. A consonant, especially one of the sonorants [l, m, n, ŋ], that can form a syllable without a vowel.

Synchronic. At one time: the method of studying a language as it exists at a particular time, disregarding how it was before (or after). See *Diachronic.*

Synecdoche. That type of metonymy in which the whole is substituted for the part, or the part for the whole.

Syntax. The department of linguistic study that deals with sentence structure and the use of forms in connected discourse.

Synthesis. The tendency in certain languages to build up morphologically complicated words, with the result that ideas are conveyed by relatively few but long terms; the trend opposite to analysis.

Tense vowel. A vowel articulated with a relatively high degree of tension in the tongue and associated muscles.

Tenuis. A voiceless stop.

Triphthong. A vocalic combination of diphthong and following vowel, pronounced within the same syllable.

Umlaut. The modification of an accented vowel through the influence of the vowel (usually the *i*-vowel) of the following syllable.

Unrounded sounds. Sounds articulated with the lips spread rather than rounded.

Uvula. The soft appendage that hangs from the rear end of the velum.

Uvular r. A variety of *r*, such as the "Northumbrian burr," characterized by vibration of the uvula.

Velar. A back consonant, that type formed by the back of the tongue in proximity to the velum.

Velum. The soft palate.

Vocalization. The process by which a consonant is made into a vowel.

Voiced consonant. A consonant produced with the vocal bands vibrating.

Voiceless consonant. A consonant produced without the vocal bands vibrating.

Vowel. A musical tone made by regular vibrations of the vocal cords, and modified by varying the size and shape of the resonance chamber.

Weak noun or adjective. A noun or adjective, in the Germanic languages, that once had a stem ending in -*n*.

Weak verb. That type of Germanic verb that forms its preterit by the addition of a dental suffix rather than by internal change.

Index